The Bramall Papers

For

Avril, Sara and Nic Bramall

Podge, Meg, Sally and Tom Brodhurst

The Bramall Papers

Reflections on War and Peace

Field Marshal The Lord Bramall of Bushfield KG, GCB, OBE, MC

Edited by Robin Brodhurst

Pen & Sword
MILITARY

First published in Great Britain in 2017
and republished in this format in 2022 by
PEN & SWORD MILITARY
An imprint of Pen & Sword Books Ltd
Yorkshire – Philadelphia

Typeset by Concept, Huddersfield, HD4 5JL.
Printed and bound in the UK by CPI Group (UK) Ltd, Croydon, CR0 4YY.

Pen & Sword Books Limited incorporates the imprints of After the Battle,
Atlas, Archaeology, Aviation, Discovery, Family History, Fiction, History,
Maritime, Military, Military Classics, Politics, Select, Transport, True Crime,
Air World, Frontline Publishing, Leo Cooper, Remember When, Seaforth
Publishing, The Praetorian Press, Wharncliffe Local History, Wharncliffe
Transport, Wharncliffe True Crime and White Owl.

For a complete list of Pen & Sword titles please contact

PEN & SWORD BOOKS LIMITED
47 Church Street, Barnsley, South Yorkshire, S70 2AS, England
E-mail: enquiries@pen-and-sword.co.uk
Website: www.pen-and-sword.co.uk
or
PEN AND SWORD BOOKS
1950 Lawrence Rd, Havertown, PA 19083, USA
E-mail: Uspen-and-sword@casematepublishers.com
Website: www.penandswordbooks.com

Contents

List of Maps

Foreword

By Sir Anthony Seldon

Field Marshal Edwin Noel Westby Bramall, Lord Bramall, must be considered one of the most significant military figures of the post-Second World War period, and I am honoured to write this foreword to his collection of papers, lectures, speeches and writing.

Born just five years after the end of the First World War, and brought up under its shadow, he is one of the relatively few figures writing today who themselves fought in the Second World War. Commissioned as a second lieutenant in the King's Royal Rifle Corps in April 1943, he took part in the Normandy landings in June 1944, serving all the way through to the fall of Germany in May 1945. He served his country with distinction in the field, being awarded the Military Cross in the final six months before fighting ceased.

Bramall decided to remain in the Army after the war was over, serving in Japan and the Middle East before being appointed to the staff of Lord Mountbatten, the incumbent of the newly created position Chief of Defence Staff, in 1963. In breadth of vision, Bramall shares much with the distinguished figure he served for the next two years. Less than twenty years later, after posts across the world and three distinguished years as Chief of General Staff, Bramall himself was appointed Chief of Defence Staff.

After his retirement as CDS in November 1985 he went on to one of the fullest and most productive of careers of any former military chief. Over the last thirty years he has absorbed himself in a wide variety of activities, including serving as Lord Lieutenant of Greater London for twelve years from 1986. He was Chair of the Trustees of the Imperial War Museum, where he was personally responsible for the establishment of the permanent Holocaust exhibition. His range of interests has been prolific, including painting, travel, charity and cricket; he was delighted to be made President of the Marylebone Cricket Club.

Very few military figures have ever painted their lives on such a broad and long canvas. The book opens with some reflections on the Normandy landings, and continues on the themes of remembrance and the Holocaust. It then takes us through the Cold War, colonial confrontations, the Falklands War in which he played such a pivotal role, and on to the First and Second Gulf Wars, Northern Ireland and Afghanistan.

The Papers remind us that Lord Bramall is one of the great thinkers of modern military history, not least with his concept of the 'Fifth Pillar' in 1983, pulling together defence attachés to form a structure for intervention in smaller countries. With his deep understanding of history, and of Whitehall, he has offered the country a series of penetrating insights over the last thirty years, including twenty-six in the House of Lords. His words on how Britain can best organize itself to meet the military threats of the modern age can be listened to with benefit by all.

His thoughts, too, on the role, nature and qualities of leadership can be read with profound interest by all involved in the exercise of that skill, whether in business, government or education. I challenge any reader who engages with the papers of such a distinguished and dignified man over such a long and well spent lifetime not to emerge more thoughtful, wiser and just a little humbler.

Ondaatje Hall
University of Buckingham
July 2017

Prologue

In a remarkably interesting and eventful professional life Dwin Bramall (later Field Marshal The Lord Bramall KG, GCB, OBE, MC) progressively established himself as one of this country's leading military thinkers, who did not confine himself, as so many academic analysts tend to do, to critical explanations of the past but also managed to look ahead and to forecast, often with uncanny accuracy, the changes in conflict situations and threats we were likely to face in the future. In formulating and expressing his thoughts he was able to draw on his own experiences gained at every level of field command and for eight years as a member of the Chiefs of Staff Committee, three of them as its Chairman as Chief of the Defence Staff (C.D.S.). He was therefore intimately involved in strategic decision making and crisis management at the highest level over a protracted period.

He was then, after his retirement from the Army, able to keep in close and informed contact with this country's foreign and defence policies through his twenty-six years of active membership of the House of Lords which enabled him to bring to bear highly relevant, and often critical, comment on the government's current policy and future intentions.

In retirement Bramall was also involved in a number of other activities of national importance. In 1987 he became Her Majesty's Lord Lieutenant for Greater London, having close contact with and giving support to national charities and, on Her Majesty's behalf, investing local industry and commerce with the Queen's Awards they had won. In 1998 he was nominated as President of the Marylebone Cricket Club (MCC), the guardian of the soul of cricket, and as Chairman of the International Cricket Conference. Finally, when in 1989 he became for nine years Chairman of the Trustees of the Imperial War Museum, he was in an ideal position to carry out in-depth research into recent military history and the lessons that should have been drawn from it.

Bramall was introduced to warfare at an impressionable age: at 16 he watched the Battle of Britain being fought overhead; at 17 he experienced the Blitz in London and joined the Home Guard, with invasion still possible; and at 18 he joined the Army in the ranks. His first experience of actual combat was not until 7 June 1944, when as a 20-year-old Lieutenant commanding a

mechanized infantry platoon he landed over the Normandy beaches immediately behind the 3rd Canadian Infantry Division. The Normandy invasion
(Operation OVERLORD) was, of course, no ordinary battle, but the largest
amphibious-cum-airborne operation of all time, brilliantly controlled and
co-ordinated by the Allies with a marvellous and successful deception plan to
help it succeed. This was to be followed for Bramall by a lightning dash into
Belgium and Southern Holland up to the Rhine, a hard-fought winter breakthrough of the Siegfried Line into Germany itself and the subsequent crossing of the Rhine, before the final push to the Elbe and the Baltic, there to link
up with the Russians from the East. From all this Bramall was to carry forward many lessons, both tactical and strategic, as well as some very poignant
memories.

Perhaps above all, those who fought in North-West Europe were to come
face to face with all the worst and most extreme manifestations of Total War:
the bombing of German cities into rubble, the Nazis' ghastly crimes against
humanity on a totally unprecedented scale, the millions of displaced persons,
the vast numbers of casualties, civilian as well as military, many of them in the
last year of the war and particularly in the east. Not long after VE Day, after
his battalion had been sent into Denmark to take the surrender of the German
forces there, Bramall went out with the Airborne forces to prepare for the recapture of Malaya (Operation ZIPPER) and ultimately the invasion of Japan,
only to find himself, after the dropping of the two atomic bombs which forced
the Japanese into unconditional surrender, occupying that country under the
redoubtable General MacArthur, who handled the occupation brilliantly. Out
there in the Far East there had been many other conspicuous examples of
total war on land, at sea and in the air, culminating in the systematic destruction of Japanese cities, initially by fire-bomb attacks and finally with the new
terrible weapons dropped at Hiroshima and Nagasaki, places which Bramall
was able to visit only a few months after witnessing equally awful European
ruins.

Of course, de-escalation from the apocalypse of the Second World War,
which had cost about 60 million deaths worldwide, would not be quick or
easy. Although some traditional seeds of conflict, notably the desire for territorial conquests in the name of *lebensraum* or economic gain, imperial zeal
or hegemony over specific areas, might no longer be as evident as they were
in the past, but deep ideological differences remained and in some cases would
become accentuated. Moreover, there were new flash points, where problems
and perceived injustices seemed insoluble except by organized violence or uneasy, potentially dangerous, confrontation. Indeed, over the next half century
the world would have to endure some still demanding, if much more limited in
scope (though certainly not in duration), forms of conflict.

First, there were the issues left over from the Second World War, such as the international and UN-backed Korean War and, in 1947, the first of the Arab-Israeli Wars. By now a staff officer in the War Office Policy Branch dealing with the Middle East, Bramall watched the latter closely as, on the abandonment of the British Mandate, the state of Israel (partly legitimized by the Balfour Declaration and given impetus by the appalling crimes inflicted on the Jews in the Holocaust) was established, developed and sustained by force of arms. This was to lead to two further Arab-Israeli wars, as well as almost endless terrorist activity, and produce a confrontation between Israel and the Palestinians, a peaceful resolution and accommodation of which still to this day provides the key to any stable and permanent peace in the largely Muslim-dominated Middle East.

Then there would be what can be described as revolutionary wars, the major ones directly linked to the readiness, or in some cases the reluctance, of imperial powers wholly to withdraw from their empires; and also, smaller minority insurrections, confrontations at various flash points and on-off bouts, mercifully brief, of limited war to protect, secure or recover what we held to be vital national interest.

Above all, dominating the defence strategy and programmes of the NATO nations and the Soviet Union there developed what came to be known as the Cold War, which although more passive in execution was extremely expensive and eventually, partly for that reason, contributed to the collapse of the Warsaw Pact and indeed the Soviet Union. That Cold War was, by the late 1950s, to be cemented by the mutual possession of large numbers of enhanced nuclear weapons of infinitely greater power than those dropped on Japan, and which could, more or less, penetrate any defences, with the result that no country, however large, could risk being subjected to them. Bramall was to have direct experience of the Cold War at three different levels: at battalion level as part of the garrison of Berlin at the time the Berlin Wall went up; at the height of the Cold War as a Divisional Commander on the Central Front of NATO in the early 1970s; and as a Chief of Staff during the Cold War's last decade.

But back now to the mid-1950s, to an entirely different area and scene: having served as an operational staff officer with one of the two divisions which had been positioned along the Canal Zone in Egypt, guarding, as the saying went in those days, 'vital imperial communications', Bramall found himself on the fringes of the planning of that ill-fated Anglo-French intervention in answer to Colonel Nasser's *coup d'état* of nationalizing the Canal. This, he recalls, not only ensured some humiliation for ourselves at that time but was to foreshadow ominously another not dissimilar operation in Iraq some forty-five years later.

The 1960s was a busy and varied period in Bramall's military life. After teaching at the Army Staff College and in 1961 serving in Berlin at one of the crisis periods of the Cold War, in 1963 he was posted, as a Lieutenant Colonel, to the personal staff of the Chief of the Defence Staff, Admiral of the Fleet Earl Mountbatten of Burma, reporting directly to him with special responsibility to set up a unified Ministry of Defence which centralized military policy and financial control, created a Defence Staff and co-located the key staff of the three armed forces in one building. Then, at the end of 1964, he was given what is the ambition of every professional soldier: command of a battalion of his own regiment, in his case the King's Royal Rifle Corps, shortly to become the 2nd Battalion, the Royal Green Jackets. He took command just as they were flying out for a two-and-a-half-year tour of duty in Malaysia, to take part, at the Malaysians' behest, in active operations in the confrontation forced on them by Sukarno of Indonesia. This involved operational tours in both Sarawak and Sabah. He was now involved in counter-revolutionary warfare. Before the 1960s were out (and after a spell writing the British Army's first post-war tactical doctrine) Bramall was given command of the 5th Air Landing Brigade, which was part of Britain's strategic reserve, with contingency planning both within and outside NATO. In particular, and more unexpectedly, it was to be the first reinforcing brigade to go to Northern Ireland at the start of the 'Troubles'. Here they were greeted with handclaps and cups of tea by the Roman Catholic population, expecting relief from discrimination caused partly by their Republican sympathies. Soon afterwards, however, the situation developed into a highly dangerous thirty- to forty-year-long insurrection; nearly twenty of these years were during Bramall's active professional life, and he was therefore to continue to keep in contact with Northern Ireland at higher levels of command.

Unlike many soldiers of his generation he had not spent nearly the whole of his military life in Germany. But at the end of 1971 he was appointed to command an armoured division in Northern Germany, with the Cold War still unfrozen. He was therefore able to plan, and to put into practice, some of the lessons he had learned from the Germans all those years ago in Normandy. From commanding the division for just over two years, with many of his units not only training for mobile warfare on the North German plain but also having to go off at repeated intervals to Northern Ireland, which was then at one of its crisis points with internment and the exceptionally violent reaction to it, he went off to the other end of the world to take command of the still sizeable joint force garrison in Hong Kong. Here he served as the number two to an outstanding Governor and as a member of the Executive Council. He was thus, in some ways, a colonial administrator concerned with economics, housing, health and employment, as much as a joint commander dealing with internal security and border unrest in the wake of Mao's Cultural Revolution. He filled this role for two and a half years, and among the main military issues he had to deal with was the future size of the garrison and the real estate they occupied, and whether it was to be the UK or Hong Kong who paid the lion's share of the cost. This therefore gave him useful insight for the future into the nature of politics and inevitable financial imperatives, because after another two years as C-in-C United Kingdom Land Forces, he was truly back in the so-called 'corridors of power' in Whitehall as a member of the Chiefs of Staff Committee for the final eight years of his active service, first as V.C.D.S., then as C.G.S. and finally as C.D.S.

As C.G.S. his first major task was supervising the Army's role in the peace process in Rhodesia, in the wake of the Lancaster House conference, and the establishment and training of the new integrated national army for the new, now legally independent, Zimbabwe. This was altogether an effective and harmonious operation, which everybody thought at the time would lead to as near as possible a multi-racial state in Africa. He saw Mr Mugabe a number of times and found him to be in favour of all we were doing, helpful and supportive; but, of course, he has now been in power far too long. His second major task, in early 1982, and very much in conjunction with his fellow Chiefs of Staff, under the leadership of the excellent C.D.S., Admiral of the Fleet Terry (later Lord) Lewin, was to put together a task force for the repossession of the Falklands Islands after the Argentinians had illegally occupied them. What a remarkable campaign that turned out to be, and from a standing start too, which has not often been Britain's strongest suit. There had not really been anything quite like it since General Wolfe, with Captain Cook as his navigator, sailed up the St Lawrence River, established his army on the Heights of Abraham and defeated Montcalm outside Quebec.

Bramall took over as C.D.S. from Admiral Lewin immediately after the Falklands campaign, which had started to make people realize that our defence needs and spending could not be confined to what were still the four pillars of our strategy: Nuclear Deterrence, the Central Front in NATO, the North Atlantic and Home Defence. The world had manifestly changed and was to continue to become more open and globalized, with many national economies intertwined and interdependent. With the Cold War beginning to thaw, which it did completely five years later, the threats we might face in the future were changing too, both in type and location. They were much more hybrid, diffused and indirect, stemming from prejudice, rivalries and perceived injustices and intended to punish and hurt those held to be responsible. They would be largely outside the southern flank of NATO. So with all constraints on using military force on a large scale becoming more and more compelling, whether economic, political (with its life's blood, public opinion) or international and legal through the UN, if we were to counter and eliminate those new threats we had to be prepared to use force ourselves in a rather different way.

Bramall therefore considered it his primary duty as Chairman of the Chiefs of Staff, now with increased powers as the Government's principal advisor on defence, to lead his colleagues into this changed (and historically more traditional) strategic balance. Moreover, in order to get appropriate funding (still virtually confined to the traditional four pillars) for these increasingly useful military instruments of softer power, he swept them all up under the heading 'A Fifth Pillar of our Strategy' and put a paper to the Secretary of State to get formal political approval, always a hard thing to achieve!

By 1986 Bramall had retired and become an informed observer, giving vent, entirely unofficially, to his personal observations and views through membership of the House of Lords. He was therefore in a position to watch and comment on, often critically, the steady decline of defence spending from (in 1981) well over 5 per cent of GDP to where it will shortly stand today at just under 2 per cent. To begin with there was a rationale for quite a substantial cut, as there would be again more recently. The Cold War had ended, with the removal of the land threat to central Europe, and not only the Treasury but the whole country naturally expected a 'peace dividend'. As always, however, it was overdone, in a number of ways, and almost at once the extent of it came to be questioned when Saddam Hussein unexpectedly invaded and occupied Kuwait. We had to put together a divisional striking force to help the Americans, the Saudis and others to kick him out, and it was only found possible to do so by massive cannibalization of other forces and their equipment. Bramall had in fact earlier warned of the likelihood of just such an eventuality. Yet even with alarm bells ringing, the full cuts were persisted with, which would lead to considerable and prolonged overstretch later on. Bramall got involved personally in Operation DESERT STORM, as the recapture of Kuwait was to be called, because he was sent out to the area, after the Iraqi invasion, with a Parliamentary delegation to report on the prospects of repossession. They saw all the leaders of the Gulf States, the American Commander-in-Chief and his British Deputy. All the Arab leaders made the same three revealing points: we want Saddam Hussein kicked out of Kuwait and the sooner the better; we want him taught a lesson, so he cannot do it again; but we do not want Iraq broken up as a country. Having talked to the commanders concerned, Bramall for one came back absolutely confident that, provided we first won the air battle, all would be well, as indeed it was in only about a week's fighting and with hardly any casualties.

One might say that the twenty-first century came in with a bang: on 11 September 2001 there occurred the most extreme and spectacular example so far of non-state operated violence, in the form of the suicide air attacks on the economic and political heartland of the United States. This, as the Cold War and nuclear deterrence once did, was to dominate, for the foreseeable future, the security thinking, action and spending in the West.

For the United States it was a uniquely traumatic experience, demanding a significantly high-profile response. They started well enough, setting about, supported by ourselves, countering this global terrorism by Al Qaeda and its leaders, correctly held to be responsible, in the best and indeed the only proper way. This was on hard intelligence and with a short, sharp, selective use of force, using pin-point bombing and specially selected ground forces to take out terrorist training camps and Al Qaeda refuge areas in Afghanistan and along the north-west frontier with Pakistan, whose tacit support had been obtained. Al Qaeda was quickly and effectively put on the back foot and soon had no more special links to Afghanistan than they were to have in other parts of the Middle East and the Horn of Africa. Unfortunately, 'the name of the game' was then changed to turning a 'failed state' into a Western-type democracy, within which no terrorist organisation like Al Qaeda could ever in the future operate. This turned out to be a wildly impractical response and it led to ourselves, at the behest of the Americans, going into Helmand Province, the most obdurate of all the Afghan areas, with 'one man and a boy', and fighting the wrong people, whose violence was directed internally at any foreign invader and not internationally motivated and inspired. This has led to massive 'mission creep' and to a highly expensive and not completely con-clusive, eight-year campaign. Nor have we done Pakistan any service either, considering their frontier and religious problems.

Moreover, in the meantime, the Americans had decided on an even higher-profile reaction to 9/11, on the rather spurious excuse that Saddam Hussein might still have and might be seriously developing weapons of so called 'mass destruction': their reaction was to invade Iraq. Bramall was one of the few senior figures to speak out openly, and more than once, in the House of Lords and in print, against such an attack well in advance (and not just, as many did, in hindsight), condemning it as 'a charge up the wrong valley' and reminding anyone who cared to listen of the repercussions of the Suez operations nearly half a century earlier.

Today, as Bramall comes to the end of a long, intimate connection with the profession of arms, he is still scrutinizing the world scene and offering guide-lines for the future. He still rates it as a dangerous world; perhaps not, for the physical security of our own country, as dangerous as the world his parents' generation had to face and live with, but still perilous, with much of the world, particularly the Middle East and Africa, in a state of huge political con-fusion, and proper political authority yet to be established in many states.

While the threats have undoubtedly changed, too, to counter such threats will require force to be used in a more subtle, selective and constrained way than was thought necessary in the past. Here his papers offer us some guidelines. None of these many changes of emphasis Bramall recognizes will make the planning of an appropriate, affordable security insurance policy (which is what in our uncertain world defence is all about) any easier, certainly not for a country like ours with significant global interests and the intention, he presumes, to remain a leading actor on the international stage, particularly as a permanent member of the United Nations Security Council. There will be organizational and budgetary problems in providing, within inevitably tight resources, the expensive equipment necessary to project credible, effective and flexible power over distance and, with others, to deter, curtail or if need be respond to threats towards the higher end of the war-fighting spectrum, and also to give us the capability to take out crucial pin-point targets. This must be combined with the substantial numbers in personnel and the units required to maintain everyday commitments, react speedily to a wide spectrum of emergencies at home and abroad, natural and man-made, and compete with the inevitable unexpected, while at the same time backing up diplomacy with effective military force. It is an intriguing and challenging prospect, which at the top level will require wise and thoughtful consideration which Bramall now hopes we will get, in our case from the newly formed and greatly to be welcomed National Security Council, which must give clear guidance on foreign policy and strategy and on what this country may require its armed forces to be able to do. Then, perhaps, we will achieve not only the appropriate size and shape for these forces, undoubtedly one of our jewels in our crown, to support our foreign policy whenever and wherever required, but also the correct funding with which to sustain them.

The aim of this book, therefore, is to bring together the Bramall Papers: his writings, extracts from his books, letters, speeches and other public observations and utterances delivered and presented in the course of his long and eventful career. These, when set out and introduced in their proper functional, sometimes historical, context, help to explain Britain's foreign and defence policies as they have developed over the past seventy-odd years, but also provide an expert analysis and overview of what predetermined these policies and how they worked out in practice, with resulting successes and failures. They also provide, with the help of chapters on the changing face of conflict, dynamic diplomacy and intervention operations, the higher organization of defence and leadership, a clear indication of how forces might be got ready, controlled and actually used to advantage in the future, avoiding some of the unfortunate consequences of recent campaigns.

Book 1

Total War and Man's Excessive Inhumanity to Man

Chronology

1939

1 September	Germany invades Poland.
3 September	Britain declares war.

1940

9 April	Germany invades Norway.
2 May	Britain evacuates Central Norway.
10 May	Churchill becomes Prime Minister.
	Germany invades France and the Low Countries.
3 June	Evacuation begins from Dunkirk.
7 June	Narvik evacuated.
11 June	Italy declares war on Britain and France.
22 June	France capitulates.
10 July	Battle of Britain starts.
13 September	Italy invades Egypt.
28 October	Italy invades Greece.
31 October	Battle of Britain ends.
9 December	British offensive in North Africa starts.

1941

4 January	British invasion of Italian East Africa.
7 February	Italian army surrenders at Beda Fomm.
28 March	Battle of Matapan (Greece).
30 March	Rommel's first offensive in North Africa.
16 May	Duke of Aosta surrenders in Italian East Africa.
27 May	Crete evacuated.
22 June	Operation Barbarossa: German invasion of Russia.
18 November	Operation Crusader: British offensive in North Africa.
7 December	Japan attacks Pearl Harbor.
	Hitler declares war on the USA.
22 December	Arcadia conference in Washington.

1942

21 January	Rommel's second offensive in North Africa.
15 February	Fall of Singapore.
8 March	Fall of Rangoon.
8 May	Battle of the Coral Sea.
4–7 May	Battle of Midway.
26 May	Rommel attacks at Gazala.
30 May	First thousand-bomber raid on Cologne.
24 July	Combined Chiefs of Staff agree strategy for 1942–3.
7–8 August	Changes in British high command in North Africa.
12–16 August	Churchill in Moscow.
23 October	Battle of El Alamein begins.
2 November	Russian counter-attack starts at Stalingrad.
7–8 November	Operation Torch: Allied landings in North Africa.

1943

14–24	January Casablanca Conference.
23 January	Capture of Tripoli.
2 February	German surrender at Stalingrad.
7 May	Capture of Tunis.
10 June	Invasion of Sicily.
8 September	Invasion of Italy at Salerno. Italian surrender.

1944

22 January	Anzio landings. First Battle of Rome begins.
12 February	First Battle of Monte Cassino starts.
30 March	Battles of Kohima and Imphal start.
11 May	Second battle of Rome begins.
22 May	Japanese withdrawal from Imphal starts.
4 June	Capture of Rome.
6 June	Operation Overlord: invasion of Northern France.
20 July	Attempted assassination of Hitler fails.
13 August	Battle of Falaise begins.
15 August	Operation Anvil: Allied invasion of Southern France.
19 August	Allies enter Paris.
8 September	Assault on the Gothic Line in Italy opens.
17 September	Battle of Arnhem starts.
1 October	Fourteenth Army offensive in Burma starts.
16–25 October	German counter-offensive in the Ardennes, the Battle of the Bulge.

1945

17 January	Russians enter Warsaw.
4–11 February	Yalta Conference.
22–24 March	Allies cross the Rhine.
2 May	Germans surrender in Italy.
9 May	VE Day.
17 June	Potsdam Conference begins.
6 August	Atom bomb dropped on Hiroshima.
2 September	VJ Day.

Introduction

On D+1, 7 June 1944, as a 20-year-old Second Lieutenant commanding an infantry platoon, Bramall landed on JUNO beach on the Normandy coast. There followed three months of fierce fighting with casualties similar to those of the First World War (a total of 500,000 on both sides), and after a crack German Army suffered a major defeat south-east of Falaise, the Allies were over the River Seine and poised to advance rapidly through North-East France into Belgium and Southern Holland, exactly as had been predicted by the land Commander-in-Chief, General Montgomery.

Bramall then took part in the hard-fought winter campaign, culminating in the crossing of the Rhine and the advance across North-West Germany. He witnessed the appalling effects of Total War on a defeated enemy, as well as the horrific evidence of the Nazis' crimes against humanity. Within two months of the end of the war in Europe he was posted to the Far East, where he saw the results of the fire-bombing of Japanese cities and the destruction wrought by nuclear weapons.

Bramall's experience of all this puts him in a rather special position to comment in depth on these events, analyse the campaign in North-West Europe and identify himself closely with the establishment of a permanent exhibition within the Imperial War Museum to remember the Holocaust, which Winston Churchill described as 'probably the greatest and most horrible crime ever committed in the whole history of the world'.[1]

Chapter 1

Normandy and the NW Europe Campaigns, 1944–5

(a) The Higher Command Structure and Commanders

At a conference at the RAF Staff College, Bracknell, on 25 March 1994 Bramall was invited to give a presentation on 'The Higher Command Structure and the Commanders' in the Normandy campaign. This was later published in Overlord 1944 *by the RAF Historical Society.*

In speaking to you about the command arrangements for Operation OVERLORD I shall start by showing how the outline Command setup looked on paper; and then explain how it was arrived at and, more importantly, how it worked in practice.

At the top of the structure was SHAEF (Supreme HQ Allied Expeditionary Force) at Bushey Park, with a Supreme Commander and a Deputy Supreme Commander. Below them – at Portsmouth, in London initially, and at Stanmore – were three Cs-in-C for naval, land and air forces, who would work together in all the planning stages, and command or control their respective forces. The land C-in-C (also C-in-C British 21st Army Group, with its US increment) was made responsible for co-ordinating the whole land battle and commanding the British, Canadian and American armies until the breakout had been achieved and a second (US) Army Group (12th Army Group) could be inserted; at this moment (still then to be determined) both those Army Groups would operate directly under the Supreme Commander.

Then under their respective Cs-in-C were:

a. **Two** Naval Task Forces, one British and one American, with assault and bombardment forces for each of the five beaches and a follow-up force for each national sector.
b. **Two** assault armies, 2nd British and 1st US, each initially of two Corps.
c. **Two** follow-up armies, 1st Canadian and 3rd US.
d. **Two** Tactical Air Forces, both at Uxbridge, 2nd British and 19th US, to give direct air support to the British and American land forces – together with an RAF airborne/transport force. The Allied Expeditionary Air

Forces also had a call on the independent strategic bomber force of Bomber Command and 8th US Air Force.

All quite straightforward, you might say, so did it work? Well, of course it did, because the whole operation was ultimately triumphantly successful and even caught up with the original time schedule – but not exactly as smoothly and harmoniously as one might have hoped. This was because, whatever command set-up you had on paper, you were dealing with powerful personalities, all with their own idiosyncrasies, likes and antagonisms; at the height of the war, with past personal experiences influencing their judgement, personal relationships could be quite significant. The result was that, although up to and including D-Day all the planning problems were solved and command decisions were taken without too much trouble (although some rather late), within the first week of the landing cracks had begun to appear in the relationships between the air and the ground commanders. First let me briefly go back to how these appointments came to be made. The top job of Supreme Allied Commander might have become an Allied tug of war, because General Alan Brooke, the Chief of the Imperial General Staff and Chairman of the British Chiefs of Staff Committee, hoped to be given the job. And indeed, Winston Churchill said he would back him for it. But the Americans were adamant that there should be an American in overall command. This was partly because, after the British Chiefs of Staff's (quite correct) reluctance to contemplate a landing in north-west Europe in 1942 or even in 1943 (preferring to develop the Mediterranean Theatre), they still had some doubts about our enthusiasm for the whole enterprise; and also because, after the initial bridgehead battle, their troops would outnumber the British and Canadians.

General Marshall (the great Chief of the US Army Staff) was at one time considered, but President Roosevelt felt that he could not be spared from Washington. So, with Churchill's eventual agreement, the popular Eisenhower, who had proved himself a good co-ordinator of diverse Allied factions in North Africa and the Mediterranean, was selected. Although Eisenhower lacked experience of the actual battlefield and of commanding land forces, as a Supreme Commander, capable of taking the big decisions and welding the Allies into a team, he was obviously a good choice. This meant that his deputy should be British and, in view of the great importance of the air plan and the air battle, it logically had to be a British airman, for which the obvious selection (as well as Eisenhower's own preference) was the brilliant, intellectual and sharp Air Chief Marshal Tedder, who had commanded successfully the Allied air forces in the Mediterranean.

The Naval Commander-in-Chief also pretty well chose himself. Admiral Ramsay had got the British Army out of Dunkirk, put the Allies ashore in

Sicily and was the Royal Navy's leading expert on large scale combined operations. Energetic, realistic and innovative, he was just the man to assemble and deploy the great armada of British and American ships, get them across the Channel without enemy interruption and land the forces safely on the other side. All this, with the Air Forces' help, he did with conspicuous success and indeed continued to support the land forces very significantly with devastatingly accurate naval bombardment in the crucial bridgehead battle.

For the assault and bridgehead battle itself, the overall land forces commander was clearly crucial. The tactical battle had to be co-ordinated by one man, working to a master plan, and since the British had both the more experienced battlefield commanders and the greater number of troops in the assault phase, it clearly had to be a 'Brit'. Eisenhower (and to some extent Churchill, who much admired him) wanted for the job the brave, urbane and laid-back Harold Alexander, because not surprisingly it was thought that he would be easier to handle than the abrasive, egotistical and supremely self-confident Bernard Montgomery. But Alexander was not a patch on Montgomery as a strategist and manager of a battlefield; this was fully recognised by Brooke, who persuaded Churchill that Alexander should remain in Italy and that Montgomery should be appointed to OVERLORD and brought back as soon as possible to put his own stamp on the preliminary plans drawn up by the OVERLORD planners under General Freddie Morgan.

What a fortunate decision this was, because I believe that as much as any other single factor the personality, self-confidence and professional leadership of Montgomery contributed to the success of this great and ambitious enterprise which, if it had failed, could have postponed the end of the war indefinitely.

What Monty did was to take a plan that would not have worked, convert it into one on a broader front (two armies up), with more assault divisions and a quicker build-up, and invigorate and give firm direction and grip to a staff which was confused and uncertain. Then, by endless morale-boosting visits to military and civilian audiences alike, culminating in the epic briefing to senior OVERLORD commanders at St Paul's School, in front of the King and the Prime Minister, he convinced everyone – commanders, the ordinary soldiers and the country at large – that the 'Second Front' was a feasible operation and was going to be triumphantly successful. Churchill had doubts, so did Brooke and Eisenhower, but Monty's self-confidence never faltered. We were going to win, and certainly all of us about to take part in OVERLORD were greatly heartened and inspired by that confidence. It was electric, and leadership of the highest quality. Little did we know what a close-run thing it was going to be in certain respects.

At the same time, particularly in his briefing at St Paul's, Monty showed that he was a realist. He knew his opponent, Rommel, respected his calibre and realised that, as quickly as possible, Rommel would use his armoured forces to try to drive the embryo bridgeheads into the sea. He appreciated that the fundamental problem was how to bring in forces fast enough over the beaches and through the Mulberry Harbours to be assembled at Arromanches, so as to match the German build-up which would benefit from their interior lines of communication. So not only did he have a deception plan to persuade the Germans that they could not weaken their Fifteenth Army in the Pas de Calais, but above all there had to be a major air effort, not only to win the air battle and create the right conditions for the landing, but also to interdict the battlefield to prevent the German forces arriving there, or at least arriving in any shape to exert their proper effectiveness. In this respect, the barriers of the Seine to the east and the Loire to the south were to prove invaluable.

Monty, despite his later contretemps with some of the air commanders, did understand air power. Indeed, he was one of the few senior army officers who did. Monty had already pontificated on changing the Principles of War by adding a new first principle: 'First win the air battle'. He also realised that the use of air power was not just the army shouting for the air support it wanted, when it wanted, but army and air force commanders sitting side by side and reading the battle together to ensure that the operations on the ground and in the air were looked on as one whole, with the air force providing the range of effort and fire power which would contribute most to the achievement of the common aim. Moreover, he did his best to inculcate this joint approach into his army and corps commanders, whom, incidentally he kept on a very close rein, always deciding himself on the overall strategy and allowing them only to plan, manage and execute particular parts of the current battle, while he turned his attention to the future. He was very lucky in having such sound, professional and loyal subordinates as Miles Dempsey with the Second British Army and Omar Bradley with the First US Army, who did everything required of them.

It is sad that Monty's own reputation as our best battlefield general, with the clearest of brains and an invariable master plan, should have lost some credibility by pretending after the event that his strong left flank, held by the British and Canadians, to attract and hold the bulk of the best German divisions, while the Americans captured Cherbourg and exploited to the neck of the Brittany peninsula (which was the basis of that plan), had not essentially included the flat high ground and the airfields south east of Caen. He always persisted with the story that every one of his limited offensives around Caen which failed to achieve this full degree of expansion had, in fact, gone exactly according to plan and achieved everything he had wanted. To some degree they had, but of course without the airfields which the Allied TAFs so badly wanted. One of Monty's problems was that he had to keep up the confidence of both his own troops and the public watching from just across the Channel, and he was extremely short of infantry, who were suffering very heavy casualties in his various offensives and who could not easily be replaced. So, he more or less had to make a virtue of necessity. However, I believe that history should recognise that he was the key figure in the planning and execution of OVERLORD and the architect of victory, and the attempts emanating from SHAEF to discredit and even go as far as removing him were never justified, even though these were bred from frustration over his self-confident boastfulness and refusal to admit any setbacks at all.

But if Monty was the key figure, the air battle in all its depth and aspects was, perhaps, the critical strategic and tactical factor in OVERLORD's success. Without the Luftwaffe being kept off their backs throughout, without the complex interdiction programme before D-Day and during the bridgehead battle, and without the power of air bombardment at the appropriate place and time, there was no way the land forces were going to get ashore, hold their bridgeheads against fierce counter-attacks and, indeed, break out to Paris and the Seine, hopefully in the process destroying the German armies facing them.

So you could say that the commander of the Allied Expeditionary Air Forces was also an absolutely key appointment. The man picked early on to fill it, Sir Trafford Leigh-Mallory, the then Commander-in-Chief of Fighter Command (later ADGB), was by no means a bad appointment. Leigh-Mallory was a quiet, frank, generous-hearted and dedicated airman who had been a successful, if somewhat controversial (because of the big wing/small wing argument), commander of 12 Group in the Battle of Britain. He believed passionately in giving the land forces all the support he could muster, in what he recognised would be a difficult and daunting enterprise. But as things worked out he found he had been given one of the most difficult jobs imaginable.

First, his responsibilities were ill-defined, in that he was not in full command or even control of all the air effort which could be used in support of OVERLORD. He did control the two Tactical Air Forces and Air Transport Force, supporting Montgomery and Bradley, but apart from that there was no overall air force chain of command, and he had to go cap in hand to the other air force commands and particularly to the strategic bomber forces if he wanted to obtain further support for ground operations.

Then there were the various characters concerned. Leigh-Mallory, with all his qualities, was not a scintillating personality, being rather stolid and, on occasions, inarticulate. For various reasons, he was sometimes resented by some of the other commanders in his own service. Friction in the Battle of Britain might have had something to do with it, but it was more that, with the SHAEF hierarchy looking exclusively at OVERLORD, other air commanders might think their own commands were being threatened, and indeed that the more classical use of air power was being put in jeopardy.

First there were the 'Bomber Barons' – Harris and Doolittle, even more, Spaatz, who was the commander of all the US strategic bomber forces – who took their orders, if they took any at all, from the Combined Chiefs of Staff for whom the British Chief of the Air Staff, Portal, acted as co-ordinator. They all thought, to put no finer point on it, that OVERLORD was the greatest strategic mistake, since Germany, according to them, was already tottering on the edge of collapse from night and day bombing, and if everyone would only leave them alone and not dissipate their effort they would win the war on their own! I believe for many reasons they were wrong over this, but it caused them to resent Leigh-Mallory, partly on the grounds that he did not appreciate the significance of the air war against Germany but, even more, because Harris and Spaatz feared that the strategic bombers were going to be hijacked by Eisenhower and taken off what they did best. Some compromise was clearly needed because although the strategic bombing offensive was still a long way from bringing Germany to its knees, it was already playing a most significant part in virtually eliminating the Luftwaffe from the skies over Normandy and the Channel by attacking German aircraft production and oil reserves.

Compromise was eventually reached, particularly through incorporating the strategic bomber force into the interdiction programme prior to D-Day and getting them to attack the north-west European, and particularly the French, railway and road network. But Leigh-Mallory was not really the man to achieve this; certainly, after D-Day, to get the bombers, who by now were even more reluctant to be taken off their primary role, to carry out direct support of various army assaults required the intervention of Tedder, who had in fact been given the authority by Eisenhower to co-ordinate the whole strategic and tactical air effort – though he was not always in favour of using bombers to destroy French targets. All this reduced Leigh-Mallory's authority further. Nor were his personal relations much better with Tedder above him, or with the Tactical Air Force commanders below him. Tedder, who was rather sharper than Leigh-Mallory, and the New Zealander, 'Mary' (from the New Zealand 'Maori') Coningham, who was a very strong personality indeed, had been together in the desert and Mediterranean; they were very experienced in every aspect of tactical air support and knew, so to speak, all the cries, which Leigh-Mallory did not. So there was an element of resentment there that he was somehow not 'one of them' – as maybe Margaret Thatcher would have said.

Then there were relations with the Army Group commanders, which added to his troubles. Although, as I said, he was passionately determined to give the land forces all the support he could, he was not invariably appreciated by Montgomery as much as he deserved. This was partly because he had refused, almost certainly quite correctly, to countenance a second airborne assault a month after the first, this time to the south of the Caen battlefield. As a result, for a time Monty thought him rather wet, but he forgave him and certainly was prepared to do business with him. The problem was that while Monty very soon set up his own tactical headquarters in Normandy, Leigh-Mallory stayed at Stanmore, which of course broke the important Commanders-in-Chief link. So Monty had to make do with a high-powered liaison officer. But this at least produced results, as did the Combined Control Unit at Uxbridge, Coningham's HQ. For it was Coningham, whom Leigh-Mallory had designated as Forward Co-ordinator of both Tactical Air Forces in the early stages of the bridgehead battle, who should have been the man to get right alongside and mark Monty. The trouble was that while Tedder disliked Montgomery, which was to become increasingly obvious with SHAEF's frustrations and machinations about the latter's slowness around Caen, Coningham positively loathed him, and the feeling was mutual. This was sad, because up to and including Alamein the two commanders – Commander, Eighth Army and Commander, Desert Air Force – had worked side by side with great success and together had defeated Rommel. But they had fallen out, partly because Monty had resented Coningham's giving him gratuitous advice on how he should conduct the pursuit and other operations (a habit he kept up in Normandy), and Coningham resented Monty for hogging all the limelight after the victory in the desert! Coningham also became particularly critical of Montgomery's failure to deliver the airfields. The result was that Monty wouldn't personally work with Coningham, who anyway, as I say, was at Uxbridge (using the well-tried 11 Group communications), and preferred instead to deal either with Leigh-Mallory or, more usually, with the commander of 83 Group, Air Vice-Marshal Harry Broadhurst, who had taken over from Coningham in the desert, and who worked extremely well with the Army. But Broadhurst really should have been supporting – and indeed was supporting – the Second British Army. Indeed, when Dempsey's Second Army headquarters moved across to Normandy, Broadhurst immediately set up his own beside him, taking command of all the RAF units over there. So poor Leigh-Mallory must have felt a bit friendless and even at times helpless in his difficult task, yet he did what he could.

Yet, despite these personality clashes, the Army/Air control machinery, the planning at Stanmore and the Combined Control Unit at Uxbridge, with 82 ASSU tentacles to all Allied Brigades and airfields at home and in Normandy and G (Air) staff down to Corps, did not work at all badly, and the Army continued to rely on, and to get, support from the Allied Air Forces in a most remarkable way. These included Bomber Command, brought in after initial resistance from Harris; his co-operation was brilliant and greatly slowed down the Germans' counter-reaction. During and after the landings, although the pre-planned programme was more uncertain and late being agreed, the Allied Air Forces continued to provide (weather permitting – and the weather was foul throughout that June) round-the-clock support with fighter ground attack and light and medium bombers, all splendidly led at wing and squadron level. This blunted many of the dangerous counter-attacks, particularly on the hard-pressed British sector, and all the time the Luftwaffe, because of the success of the overall air battle, hardly showed up at all.

But as the bridgehead became established and the breaking out became more urgent and difficult, the army looked more and more to the strategic bomber force to help them punch a hole, and the bombers, with some justification and by now with more and more support from Tedder, became less and less enthusiastic about diverting their effort from the German cities and industries. They had a point, because when they were used in close support of the land forces they were not always entirely successful, either because they weren't properly followed up with artillery and armoured forces or, on at least two occasions, St Lo and Falaise, the bombs landed in the wrong place (a case of blue on blue). In one case, Caen, which I watched myself at quite close range, they produced so much rubble in the city that actually it made it easier for the defenders and more difficult for us attackers. But they were used; the bombing did numb the German defences for a period and certainly gave them a hard time and contributed to the heavy casualties and strain the Germans were suffering all along the line.

To summarise, the command system, although fraught with difficult personal relations, did eventually work; the air forces knew what they had to do, and the staffs at the highest levels and the leadership at the lower levels got on with the job of destroying the German war material. Moreover, continuous and accurate updating of the bomb line proved most important, for it gave the air forces the freedom to attack whatever moved behind them, with whatever was available within the overall mission.

Gentlemen, without the air forces the staggering victory in Normandy, culminating in the Falaise pocket, could not have happened as it did, and as one of those on the ground who benefitted, I salute them.

(b) Operation Overlord and the NW Europe campaign

In 1994 Bramall was asked by the Warden of Radley College, of which he was a governor, to talk to the school about his experiences of the Normandy campaign on the 50th anniversary of D-Day. Due to his many commitments, he gave his talk just before Remembrance Sunday, on 1 November 1994. This was also the basis of his lecture 'Lessons from Overlord and the Campaign in North West Europe', delivered to the RUSI the same year.

When the Warden[2] (way back in June) asked me to speak today on the D-Day landings in Normandy, my first concern was whether I could still hold your interest several months after even the 50th anniversary. Well, I hope I can, because Operation Overlord, as those landings on 6 June 1944 were named, was certainly no ordinary battle. It carried all the hopes and fears of the whole Allied cause, some of whose members had already been fighting for nearly five years, and it forged the history of Europe as we have come to know it today.

For not only did it, in the event, put beyond doubt victory over Hitler's Nazi Germany, with all its cruel and callous oppression, but had we failed, in those storm-swept June days all those years ago, to secure and retain a foothold in Northern Europe, and at times early on it was very much touch and go, the end of World War II might have been postponed almost indefinitely. Hitler might well have been able, if he'd listened to his generals, to stabilise his Eastern Front with Russia, he could have continued with far greater impunity with his V weapons – V1 flying bombs and V2 rockets – and their terror attacks on London and South East England. And, who knows? He might have even found the secret of the atomic bomb before the Americans did, with untold consequences. The landings also, of course, constituted the greatest and most complicated combined and amphibious operation the world has ever seen, or thankfully, is ever likely to see.

It was, therefore, an event of the greatest possible historical and military significance, quite on a par with the Battle of Hastings, the Armada and Waterloo, because however important was the clearance of the North African coast and putting Italy out of the war, however essential the Allied bombing offensive on Germany continued to be, and it was very essential, until an Allied army could be put on the continent of Europe near enough and with sufficient strength to strike directly at the heart of the Third Reich and ultimately to link up with the Russians from the east, there was no way victory could be guaranteed, or, indeed, more immediately, the Russians persuaded that we were in earnest and not going to leave all the serious fighting to them.

So, ever since the Germans, frustrated by the Battle of Britain, had, in the summer of 1941, invaded Russia, initially with much success, until stopped at Stalingrad two years later, the creation of a 'Second Front' in Western

Europe had become an essential part of the Coalition (United States and United Kingdom) strategy. It was never a matter of if, but of when and where. The Americans had a strange idea that such an operation which, with the German interior lines of communication, was always going to be very difficult, could be done as early as 1942. It took all the power and persuasion of the British Chiefs of Staff, backed by our Prime Minister Churchill, to convince the Americans that it would be a sure recipe for disaster, just as the large-scale raid on Dieppe was in that same year. Then they wanted it in 1943, and again the British view prevailed in favour of developing operations in the Mediterranean Theatre after the victories at El Alamein and Tunis, putting Italy out of the war, (with the bonus of gaining air bases there) and sucking more and more German forces into Italy and Southern Europe and away from any projected Second Front. But by the spring of 1944, with all these preliminary and softening up moves under way, the Russians firmly on the offensive and sufficient Allied forces, particularly American forces and landing craft, now available, the stage was set for this great adventure across the Channel, which Hitler understandably so dreaded and was determined to resist at all costs.

In preparation for it a planning team known as COSSAC (Chief of Staff to the Supreme Allied Commander) was assembled in London in early 1943 to start making a firm plan for Overlord, based on the troop ships and landing craft thought to be available. It was at this point that Normandy was selected in preference to the area more expected by the Germans, the Pas de Calais, as the best compromise between being near enough to England to enable there to be air cover over the invasion beaches and far enough away from Germany and their reserves to make their quick reaction to the landings that much more difficult. Soon afterwards, around Christmas 1943, the commanders of this great enterprise started to be appointed.

The Americans, who, after the initial beachhead battle would considerably outnumber the British and Canadians, were adamant that there should be an American in overall command. And so, with Churchill's eventual agreement, the popular Eisenhower (who was later to become the President of the United States) and who had proved himself a very good co-ordinator of diverse Allied factions in North Africa and the Mediterranean, was selected. Although he lacked experience of the actual battlefield and commanding land forces, as a Supreme Commander – capable of taking big decisions and welding the Allies into a co-operating team, he ('Ike' as he was so often known) was clearly an excellent choice.

This meant that his deputy should be British, and in view of the great importance of the air plan and the air battle (as I'll explain in a moment) it logically had to be a British airman, for which the obvious selection, as well as

Eisenhower's own preference, was for the brilliant, intellectual and sharp Air Chief Marshal Tedder, who had successfully commanded the Allied Air Forces in the Mediterranean.

The Naval Commander-in-Chief also pretty well chose himself. Admiral Ramsay had got the British Army out of Dunkirk, put the Allies ashore in Sicily and Italy and was the Royal Navy's leading expert on large scale combined operations. Energetic, realistic and innovative, he was just the man to assemble and deploy the great armada of British and American ships, get them across the Channel without any enemy interruption and land the forces on the other side. All this, with the help of the Allied Air Forces, he did with conspicuous success, and indeed continued to support the land forces very significantly with devastatingly accurate naval bombardment in the crucial bridgehead battle. For the assault and bridgehead battle itself the overall land forces commander was clearly going to be crucial. The tactical land battle had to be co-ordinated by one man, working to a master plan. And since the British had at the time both the more experienced battlefield commanders and, initially in the assault phase, the greater number of troops, it sensibly had to be a Brit. Eisenhower, and to some extent Churchill, who much admired him, wanted for the job the brave, urbane and laid back General Harold (later Field Marshal) Alexander, late of the Irish Guards. This was not surprising because it was thought that he would be easier to handle than the abrasive, egotistical, supremely self-confident Bernard Montgomery of Eighth Army fame and the victor of El Alamein. But Alexander was not a patch on Montgomery as a strategist and manager of a battlefield, and Churchill was therefore persuaded by his military advisers, principally General Brooke, the CIGS, that Alexander should remain commanding the land forces in Italy and that Montgomery should be appointed to Overlord and be brought back as soon as possible to put his own stamp on the preliminary plans drawn up by the Overlord planners.

It was Montgomery who had earlier revived the fortunes of the Eighth Army in North Africa and in October 1942 had won that proud victory at El Alamein. And what a fortunate decision this was, because I, and I believe most historians, now believe that, as much as any other single factor, the personality, self-confidence and professional leadership of Montgomery contributed to the success of this great and ambitious enterprise. What Montgomery did, 'Monty' as he was always known, was to take a plan of only three assault divisions, supported by two airborne brigades, controlled by only one Corps and one Army Headquarters, which would not have worked because the build-up would have been too slow, and enlarge it into one on a broader front with five assault divisions, commanded by two Corps and two Army Headquarters, and with three airborne Divisions, which could make reinforcement through each bridgehead far quicker. That change took some doing, with the planning so far advanced. He then invigorated and gave firm direction and grip to the staff, which was confused and uncertain, and, finally, by endless morale-boosting visits to military and civilian audiences alike, culminating in an epic briefing to senior Overlord Commanders at St Paul's School, in front of King George VI and the Prime Minister, Winston Churchill, convinced everybody, commanders, military formations taking part, the ordinary soldier like me, and the country at large, that the Second Front was a feasible operation and was going to be triumphantly successful. Churchill had doubts, so did Eisenhower, as did Alan Brooke, but Monty's self-confidence never faltered. We were going to win, and certainly all of us about to take part in Overlord were greatly heartened and inspired by that confidence. It was electric and leadership of the very highest quality. Little did we know what a close-run thing it was going to be, in certain respects. At the same time, Monty showed that he was a realist. He knew all about his opponent, Field Marshal Rommel ('The Desert Fox') whom he had fought and defeated in the desert, respected his calibre and realised that as quickly as possible Rommel would use his armoured forces to try to drive the embryo bridgeheads into the sea. He appreciated that the fundamental problem was how to bring in forces fast enough over the beaches and through the artificial 'Mulberry' harbours, to be assembled off Arromanches, because it was going to take too long to get Cherbourg into operation, to match the German build up, benefiting from their interior lines of communication. In fact, Cherbourg was in the event never used for supply because by the time it was cleared we were able to use Antwerp.

So not only did he have a deception plan to persuade the Germans that they couldn't weaken their Fifteenth Army, in and around the Pas de Calais, but above all there had to be a major air effort, not only to win the air battle and create the right conditions for landing, but also to interdict the battlefield to prevent German forces arriving there, or at least arriving in any shape to exert their proper effectiveness. In this respect, the barriers of the Seine to the east and the Loire to the south were to prove invaluable.

Despite his later contretemps with some of the air commanders, or they with him, for there was mutual dislike between Monty and one of his tactical Air Force Commanders, 'Maori' (or as he was known, 'Mary') Coningham, dating back to the desert, when Coningham thought Monty had hogged the limelight, and there was no love lost between Monty and Tedder, Monty did understand air power. Indeed, he was one of the few Army officers who did. He had already pontificated on changing the principles of war by adding a new principle to the existing ten: 'first win the air battle'. He also realised that the use of air power was not just the Army shouting for the support it wanted, but the Army and Air Force commanders sitting side by side, reading the battle together to ensure the operations on the ground and in the air were looked on as one whole, the Air Force providing the range of effort and fire power which could contribute most to the achievement of the common aim and the master plan.

So, what was the master plan that Montgomery had approved and saw through with such single-mindedness? Well, it was to land five assault Divisions, two British, one Canadian, two United States, with assorted commandos and Special Forces, on the Normandy coast between just east of the River Orne, running through Caen in the east, to just into the base of the [Cotentin] peninsula in the west, a frontage of some 50 miles, with airborne Divisions, one British and two United States, on either flank, to secure the eastern flank, hopefully out to the River Dives, and including the famous Pegasus Bridge across the Orne River and Canal, and on the western flank to secure the exits from the western United States beach (Utah Beach).

These assault Divisions, under their respective four Corps and two Armies, British and Canadian in the East and American in the West, would have to overcome the beach defences (Hitler's much vaunted Atlantic Wall) and with the help of armoured columns stake out as large a bridgehead as possible in the first few days, including the large city of Caen. The plan was then (and he set all this out quite clearly in his St Paul's briefing in April), for the British and Canadians to establish a strong 'hinge' around Caen with the high ground and the airfields immediately to its south and west, on the shortest route to Paris, and therefore the most dangerous one in the German eyes, which would attract and hold the vast majority of the German counter-attack effort. This would leave the Americans comparatively free to swing north up the [Cotentin] peninsula to capture the important port of Cherbourg and then to break out south to the neck of the Brittany peninsula and with their follow-up Third Army, commanded by the flamboyant pistol-packing General George Patton, to exploit west into Brittany and particularly east towards Paris. The whole line would then swing east like an open door, and the timings were those that Montgomery had forecast in his April briefing (90 days to reach Paris and the Seine). The timings that Monty had included in that briefing were not strictly adhered to, getting as much as a month and a half behind in the early stages, but the principle of the 'hinge' remained, and by the end of August/beginning of September the schedule had been caught up and the Allied Armies were lined up along the Seine and were in Paris, exactly as Monty had predicted.

So, let us follow together how the Battle of Normandy developed. Early on 6 June, in fairly bad weather and after one 24-hour postponement because of even worse weather, the great armada of over 4,000 warships and landing ships, an amazing sight as I can vouch for myself, which had started the day before from harbours and inlets from Falmouth in the west to Newhaven in the east, with follow up echelons coming from as far round as Tilbury and Harwich, and all assembling south of the Solent and the Isle of Wight area, started to disgorge the assault Divisions on their assigned beaches: from the west to east, Utah, Omaha, Gold, Juno (where I landed the day after D-Day, D+1) and Sword. The *coup de main* parties had landed shortly after midnight (including at Pegasus Bridge, taken by a glider-borne company of the Oxfordshire and Buckinghamshire Light Infantry), parachutists (British 6th Airborne Division and US 82nd and 101st Airborne Divisions); on the flanks the beach obstacle removal parties went in while it was still dark, and the assault troops with their floating DD tanks and specialist armour to deal with beach defences started to land from first light on a rising tide between 05.30 and 07.00, supported by the massive fire support of Allied aircraft and naval gunfire and rockets. It was a fantastically well-organised operation, and although there was some very heavy fighting, as the beach defences of the Atlantic Wall had to be overcome, particularly on Omaha Beach, where the 1st US Division took nearly the whole day to get off the beach area alone and suffered at least 3,000 casualties (you may remember the scenes in the film *The Longest Day* with Robert Mitchum as the Deputy Divisional Commander).[3] By the end of D-Day 156,000 men had been landed by sea or air at the cost of some 10,000 casualties, and two individual bridgeheads in the United States area and one large consolidated one in the British and Canadian area had been established.

Six days later, by 12 June, all the bridgeheads had been linked up and extended to a depth of 15–20 miles inland. Although one pocket of German resistance at Douvres held out until the 16th and the city of Caen had not been captured. In those six days which, as it was, were quite dicey enough, particularly on Omaha Beach and then later in the British sector, north of Caen, where the bridgehead was only 10 miles deep, it might have been an even closer run thing if the Germans had reacted sooner and with greater strength. Here it is worth pausing and looking at the German situation on D-Day and immediately afterwards.

The German Army at this time was probably the most formidable and effective fighting machine since the Roman legions. Immensely battle-experienced in Poland, the fall of France, North Africa, Italy and, above all, Russia; superbly well-equipped, intensely fanatical and, above all, literally fighting for their lives and future, for they realised that if the Allies were not pushed into the sea or at least contained in a small lodgement area, this was the end of Hitler and their Nazi world, in which most of them had grown up and become enthusiastic followers. This, constituting as it could, a second defeat for Germany in less than thirty years, would have meant that, for them, life would not be worth living. This particularly applied to the Waffen SS formations, the fighting arm of Hitler's Party elite, of which there were a very high proportion in Normandy, and none more fanatical than the 12th SS Hitler Youth Division, made up of young Nazis, no older and in some cases much younger than all of you.

But balancing this was the fact that the German High Command was not in the best state to deal quickly with a landing. Only the Seventh Army of some three lowish-grade Infantry Divisions and one good Armoured Division, the 21st Panzer, were actually facing the invasion beaches. A much larger number were held in the Pas de Calais, which was always thought by the Germans to be a more likely area for an invasion – an idea cleverly fostered by a brilliant Allied deception plan in which a mythical Army Group (FUSAG), commanded by the dangerous Patton, was created in the Dover area and made ominous noises (through a lot of totally bogus wireless traffic) while appearing ready to descend on north-eastern France. This was supported by the clever selection of Air Force interdiction targets, in which for every bomb dropped on Normandy three were dropped on the Pas de Calais, seeming thus to point to that area as the target for invasion. This tied down a number of the Fifteenth Army Divisions away from Normandy. On top of that, the real striking power, the Panzer Divisions, controlled by Panzer Group West, was held back centrally, and there was also a major disagreement about their use. Field Marshal Rommel, the Army Group Commander, realising the power of the Allied air effort and the difficulty his troops would experience moving at all, and particularly in daylight, wanted to defeat the invasion on or near the beaches, with immediate armoured counter-attacks by armour held far forward. The Commander-in-Chief, West, the elderly patrician Field Marshal Rundstedt, however, wanted to hold the reserves back until the Allied weak points had been identified and then make a large concentrated counter-attack. In any case, no decision on reserves could be taken without Hitler's personal authority and he often could not be disturbed by his sycophantic staff. Much play was made of this in the film *The Longest Day*.

All this slowed things up, and to top it all, Rommel was taking advantage of what he was informed was unsuitable weather for an invasion and was in southern Germany on D-Day for his wife's birthday, and the commander of 21st Panzer Division, based in Caen, was in Paris with his girlfriend. So all in all, and for a number of hours, there was almost total paralysis of the German High Command, first not believing it was the main invasion at all and then not being certain what to do. The only real counter-attack on that first morning was by 21st Panzer Division, stationed in the city of Caen itself, but without its commander. Of course, all that changed with the arrival back of Rommel on the evening of D-Day, and from then on it became a really vicious dog-fight and blood-letting on both sides, of which my own personal memories, still so vivid even after fifty years, are of lush Normandy country-side, with its standing corn nearly chest high, interspersed with chunks of sinister impeding *bocage* (deep ditches and high hedges), today, because of modern farming measures, largely disappeared, all suddenly blighted by the terrible sights and smells, thunderous noises of guns and mortars going on both sides, and the congestion of war: the blackened corpses, the bloated and stinking dead cattle and horses, the savage no-quarter fighting, with stay-behind snipers everywhere, and the appalling destruction of so many hamlets, villages and towns. Normandy quickly became a hellish battle, with the elite Panzerlehr Division, made up of Army instructors, the 1st, 2nd, 9th, 10th and 12th SS Panzer Divisions, and also the 2nd Panzer Division – seven elite Divisions, Nazi fanatics, with far better tanks and anti-tank weapons than we had – all started to pour into the battle, and all of them against the British sector. It was only fortunate that so much of their original power had been reduced by our own air support, on their way to the fight.

To keep to his master plan, even against all that lot, Montgomery had to keep up the pressure, seize Caen and the high ground to the south and west, which he had promised to capture early for the Air Forces' airfields, and continue to pose a severe threat to Paris and the Seine, to which the Germans had to continue to react. And yet, unlike the Americans, he was very short of infantry and could not easily replace the high infantry casualties he was steadily suffering. So, between mid-June and mid-August he mounted a series of short sharp attacks, backed by massive ground and air bombardment around the Caen area. First on 14 June he tried a right hook to seize a village in a valley called Villers-Bocage, 15 miles south-west of Caen, and here our 7th Armoured Division (the 'Desert Rats') got a very bloody nose from a German regiment of heavy Tiger tanks,[4] which arrived on the battlefield at a critical moment. Then on 26 June he put in a Corps attack of three Divisions (called Operation EPSOM) to cross the River Odon and try to get across the River Orne and isolate Caen from the south-west, and this continued on into July when, behind a massive bombing raid by Bomber Command which virtually flattened Caen itself, the northern part of that city was captured and further efforts were made from the EPSOM bridgehead to surround the rest of the city and to cut it off from the south.

Then in mid-July Montgomery launched a massive armoured attack by three Armoured Divisions east of Caen (Operation GOODWOOD) to get onto the high ground to the south-east of the city, known as the Bourgebus Ridge. This, too, was supported by Bomber Command and made some ground, but failed to reach its objectives and lost 240 tanks in the process, all, I may say, replaced within a few days, which could not have been done if the attack had been made by Infantry Divisions and it had been infantry casualties that had to be replaced. Finally, in the first week of August he launched a two-pronged movement (Operation TOTALISE) by the British, Canadians and Poles down the Caen-Falaise road and, in the west, an armoured drive, also British, towards Vire on the boundary with the German armies.

None of these, despite Montgomery's optimism, achieved all their objectives or fulfilled the high hopes he had created for them, and I think he lost some of his reputation as our best battlefield commander by always trying to make out that everything had gone exactly according to plan, when it clearly had not. But then he had to keep up the morale of his troops and the whole home population, and the Germans were being kept on the defensive and were being forced to put more and more of their high-quality armour against the eastern hinge to prevent a complete breakthrough there, and, to suffer heavy losses from the full range of Allied defensive fire when they deployed to counter any British or Canadian gains, so that as a result, less and less could be deployed against the Americans. All this was to pay dividends when the immensely taut elastic finally snapped. So the master plan was being maintained, even if Montgomery's arrogance was making him extremely unpopular in certain sections of General Eisenhower's headquarters, fuelled regrettably by Tedder, Eisenhower's deputy. There was even at one time, and most unfairly, talk of his dismissal for his failure to make more progress in the east.

But eventually it all worked. On the last day of July the Americans did break through in the west, around St Lo, again supported by heavy bombers, some of whose bombs fell initially short on their own troops, not the first, nor the last case of 'blue on blue', but once they had recovered from that, unlimited possibilities opened up. Once through the thin German crust, Patton's Third US Army was passed through Hodges' First US Army and in an American-style blitzkrieg went like a bat out of hell, not only exploiting into Brittany, but also south to the Loire, east to Le Mans, Chartres, Orleans and even to the north, to Argentan, threatening to cut off the whole German Seventh Army facing north in Normandy.

Indeed, with the British, Canadians and Poles now advancing southwards down the road from Caen to Falaise, and later, beyond, to the east, and the Americans coming up from the south, as well as exploiting to Paris, the German army was becoming trapped in a huge pocket in the centre, from which escape was becoming increasingly difficult; and virtually impossible after Hitler had given futile orders not to retreat but to counter-attack westward, across the base of the US breakthrough, towards Avranches, putting the German head further still in the noose. This was comprehensively defeated with the help of a massive Allied ground attack air effort in perfect weather, and the Germans were then doomed. On 19 August the Falaise pocket was finally closed at a place called Trun. Very few Germans escaped, and certainly no equipment to speak of; 400,000 Germans were killed, wounded or taken prisoner, and it was one of the most comprehensive military defeats in history. The way was now opened to a broad advance to the Seine, a crossing against the lightest opposition and the rapid liberation of northern France, Belgium and southern Holland.

There was still, of course, heavy fighting to come at Arnhem, undoubtedly, in the event, 'a bridge too far', but no doubt influenced (even if you believe that higher headquarters knew, or should have known, that two SS Panzer Divisions had just moved into the area) both by the morale problem of standing down 1st Airborne Division yet again after so many false starts, and by Montgomery's obsession with the single northern thrust to Berlin, at the expense of Bradley and Patton. Then the Ardennes (the Battle of the Bulge) a brilliant tactical counter-stroke by Hitler, but one which, unless the Allies lost their nerve, which they did not, thanks to the Americans fighting performance at Bastogne and elsewhere, Patton's remarkable counter-attack from the south and Monty's clear leadership in command in the north, was bound to fail; and indeed, by exhausting its final effective reserves sealed the fate of the Third Reich both in the east and in the west. This was followed by the wet and dangerous fighting through the Reichswald Forest on the German Dutch border, as the Siegfried Line was penetrated, and the Allied forces closed up to the Rhine, leading to the crossing of that mighty river itself, helped by a very daring use of Airborne Forces, and the debouching across the North German Plain and the isolation of the Ruhr.

And all the time there continued the remorseless air bombing of German cities by day and night, with heavy casualties to our gallant Allied aircrews, as well as enemy civilians on the ground. But this, for two to three years, had been the only method that first the British and then the Allies had of hitting back and had been more than morally justified by the overriding need to defeat one of the most evil and amoral regimes the world has ever seen; although from early 1945 there were some other options available for selecting targets, which could have equally contributed to the Allied victory and which might have made the attack on Dresden, for instance, unnecessary. It is easy to see why Dresden happened, with the Russians pressing so strongly for it, as a communications centre, contributing munitions to the east, and in the context of the momentum of the earlier strategic bombing policy, but I personally believe we did lose a little of the moral high ground by carrying out the attack as we did in February 1945, which, incidentally, and for different reasons, Harris was against.

But it had been the success of the Battle of Normandy, in conjunction with the Soviet successes in the east, that set the scene for all these things, and meant that by the autumn of 1944 the victorious end was not only in sight, but inevitable. Indeed, only eight months after Falaise, Hitler committed suicide and Germany surrendered unconditionally.

Normandy was a triumph for Montgomery, who was undoubtedly the architect of that victory, but it was only made possible by the Allied air superiority and its brilliant and sustained use in support of the land battle. For despite the personality clashes and the command problems I mentioned earlier, the Air Forces (gallantly led at Wing and Squadron level) knew what they had to do, and got on with the job of destroying German war material and communications wherever they found them the other side of the bomb line, and without that, this staggering victory would not, I am sure, have been possible. Yet even then the cost had been high. In the three months, June to September, 200,000 casualties had occurred on the Allied side, including 30,000 dead, and many of these were the bravest and the best compared with those of us left behind. So we must never forget their sacrifice, for with fifty years of peace under our belt and Europe an infinitely safer place than it was in the Thirties, we do indeed owe them a very deep debt of gratitude.

(c) Staff College battlefield tour to Normandy

In 1961 Bramall was on the Directing Staff of the Staff College, Camberley, and produced the programme for the annual battlefield tour to Normandy for the students. However, he changed the format slightly, making the discussions much more focused than heretofore. This is his briefing document for syndicate leaders, with military abbreviations removed! The Staff College Battlefield Tour utilized veterans, including Bramall himself, of course, who had commanded units in 1944, e.g. General Sir John Mogg, who had commanded 9 DLI, Captain Alastair Morrison, a troop commander in 4/7 RDG and his squadron commander Major, later Major General Sir, James d'Avigdor-Goldsmit, and Lieutenant Colonel Robin Hastings, who commanded 6 Green Howards on D-Day and later 2 KRRC, including Lieutenant Bramall. Although it looked at operations Goodwood and Epsom and the parachute and glider landings at Pegasus Bridge and Renouville (apparently in reverse order), they also spent time on the actual beach landings at Sword, Gold and Juno.

DIVISIONAL DISCUSSIONS

Form of Discussions

1. This year, for the first time, there will be div discussions on the Battlefield Tour on the day after we return from France. 1030–1230 on Thursday 15 June has been allocated, which should give:

(a) Time for preparation after returning from France.

(b) Ample time for discussion.

(c) Time to get to Ascot!

2. There are five questions included in the Questionnaire attached to the three Annexes of the Tour folder as follows:

(a) OVERLORD – 2
(b) EPSOM – 1
(c) GOODWOOD – 2

These questions have been redesigned to make students look to the future as well as pondering on the past.

3. I suggest that you will wish to spend 90 minutes on these Questionnaires. Each team leader will detail one member of his team to assist you in running the discussion on his particular battle.

4. In the remaining 30 minutes, you may wish to sum-up and try to put the three battles in proper perspective in terms of time and effort. The aim would be to rub home to inexperienced students the 'facts of life' of the battlefield (the lamentable conditions of war), so that when they are trying to evolve new tactics in the future, they will not have their feet too far off the ground. In this way, valid battle experience will be kept alive.

5. Maps suitable for discussing all three battles are being prepared by the Drawing Office.

Analysis of the Battles

6. In the hope that they will be of some use to you in your summing-up, I attach some short notes on the three battles. These try to analyse why there was success or failure in any particular battle or phase of the battle, and what exactly was achieved in relation to the effort in men and material expended.

7. The battles are considered in the reverse order in which they took place as follows:

(a) Annex 'A' – GOODWOOD
(b) Annex 'B' – EPSOM
(c) Annex 'C' – OVERLORD

Main Lessons

8. Of all the lessons discussed in the Annexes, I would select the following as the most significant:

(a) Good intelligence and planning are vital to successful operations.
(b) To succeed in an attack one must either have decisive superiority or achieve surprise by speedy deployment and skilful use of ground and fire and movement. It is worth taking risks to achieve real surprise.
(c) Correct grouping and a proper balance of arms is of the utmost importance.

(d) Without depth there is no defence and the key to a successful defence is good close artillery support.

(e) With the great increase in fire power available on the battlefield, ground forces are still required to exploit. Fire power alone cannot destroy a determined enemy dispersed over the battlefield and deployed in depth.

(f) The outcome of battles often turns on the fighting spirit of the soldier. High morale and a determination to win can only be developed by good leadership and tough and imaginative training. This is our main responsibility in peace time.

(g) A battle can easily be lost in the mind of a commander and his staff irrespective of what is going on, on the ground. There are many examples of this in the South African War, and in EPSOM the push towards the River Orne was called off not because 11 Armoured Division had suffered undue casualties and were unable to get forward, but because the British command had reacted unduly to the German threat to the salient and had become defensively minded. Generals like Rommel would probably have been prepared to take greater risks in a situation like this.

(h) Winning air superiority is an essential pre-requisite to fighting a successful land battle.

(Signed) E.N.W. Bramall
Lt. Colonel.
CAMBERLEY
31 May 1961

ANNEX 'A'

BATTLEFIELD ANALYSIS

OPERATION GOODWOOD

Success or Failure?

1. In the light of Montgomery's Master Plan, it can be argued that strategically GOODWOOD was worthwhile, but tactically I think we must rate it as a failure in that three divisions supported by 2,000 aircraft and 750 guns failed, after three day's fighting, to establish themselves on their objective and lost 413 tanks in the process.

2. The main cause of the failure was undoubtedly:

(a) A faulty appreciation of the strength, and particularly the depth, of the enemy position.

(b) The undue confidence placed in the effect of the air bombardment.

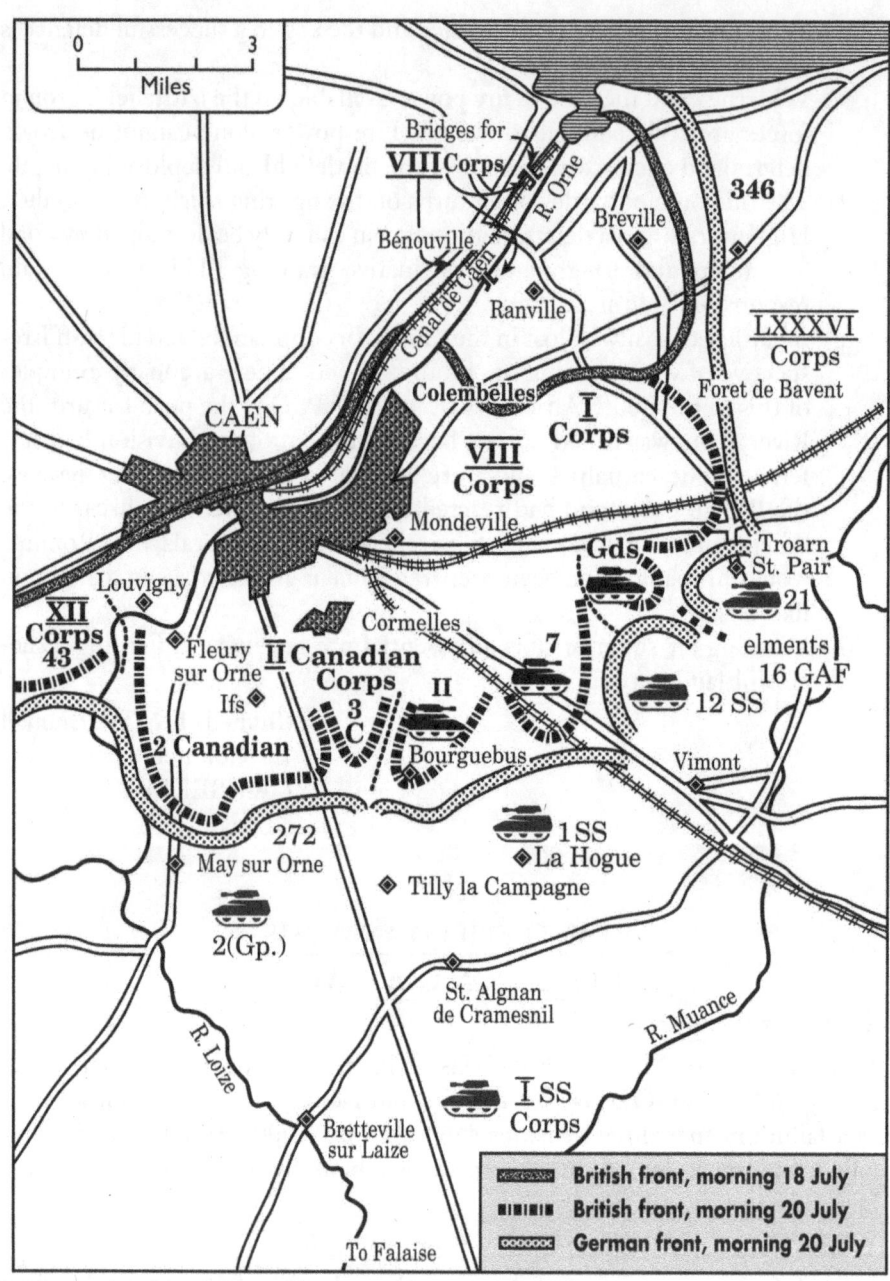

OPERATION GOODWOOD, July 1944.

(c) A wrong conception of how to operate an armoured division in European countryside resulting in separate tasks for armour and infantry and a lack of balance in grouping.

Ratio of Strength Between Attacker and Defender

3. Infantry. Despite the fact that the German infantry divisions in the line were caught by the initial air bombardment, the narrowness of the front and the fact that the armoured regiments had only one company of infantry grouped with them contrived to ensure that:

(a) Only in the early stages (the attack on CUVERVILLE and DEMOU-VILLE) was the balance of infantry effort in our favour.
(b) Towards the end of the battle it was never better than 'evens'. If proof were needed of how useful a superiority of infantry would have been at this stage, one has only to look at the effectiveness of 8 Rifle Brigade's attack at BRAS and HUBERT FOLIE.

4. Tanks. Although staff tables would have shown a British superiority on the 8 Corps front of over 3:1, the narrowness of the assaulting area so restricted manoeuvre on the first day that the ratio was reduced to about 2:1 and this was quickly offset by natural obstacles (the lateral railway lines produced surprising hazards) and excellent enemy observation and anti-tank shoots from mutually supporting areas of cover. It is interesting to note that in order to hold the front, the Germans committed only one third of their tank strength for an immediate reserve to the forward infantry. This was von Luck's battle group. The remaining two thirds were held back in reserve behind the BOURGEBUS RIDGE. Few, if any, of the tanks were actually sited in the forward locations.

5. Artillery. Apart from 272 Nebelwerfers, the enemy had 250 field, medium and assault guns untouched by the initial air bombardment. Against this, we could put 750 guns or a ratio of 3:1; but because of the mis-appreciation of the enemy layout which was 10 miles deep (with 4–5 defensive belts), instead of the 3–4 miles which had been supposed, the latter part of the battle was fought with most of our guns firing at maximum range.

6. It is a sound military principle that unless you are able to achieve complete surprise, or you have greatly superior equipment, or your fighting ability is greatly superior to the enemy (as at SINAI and SUEZ), you must concentrate clear numerical and fire power superiority if you are to have decisive success at any particular point. With the observation from the BOURGEBUS RIDGE and the towers of COLOMBELLES there could be little question

of surprise, and as things turned out, we failed to produce that significant superiority in ground forces.

Air Bombardment

7. It does not need a great stretch of the imagination to compare the massive air bombardment of GOODWOOD to one or two nuclear weapons producing the same tonnage in High Explosive. What applied to the one might easily be applied to the other.

8. The air bombardment was, by all accounts, nerve-shattering to the forward divisions, but the corridor it carved was not deep enough and failed to neutralise the enemy reserves or gun areas. The use of strategic aircraft in the direct support of ground troops failed at CASSINO and CAEN and had only limited success during GOODWOOD. The lessons seem to be:

(a) Such an attack is demoralising for those who happen to be underneath it but against a dispersed army, deployed in depth, the effect will not necessarily be crippling.

(b) The effects of bombing do not last forever and determined, well led troops moving back into the devastated area and taking advantage of the obstacles created by the bombing, can cause untold delay. A quick follow-up is therefore essential.

(c) The corridor made by the bombing (or by a nuclear strike) must be sufficiently long to penetrate right through the enemy defensive area or be deepened by subsequent strikes.

(d) Reserve and gun areas are every bit as important as targets as forward troops.

(e) Follow-up troops must be prepared for resistance from enemy units, which, because they were so close to our own troops, were untouched by the bombing, and by mobile armoured forces which re-enter the area after the bombing has stopped. They must have balanced grouping with the necessary fire power to deal with these enemy units.

Grouping

9. GOODWOOD began with 11 and 7 Armoured Divisions operating in the normal Western Desert way with the infantry brigade acting as a firm base allowing the armour to manoeuvre. The brigades were fought as separate entities and separate tasks were sought for each. This meant that both brigades were severely hampered – the armour by lack of infantry and the infantry by lack of tanks.

10. After GOODWOOD it was quickly realised that not only in close '*bocage*' country but in more open country as well, the Armoured Regiment/Infantry

Battalion provided the best possible fighting combination. It could carry out effective reconnaissance and deliver a quick heavy punch, particularly against an enemy organised in successive defensive belts in depth.

11. By 1946 it had become standard grouping, only to be forgotten again in the 1950s. Now once again it is being advocated. If the lesson had been learned before GOODWOOD the result might have been different.[5]

Main Lessons from GOODWOOD

12. To sum up, the main lessons from GOODWOOD seem to be as follows:

   (a) Good intelligence is vital to any operation.

   (b) There is scarcely a single situation on the modern European battlefield which does not demand a proper balance of infantry and armour.

   (c) In the absence of other factors, such as variety of fighting qualities or complete surprise, an attack which is not launched with adequate superiority at the decisive point is likely to fail.

   (d) Small, natural obstacles, particularly those which are unforeseen, can impose delay out of all proportion to their size.

   (e) Mutual support and depth are essential to successful defence. In fact, without depth there is no defence. This point emerges time and time again from the study of World War II and is evident again in the study of EPSOM.

   (f) In deploying armour in defence a proper balance must be held back and the minimum deployed forward to support the forward localities.

   (g) An attack must be planned and maintained in depth. Although there must be flexibility to take advantage of new situations, the battle must not develop into an *ad hoc* arrangement immediately the initial assault has been completed.

   (h) Massive air superiority or nuclear support can be a battle winning factor if used properly, but it has limitations which must be recognised. Its use does not dispense with the need for a sound plan for the ground forces.

ANNEX 'B'

BATTLEFIELD ANALYSIS

OPERATION EPSOM

Success or Failure?

1. Strategically EPSOM had a similar significance to GOODWOOD but tactically it can be rated more of a success, even though this success was hard-won and the reward, in terms of ground, limited.

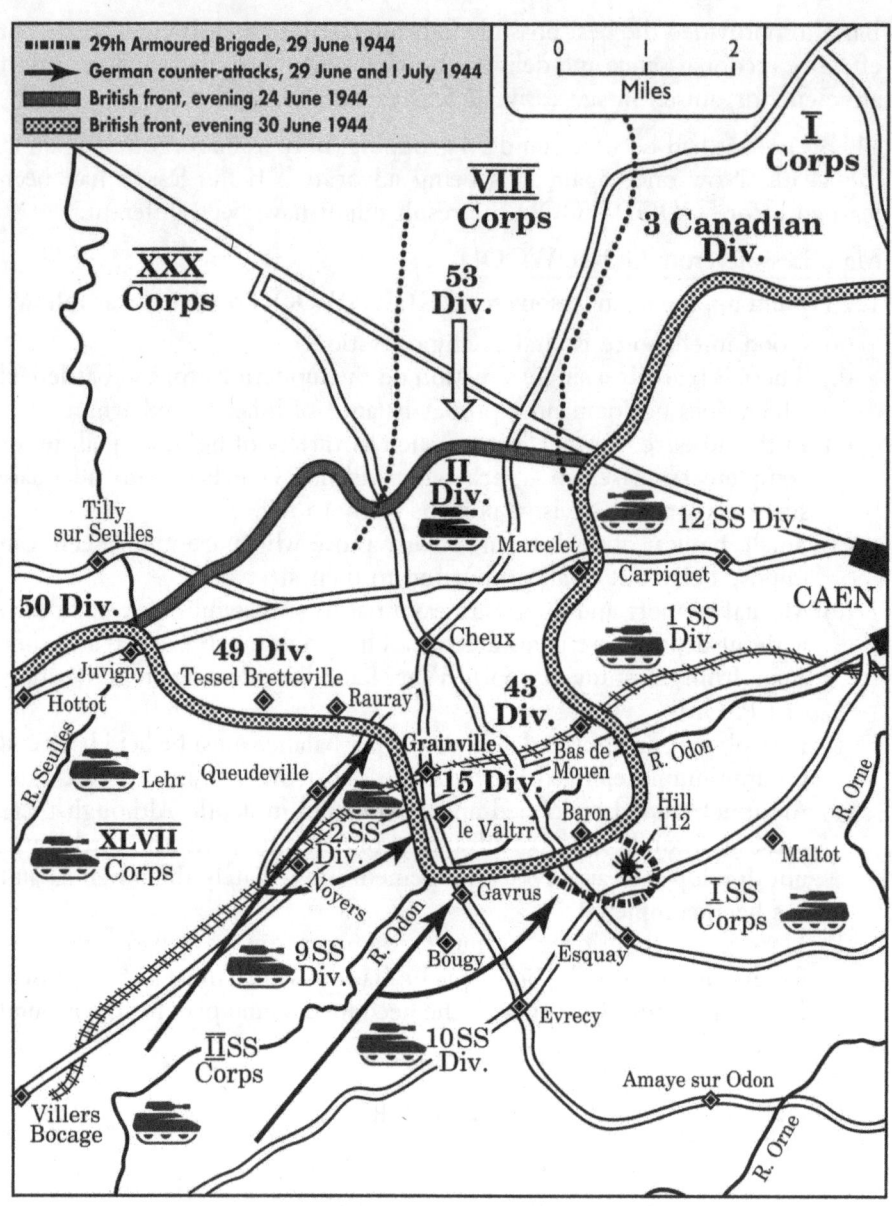

OPERATION EPSOM, June 1944.

2. For the purposes of analysis, EPSOM is three different battles:
   (a) The attack on CHEUX and HAUT DU BOSQ and the other two villages to the north-east – the first phase of EPSOM.
   (b) The capture of the bridge over the river ODON by the Argyll and Sutherland Highlanders on the right, and the capture by the 11 Armoured Division of the 112 feature on the left.
   (c) The defence of the Western side of the salient against concerted German counter-attack.

First Phase of EPSOM

3. In the set-piece attack, the objectives of the assaulting battalions, which in each case were about the size of one map square, were only captured at the expense of 30% killed, wounded and missing and with a rate of advance as slow as 100 yards in six minutes. This was despite a superiority in both infantry and tanks of 4:1 in favour of the attacker and despite support from 900 guns and 4 Royal Navy ships, of which nearly half were used in the opening barrage. The only factor in favour of the defender were the good cover for defence and the bad weather which restricted allied air support and hampered the preparation and reconnaissance for the attack.

Capture of Bridgehead over the River ODON by 2 Argyll and Sutherland Highlanders

4. In contrast with the frontal attack and heavy pounding of the first day's battle, 2 A & SH thrust to the ODON made remarkably quick progress and suffered extraordinarily lightly. Their total casualties for the operation were only 2 officers and 15 other ranks, and for this they achieved an advance of 100 yards in 10 minutes. Although they undoubtedly had numerical superiority on the narrow front on which they attacked, they had, because of the speed with which the attack was laid on (approximately 2 hours), negligible artillery and tank support. I think there were three reasons for their success:
   (a) As a result of the heavy pounding of the previous day, the German containing forces had been stretched to breaking point round the salient and only needed one sharp thrust to puncture their front line. In fact, they were concentrating their efforts in forming yet another containing line supported by reserves, behind the river ODON.
   (b) Good minor tactics consisting of fire and movement and skilful use of ground on the part of the A & SH.
   (c) The speed and informal way in which the attack was laid on had the advantage of not drawing attention to the start line and axis. Thus, the attack, by means of quick company and platoon attacks, fought its way

through the German Forward Defence Lines to its objective before the Germans could react.

5. From this encouraging episode I think the following points emerge:

(a) The frontal attack which lines men up on the start line and moves deliberately behind concentrations or a barrage may make it easy for an unimaginative commander and indifferently trained troops, but it will always prove the most expensive in casualties. It will normally take longer and will always depend on a very heavy weight of fire which in the future will not be available.

(b) The infiltration type of attack even if hastily mounted and lacking in outside support, may achieve results out of all proportion to its numbers, provided the infantry are well led and trained and can execute skilful and dynamic minor tactics.

(c) If deployment is too ponderous and reconnaissance is too prolonged, and there is too much marrying up between infantry and tanks in the forward areas, surprise is likely to be forfeited. As a result, the attack may be brought to a halt before it has hardly started. Opportunity to exploit seemed often to be lost in Normandy because of too rigid phases and objectives. It is a question of striking a balance between proper briefing and reconnaissance and surprising an enemy as to the timing and direction of a thrust.

Defence against German Counter-Attack

6. This phase took place on 29/30 June when 2 SS Panzer Division was directed north-east in the direction of HAUT DU BOSQ and CHEUX and ran into British positions down the west side of the salient at GAVRUS, LE VALTRU and GRAINVILLE. It was a complete failure and all it achieved was the elimination of the small bridgehead at GAVRUS.

7. The two defended areas most heavily affected were:

(a) GAVRUS, where 2 A & SH were deployed either side of the river in a box 400×300 yards. Troops south of the bridge, in a small bridgehead, were in a reverse slope position.

(b) LE VALTRU, where owing to its weak strength (each company only had 2 officers and 4 sections) 7 Seaforths occupied a diamond position no more than 300 yards across.

8. Against this, 2 SS Panzer Division put:

(a) The equivalent of one brigade group (in fact one tank battalion and two motorised infantry battalions) on GAVRUS.

(b) A mixed battle group of one tank battalion and one infantry battalion on LE VALTROU.

9. The fighting was very heavy, with enemy tanks and infantry working closely together and trying to infiltrate into the British positions. Bearing in mind the weak strength of the battalions and the fact that the whole weight of the attack on GAVRUS fell on one company on the far side of the river, the ratio in both armour and infantry in favour of the attacker was overwhelming. The British armour which barred the way to the final German objectives of CHEUX and HAUT DU BOSQ was held concentrated in reserve and was not available to support the forward infantry. Yet LE VALTRU was never taken and the bridgehead at GAVRUS only evacuated after two days' successful defence, in which severe casualties were inflicted on the enemy.

10. The action at LE VALTRU and GAVRUS brought the German counter-attack to a halt and air support later hit it hard and prevented the tanks from reforming. These key positions were undoubtedly held because of:

(a) Excellent artillery support.
(b) Determined fighting by the infantry which can be measured by the number of casualties:
  (i) At GAVRUS, 172 killed, wounded and missing.
  (ii) At LE VALTRU, over 300, although this includes the action in the earlier part of the battle.

Main lessons from EPSOM

11. To sum up, the main lessons seem to be as follows:

(a) The superiority of the defence in any deliberate, hard-fought, set-piece battle. This particularly applies in country which offers good cover for siting weapons.
(b) The potentialities of the infiltration type of attack in which full use is made of ground and fire and manoeuvre.
(c) The need to allow infantry to exploit where conditions allow instead of waiting for the next deliberate phase to start.
(d) Once again, the value of defence in depth. As in the case of GOOD-WOOD, the German defence was in four separate belts (in front of CHEUX, on the reverse slopes of ring contour 100, along the CAEN–LE VALTRU road and behind the River ODON on Point 112). Every time there was breakthrough in one belt, the Germans were able to reform and produce a containing line of a few tanks, SP guns and some protecting infantry. These tactics prevented 11 Armoured Division exploiting 2 A & SH's bridgehead and gave the Germans time to

assemble a counter-attack force as a threat to the salient. It was this threat to the south-east which forced 8 Corps commander to lose his nerve and withdraw 11 Armoured Division into the salient.

(e) The tremendous value of good, close artillery support in defence.

(f) The value of good junior leadership in war. 7 Seaforths arrived piecemeal at LE VALTRU having already suffered heavy casualties (three company commanders had already been killed). The battalion then had to meet strong enemy counter-attacks which put great strain on the 2nd and 3rd XIs who had to carry out tasks one or two up from their normal functions.

(g) The problems of relief in the line, particularly when a full-strength battalion takes over from a weak one.

ANNEX 'C'

BATTLEFIELD ANALYSIS

OPERATION OVERLORD

Success or Failure?

1. 6 Airborne Division's operation to secure the left flank of the British an undoubted success; despite adverse weather conditions and a scattered drop, the division achieved its primary and secondary tasks and was able to secure and defend a bridgehead east of the River ORNE.

2. The main reasons for this success were undoubtedly:

(a) The high quality of the airborne troops as demonstrated by their high morale, fitness, toughness and standard of training.

(b) The thoroughness of the planning and briefing.

(c) The degree of surprise obtained from the night landing.

(d) Poor German command arrangements which prevented them from launching a concerted counter-attack while the troops of 6 Airborne Division were still very vulnerable.

Balance of Forces

3. In an operation of this sort, it is impossible to equate the strength of the opposing sides as has been done with the other two battles. Initially, two parachute brigades were launched into an area held by two German infantry divisions and two squadrons of tanks, supported by some 100 guns, many in fixed positions; and they might therefore have been considered to be at a disadvantage. On the other hand, the troops of 6 Airborne Division were of an infinitely higher calibre than the two low category German divisions, and

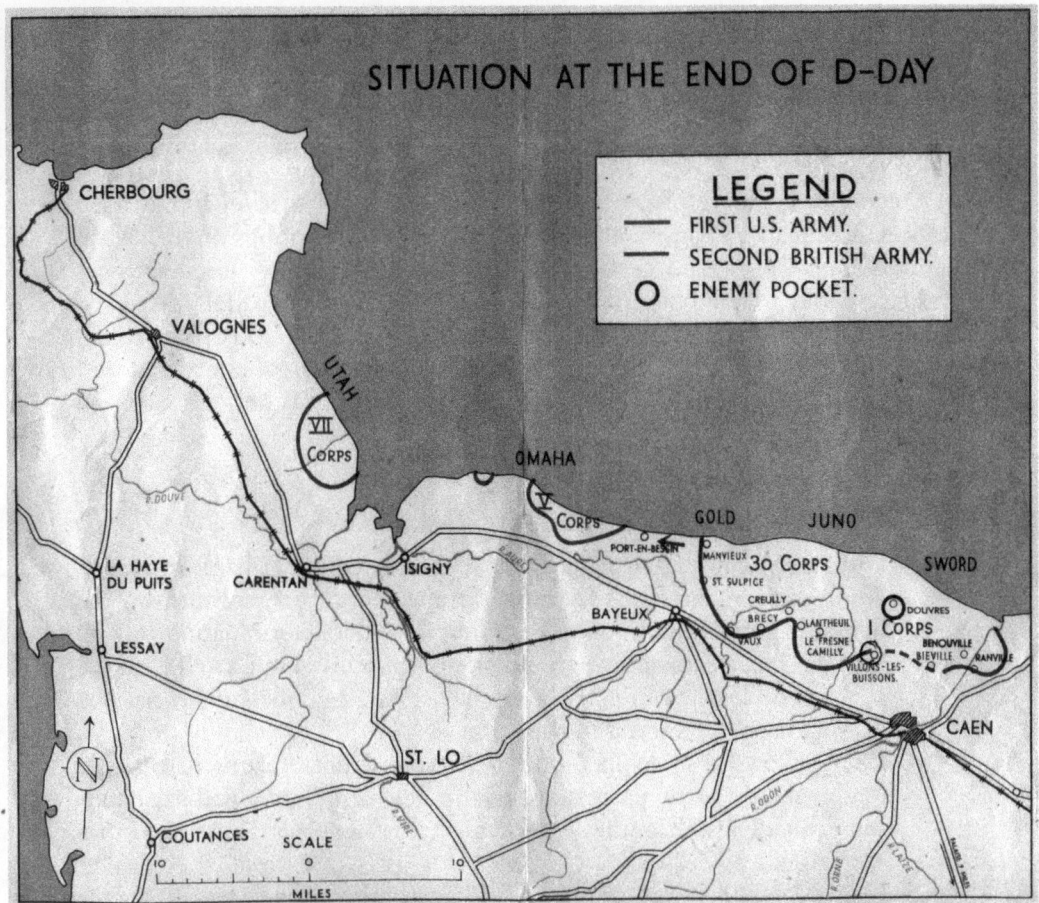

OPERATION OVERLORD, The situation at the end of D Day.

with the help of surprise, clear-cut objectives and great determination, the Airborne troops were able to press home their attacks and capture their objectives without undue difficulty. Their weakness in organic artillery was to some extent offset by air support and support from the guns of the fleet. In the reorganisation phase of the operation, they were undoubtedly helped by reluctance on the part of the German High Command to commit the Panzer Division which was in the area, in a counter stroke. Altogether, this was an operation in which surprise, a variety of fighting qualities and other factors, all contributed to invalidate the numerical superiority normally required for successful offensive operations.

4. One point however does emerge very strongly, and that is that without air superiority the operation would have been impossible. Air superiority not only enabled the assault and immediate re-supply to take place without undue casualties, but also ensured that enemy reserves were committed into battle badly disorganised and piecemeal.

Defensive Phase

5. Once the defensive phase had started, 6 Airborne Division found itself having to hold a very wide front with few men and little armour or artillery in support. That they were able to hold their position under these circumstances was largely due to good briefing and leadership amongst the widely-dispersed groups and to the offensive and aggressive patrolling which took place round the BOIS DE BAVENT. This gave a false impression of the defenders' strength and prevented the enemy from infiltrating into the gaps between battalions.

Main Lessons from OVERLORD

6. The main lessons from OVERLORD seem to be:

(a) Ultimately, battles, particularly those conducted under hazardous conditions and in the face of a numerically superior enemy, turn on the fighting spirit of the soldier. High morale and a determination to win, can only be developed by hard, tough, purposeful training and with the aid of good leadership. 6 Airborne Division is an outstanding example of what can be achieved in this respect.

(b) If time allows, as in an operation of this sort, detailed planning, realistic rehearsals and particularly thorough briefing of all ranks, will pay handsome dividends. Eighth Army came to realise this in 1942 before ALAMEIN.

(c) In order to obtain real surprise, it will nearly always be necessary to take a calculated risk which might not come off. As at QUEBEC, where Wolfe might not have been able to reach the top of the Heights of Abraham unobserved, so in Normandy the night landings might have been so dispersed by the wind as to be completely ineffective.[6] (As it was, their effectiveness was much reduced by the dispersed landings.) It is in judging these risks properly that a commander reveals his true quality. One thing is certain; every effort must be made to achieve surprise because, with surprise on his side, a commander can achieve results out of all proportion to his strength.

(d) Airborne forces are particularly vulnerable when they first land. A quick counter-attack at company or battalion level, particularly if supported by armour, may be far more effective than a much larger counter stroke delayed until the next day.

(e) Air superiority is truly one of the principles of war. It enables airborne forces to be used, air supply to take place, and it delays and disrupts enemy counter-attacks. An unfavourable air situation can make it virtually impossible for a commander to hold and manoeuvre a large armoured reserve.

(f) Defence on a wide front can be greatly facilitated by offensive aggressive patrolling, operating deep into enemy held areas.

(g) The effectiveness of well-planned *coup de main* operations carried out by highly trained, well briefed troops with a high morale.

(h) The advantages of holding a reverse slope position, particularly where, as at Ring Contour 30, there is little cover.

(d) 50th anniversary speech to Normandy veterans

Bramall was asked to speak at the Normandy Veterans Reunion on 25 June 1994 at the Royal Albert Hall.

Your Royal Highnesses, Normandy Veterans, My Lords, Ladies and Gentlemen,

Perhaps after all that I could just try to sum up why it is we've all been here this evening, responding to the wonderfully inspiring and most moving programme, and, indeed, why many of us have attended those stirring events in Portsmouth and Normandy, and in doing so I will be echoing some of the words of the Lord Bishop in his most inspiring address.

The first reason is understandable pride. The Battle of Normandy was no ordinary battle. It certainly started as the greatest combined and amphibious operation the world has ever seen, or thankfully is ever likely to see; and in the event, it did, as nothing else could have done, put beyond doubt victory over Nazi Germany with all its cruel and callous oppression. But had we failed in those storm-swept days of fifty years ago, when we were all young lads, to retain a foothold on the Continent of Europe (and there were times, early on, when it was a close-run thing), the end of the war would have been postponed almost indefinitely.

It was therefore an event of the greatest historical and military significance, and all of us who contributed in any way, however small, to making it possible and seeing it through, have reason to feel proud and conscious that we were part of history in the making. Secondly, what a unique opportunity it has been to meet old comrades in arms, and to share with them memories of those stirring days.

Do you remember Monty's pep talks to us on the eve of the invasion? Then the emotional feeling as we threaded our way through the English countryside, heading for our embarkation points. I can recall some barracking dockers as we approached Southampton, shouting to us, 'Are we downhearted?'

To which, of course, we all shouted back, 'No!'

'Well you bloody soon will be!' came the encouraging reply.

And then the great Armada of over 4,000 warships and landing craft – as far as the eye could see; the wonderful support from the Royal Air Force, ensuring virtually Luftwaffe-free skies and the splendid Royal Navy beach-masters, contriving to produce some order out of the chaos of those obstacle-strewn beaches.

And then on into the Normandy countryside, with its standing corn nearly chest high and its sinister impeding *bocage*, all suddenly blighted by the terrible and incongruous sights and smells, the thundering noise and the congestion of war – the blackened corpses, the bloated and stinking animals, the dead horses, the savage fighting and the appalling destruction of so many hamlets and villages and towns, as Normandy became a hellish battlefield.

And what about those emotive cries: 'Tiger!', 'Sniper!' or 'Panzerfaust!' which set our adrenalin running and our hearts pounding, and the 'Moaning Minnies' and the 88s, and the very short nights with Stand To's only some four or five hours apart and little chance of sleep; and not forgetting, on a lighter note, the pitfalls of taking a shovel, or of drinking raw Calvados when by some extraordinary chance we came across it. So many memories which will have remained with us all our lives and will, no doubt, have formed the basis of many 'do you remember?' stories tonight, and over the last few weeks. And why not?!

But finally, fellow veterans, the most important reason of all for us being here, has been that, through this gathering, and other events round the country, the drumhead service at Portsmouth and our pilgrimage to Normandy, we are able to honour and remember those who, in the course of the battle, which lasted until late August and accounted for over 200,000 Allied casualties, including nearly 40,000 dead, made the supreme sacrifice, as any true warrior must be prepared to do. They didn't have the chance to grow old, as we who are left, and amongst them were the bravest and the best compared with those of us left behind. I am sure we all have many memories of personalities, and of anecdotes and incidents surrounding those who fell, even to the very moment that they were struck down. I know I do.

But had it not been for their collective sacrifice and that of others on battlefields as far removed as Alamein, Kohima, Cassino, and the Rhine, all our country's efforts might not have been sufficient to pull off the victory which was so essential if civilisation was to survive.

So it has been an excellent gathering and one of proud commemoration, nostalgia and reminiscence, and of meeting old comrades in arms in good fellowship, yet always remembering with honour and respect those who still lie in Normandy and whose beautifully tended graves some of us saw recently. And now, who better to round off this remarkable evening than a very special person, whom those of us who fought in the war will never forget for the part she played in her songs and with her personality in typifying all that was best in Britain, and in raising our spirits when things looked bleak? I refer, of course, and am delighted to welcome, the Forces Sweetheart – Dame Vera Lynn.

Chapter 2

Remembrance Sunday Address

In November 2007 Bramall was asked to give the address at the Remembrance Sunday service in his local village church.

I consider it such an honour to have been asked to share my thoughts, on this Remembrance Sunday, with my fellow parishioners, particularly as the pulpit is not my scene! Remembrance, of course, is a very personal emotion, but I can only hope that what's in my heart today will strike a chord with some of you as well. I, of course, belong to a generation, shared by a number in this congregation, in which war played a very dominant part in our lives. My father had served and suffered throughout the First World War, during which, by the time the guns fell silent eighty-nine years ago on this very day, over a million men from the United Kingdom alone had died in the service of this country, and countless more were maimed or seriously wounded in the appalling slaughter of the Somme, Passchendaele, Gallipoli and elsewhere. Some would be tempted to ask 'for what purpose?' but our country had established where its interest lay and it needed these men and their sacrifice to bring victory, and in those days, that was quite enough. But a million men, with no fewer than sixty from this one, then small, village of Crondall, whose names have just been read out. Just think of that!

Then, when I was still in my teens, war came again with a vengeance, because it was spread so much more widely; and the whole population was swept up in the imminent threat of an invasion, the Battle of Britain and the horrors and traumas of all-out war, whether on the Home Front, with the Blitz and the V-weapons, or in the various operational theatres.

And soon, like so many others of my age, I was to experience the realities of battle at first hand and see friends and comrades-in-arms lose their lives or be seriously injured in close proximity to oneself; and of course, because of my profession I was often to find myself leading people, or latterly sending them into battles of one sort or another, from which I knew that a number would not return. So when I remember the Fallen, as we are all exhorted to do on this day, there are often actual faces and personalities and incidents which are etched indelibly on my mind.

Those my generation mourn came from all parts and sections of the country and community, irrespective of upbringing or education, and not all, of course, were heroes. Most of them would have been the first to pooh-pooh the idea, and certainly none of them wanted to die, although, in fact, many who did were the bravest and best, compared with those of us left behind. War, of course at best and however sometimes necessary, can never be other than the lesser of two or more evils; but if there was ever such a thing as a just war, World War II was one of those, because we were up against one of the most evil regimes the world has ever seen, in which the sort of things which happened later in Bosnia, Croatia, Kosovo and worse were commonplace, and even institutionalised, and it had to be overcome if civilisation was to survive; and convinced of the righteousness of that cause, many of those whom we remember today did display at one time or another at least a readiness to face danger and accept the risks and, if need be, make the final sacrifice.

And please remember (because it is often forgotten) that it was only by the skin of our teeth that we were able to survive the first three years of the war, and ultimately get the right result. Had it not been for the collective efforts and sacrifices of those who gave their lives we would not have been able to keep the way open for civilised society; and all the hallmarks of Nazi tyranny would have never been kept at arm's length from this country. The world would have been an altogether more barren and brutal place for all of us, our children and grandchildren to grow up in. So it's hardly surprising, therefore, that so many of us older ones feel a deep obligation not only to remember but to say 'thank you'.

But what about the young, how should they feel about it all? Well, of course, war has not stopped there, and since those days no one, whether in or out of uniform, can be said to be strangers to conflict. Indeed, there has only been one year since 1945 when members of the Armed Forces have not been killed or died doing their duty in action, 16,000 in all since 1945, within conflict situations as diverse as Korea, Malaysia, Aden, Northern Ireland, the Falklands, the Balkans and, of course, more recently, in the ghastly and ongoing wars in the Middle East, most emanating from the dramatic horrors of 9/11, which elevated terrorism to the highest international level, and which has affected all our lives. While thanks particularly to television, the horrors and anguish of war, its effects on human beings and what sacrifice really means have been brought home to every one of us so much more graphically than in years gone by. Indeed, this year, twenty-five years on, we've been particularly remembering the Falklands, another just war, I believe, in which over 260 lost their lives regaining the Islands which had been illegally seized from our own kith and kin, and in which great valour was displayed, as is still being done in Iraq and Afghanistan, and which has brought the total of post-war Victoria and George Crosses up to eight.

It was in St John's gospel that Jesus is recorded as saying that 'Greater love hath no man than this: that he lays down his life for his friends.' Well, many of our young warriors did so, primarily in the line of duty or for the sake of total strangers, which, perhaps, makes their sacrifice even greater.

So perhaps we can all, young as well as old, accept this obligation: to remember before God those who fell, particularly those with whom we are in some way more directly linked and familiar, through our families, our schools, our neighbourhood, our corps or regiment, our livelihood – indeed, it is an obligation we seem to accept readily enough when we echo the words of Laurence Binyon's famous poem *For the Fallen*, said again this morning when we firmly promise that 'At the going down of the sun and in the morning we will remember them.' Although, if we are honest with ourselves we have to admit that many a dusk and dawn passes with our minds entirely on other things. But once a year, on this day, it is the very least we can do, for truly, as that lovely inscription on the war memorial at Kohima on the India-Burma border reminds us:

When you go home
Tell them of us and say
For your tomorrow
We gave our today.

Those who went to war and didn't come back, and many who are still going to war and not coming back, were prepared to sacrifice their 'today' for our 'tomorrow'. We owe them all so much. As indeed we also owe to their serving comrades fighting bitter battles in the line of duty and suffering severe wounds as well as risking their lives, – on a ratio of about ten wounds, rarely heard about, to one fatality. They, too, deserve our thoughts and prayers and all the support and honour we and our government can give them.

But finally, although there is much, and many, to remember on this day, it would be a tragedy if we were to see their deeds and sacrifices simply as something remote, to be consigned to history, inert memorials and recognition but once a year, instead of a living and shining example of what can be achieved in the face of odds and adversity and when selfish motives are subordinated to a wider benefit.

I suggest to you that Remembrance Sunday gives us a unique opportunity to carry forward some of that character and sacrifice of those who, when put to the test, were not found wanting, for the benefit and inspiration of us all and particularly of the younger generation who will have many difficult problems to solve and will need all the help, inspiration and strength they can get.

The challenges may not be the same, I hope they won't be, as those that faced us older ones, but they will be no less urgent and will require the same degree of unselfishness if they are to be overcome.

For these days, it's not just power-hungry dictators, sinister aggression, ethnic cleansing and now international terrorism that have to be stood up to, although recent events have shown that this still has to be done in a dangerous world. Because, apart from great privations in our world there are so many other dragons, some much nearer to home, waiting to be slain by latter day St Georges, some of them also requiring considerable courage, certainly of the moral sort. I refer, of course, to bigotry, envy and hate, to mindless civil and criminal violence, to the disproportionate power of the popular media and the degrading impact it can have on standards and values in our lives, to greed, to despair by those without fulfilling work or affordable homes, or those who are seriously ill or disabled, the old who are lonely, the young who are on drugs, and other evils just as serious, those of apathy and complacency. We can't all be like that great war and peace hero, Leonard Cheshire, but at least the up and coming generations can try their utmost to make the best of a world which with all its beauty, love and enchantment is bound to be full of human frailties, tragedy, wickedness and conflict of one sort or another, and only pray that when they are put to the test, in whatever field of endeavour, they are not found wanting any more than those we remember today.

So there's no better time than this Sunday, not only to remember with grateful hearts, but also to obtain strength and inspiration for the challenges which lie ahead. And no better place than this lovely church of ours, where we are constantly reminded of Christ's own death for our sakes and of the help and inspiration His sacrifice and teaching can give all of us in leading out our lives, and remind us, too, if we pause to think about it, of the undoubted truth that without God's love, mercy and protection no endeavours of a lasting nature are really possible.

Chapter 3

The Holocaust

In April 1998 Bramall announced, to a distinguished audience, the setting up of a permanent Holocaust Exhibition within the Imperial War Museum. The Exhibition was not without controversy, but as the Chairman of the Museum's Trustees he drove through the whole concept and for his work was awarded the Interfaith Gold Medallion. The Holocaust was, after all, the most extensive example of 'Man's Inhumanity to Man', and became an essential part of Hitler's war aims. It has therefore come to symbolize the horror and totality of the Second World War and it is now part of the National Curriculum taught to all schools. For a soldier who had the almost unique experience of witnessing not only the uncovering of Belsen concentration camp but also the ruins of both Hamburg and Hiroshima, this manifestation of Total War has a particularly strong resonance.

May I, as Chairman of the Trustees of the Imperial War Museum, welcome you all here this morning on behalf of all of us, and thank you very much for coming? I and the Director General have invited you here to tell you why the Imperial War Museum has decided to take the important step of establishing a permanent Holocaust Museum within the Museum's Headquarters building here in Southwark, and how in general terms we are going to go about it.

The remit of this museum is Twentieth Century Conflict (from 1914 to be precise), i.e. the study and recording of it, and the graphical portrayal, to public and nation, of all aspects of it and its impact on individuals and societies. We record and portray, hopefully objectively and historically, so that others can learn and take note.

We do this in a variety of ways: here at the main museum, at the Cabinet War Rooms, on HMS *Belfast* in the Pool of London and at Duxford, near Cambridge. Particularly, we do it through our research facilities and our permanent exhibitions on the First and Second World Wars, on conflict since 1945, from Korea to the Gulf (to be opened in June); and at Duxford, to be opened next summer, also an American Air Museum which will commemorate principally the major US air effort, with all its sacrifices, mounted from this country in World War II, but also covering the contribution of US air power in support of NATO and in the Cold War. We also have many temporary exhibitions covering such things as 'London at War', 'Occupation of the Channel Islands', 'Evacuees' and much, much else, ranging from the deadly serious and traumatic to the lighter hearted and more nostalgic.

Now the Director General and I, and all the Trustees, believe the time has come to record permanently for future generations that horrific chapter in European history – Hitler's calculated and systematic extermination, by gassing in death camps or mass shooting by police battalions, of over 6 million Jews in Europe, which has come to be known as the Holocaust.

We believe that for two main reasons this falls completely within our remit, and that we, with all our experience in the exhibition field, are in the best position nationally to carry it out. The first reason (and I say this as part of the wartime generation, like Lord Runcie, which took part in the Normandy invasion and the final conquest of Nazi Germany) is that nothing convinced us more that we had been fighting a just war, and that whatever harsh steps we had had to take to achieve victory were justified, because Hitler and his most evil regime had to be beaten once and for all, than the discovery by us, a half-century ago, of the concentration camp at Bergen-Belsen (and Lord Runcie may have more to say on this), of Dachau and Buchenwald by the Americans, and Majdanek and Auschwitz by the Russians, to say nothing of all the slave labour camps set up for the benefit of the German armament industry.

And the second reason is that the Holocaust constituted an integral part of Hitler's war aims and the sort of 'Thousand Year Reich' he wanted to establish as a result of the war. Aryan Germans were to be the master race, with all the Eastern lands subjugated and colonised and their indigenous inhabitants reduced to being *Untermenschen* and slave labour, with the 'Final Solution', harping back to his obsession exposed in *Mein Kampf*, reserved for Jews, not only in Germany, but in Poland, Russia, Czechoslovakia and Hungary as well, and indeed in any part of Occupied Europe where the Nazis held sway.

Of course, in this onward march of Nazi tyranny, it was not only the Jews who suffered. In Nazi Germany there was persecution, starvation, cruelty and often death for those in many other groups; there was euthanasia of the mentally ill and infirm; and in the wake of the military campaign in Russia, Poland, Yugoslavia and Greece, the civilian population was brutally treated and often slaughtered, particularly by the SS. The Holocaust Exhibition, being the history of these terrible times, will naturally reflect all this as well.

But it was that 'Final Solution' for the European Jews which was at the heart of the whole thing, and unique in the sense that, although there had been before, and have been since, and may sadly be again, other ghastly examples of man's inhumanity to man, in which troops have run amok, where there has been 'ethnic cleansing', and occasions when thousands and even tens of thousands have been murdered in sudden surges of revenge or blood lust, and which have been covered up or condoned, instead of perpetrators being brought to justice; and you will be able to recall what occurred in Russia, Armenia, Cambodia and those in much more recent memory still (and some of these will be covered in a small exhibition, called Total War, dealing with the abuses of civilian populations and those in captivity), there has never been such a cold, calculated exercise as the Holocaust, to wipe out a whole people, organised by tidy-minded staff officers, who went home to wives and children in suburban homes, and carried out and perpetrated, in the most callous and depraved way possible, by officers and men of disciplined agencies who actually got applauded, promoted and decorated for these ghastly crimes. Nor ones at which, for a variety of reasons, a whole population of a Western, developed nation, many of them decent, honourable people, and who certainly would have displayed those more honourable traits if they had been brought up under a different regime, looked on with complete indifference, preferring to pretend they knew nothing about it, and, tragically, in a number of cases, collaborating. Such was the forward path and vice-like clamp of tyranny.

And students of human nature will realise only too well how, under certain circumstances, these ghastly manifestations of hate, envy, cruelty and indifference can come to the fore or be stirred up, which is why it is so vital that the truth about this particular tyranny, brutality and genocide should never be forgotten by future generations.

Certainly, as you can see from the brochure, this is the unanimous view of all the leaders of our main political parties – the Prime Minister, John Major, Tony Blair and Paddy Ashdown – who together have given the project their firm all-party support. For not only is vigilance the price of peace, the main theme of this Museum, you might say, but also, as Mr Blair has put it, 'Our vigilance and diligence must ensure that man's innate capacity for evil must never be allowed again to have such despicable and depraved consequences.'

This important new facility will be housed in a major extension to this building, which the Director General will describe in a few moments, and for which we now have planning permission. The cost of this extension, which as well as housing the Holocaust exhibition will provide space for two other similar exhibitions and, very importantly, a new education complex, because so many young people come here, is just over £13 million. We are entirely confident that we shall raise this sum. We have made a submission to the Heritage Lottery Fund,[7] and have had promises of very generous donations from the private sector.[8] The outcome of our application to the Lottery Fund is not yet known, but we are very optimistic that a scheme which completes the long-awaited redevelopment of this greatly regarded Museum and gives Britain a permanent exhibition on the Holocaust will be of enormous benefit to the nation and future generations.

On the platform with me to make their own points and help answer any queries are, as you can see, from left to right, Lord Runcie, who, apart, of course, from being a one-time Archbishop of Canterbury, was an officer in the Scots Guards at the time of the appalling revelations at Belsen (which is already the subject of a small exhibition here); Rabbi Hugo Grynn, himself a survivor of the Holocaust, the Director General, Robert Crawford, and the very distinguished historian of the twentieth century and Churchill biographer, Martin Gilbert.

But first I am going to ask the Director General to say something about how we are going to go about designing the Exhibition itself.

Book 2

Cold War and Nuclear Deterrence

Chronology

1946

March	Churchill's 'Iron Curtain' speech at Fulton, Missouri.

1947

January	Attlee authorizes British atomic bomb production.
June	Marshall Plan for the reconstruction of Europe announced.

1948

February	Communist coup d'état in Czechoslovakia.
June	Berlin Blockade starts, and Airlift.
November	Montgomery becomes Chairman of Western European COS.

1949

April	North Atlantic Treaty signed.
August	Soviet atomic bomb exploded.

1950

June	Korean war begins.
December	First V bombers ordered.

1951

April	Eisenhower appointed SACEUR (Supreme Allied Commander Europe), with Montgomery as Deputy.

1952

October	British atomic bomb successfully tested.
November	US hydrogen bomb successfully tested.
December	Decision to start work on investigating British hydrogen bomb.

1953

January	First 'Radical Review' of British defence policy.
August	Soviet hydrogen bomb successfully tested.

1954

May	Foundation of SEATO (Southeast Asia Treaty Organization)
July	Cabinet decision to build British hydrogen bomb.

1956

October	Operation Musketeer: Anglo-French invasion of Egypt.

1957

March	Eisenhower/Macmillan Bermuda meeting.
April	Sandys Defence White Paper.
May	British hydrogen bomb successfully tested.
June	Mountbatten/Rickover submarine agreement.

1958

June	Chief of Defence Staff established.

1959

July	SSN *Dreadnought* laid down.

1960

February	French atomic bomb successfully tested.
March	Camp David meeting on Skybolt, Polaris and Holy Loch.
June	Skybolt agreement with USA.
October	Hugh Gaitskell's 'Fight, fight and fight again' speech.

1961

March	Macmillan/Kennedy meeting at Key West.

1962

August	Cancellation of Blue Water.
Berlin	Wall erected.
October	Cuban Missile Crisis.
December	Macmillan/Kennedy Nassau Agreement on Polaris.

1964

October	China atomic bomb successfully tested.

1968

January	NATO 'Massive Retaliation' replaced by 'Flexible Response'.
August	Soviet invasion of Czechoslovakia.

1971

August	Polaris improvement programme approved.

1972

January	SALT 1 agreement.

1978

December	Chiefs of Staff recommend Polaris replacement.

1979

December	NATO decision to deploy Cruise missiles. Soviet invasion of Afghanistan.

1980

July	Decision to buy Trident announced.

1981

January	Reagan sworn in as President of USA.

1982

January	Cruise missile deployment in UK begins.

1985

March	Gorbachev becomes Soviet Head of State.
November	Reagan/Gorbachev Geneva Summit.

1986

September	Keel of first British Trident submarine laid.
October	Reagan/Gorbachev Reykjavik Summit.

1987

December	Reagan/Gorbachev Washington Summit. Intermediate-Range Nuclear Forces Treaty.

1988

June	Reagan/Gorbachev Moscow Summit.
November	USSR ceases to jam all foreign radio stations.
December	Demonstrations in Baltic, Caucasian and East European states against USSR.

1989

June	Tiananmen Square massacre. Solidarity win Polish elections.
November	Berlin Wall comes down.

1990

| October | German re-unification. |

1991

| August | Attempted coup to remove Gorbachev. |
| December | Final collapse of Soviet Union, Gorbachev resigns and is replaced by Yeltsin. |

1997

| March | Poland, Hungary, Czech Republic join NATO. |

2003

| April | Poland, Czech Republic, Estonia, Hungary, Latvia, Lithuania, Slovakia and Slovenia join European Union. |

2004

| March | Bulgaria, Estonia, Latvia Lithuania, Romania, Slovakia, and Slovenia join NATO, i.e. NATO now on the Russian border. |

2007

| January | Bulgaria, Romania join European Union. |

2009

| April | Albania and Croatia join NATO. |

Introduction

In late 1946, with the Soviet Union bringing down what Winston Churchill described in his Fulton speech as an 'Iron Curtain' across Central Europe, the Western nations (NATO) and the Eastern European nations (the Warsaw Pact) faced each other in what came to be called the Cold War, a period of worldwide tension made more extreme by the fact that both sides possessed nuclear weapons.

NATO therefore now perceived that what was necessary to counter any potential land threat on the continent of Europe was an ever-ready and manifest linkage between committed conventional forces, which if ever too hard pressed to defend successfully and halt any aggression, had a clear call on the possible use of nuclear weapons in some shape or form. This, it was firmly believed, would constitute too big a risk for any aggressor to take; and since the prize which had to be made not worth the risk was the total ideological domination of Europe, the strategy carried just enough credibility to bring about stability and protected peace in Europe, something which could not have been achieved so cheaply in any other way. Moreover, since Britain's comparatively small contribution to the US/NATO deterrent carried an independent tag, it was held to provide a belt and braces guarantee for our homeland security, should some sort of nuclear exchange be embarked upon by either side. So, over the next decade we all came to believe in and live with the strategy of Flexible Response as our basic philosophy, or, you might almost say, theology.

Bramall was to have experience of the Cold War at three levels and was therefore in a good position to ensure that those involved had a clear understanding of the complexity of Flexible Response and the basis on which NATO forces were deployed and might have to fight. Once he had retired and taken his seat in the House of Lords he continued to observe the Cold War and to comment in his speeches on the issues he had already lived through, bringing to bear his knowledge and experience to make relevant and often critical comment on government policy, both present and future.

Chapter 4

The British Army's Role in Germany

While commanding 1st Armoured Division Bramall regularly spoke about why B.A.O.R. existed and its purpose. There follow two examples of these speeches, one to soldiers and the other to civilians. The first was given at an 11th Armoured Brigade study period on 11 September 1973 about the role of BAOR. He felt it was important that all knew the basis on which they were required to operate and why the British stationed an Army in Germany

(a) 1972 speech to 1st Armoured Division

I thought I would say something about how I see our role in Germany; what, if anything, we are achieving and in what way the situation could change in the next three or four years.

Why are we here? The answer is simple: to prevent war, not to fight it.

(a) We help provide the outward and visible manifestation of strength and involvement and determination to defend the NATO area, and resist unacceptable political pressures, in a way which the presence of strategic nuclear weapons **alone** could never do; and the reason, of course, why nuclear weapons alone could not convey the same conviction of comprehensive protection to our friends and effective dissuasion to any potential foe is that although possessing nuclear weapons, in all crises between the super powers, such as Korea in 1949, Berlin in 1961, Cuba in 1963, the Middle East, Indochina, has produced very **real** restraint on aggressive intentions, and no one should underestimate the restraining influence in all cases – restraint on ally as well as enemy – no one could easily get themselves to believe that an American President, or for that matter, a British Prime Minister, would risk national suicide for the sake of something in Europe which had not, up to that point, involved a direct and urgent threat to the heart of America or the United Kingdom.

(b) Which brings me to the **second** and more specific role, which is, with that of the other Corps of Northern Army Group and the Central Front, to provide specific tactical deterrent against those who otherwise might feel that if they limited their aggression in terms of time and space, they would surely be able to achieve some expansion of power and influence without incurring the nuclear retribution which everyone naturally seeks to avoid. So it might be worthwhile. For here in Germany we continually present to any would-be aggressor a thoroughly realistic prospect that tangling with us, as they would have to, could well initiate the process of escalation to the unthinkable holocaust. Of course, at what stage and in what order such a stumbling forward to nuclear war would occur, must remain, I am sure you would agree, part of the uncertainty that surrounds the whole theology of the nuclear deterrent and makes it that much more effective and awe-inspiring. But we **do** deliver a comprehensive message which is both plausible and unmistakable: if you start anything, however limited, those of us who are here will fight and promise you an unspecified number of days – five, six, a week – perhaps even ten days of hard battling, which we are well capable of doing and moreover, if we **do** clash together, it is almost certain that nuclear weapons in some shape or form will be used in our support, and then who can judge the consequences? Is that really what you want? The onus is then on them to say whether they want to risk it, not on us to say that we will necessarily fight to the death for this or that cause or piece of real estate. This is what we say we can do. This is what we can do. Because except in Air Defence we are very well equipped.

If you don't think that is a good enough deterrent, then we haven't got a good enough deterrent; if you think we would never get nuclear release, then perhaps we should increase our strength so that we could fight unsupported for say twenty or thirty days, or more, but that would cost a lot more money and involve all sorts of political problems. But is what we have got now, which is what General Carver called 'credible strategy', really credible? **I** think it is credible, because in a comparatively short time in the event of a major attack, the British and particularly the American troops would have started to get killed, the threat would have been identified, and the fundamental truth, that America and Great Britain can only be defended in Europe would be obvious for all to see; nuclear weapons would have some possible justification, and if it is only a minor excursion, then our twenty-odd divisions should be able to cope. Do you think it is credible, and what is more important, do the Russians think it is credible? If they do, our insurance premium is high enough; if they don't, we have got to do more about it. The indication so far is that it has done its job and is still doing so.

(c) Finally, of course, our third role is that we have got to be trained and equipped actually to do the things we threaten to do. To give battle should our deterrent fail; to counter aggression, with the appropriate degree of force (and the range of options may be bigger than is envisaged) in order to identify, delay and deal with minor infringements; to win time for diplomatic action to be instigated, for international pressure to be applied, for calculated political decisions to be taken on nuclear weapons and, if we are lucky, for wiser counsels to prevail; and the longer we can fight, eventually the more flexibility our politicians have.

What would happen at the end of five or six days battling in an all-out assault is difficult to predict and scarcely worth the speculation, but we would have done our job, and indeed our ability to do just that is one of the essential pillars on which the credibility of our deterrent is based. Perhaps in the past this role for BAOR has not very often been so starkly put; but the Japanese, who are realists, give their armed forces exactly this sort of task. Quite simply, they must be prepared to fight for ten days, no more, no less. At the end of that time nuclear war would either have taken over or they would surrender.

Wet? Not at all. Enough is enough, and our ability to fight four, five or six days, cause heavy losses to the enemy and introduce a nuclear war, is, to my mind, in the context of NATO and the East/West balance, quite sufficient today to meet our aim and make our strategy credible.

But what of the future in a Europe dominated by a possible US withdrawal, MBFR [Mutual and Balanced Force Reduction], European Security Conferences, etc? Can we go on playing the same old record in the same old way, with the same old and higher costs?

The Security Conference is unlikely to lead to anything except the running of pet hobby horses, but what if the Americans, as seems quite likely, take out two Divisions? What does NATO and particularly Europe do then?

Abandon defence altogether, on the basis that the use of force is so circumscribed by restraints that it is almost impossible to use, and no one wants war anyway? Take, for example, the British Aircraft Corporation TSR-2 (Tactical Strike and Reconnaissance Aircraft, version 2), which was a cancelled Cold War strike and reconnaissance aircraft developed by BAC for the RAF in the 1950s and 1960s. It was designed to penetrate a well-defended forward battle area at low altitudes and very high speeds, and then attack high value targets in the rear with nuclear or conventional weapons. It also had a combat role as a high altitude stand-off, side-looking radar and photographic imagery and a signals intelligence reconnaissance role. It was a victim of ever-rising costs and inter-service squabbling over Britain's defence needs, and was cancelled by the new Labour government in 1965. It was originally to be replaced by the F-111, another decision scrapped for financial reasons, and eventually replaced by the Buccaneer and Phantom and eventually the Tornado. Sir Sidney Camm (designer of the Hurricane) said, 'All modern aircraft have got four dimensions: span, length, height and politics. TSR-2 simply got the first three right.'

Well, that allegory is no doubt attractive to the extreme left, but to take it seriously hardly adds up to good government. For if anything, we are seeing the balance of power swing away from us and towards the Soviet Union, both in Europe, where her capabilities to launch an attack with little or no warning and with at least a 3-to-1 superiority seems, if anything, to be increasing both in quality and quantity (and why, if no dark intentions?), and in the Middle East and elsewhere, where she gets more confident in her exploitation of vacuums, just at the time when the other super-power, the United States, gets more compulsively introverted over her own internal problems. No, to fail to keep any sort of balance in Europe would lay oneself open to intolerable political pressures and abandoning the minimum freedom of action which **guarantees** independence; a situation which no self-respecting government or community is likely to accept.

Well then, just admit that there are to be fewer troops to hold the same frontage, on the basis that, as the aim of the exercise is prevention rather than fighting, our actual capability does not matter too much, and we have always got the potential in the form of nuclear weapons behind us, and the capacity to reinforce. Well, even for deterrence purposes one needs credibility in the eyes of friend and foe, friend as much as foe, and at the present we are so thin on the ground while operating a forward strategy that any further reduction of NATO forces must quite clearly blow this credibility sky high. If we were prepared just to be a trip-wire it might not matter, but then the options would be to use nuclear weapons at once or surrender without any resistance at all.

Then there is the option that we have light covering forces and such forward formations, as we have in Europe, so that we concentrate in a central point to move to the particular threatened area in the belief that the enemy would not attack everywhere. This might make some theoretical military sense on the basis that the wider and weaker their front, the greater the depth you must have, but there would seem to be two overriding objections. First, could you get this mass of manoeuvre into action where it was wanted in the face of an adverse air threat, and secondly, more urgent, are you prepared to back down on the steady movement of the last three years to defend further and further westwards to appease German susceptibilities and to avoid giving the impression that you were prepared to sacrifice large chunks of German real estate and population in order to win some classic military victory in the heart of Europe. I hardly think that such a solution is possible if the European community is to hold together.

So finally, is there anything else we can do to compensate for the American withdrawal? If we could be certain that the Russians would reduce their superiority, having made allowance for their quicker ability to reinforce, the situation might not be so urgent, but there seems little likelihood of this happening. Is there any way we can improve the size and effectiveness of the European forces? Some people say that if we made our Divisions blatantly defensive units, strong in anti-tank weapons, both mobile and hand-held, we could bring the enemy to a grinding halt, but then our Divisions are by necessity defensive forces with little real offensive capability in view of their inferiority of numbers, and to abandon all offensive performance altogether would hardly serve the interests of defence when the chips are down. The best anti-tank weapon is the tank; what we want is more tanks and more weapons for infantry to use in close country. Could we make use of German Home Guard or Territorial forces to turn Hanover, Celle, Brunswick and Hildesheim into fanatical pivots of resistance around which our mobile forces could operate to a greater advantage? It is hardly compatible to the open city policy but worth thinking about. Could we increase the size of our own 1st Corps by one Division and the Germans by two or three, and the Dutch and Belgians by a Brigade or two? Well, it is a nice thought, and no doubt the Americans would like us to do just this, but not only is a great deal of money involved, putting our increased spending at well over 5% or 6% of GDP, and in the case of the Germans', Dutch and Belgians' hostility to conscription even at its present level, but in our case we would have to take the very large and deliberate step of abandoning all voluntary forces and going back to the system of conscription which we had for over twenty years from 1939, including through the Second World War. This would be costly, uneconomical and unpopular. Is the threat worth the price? There would certainly be no other way to increase significantly our forces in Europe.

Finally, are there any political compromises, sacrifices, almost international indignities that we would be prepared to undergo in order to get the French Army back in the firing line? This could be done perhaps by means of a complete break with the United States, probably by a French Supreme Allied Commander in Europe and a nuclear deterrent not underwritten by the fantastically formidable nuclear resources of the United States but only by the far smaller and less plausible resources of France and Great Britain, who would be threatening to throw their stones from an all too vulnerable glass house.

It is a fascinating problem and dilemma, which is going to face military men over the next few years, and the trouble is that, square as it sounds, whenever one tries to produce a new military strategy to keep the peace as this one has done for close on thirty years, through some difficult times and touch-and-go moments, it is very difficult to think up a more satisfactory one than the present system. But perhaps after this some of you will be able to produce one, and I would be more than interested to hear it.

I myself am a balance of power man, with which to date we have just kept pace – more complicated because of non-aligned nation blocks. When people talk of constraints on military force and the non-utility of military force and of there being no threat, it is usually within the confines of a certain balance of power. Scrap that balance and the situation could be radically transformed, with those in the ascendancy suddenly in a position to reap the rewards which come from military power when others have none. Indeed, I would not disagree with that crafty Chinese philosopher Mo Tzu of 400 BC, who preached universal love but founded a society of fighting freemasons on the basis that the truculent were deterred less by the moral reprimand of the turned cheek than by its perfect system of defence which would make them pay dear for aggression.

*   *   *

So much for the moment on the balance of power in Europe which, because we have got it more or less right, is perhaps the least potentially explosive area in the world. Is Europe the only place in which we in Britain, and perhaps we should now say we in Europe, have a contribution to make?

Well, Britain's top priority is undoubtedly Europe, but this does NOT, I believe, mean that the British Army is necessarily and forever confined to the Westphalian Plain. One thing that all contingencies have is that they are largely unexpected.

First it is easy to forget what a large place Europe is. Traditionally, Britain's more effective role in Europe has been as part of an alliance employing a maritime strategy on the flanks and I believe that NATO responsibilities in Scandinavia and possibly in Southern Europe could become increasingly interesting and testing. It is, after all, in those areas that marginal confused situations with implications of political blackmail can be so dangerous. And with the build-up of the Soviet Fleet in the Mediterranean and the North Sea, these areas, and places like Cyprus and Malta, look uncommonly like the front line.

Secondly, although the world is indeed getting more permissive than it was in the old imperial days, and although we no longer have the means or the inclination to carry out an independent policing policy in traditional areas of influence, there are some military responsibilities outside Europe we in Britain cannot escape or wish to escape.

We are responsible for the IS and external security of our remaining colonial possessions, of which Hong Kong, Fiji, British Honduras, Bermuda and Gibraltar all have internal or external problems of one sort or another. Hong Kong, of course, has already given us serious civilian disturbances, and in Hong Kong the Army also has the important task on the frontier to make it clear that if Peking wants to knock off Hong Kong, they might have a full-scale war on their hands.

We also have treaties and responsibilities to ex-allies and to other commonwealth and ex-colonial countries. The degree of obligation, of course, varies from the completely binding, but admittedly very remote, contingency of coming to the aid of Australia and New Zealand if the need arose, to those in which we reserve the right, in any situation, to say what aid we would give, but where it would be difficult to refuse altogether a genuine call for help, particularly if earlier administrative arrangements on our part had contributed to the problem, e.g. Borneo or Brunei, and in the Arabian Peninsula.

We are still required to retain some permanent military presence in SE Asia in a Commonwealth Brigade (albeit a small one of a battalion group and aircraft and ships on station), described at one time as part of the five-power 'posse' rather than the Imperial sheriff. This commitment is important and significant for two reasons:

(a) The consensus of local opinion is that our presence inspires confidence, contributes to stability in the area and stops internal friction, and as long as they think that, there is a good chance that it does.

(b) One should not underrate the power of even quite small forces to make a political point (rather better than diplomacy) and improve a nation's bargaining position.

For effective use and deployment of military forces need not necessarily mean heavy engagement in ground combat (in fact paradoxically they lose some of their latent power when they are so engaged). If a nation retains its forces in an area of traditional concern when it is wanted, or moves into an area where it had not been previously, it may or may not pose a substantial threat to a potential enemy, and this depends on many things. But such forces can give moral support; they can show a continuing or novel interest in local politics and trade; they can confirm or establish their nation as a power to be reckoned with and strengthen its bargaining position; and they can balance the excessive influence of others. They can in fact, as a deployment of Soviet naval forces in the Eastern Mediterranean and Indian Ocean has so clearly indicated, play a significant part in adjusting the balance of power without unacceptable escalation. (As you see, I am a balance of power man).

Now how much our forces in the Middle East or Suez would actually be able to achieve if their stability value failed and violence erupted would depend on a great many factors. They will, of course, be very small and they would need a scale of reinforcement and logistic support which could only be achieved over some weeks, if the **will** of the Nation was really behind it and if our commitment to Ireland had subsided. We would, of course, need to be very certain about what it was we were protecting and from whom and why (i.e. were we backing the right horse morally and in terms of self-interest, and preferably both?) and we would require allies to be in on the act.

Under certain circumstances we could I think still play a useful role on the lines of Brunei and Borneo – part deterrent to widening the conflict, part moral support, part counter-insurgency inside the host nation and part frontier protection from outside threats – and we would then hope to contribute towards a constructive political settlement, as we did there. But we must face the fact that our response would inevitably be smaller and slower, and then any intervention on our part must be more in the nature of supplying equipment, training teams, seconding officers and perhaps at the most sending token forces. Such a policy is more flexible and, as the United States have found, less liable to quite unnecessary escalation.

Next, of course, our support of the UN requires us to be prepared, whenever we are considered acceptable, to provide observers and contingents to the UN Peace Keeping Forces, whose important role allows nations to back down on bigotry and prejudices without too much loss of face. It has proved an essential service and safety valve in the past – Suez and Cyprus are cases in point – and could do so again in the future, e.g. the Middle East, and Britain's contribution has always been very effective **when** it has been acceptable. Indeed, in **theory** at any rate, what Palmerston said about it 'not being fitting for a country like Britain with such wide and extensive interests to lock herself up in a single regard to her own affairs of state', could still hold good to some extent today, and could start to apply to the EEC, particularly with the Soviet Union usurping previous influences in the Middle East and showing every inclination to extend to its south-east.

We will always need allies; we may bring all Europe to accept a common strategy for Peace in these peripheral areas, but the unique 'Have Gun Will Travel' ability of the British Army could be a continuing asset for Europe and what is loosely called the free world for some decades to come.

The Use of Force

Against this background, the function and duty of our profession is the organised application of armed force – its control and management under the properly constituted authority and, as I have tried to point out to you, this force may be required in a number of forms:

(a) As a deterrent.
(b) As a back-up to diplomacy, psychological operations, and economic trade aid and military advice in order to achieve an acceptable balance of power without precipitating an escalation of conflict.
(c) In the form of limited and tightly controlled violence, when a particularly deep conflict of interests exists and when it is necessary to

combat or undertake operations designed to hurt and give warnings of what **could** be worse to come, i.e. deterrent plus.

(d) In the handling of revolutionary situations and internal violence, which must be by far the greatest threat to nation status in the 1970s and 1980s.

In carrying out its responsibilities the British Army may encounter all sorts of violence against it, although it is likely, assuming the balance of power is right, to be on a smaller scale than the set piece battles of the first half of the century: sniper, grenade, mine, bomb and machine guns rather than air bombardment and artillery barrage. But the problems violence will pose and the demands it will make on professional skill will be just as great. To counter it will require, as illustrated in Ireland, patience, profound thought and often a comprehensive political and social programme, with which military plans must be closely co-ordinated. Indeed, politics will usually interpenetrate military plans at every level, and the demands on military discipline and self-restraint will be heavy.

In such a climate, in which the errors of a single soldier can unbalance a delicate political situation, a military man requires a degree of political wisdom to appreciate the implications of his plans and actions and to be able to deal with politicians and civil administrators on a frank, firm but harmonious basis; he must have sound military plans but try to see political requests as not prejudiced; and although **courage** will be as important as ever, there will be no place for the irresponsible heroics, and regiments may have to get as much satisfaction from the incidents and violence they have averted as from enemies they have put to flight.

Generally, with **one** exception, the British Army's record since World War II has been very good in this sort of situation, and the military seem to have completely accepted that the military reaction to violence will invariably have to be in no higher currency than the original act of violence, that it may have to be completed in a reasonable time frame if it is not to lose its effectiveness and that it will **always** be in a glare of publicity. Such constraints put a high premium not only on professional skill and political awareness, but also on the ability to be **articulate** in dealing with home and foreign officials, press and TV.

So, as you would expect, I remain a confirmed believer in the need for, and under certain circumstances, the utility of military forces. I believe we have a career which not only can we be proud of, as being in the forefront of public service, but one which produces immense satisfaction, variety, intellectual as well as physical challenge, the pursuit of private excellence, congenial companionship, and, perhaps above all, fascinating problems of human relationships which have to be solved in practice not just in theory (such as how do you make changes to conform with society while preserving what needs to be preserved).

As long as we can keep our ranks filled, and this will be our biggest problem, the profession of arms shall continue to make a vital contribution to the gradual progress of civilisation and, with others, to act as a restraint on mankind from utterly destroying itself.

(b) 1973 speech to Consul General, Hanover

As GOC 1st Armoured Division Bramall played host to many visitors, both official and unofficial. For all of them he had to provide a briefing. This was one delivered to the Consul General, Hanover on 14 June 1973.

May I welcome you most warmly to the 1st Division and say how pleased we are to see you in Verden?

We will keep it very informal, but I hope in the time available we will be able to give you some idea of deployment, equipment and the various small problems which crop up from time to time, although from the outset I should make it clear that here in Niedersachsen we operate within a fund of goodwill and cooperation from the *Land*, *Kreis* and *Stadt* administrations, and this, I know, in no small part is due to our diplomatic representation in Hanover. We are very grateful for this general goodwill which makes our job so much easier and we will do our best, in cooperation with your office and the SLOs [Service Liaison Officers], to continue to foster it. Indeed, really the problems vis-à-vis the local population are absolutely minimal.

1st Division, which is deployed to the north-east part of the British zone, is one of three Divisions of the British Corps which forms the bulk of the 50,000-odd men of BAOR (doubled after reinforcement from the UK). The Divisional administrative area covers the whole of Schleswig Holstein, virtually all Niedersachsen east of the Weser, and down to and including the Hartz and the Minden enclave of Nordrhein-Westfalen. The exact area we occupy will be given to you later.

Within this area, we live and train and administer ourselves, and from this area we deploy in war to take our place on the left of the British Corps, and on the right of the 1st German Corps in the general area of Hanover.

You know the reason for our presence here as well if not better than I, but I think it is not an unhelpful intellectual exercise to re-state our roles, because to some extent they do influence everything that we do out here.

(a) We help to provide the outward and visible manifestation of strength and determination to defend the NATO area, without which the presence of strategic nuclear weapons alone could never convey the same conviction of comprehensive protection and of effective dissuasion to any potential foe.

(b) Secondly, with the other Corps of Northern Army Group and the Central Front, we provide the specific tactical deterrent against those who might feel that if they limited their aggression in terms of time and space, they might be able to achieve some expansion of power and influence without incurring the nuclear retribution which everyone seeks to avoid. For we continually present to any would-be aggressor a thoroughly realistic prospect that tangling with us could well initiate the process of escalation to the unthinkable nuclear holocaust. Of course, at what stage and in what order such a stumbling forward to nuclear war would occur, must remain, I am sure you will agree, part of the uncertainty that surrounds the whole 'theology' of the nuclear deterrent and makes it that much more effective and awe-inspiring.

(c) Finally, should our deterrent fail to prevent aggression great or small, we have to be ready to give battle with the appropriate degree of force in order to identify, delay and if possible deal with any infringement of the DML [Demarcation Line].

Any threat, of course, is a blend of capability and intention, and in any case the spectrum of incidents which could demand some reaction by NATO forces could be fairly broad. In the worst case, however, we could be faced with a Soviet attack (nuclear or conventional) which was delivered with little warning, and of which the first echelon alone would be capable of producing, at any point on the ground, at least a three to one superiority against us; and in the air the preponderance would be considerably more than that. Moreover, with the great capacity to reinforce which the Warsaw Pact possess, there would be plenty more divisions quickly available to follow up the first echelon. I am bound to point this out to you, because however unlikely an attack may seem, the Soviet Union most certainly has the capacity to do everything I said, and if anything this capability is increasing not diminishing, as the Russians get more self-confident in their exploitation of the vacuum in the Middle East and elsewhere and the USA gets more comparatively introverted over their own internal problems.

Under these worst-case circumstances there must be a limit to what we on our side could achieve. We could certainly give a good account of ourselves, because we are, by and large, except as yet in the important air defence field, extremely well equipped; and there is plenty of professional skill and experience. We could win some time for diplomatic action to be instigated, psychological and international pressures to be applied and, if we are lucky, wiser counsels to prevail; if nuclear were not used against us from the outset, we could also win time to threaten and get calculated political decisions on the use of our own nuclear weapons. We would be deeply conscious that the longer we fought conventionally, the greater flexibility we would give to our political leaders, but at the same time, if the attack was pressed home with fresh troops and heavy air support, it is difficult to see how we could endure for very long without resorting to nuclear weapons at some stage and in some form. And indeed, such a progression is all part and parcel of our deterrent capability to keep the peace.

To carry out the first two deterrent roles may require latent and political power rather than actual power, a point which is some cause for comfort when we see how reduced we are by the withdrawal of troops on temporary tours in Northern Ireland; but even these roles demand a credibility in the eyes of friend and foe, and we are at present so thin on the ground when operating a forward strategy that any further reduction of NATO forces must quite definitely threaten this credibility. If we were only a trip-wire it might not matter, but then it would have to be nuclear or surrender. Moreover, for the role of fighting we need not only an actual capability and adequate warning, but also stemming from that, and of crucial importance, timely political decisions which will ensure that the massive reinforcements we need so badly to mobilise our logistic resources, to bring us up to battle strength and to protect our rear areas, do arrive in time, otherwise we will be a shadow of our proper self.

One of the most interesting dilemmas that is going to face us if the Americans withdraw in significant numbers is this: should we now reverse the process of being slower on the nuclear draw and basing our defence as far east as possible and go once again for a nuclear trip-wire and reserves held back in depth (which might be the best military answer but with all the political complications that this would bring)?

Even in BAOR it is impossible to conduct a briefing without mentioning Northern Ireland. As at today's date there are seven Regiments over there, with the likelihood of maintaining this commitment for an indefinite period, and this means that about once every year or sometimes more frequently every unit, armour, artillery, engineers, as well as infantry, has to prepare itself for Ireland and serve four months there.

As a result, tactical and special to arm training in the skills of mechanised warfare is inevitably suffering, and so, of course, is our readiness to take the field at short notice. At the same time, we are gaining an immense amount in the fields of morale (the sense of purpose is so much more urgent to the ordinary soldier), junior leadership and battle 'know how' generally, that on balance I believe that our overall professionalism and quality is being enhanced rather than the reverse. I think you would find the more you went round units that the blend of the two types of soldiering (counter-revolutionary warfare on the one hand and training for mobile warfare on the other) is leading to a particularly high state of morale. How long this state of affairs would continue is hard to judge, and I could see a time when continued repetition of service in Northern Ireland could lead to falling in standards and morale all the way round.

My last point has nothing to do with operations at all but with our responsibilities towards the management, administration and morale of a community of over 100,000 souls (including women and children) – something the size of Exeter – with all its associated problems of schooling, hospitals, transport, law enforcement, housing and social services which fall to local government at home, and all the inroads to the Defence Budget which these make in competition with equipment. We have to be ready for our operational tasks, but at the same time we have all the time to be town clerks and local government officials as well, and I think you would be comparatively impressed with what is achieved in those fields, in spite of the inevitable shortages of money. I believe it is this side of life where our attitude on the man management, family management side is quite unique and has been one of the reasons why, almost alone, we have been able to sustain our all Regular Army on our peacetime deployment.

I will now ask Roger Plowden[9] to say something about our peacetime deployment and our main operational problems, and afterwards the Col. AQ, Tom Jackson,[10] will tell you more about our administration in peace.

We will then, I hope, have time for general questions and discussions.

Chapter 5

Preserving Peace: Maiden Speech in the House of Lords

Bramall remained interested in the problems of the Cold War, not just as C.G.S. and C.D.S., but also when he retired and took his seat in the House of Lords. In his maiden speech to the House of Lords in March 1987, Bramall spoke about the Cold War and how it helped to preserve the peace.

My Lords, I am sure that many noble Lords will have felt a deep sense of diffidence when addressing your Lordships' House for the first time, and I am certainly no exception. However, I feel proud that my presence in the House seems to indicate continuing recognition of the valuable and constructive role that the armed forces of the Crown play in the service of the nation in peace, which thankfully, but not accidentally, has come to be the more normal state for the British people, as well as in more war-like operations.

It is on this theme of continuing peace that I offer my initial contribution in the context of this debate. It is, of course, difficult at this time to say anything with defence connotations that is not considered controversial by some: so I know that I must proceed delicately, like Agag, and can only hope that, with your Lordships' indulgence, I avoid his subsequent fate of being hewed into pieces!

I just belong, as do so many others in this House, to the generation which experienced at first hand the realities and dangers, and not infrequently the horrors, of modern warfare both on the home front and with the field armies, in the latter case under the distinguished command of the noble and gallant Lord, Lord Carver. At the end of the war, I had the somewhat unusual experience, in the space of only a few months, of seeing for myself the ruins of both Hamburg and Hiroshima, the first no less horrifying than the second. Perhaps as a result of such experiences, I have never found myself impressed by the argument, however understandable, that if you totally removed nuclear weapons from Western armouries or, indeed, from both West and East, you would somehow be serving the cause of peace, because then the risks and general panoply of so-called conventional war would have become more respectable and even tolerable.

Modern warfare with modern weapons, with forty years' improvement over those that we experienced, would be quite disastrous enough for our country's future. This is why peace, with honour and territorial integrity unimpaired, must be preserved, and why all aggressive war must be made too difficult and dangerous for rational men to contemplate and thus eradicated as a viable extension of foreign policy by other means as, we must never forget, the Kaiser held it to be in 1914 and Hitler in 1939. You started a conventional war because you believed you could win it. Even the remotest prospect of nuclear conflict encourages no such dangerous thoughts, not even – perhaps particularly not – in retired field marshals. I hope that noble Lords will not believe all those stories about field marshals never retiring. Their active duty, I assure your Lordships, is almost entirely confined to attending each other's funerals. But I am digressing.

When I was in China recently a senior Minister said to me that the will of the people all over the world was for peace, and I am afraid that I had to take issue with him. Certainly, I said, those who lived under the protection, or, if you prefer, the shadow, of nuclear weapons undoubtedly wanted peace because the consequences of not having it were obviously too awful to contemplate. But where such constraints do not apply, the human race seemed all too willing to fight each other, given half the chance, and local fighting can all too easily, if unrestrained by those with more to lose, lead to all-embracing conflict.

So I would suggest, my Lords, that with man as belligerent and competitive as he naturally is in this dangerous world, there must still be strong restraints. Berlin, that outpost of a free society, is a good case in point. The West can only defend Berlin, as it must, by ensuring that it is not attacked, because the price of attacking it in terms of wider proliferation within the NATO alliance, and even escalation into the realms of some just possible but unspecified nuclear release, must be, and would be seen to be, far too high, and greatly to outweigh any advantages that might accrue to those who would wish, as some undoubtedly do, to change the status quo.

That is why I have always believed that a manifest – not a precipitous trip wire, but a manifest – linkage between the shop window and credible conventional forces on the one hand and some background and preferably invulnerable nuclear weapons on the other provides just that mix of commitment and restraint that is needed to be assured of maintaining peace while retaining territorial integrity and freedom of thought and action. The last forty years of such peace, which may seem commonplace to our children but, to our generation and to our fathers' generation, constitutes no mean achievement, has not dissuaded me from that view, nor discouraged me for the future.

The question, therefore, that we should perhaps be asking ourselves is whether the NATO alliance, with its strategy of flexible response – which, I need hardly point out, not only keeps potential aggressors out but comfortably ensures that any allies remain firmly in – continues to provide that required mixture, or whether that wind, if not of change, then of more open debate and presentation, which seems to be blowing across the Soviet Union, and the somewhat erratic content of some of the policies that sadly have recently been evident across the Atlantic, should somehow be changing what we do.

In general terms, I am sure that the answer to the second question is emphatically no. With the Middle East remaining so volatile and so dangerous for miscalculated superpower confrontation; with Europe still the key area in any ongoing ideological competition; with the undoubted numerical superiority and technological potential of the Warsaw Pact, as yet un-dented by any balanced force reductions; and with our strongest ally in some disarray, albeit, I hope, only temporary, this is surely no time for NATO to drop its sensible guard if we are to face the future with confidence and negotiate from a position of strength; nor, incidentally, to do anything which would risk throwing away that one great advantage that we have today over 1914 or 1939, and to which the noble Lord, Lord Home of the Hirsel, with all his experience, has so clearly drawn the attention of the House – a firm United States commitment to Europe.

What these new developments – some encouraging, some rather discouraging and even conflicting – must surely do is to make us look again most critically at the type and number of nuclear weapons that are really needed in order to meet that precise NATO aim of deterring attacks and pressures in all parts of the alliance; no more and no less. Certainly no one could possibly be satisfied with the 45,000 or so nuclear warheads which, at the last count, were available to the two power blocs, when, if only 45 were used, the consequences would be too awful to describe. As someone who has been connected with the problem for seven or eight years, I firmly believe that in the light of Mr Gorbachev's so-called initiative – which only seems to say what many in the West have been wanting for some time – it makes considerable sense to start by mutually reducing or eliminating medium-range missiles, which have always had more useful political and bargaining potential than real military value.

Of course, it would still be necessary to maintain some bridge between the purely conventional and the largely strategic weapons, but there are other weapons systems which can cover this. Difficult as it is, an attempt should be made to bring chemical weapons into the equation; otherwise we could indeed find ourselves highly vulnerable. But I believe progress can be made if the will is there. I believe that we in the United Kingdom must not only try to help bring about a significant breakthrough in regard to these missiles, as I am sure we will, but we must actually succeed.

Perhaps the greatest danger in our international relations is that if this present opportunity is not taken and if the overkill – which can only have been designed for mutual obliteration – is allowed to persist and if the escalation of the nuclear arms race is not halted or even reversed, the revulsion and impatience of the ordinary general public may become so great that it will start to question the whole basis of deterrence. If that were to happen, then out with the ridiculous overkill bathwater may go a really indispensable baby in the shape of a much more modest but adequate and balanced stockpile on both sides, with the risk that the world would become not a safer place but a less safe one for future generations to grow up in.

Book 3

The Changing Face of Conflict: De-escalation from an Apocalypse, Limited and Revolutionary War, Insurgency, Terrorism and Peacekeeping

Chronology

1945

May	VE Day.
September	VJ Day.
October	Jewish revolt begins in Palestine.

1947

October	India granted independence.
November	Britain begins withdrawal from Palestine.

1948

June	State of emergency declared in Malaya.

1949

October	Chinese People's Republic declared.

1950

June	Korean War begins.

1951

May	Abadan crisis (Iran).
October	Churchill becomes Prime Minister again.

1952

January	Rearmament programme slowed.
April	Chiefs of Staff strategy review.
October	Mau Mau rebellion starts in Kenya.

1953

July	Korean War ends.

1954

February	Dien Bien Phu falls to Viet Cong.

1955

February	Baghdad Pact signed.
April	EOKA terrorist campaign begins in Cyprus.
October	Soviet-Egyptian arms deal announced.

1956

June	Last British troops leave Egypt.
July	Nasser nationalizes the Suez Canal.
October	Anglo-French landings at Port Said.

1957

March	Treaty of Rome signed.
July	Dhofar campaign in Oman begins.

1958

July	Iraqi Hashemite dynasty overthrown in Baghdad. Anglo-US intervention in Jordan and Lebanon.

1960

February	Macmillan's 'Wind of Change' speech in Cape Town.

1961

July	British intervention in Kuwait.
August	British application to join EEC rejected by de Gaulle.

1962

October	Nasser-inspired revolution in Yemen.

1963

April	Confrontation with Indonesia begins.
May	Last national serviceman leaves the Armed Forces.
December	State of Emergency declared in Aden.

1964

January	East African mutinies quelled. Radfan campaign starts in the Aden Protectorate.
July	Independence for South Arabia by 1968 announced.
October	Denis Healey becomes Secretary of State for Defence.
November	Healey Defence Review starts.

1965

February	US bombing of North Vietnam starts.

September	Indo-Pakistan war over Kashmir.
November	Rhodesian UDI.

1966

August	Confrontation with Indonesia ends.

1967

June	Arab-Israeli Six Day War.

1968

January	Viet Cong begin the Tet Offensive in South Vietnam.

1969

August	British troops intervene in Northern Ireland.
September	Gaddafi seizes power in Libya.
December	Harrier enters service with the RAF.

1970

July	Dhofar campaign starts in Oman.

1971

October	China admitted to UN.
December	Indo-Pakistan war over East Bengal (Bangladesh).

1972

July	Operation Motorman in Northern Ireland.

1973

January	Britain enters the EEC.
	Withdrawal of US forces from Vietnam begins.
October	Arab-Israeli Yom Kippur War.
December	Sunningdale Conference on Northern Ireland.

1975

July	End of internment without trial in Northern Ireland.
October	Healey cuts back Defence Vote.

1976

April	Last British forces leave South-East Asia.
May	Callaghan accepts NATO 3 per cent increase in defence spending.
November	Nuclear submarine sent to Falkland Islands as a deterrent.

1978

April	First stage in restoration of service pay comparability.

1979

January	Fall of the Shah of Iran.
May	Margaret Thatcher wins general election.
August	Earl Mountbatten murdered by the IRA.
December	Soviet invasion of Afghanistan.

1981

June	John Knott's Defence Review proposes cuts to Royal Navy.

1982

March	Argentine scrap-metal dealers land on South Georgia.
	SSN *Spartan* sails for the South Atlantic.
2 April	Argentine invasion of the Falklands.
5 April	Task Force sails from Portsmouth.
25 April	South Georgia retaken.
1 May	Vulcan strike on Port Stanley airfield.
2 May	Sinking of *Belgrano*.
4 May	Sinking of HMS *Sheffield*.
19 May	Landing authorized by War Cabinet.
21 May	Landing at San Carlos Water.
25 May	Sinking of *Atlantic Conveyor*.
28 May	Battle of Goose Green.
8 June	Bluff Cove disaster.
11 June	Attacks on main Argentine positions begin.
14 June	Argentine surrender at Port Stanley.
December	Falklands lessons published.

1983

June	Thatcher wins second general election victory.
October	US invasion of Grenada.

1984

October	IRA bombing of Grand Hotel, Brighton.

1986

January	Evacuation of British refugees from Aden.
April	US bombing of Libya.
	NATO 3 per cent annual budget increases end.

1987

April	US/Soviet agreement on withdrawal from Afghanistan.
August	Iran/Iraq armistice signed.

1987

November	Enniskillen Bomb.

1989

May	Withdrawal of Soviet troops from Afghanistan.

1990

July	Republic of Kosovo proclaimed.
August	Iraq invades Kuwait.
	UN economic sanctions on Iraq.
	Operation Desert Shield starts.

1991

January	Aerial and naval bombardment of Iraqi positions begins, targeting Iraqi air force, command and control and military targets.
February	Operation Desert Storm. Allied troops enter Iraq.

1992

February	UNPROFOR created for operations in Bosnia.

1993

June	UN authorize air operations against Bosnian Serbs.
December	Joint Declaration on Peace signed by Prime Minister John Major and Taoiseach Albert Reynolds.

1994

August	IRA announce 'cessation of military operations'.
Summer	Taliban formed in Afghanistan.

1995

August	Srebrenica massacre.
December	Dayton Peace Accords signed.

1996

January	Mitchell Report outlines principles on arms decommissioning.

February	IRA end ceasefire and detonate bomb at South Quay DLR station, London.
June	Massive IRA bomb in Manchester.
September	Taliban seize control of Kabul.

1997

July	IRA announce the renewal of ceasefire.
August	Sinn Fein invited into multi-party talks at Stormont.

1998

January	Prime Minister Tony Blair announces the Saville Inquiry into 'Bloody Sunday'.
April	Good Friday Agreement. Includes a devolved, inclusive government, prisoner release, troop reductions and civil rights measures.
May	Referendum endorses the Good Friday Agreement in both Eire and Northern Ireland.
August	The 'Real IRA' explode bomb at Omagh, killing 29.

2001

9 September	Attacks on World Trade Center in New York and Pentagon in Washington.
20 September	President George W. Bush announces his new 'War on Terror'.
26 September	First US Special Forces deploy to Afghanistan.
October	Operation Enduring Freedom launched. Taliban driven out of Afghanistan or underground, by US and UK forces.
December	UN authorized International Security Assistance Force (ISAF).

2002

November	UN Resolution 1441 passed, demanding Iraq comply with disarmament demands.

2003

March	USA and UK forces invade Iraq.
7 April	7 Armoured Brigade clear Basra.
June	Six RMP soldiers killed near Basra.
August	NATO takes command of ISAF.
December	Saddam Hussein captured.

2004

May	Large scale demonstrations against British troops in Basra.

2005

September	Final IRA arms consignment 'put beyond use'.

2006

January	British take responsibility for Helmand Province, with 16 Air Assault Brigade.
May	Month-long state of emergency declared in Basra.
December	Saddam Hussein executed.

2007

February	Iraqis take lead in Basra security.
May	Democratic Unionist Party and Sinn Fein form government in Northern Ireland.
July	British Army formally ends Operation Banner, begun in 1969.
August	First British troops withdraw from Basra.
September	Last British troops leave Basra.

2009

January	British troops hand over full control of Basra International Airport, formerly a British military base.

2010

Spring	'Surge' of US reinforcements to Afghanistan. Saville Report published.

2011

March	British intervention in Libya.
May	Osama bin Laden killed by US Special Forces. Last British troops leave Iraq.

2012

May	NATO leaders endorse withdrawal strategy from Afghanistan.

2014

October	Combat operations in Afghanistan officially end. Camp Bastion handed over to Afghan forces.
December	NATO officially end combat operations in Afghanistan.

Introduction

The end of the Second World War did not mean the end of conflict, which continued in many parts of the world and took various forms: ideological clashes against the background of the Cold War, such as Korea and Vietnam; post-colonial or revolutionary uprisings, such as Suez, or Mau Mau in Kenya; and more 'traditional' conflicts caused by territorial aggression or conflict of national interests like the Iran-Iraq war or the Arab-Israeli confrontations.

Bramall was involved with many of these, in particular the Cold War and the Suez Operation, and in the mid-1960s he got command of a Battalion of his own Regiment – the King's Royal Rifle Corps, shortly to become the 2nd Battalion of the Royal Green Jackets – in the jungles of South-East Asia. He took command just as the battalion was flying out on a three-year tour of duty in Malaysia which included two operational tours in Sarawak and Sabah in the Confrontation forced on the Malaysians by President Sukarno of Indonesia. In fact, the Borneo campaign proved to be a most effective and economical use of force. It did all that was needed to be done to abort Indonesian oppression, avoiding any mission creep and positively contributing to the ultimate resolution of the conflict and to a more benign aftermath. Bramall was therefore ideally placed to describe the campaign in detail and analyse and assess the important lessons to be learned from it.

Later, Bramall commanded the first reinforcing Brigade sent to Northern Ireland at the start of the Province's 'Troubles'. This was to develop into a lengthy commitment for the British Army and one with which Bramall was intimately connected for two decades at higher levels of command. Indeed, even after retiring he made a formal contribution to the ultimate Peace Process when from the benches of the House of Lords he commented emphatically on the Saville report on 'Bloody Sunday'.

When the Argentines invaded the Falkland Islands, Bramall was Chief of the General Staff and responsible, together with his fellow Chiefs, for the planning of the campaign to repossess the Islands. Despite the inherent difficulties of distance (8,000 miles) from the UK and initially a very unfavourable air situation, this was a brilliant and triumphant success, revealing the high quality and morale of our three Armed Forces and Merchant Marine, and also showing our politico-military interface and command and control to be of a very high order. Being at the heart of the planning and mounting of the operation, Bramall was in an excellent position to describe the entire campaign in its proper perspective and analyse every aspect of the battle as it developed.

In January 1986 Bramall retired from the Army after forty-three years of active duty and next year was elevated to the House of Lords as Baron Bramall. He was thus able to continue to keep in close and informed contact with the country's foreign and defence policy, and where necessary bring to bear highly relevant and often critical comment on current policy and future intentions, particularly as regards plans for Defence cutbacks desired to obtain the publicly long awaited and expected 'peace dividend' from the ending of the Cold War.

Bramall was also asked to join a Parliamentary delegation sent out to the Gulf Area to assess the practicability of recapturing Kuwait after it had been invaded by Saddam Hussein, the dictator of Iraq. The delegation saw all the Arab rulers in the area, together with the American C-in-C, and his British deputy, of the Coalition Forces being assembled in Saudi Arabia; and Bramall came away convinced that provided the air battle was won first, the ground operation would be completely successful, as indeed it turned out in a remarkably short period of time and with very few own troop casualties. Bramall was therefore in an ideal position to speak in an informed and positive way in the House of Lords on the limited war which was to follow and later to lecture on Operation Desert Storm to a wider audience.

The new millennium brought in yet another dimension to the shape and face of conflict; on 11 September 2001 (for ever after known as 9/11) there occurred by far the most extreme example so far of non-state operated violence and international terrorism, with suicide air attacks on the political and economic heartland of the United States. The potential of this enhanced terrorist threat was, like the Cold War earlier, to dominate defence thinking and preparation and retaliatory action for the foreseeable future. For the United States, 9/11 was a uniquely traumatic experience which demanded a high-level military as well as a political response. This was to start off sensibly enough, countering this global terrorism in the best and indeed only proper way, based on hard intelligence and selectively using Special Forces and precision air attacks. Bramall strongly supported this comparatively low-key and constrained reaction, but became increasingly critical when the aim appeared to change to that of turning Afghanistan into a western-style democracy. This was palpably an unrealistic aim, which led to the coalition fighting the wrong people, whose violence was directed internally at any foreign invader or their own kith and kin, and was not internationally motivated. This, inevitably, led to mission creep and a highly expensive eight-year war. It was also responsible for the incoherent decision to commit totally inadequate UK ground forces into Helmand province, the most obdurate in all Afghanistan, because no larger or stronger forces could be made available. At an MoD briefing of ex-C.D.S.s Bramall personally warned the Secretary of State for Defence and Army Council against doing this.

In the meantime, the Americans had started to mass troops with the intention of invading Iraq, on the basis that Saddam Hussein was defying UN resolutions and still holding or even developing weapons of mass destruction. In numerous speeches Bramall gave cogent reasons for not doing so, describing the war on terrorism as 'charging up the wrong valley', making terrorism infinitely worse and encouraging Al Qaeda recruitment. It would also, Bramall emphasised, have serious consequences for the balance of power and ideological equilibrium of the whole of the Middle East. That is, of course, exactly what happened.

Bramall's speeches and letters make fascinating reading in the aftermath of the Iraq fiasco, which was later roundly condemned by the Chilcot Inquiry.

Chapter 6

The Balfour Memorial Lecture, 1996

In November 1996 Bramall was invited to Tel Aviv to deliver the Balfour Memorial Lecture. He used the opportunity to look back over Britain's relationship with Israel and to look forward by presenting to this audience the concept and the reasoning behind the decision by the Imperial War Museum, of which he was the Chairman of Trustees, to build a Holocaust Exhibition. He encouraged Israel to seek a permanent peace through the acceptance of a two-state solution, as Balfour had outlined. The response to this speech was delivered by Ehud Barak, previously Chief of Staff of the Israeli Defence Force and future Israeli Prime Minister.

Chairman, Chief of Staff, Your Excellency, Ladies and Gentlemen,

I feel immensely honoured to have been asked, after this excellent and congenial dinner, to give what is termed the Balfour Lecture, which over the years has been given by many distinguished speakers, so much more eminent than I, with perhaps Malcolm Rifkind, who could speak on behalf of the British Government, or Gordon Brown, on behalf of Her Majesty's Opposition. I will of course speak to you as a private individual and not in any official capacity, and I only hope there won't be retribution for those who have extended the invitation to me, because I recall that story of the man who was asked to speak in one of the more unruly parts of the Western United States. After he had been speaking for five minutes he was alarmed to see a man in the front row draw a gun and place it on his knee. After another five minutes he saw another man do the same, with the barrel pointing ominously in his direction. By now the speaker was, not unnaturally, absolutely terrified and he looked quizzically, nay pleadingly, at the Chairman sitting just beside him on the platform, who leaned over to him with a reassuring smile and said, 'Don't you worry, Sir. It's not you they're after but the guy who invited you!' So, Lewis Harris, watch out!

But seriously, Arthur Balfour was indeed a remarkable man, and I think a much-underestimated statesman, and so I am proud to be speaking in his honour. I am, however, conscious that, leaving aside the large amount of goodwill that exists today between our two countries (and I am so delighted that your esteemed President is making a State Visit to Britain early next year), standing before you as an Englishman, or a Briton, does, I know, inevitably carry a certain stigma in relation to parts of your nation's history and the suffering of your people. I know, for instance, that it can be asked, and indeed is asked, why British policy towards Zionism often appeared to be so contradictory and vacillating from 1915 to 1948; with, in October 1915 the British High Commissioner in Egypt's letter to Sherif Hussein of Mecca, effectively recognising the latter's claim to an Arab Empire; the Sykes-Picot agreement with the French in the spring of the next year, and, of course, Arthur Balfour's letter to Lord Rothschild in the following year, 1917; and then, at various times during the nearly thirty years of the British Mandate of Palestine. Why, for instance, in the light of that Declaration, and since a Jewish Homeland was one of the *raisons d'être* for the Mandate itself, was there so much control of immigration, both before Hitler's War, and after it, for example in the sad saga of the *Exodus* incident? All of this caused more suffering in Europe and hampered the setting up of a viable partition of Palestine under the Mandate, and forced some of your countrymen to adopt measures of violence which Israel has often since and understandably condemned in others, although in both cases the aim of that violence was the same: to draw the attention of international opinion to their perceived cause, and put pressure on the ruling administration to give the perpetrators what they wanted. Something that, in the long run these days, is often counter-productive because it loses much international goodwill. And what about the way some of the Jewish refugees who had fled from Hitler, were treated, for a time, as enemy aliens in Britain when World War II broke out? And why was Auschwitz not bombed? And so on and so on.

Well, of course, all these and others deserve to be answered, and I believe can be answered; and although there is clearly not the time, nor is it the occasion, to do so here, I would like to say just a few things in defence of my country.

First, in the years before 1914 Britain was almost alone among the leading powers in showing serious interest in Zionism, with as far back as 1840 Foreign Secretary, later Prime Minister, Palmerston trying hard but unsuccessfully to persuade the Turks that the settlement of Jews in Palestine would be to their advantage. Secondly, that although the British Government acted initially and perhaps largely for such strategic reasons as keeping Russia out of the Middle East, keeping her Imperial Muslim subjects at least quiescent, appeasing her French allies and, later, the need to knock Turkey out of the First World War, Britain did create between 1915 and 1921 that complex web of promises and agreements, which in the event created a further set of intractable problems for the future, although they did not at the time, I think, consider any of these as being incompatible. Indeed, they saw them, and perhaps some of you would say that they should have continued to see them, as largely unrelated: the French influence intended to be well to the north in Lebanon and western Syria; the Jewish homeland confined to, and easily accommodated by the local inhabitants in a part of Palestine west of the Jordan, and the Arab Empire, the sop for the Hashemite involvement in the Arab Revolt against the Ottoman Empire, to stretch eastwards from the Jordan to the Persian frontier.

Moreover, thanks to the conviction and influence of the very impressive Doctor Chaim Weitzman, who having left Russia at the turn of the century and settled in Manchester did so much for the British war effort in 1914–18, and the integrity, conviction and political skill of Arthur Balfour, the policy and principles embodied in that so-called Balfour Declaration were sincere enough, and, in fact, remained substantially in place as Government policy for at least thirty years after it was made.

And for this one must also thank two of Britain's renowned statesmen, David Lloyd George and Winston Churchill, who although perhaps initially for pragmatic reasons, did increasingly and sometimes passionately, if not always consistently (particularly Churchill, after his great friend Lord Moyne was assassinated in Cairo in 1944) support both on the domestic and the international stage the establishment of a Jewish homeland.

I should also point out that in the rather general apathy that existed in Europe and elsewhere in the world as to what was happening in Germany under the Nazis and thus to the plight of the refugees, particularly Jewish refugees, Britain's record was the best in Europe and something of which we can be quite proud.

Finally, if it hadn't been for the British Mandate and its termination when it occurred, the State of Israel might never have come into being, and perhaps above all, of course, without the sacrifice of 400,000 lives from the British Empire and Commonwealth Forces, including many Jewish people, and not forgetting the contribution of the Jewish Brigade, Hitler could not have been beaten, and then what sort of world would it have been for any of us, our children and grandchildren? So I do not feel so ashamed, standing before you, and, of course, the Balfour Declaration is a remarkable document. It is short, well written, saying exactly what it means, and I believe meaning exactly what it says, and which with only minor rewording could, indeed, today project forward Britain's conviction and commitment to the permanency of the State of Israel. But as I said, it read, and some of you may well know it by heart, and I quote:

Dear Lord Rothschild, I have much pleasure in conveying to you on behalf of His Majesty's Government, the following declaration of sympathy with Jewish Zionist aspirations, which has been submitted to and approved by the Cabinet. His Majesty's Government view with favour the establishment in Palestine of a home for the Jewish people, and will use their best endeavours to facilitate the achievement of this object, it being clearly understood that nothing should be done which may prejudice the civil and religious rights of existing and non-Jewish communities in Palestine, or the rights and political status enjoyed by Jews in any other country. I should be grateful if you would bring this Declaration to the knowledge of the Zionist Federation.

It says it all, and the problem today, of course, is how in the modern world and in the existing international scene those principles can be best accommodated for the peaceful permanence of the whole area, and that of course is well beyond the scope of this talk. But our hearts go out to you and we wish you God Speed in your efforts to ensure a lasting peace for the State of Israel.

But I think the main reason you have invited me to address you is that as Chairman of our national, rather anachronistically titled, Imperial War Museum, our national museum of conflict in the twentieth century (including its impact on individuals and societies), I and the Museum's Director General have decided with the unanimous support of the Trustees to create a national Holocaust Museum within our enlarged headquarters building at Southwark, just near Waterloo Station. Truly, at 1,400 square metres, the equivalent to Yad Vashem here in Jerusalem, it will be a museum within a museum.

I'd like to take this opportunity to say why we think it's so important that Britain should have its own record at national level of those terrible events which Winston Churchill described as the most horrible crime committed in the whole history of the world, and be able to disseminate the vital lessons of those ghastly days to as wide a public as possible, and particularly, as we approach the next Millennium, to the young who already have it in our National Curriculum. Of course, the Imperial War Museum has already over a million visitors a year and rising, so we will be spreading the net wide and not just preaching to the converted.

The first reason why we think it is not only vital for future generations to learn about the Holocaust, but it is entirely within the remit of our Museum is that, and here I speak as part of the World War II generation which took part in the Normandy invasion and the final conquest of Nazi Germany, nothing convinced us young soldiers more that we had been fighting a just war, and that whatever harsh steps we had to take to achieve victory were justified because Hitler and his most evil regime had to be beaten once and for all, than the discovery by us, half a century ago, of the concentration camp at Bergen-Belsen, Dachau and Buchenwald by the Americans and Auschwitz and

Majdanek by the Russians, to say nothing of all the slave labour camps set up for the benefit of the Nazi war machine.

The second reason is that the Holocaust historically constituted such an integral part of Hitler's war aims and the sort of 'Thousand Year Reich' he wanted to establish as a result of that war. Aryan Germans, as we all know, were to be the 'master race', with all the eastern lands particularly subjugated and colonised, and their indigenous populations reduced to being '*Untermenschen*' and slave labour, with the 'final solution' harping back to his obsession, exposed fully in *Mein Kampf*, reserved for the Jews, not only in Germany, but also in Poland, the Baltic States, Russia, Czechoslovakia and Hungary as well, and indeed in any part of occupied – and in some cases unoccupied – Europe where the Nazis held sway. If the Allies had lost the war, or Britain had become marginalised, and it's appalling to think of the barren and brutal world which succeeding generations would have inherited if they had, the 300,000 Jews in Britain, specifically mentioned in the minutes of the Wannsee Conference, would undoubtedly have faced the same fate, although I only hope there would have been just a few more people to help them and hide them away.

Of course, in this onward march of Nazi tyranny it was not only the Jews who suffered. Under the Nazis there was persecution, incarceration, starvation, cruelty and often death for those in many other groups. There was euthanasia of the mentally ill and infirm, and in the wake of the military campaigns in Russia, Poland, Yugoslavia and Greece, the civilian populations were brutally treated and often slaughtered, particularly, but not exclusively, by the SS. The Holocaust Museum, being the history of these times, will reflect this as well.

But it was the 'final solution' for the European Jews which was at the heart of the whole thing. It was unique, in our view, even though there had been before, and have been since, and sadly may be again, other ghastly examples of man's inhumanity to man, in which troops have run amok, where there has been local 'ethnic cleansing' and indeed occasions when thousands, tens of thousands, even hundreds of thousands, have been murdered in sudden surges of revenge or blood lust. Many of us can recall what occurred in Russia, Armenia and Cambodia, and those in more recent memory still (just look at Rwanda and Zaire), but there has never been such a cold, calculated exercise as the Holocaust to wipe out a whole people, organised by tidy-minded staff officers who went home to loving wives and children in suburban homes, and carried out and perpetrated, in the most callous and depraved way possible, by officers and men of disciplined agencies who actually got applauded, promoted and decorated for those ghastly crimes. Nor, one has to say, one which for a variety of reasons, a whole population of a western, developed and cultured nation, many of them decent, honourable people, and who certainly would have displayed those more honourable traits if they had been brought up under a different regime, largely looked on with complete indifference, preferring to pretend they knew nothing about it, and, tragically, in a number of cases, actually collaborated with it. Such was the forward path and vice-like clamp of tyranny.

Students of human nature will realise only too well how, under certain circumstances, these ghastly manifestations of hate, envy, cruelty and indifference can so easily come to the fore or be stirred up, which is why it is so vital that the truth about this particular, undeniable and well-chronicled tyranny, brutality and genocide should never be forgotten by future generations. This must include some of the apathy shown at the time by the rest of the world.

So we firmly believe that our Imperial War Museum, with all its experience in the exhibition field and in the recording of conflict with its wider impact on individuals and societies, and also because of its reputation as a national institution, is the right place for our country to relate this terrible historic event and ensure the vital lessons are disseminated to the widest possible public. Certainly, this is the unanimous view of all the leaders of our main political parties – the Prime Minister, John Major, Tony Blair and Paddy Ashdown – who have given the project their firm all-party support in writing. For not only is vigilance the price of peace – the main theme of the Imperial War Museum you might say – but also, as Mr Blair put it, our vigilance and diligence must ensure that man's innate capacity for evil (as well as, of course, for good) must never be allowed again to have such despicable and depraved consequences. This, indeed, is perhaps one of the reasons why the British and others are in Bosnia today, and may well be in Central Africa.

We hope shortly to have the funding of £7 million in place and then, backed by a very strong Historical Advisory Group and in close contact with your own splendid Yad Vashem and the equally splendid museum in Washington, we will be all set to go full steam ahead. Please wish us God Speed.

Finally, as you've done me the honour of producing as my co-speaker a very distinguished Israeli soldier, I would like to say something about our mutual profession of arms.

Having been brought up, gone to school and served in our local defence Home Guard in the dark days of World War II, when invasion appeared imminent, the Blitz was taking place on London and many other cities, I can appreciate what Israel must have felt like in 1967 and 1973, and indeed at many other times when it appeared to be threatened, and not least, and much more recently, when Scud missiles started to land in Tel Aviv. It also prompts me, for which I may say I have had to pluck up some courage, to tell a Jewish story, which is about those days before the tide began to turn. Apparently, King George VI had invited the Chief Rabbi to lunch at Buckingham Palace, and the very worried King asked the Chief Rabbi how he felt Britain was surviving in those days before the Battle of Britain, Alamein and other turning points, and how he thought it was all going to work out.

After a pause the Chief Rabbi was supposed to have said, apocryphally no doubt, 'Well, your Majesty, I'm sure it will be all right in the end, but have you thought of putting a few of your colonies in your wife's name?'

They were indeed dark days, if quite stirring and exciting for a teenager.

But back to the war, when both your President and I, in our different fields, air and land, were fighting against the Nazis. We both joined the Services in 1942. I myself, as I indicated earlier, seeing prolonged combat from the Normandy beaches to the Baltic against some of the most fanatical SS elite that the Germans could put into the field, and I ended the war, having been wounded twice, in bomb-blasted and shattered Hamburg.

Since then, although my active service and combat experience have been of a rather lower intensity, I've been lucky enough to command every level of Army formation, from that first platoon in Normandy to a company in the desert at the time of the Suez Crisis in 1956, a battalion in the jungles of Malaya and Borneo during the Confrontation with Indonesia, an airborne brigade in our strategic reserve, in which capacity my brigade was the first into Northern Ireland at the start of the so-called 'Troubles', and an armoured division in NATO. I also commanded our Joint Forces in Hong Kong, where as a member of the Executive Council I was as much a member of the Government, dealing with budgets, investment, taxation, social welfare and trade as I was a military commander, and then our Land Forces in the United Kingdom. And for eight years, of course, I was a Chief of Staff – Chief of the General Staff (professional head of the Army) at the time of the ceasefire in Rhodesia and the re-training of the new Zimbabwean Army, and of course over the period of the Falklands Campaign, and then Chief of Defence Staff when we had peacekeeping troops in Lebanon, and other alarms and excursions. The Falklands Campaign, which I suppose to some extent was a highlight in my career, was, I think you would agree, a very remarkable operation in that it was conducted so far – 8,000 miles – from home against numerical odds and without air superiority, which would normally have been essential in this sort of operation. We had to win that air superiority as we went along, but the quality and professionalism of our Forces did shine through, and I believe our soldiers, sailors and airmen did display the true qualities of the

Warrior: the will to face danger, the will to take risks and the will, if necessary, to make the ultimate sacrifice.

Throughout my service I've not only, like Arthur Balfour, been impressed
by the remarkable concentration of genius in the Jewish race, but I've watched
the Israeli defence forces with enormous professional interest. Sometimes it
has been with sympathy, because I know so well from personal experience the
inherent problems and difficulties of military forces operating in support of a
civil power, when restraint and minimum force has to be the order of the day,
despite intense provocation, and when Intelligence is the key to success. But
also, and so very often, I have watched them with enormous admiration and
respect for what they have achieved in fierce combat and against odds and
after remarkable feats of mobilisation.

Particularly, my (I hope) trained military eye has noted the all-round fighting qualities of the Israeli soldier, sailor and airman, not least the doggedness
and straight shooting of the tank crews, always a key battle-winning factor.
The relentless pursuit of the tried Principles of War, not forgetting the one
which our own Field Marshal Montgomery added to the other ten: 'First win
the air battle'. A principle so amply illustrated in the recent Gulf War to
throw Saddam Hussein out of Kuwait, as well as, of course, in 1967, when
your President was in charge of the Air Force. Above all I have noted with
approval the dashing and classical use of armour, in conjunction with helicopters, to exploit an open flank, and airborne forces to seize key points in
depth and ahead of any armoured thrust as in the Six Days War, and also in
the Yom Kippur War, the use of armour most effectively in mobile defence to
draw the attacker on and defeat him in chosen killing areas (having initially
underestimated him) and then exploit the weak points and vacant areas so
created in order to strike deep into the attacker's rear areas and straddle his
communications. All these operations have ranked among the epics of military history and are classic examples of brave and effective tactics.

Moreover, when I was Commander-in-Chief of the United Kingdom Land
Forces I instructed all officers to study in depth and in detail that remarkable
feat of arms – the Entebbe Raid of 1976 – just in case one day one might have
to undertake a similar operation. I thought that no one could have planned it
or executed it better. Since then, of course, we've had some success with our
own Special Forces.

All these instances, leaving aside politics and the international scene, which
of course you never can, stir the hearts of a military man, like myself, full of
admiration, but as our great poet Milton once wrote, 'Peace hath her victories
no less renowned than war',[11] and I realise that it is to peace that today
your country needs to apply itself, with all the courage, resolution and

determination that Israelis with their martial tradition going back to Masada, have shown in battle.

Our hearts go out to you in your noble enterprise; I wish you, as I said before, God Speed in your determination to bring about a lasting and enduring peace for the state of Israel in the modern world, as an essential prerequisite, I may say, for a proper balance of power in the Middle East.

Shalom.

Chapter 7

The Borneo Confrontation

At the time of the Confrontation in Borneo Bramall was a Lieutenant Colonel, commanding initially the Kings Royal Rifle Corps and then the 2nd Battalion of the newly created Royal Green Jackets, which had been formed out of the amalgamation of the King's Royal Rifle Corps, the Rifle Brigade and the Oxfordshire and Buckinghamshire Light Infantry. Stationed in Penang in Malaya, he led them on two operational tours in Sarawak and Sabah in 1965 and 1966. Shortly afterwards he wrote an analysis of this interesting campaign which was later published in Volume VII of The Annals of the King's Royal Rifle Corps,[12] *as part of Chapter 12. The following is an extract from that analysis.*

Borneo in Perspective

Indonesia was formerly a Dutch colony, but gained independence after a long struggle under the leadership of Achmed Sukarno. In 1961 Britain backed a proposal to create a federation of Malaysia, uniting Malaya and Singapore with Brunei, North Borneo and Sarawak. Sukarno wanted instead to unify Indonesia with Malaya, North Borneo and the Philippines. A rebellion, backed by Sukarno, in 1962 in Brunei was quickly crushed by British troops, but rebels continued to operate in Sarawak.

The Malaysian Federation was founded in September 1963 and Sukarno promised a 'Konfrontas'. Indonesian Army 'advisers' began to fight alongside the rebels in North Borneo. British and Commonwealth forces mounted a successful 'hearts and minds' campaign to isolate Indonesians and gain intelligence about their movements. The conflict was contained mainly as jungle warfare.

Royal Navy warships were used in support of the land campaign and to deter the Indonesian Navy from putting to sea. Australian and New Zealand naval, ground and air forces played major roles in the campaign.

As the confrontation developed, British forces launched Operation Claret, a series of secret, highly effective operations in Indonesia and Borneo (Kalimantan). Military defeat led to Sukarno's downfall. A cease fire was agreed in June 1966, following a conference in Bangkok. By early 1965, shortly after a substantial British and Commonwealth reinforcement of Borneo Territories, the threat across the border from Indonesia, particularly in the 'First Division' of Sarawak, was considerable. The enemy regular strength had

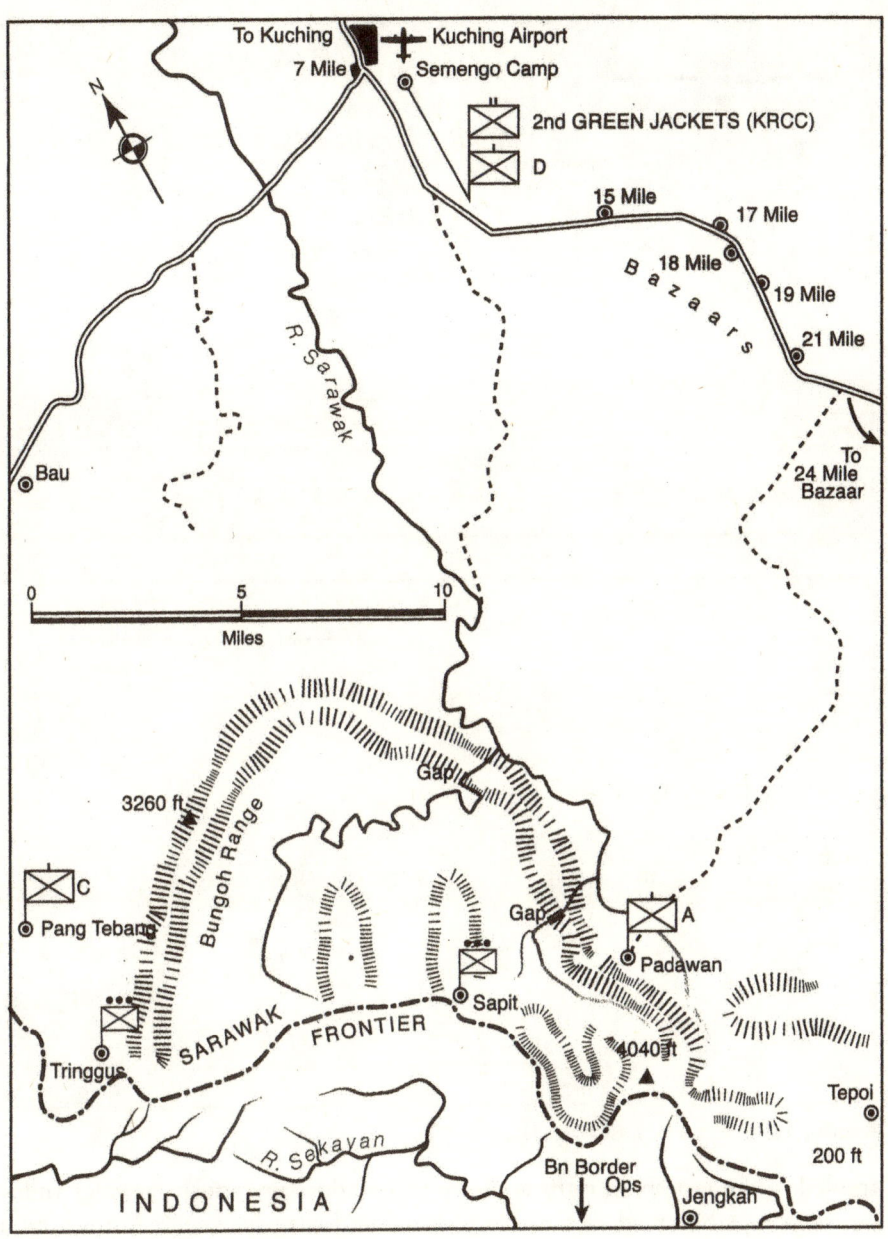

Borneo, Central Sector of West Brigade area, 1965.

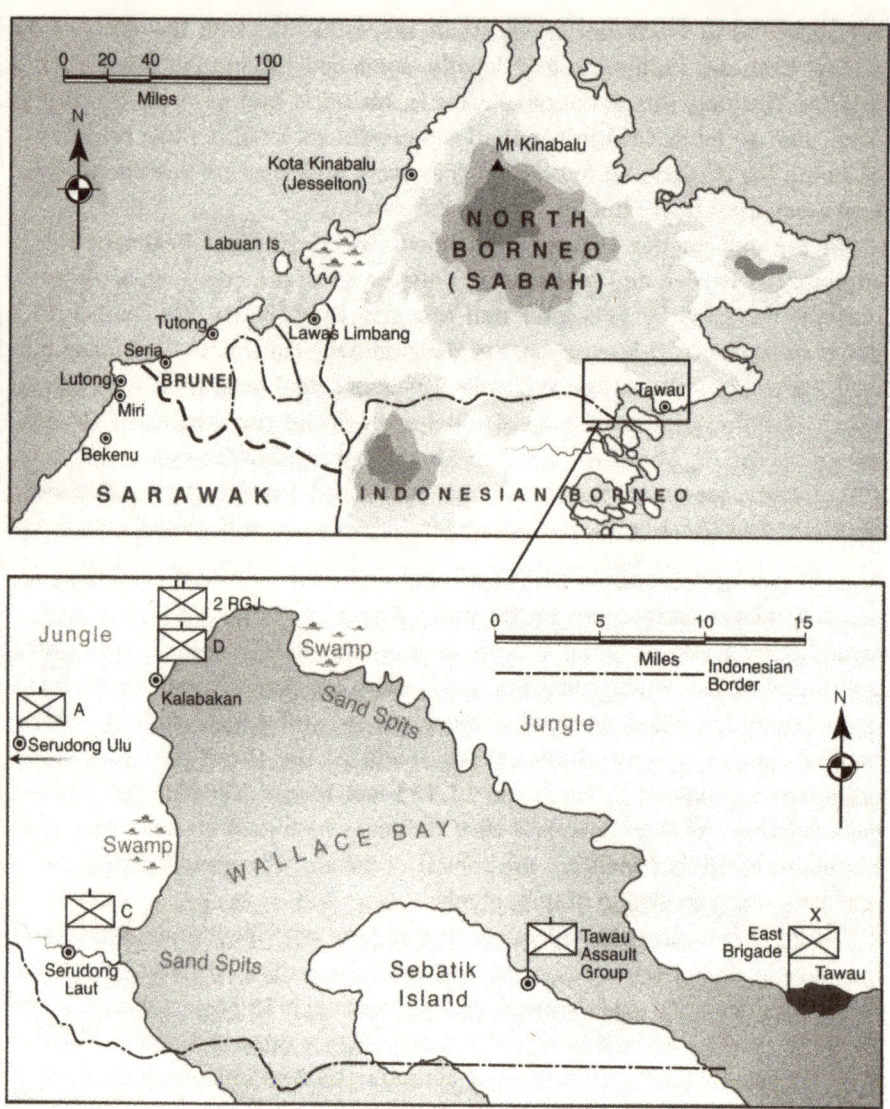

Borneo, Tawu Sector of East Brigade area, 1966.

trebled in the last six months and, only a few days previously, regular Indonesian troops had made a skilfully planned and bravely executed attack on a forward patrol base held by 2nd Parachute Battalion, and only great gallantry on the part of the defenders had prevented the post being overrun. There was indeed a very real threat that the Indonesian Army might make a concerted thrust against the town of Kuching, which lay only 25 miles from the border.

Had this occurred, or indeed in order to deter it or any preliminary moves from happening, the overall defensive plan was to take the fullest advantage of the mobility provided by the helicopters of the Royal Navy and the RAF. The forward patrol bases comparatively close (1,000 to 5,000 yards) to the border were to be held securely and maintained as necessary by helicopter and with the help of airdrops. From these forward bases, offensive patrols would be launched to harry any enemy columns, firm bases or subsequent reinforcements which might be part of a preliminary drive towards Kuching. With these barbs firmly planted in the enemy side, reserve companies of forward battalions and any other reserves which commanders could muster would be moved by helicopter to block and cut off any enemy who were threatening to break through. Given a good measure of air support, which would have undoubtedly been received from the RAF Tactical Group – No. 224 Group – and Royal Naval helicopters, this plan should have been successful and sufficient in preserving the integrity of Sarawak. It was the classical pattern of defence under limited war conditions when there is little heavy equipment, but where the three Services are obliged to work in close harmony and when we possess the priceless mobility and ability to re-supply provided by helicopters.

As it was, the threat never developed. Our own build-up of ground and air forces deterred a major effort by Indonesian regular units, and the constant and aggressive activity of our patrols limited the infiltration across the border to manageable proportions. Subversion in the rear areas, which were inhabited by Chinese near Lundu, Bau and Kuching itself, remained a serious problem, for there any infiltration which did penetrate to any depth could be given a refuge from which to carry out assassinations and sabotage; and later on, considerable military effort had to be put into supporting the police, in resettlement operations, cordon and searches and following up reports of terrorist bands. The primary task of each battalion remained, however, to deter, by active patrolling, any would-be infiltration across the border, and should this fail, to get the maximum information of the enemy's movements so that he could be cut off and destroyed by helicopter-borne reserves.

The patrol base
To achieve their aim, battalions adopted a fairly set pattern of defence behind the border, the first element of which was the forward patrol base. This was established comparatively close to the border itself, anything from 1,000 to 5,000 yards, to provide a springboard from which patrols could operate and a haven to which they could return, in comparative security; also, to provide protection for border villages and a focal point for the gathering of intelligence on the activities of the enemy on the other side of the border.

The minimum economical size of these patrol bases turned out to be a company. Anything less than this would have been vulnerable to a determined enemy supported by mortars, and would only have allowed for a very few men to be out patrolling along the border at any one time. In many ways, two companies were ideal. This allowed adequate protection of the perimeter with at the same time a reasonable ratio free for patrolling.

The bases had to be prepared to withstand attacks by a battalion group supported by mortars, and much attention therefore had to be paid to field works, fields of fire and defensive devices to hinder an assault. All troops slept protected by overhead cover, or at least by thick blast walls, and all were within easy reach of their fighting trenches. All trenches were linked by telephone to a central command post. To the observer, the finished article looked like a cross between a sector of a World War I trench system and a 'Wild West' fort occupied by the United States Cavalry in some past Indian war. The important thing was to maintain constant vigilance because with the border so close, the risk of surprise attack was considerable.

Apart from patrolling, life for the rifle companies in the forward patrol bases was always varied and interesting. To make life secure, and as comfortable as possible, required imagination, industry, discipline and good organisation. Field works had to be dug, fields of fire and helicopter pads cleared, obstacles and devices invented and constructed, and local civil labour had to be recruited, organised and paid to help with this work under supervision and thus release soldiers for active patrolling.

As I have already mentioned, the patrol base was also valuable as a focal point for gathering intelligence. There was a certain amount of legal cross-border trade, and in any case the border itself was in places very vague and undefined. The practice amongst the local people of visiting relatives 'on the other side of the hill' had never properly ceased, and there were plenty of freelance agents ready to give information, if the money was right and they approved of our methods. There was always, of course, a risk that such agents might be working for both sides, but by carefully graduating the tasks given to each, checking the credibility of the information against other more reputable sources and, above all, by picking and paying well, we gained more than we ever lost.

All this kept everyone on their toes, with company second-in-commands and support platoon commanders fully engaged respectively on administration and on the task of battle adjutant with special responsibility for intelligence. Despite the full complement of mud and rats, which always characterise such fortifications, the British soldier quickly adapted himself to the very primitive conditions. Safely out of the orbit of Battalion office and the RSM, he seemed cheerfully prepared to live in the jungle indefinitely.

Patrolling and ambushes

An important element in the pattern of defence was the offensive patrols operating from the patrol bases. Indeed, as the defence of the patrol base got progressively stronger, it became increasingly important to resist any temptation to Maginot-mindedness. The bases were in no sense blocking positions because of the ease with which the enemy could circumvent them. The enemy could only be deterred, harried and destroyed by continuous patrolling along the border, which was carefully planned and resolutely executed. The patrols had three tasks:

(a) *Reconnaissance.* To discover, with the help of experienced trackers, if certain routes had been recently used by the enemy and, if they had, to follow up these tracks and report on enemy movements.

(b) *Ambushing.* To anticipate the enemy's likely movements, possibly based on information received in carrying out the first role, and to move into a position where an effective ambush could be laid.

(c) *Harassing.* To destroy any enemy patrol or firm base or bivouac areas which the enemy might be inclined to establish on our side of the border.

Patrols varied in size from six to ten men for comparatively local reconnaissance, to a full company strength for large patrols, when contact with the enemy was likely. By no means a complete company was required in the ambush itself, which probably only called for ten riflemen to cover the main killing area at any one time. Allowing for rest and relief, stops and warning parties on either flank, subsidiary ambushes and firm bases in depth on the routes to and from the ambush, a whole company could be quickly absorbed.

A golden rule was to ensure that whenever possible an ambush was planned to lie within range of our Battalion's mortars or supporting field artillery (105mm Howitzers). Because of the length of a battalion's front (anything between 20 and 50 miles) and the sparsity of forward bases, this was not always easy to arrange. Special sites in inaccessible jungle had sometimes to be cleared, and the guns and mortars then flown in by helicopter.

Much of the country in Sarawak and Sabah, the other Borneo territory, was immensely hard, with jungle-covered hills rising to 4,000–5,000 feet, knife-edge ridges and precipices, and rivers in the valleys capable of becoming raging torrents five to six feet deep in a few hours after the invariable heavy afternoon rain. Wherever there had been an old habitation, cultivation or logging area, the primary jungle would have deteriorated into the most unpleasant secondary jungle, where visibility was often down to a few feet and where a few hundred yards of movement took an hour or more. In these areas – and this particularly applied to the valley floors – there was a great temptation to use the established tracks and jungle paths in order to speed up movement and reduce effort. However, never can an old infantry saying that 'sweat saves blood' have been more applicable. Until a track had been blocked near the border and fully proved to be unheld and unmined, there was always a risk of ambushes and mines and of giving away surprise. Indeed, even if a physical block had been established, there was no certainty that the enemy had not circumvented it and cut in behind. Initially, and until patrols became really familiar with the area, it proved sound policy to avoid established tracks and to cut in on these at intervals from the flank, even if this involved an extremely arduous cross-country move. Jungle can be singularly unpleasant, but is seldom impenetrable.

When planning these patrols a commanding officer had to consider a number of factors. First, every effort had to be made, by studying the intelligence available, to anticipate the enemy's next move. Often this was a matter of backing a hunch, because other pointers were misleading and contradictory. Then the tasks allotted had to be matched to the state of experience and local knowledge of the troops and their commanders. This was a very strange environment for British troops, and it was necessary to graduate the tasks in order to build up confidence and ensure the steady progression of successes, which does so much for morale. Next, the best way of applying the techniques which I have described to the particular piece of ground had to be worked out in considerable detail, after careful discussion with the company or platoon commander who was to carry out the operation. Finally, the risks had to be weighed most carefully to see whether they were justified in the context of the Confrontation and in the light of the situation at the time. Nothing would have been achieved without some degree of risk, but the risk of losing British lives had to be weighed against the urgency of the enemy threat and the possibility of political settlement. Although the Indonesian threat was pernicious and serious enough if unchecked, it never materialised in so drastic and urgent form as to justify really heavy British losses. The initiative had to be won along the border, the enemy's aggression blunted, and the hearts and minds of the border people won and maintained. But the real challenge which faced commanders at every level was to do this without sacrificing valuable world opinion, without escalating the conflict beyond our resources and without incurring large casualties on our own side.

Air-mobile operations

The last element in the defensive plan was the reserve company or companies, which were moved into battle by helicopter to block and encircle located enemy infiltrations. Sometimes the reserves would be moved to reinforce or relieve forward companies in their patrol bases so that the tactical deployment could take place from there, thus taking advantage of the short helicopter turn-round and the local knowledge of the forward troops. Sometimes reserves were deployed direct from a base area. In either case, the response had to be quick if the operation was to be successful. Although we could have done with more of them, helicopters certainly proved their value and gave the British Commonwealth Forces a mobility completely denied to the enemy. Without them far less would have been achieved.

Lessons for the future

The campaign in Borneo, and especially in the western parts of Sarawak known as the 1st division, was a very satisfactory campaign from the point of view of a professional soldier. There was a clear-cut and worthy aim, for we were helping friends who had asked for help. The physical challenges imposed by the country and the climate were tough and demanding, and the successful surmounting of them correspondingly rewarding. There was plenty of opportunity for young men to prove their nerve and endurance in contact with a tough and brave enemy, and there was considerable scope for initiative and intelligence as well. There were short moments of high excitement, and even when there were no contacts the business of patrolling and living in the forward bases was never dull. Above all, although the risks and hazards were real enough, not too many soldiers got hurt, and fewer still lost their lives.

Perhaps even more significantly, Borneo was an encouraging example of military force contributing to a political solution. Instead of the progressive escalation that was often so inevitable, military force intelligently deployed produced conditions which helped and perhaps even promoted sensible negotiations. It did this by decisively rendering Confrontation ineffective, while not using more force than was necessary to achieve this and retaining the sympathy of world opinion throughout – no mean feat, which reflected great credit on the skill and sagacity of the higher command. Borneo served to confirm that British and Ghurkha troops had a very real talent – perhaps genius would not be too strong a word to use – for this type of campaign, in which aggression, robustness and successful anticipation had to be subtly blended with restraint, humanity and sensitivity to the aspirations and to the hearts and minds of the local people.

Lt. Col. E.N.W. Bramall OBE, MC

Chapter 8

The Falklands War

(a) The Falklands Lecture

In 2012 Bramall was invited to lecture on the Falklands War at Winchester Guildhall.

Ladies and gentlemen, exactly thirty years ago there took place a military campaign in the South Atlantic involving all three of our armed forces which was remarkable by any standards. I don't think there has really been anything like it since Wolfe went up the St Lawrence River with muffled oars and Captain Cook as his navigator to storm the Heights of Abraham and defeat the French outside Quebec over 250 years ago. I thought it might be of interest if I were to tell you something about it. There have been some excellent programmes on the battle itself on the History television channel, notably one presented by Peter Snow and his son Dan, but I shall be putting particular emphasis on the political and broader strategic aspects of the campaign as seen and, to some extent, influenced from the safety and comparative comfort of Whitehall when, as CGS, I was head of the Army and therefore a member of the Chiefs of Staff Committee.

The whole campaign was, I think, remarkable for a number of reasons. First, and most obviously, it took place 8,000 miles from home, with all the inherent logistical problems that such a long and unhelpful line of communications inevitably brings. Then, it was launched from a 'standing start' with virtually no warning, something which British military history has shown that we have not always been all that good at. Look at the disasters in Norway in 1940 and Singapore and Malaya in 1941, in both of which we should have done better than we did. We win the last battles, but not too often the first ones. It was, moreover, completed successfully against an enemy who had many advantages on their side; and in a remarkably short period of time, as all modern conflicts should be if they are not to attract often insurmountable problems later on. In fact, it took barely two months, including the initial naval deployment to the South Atlantic, while the actual land battle lasted only three weeks.

It was also a conflict, unlike some recent ones, when the politico-military co-operation and the clarity of the command chain worked excellently in an

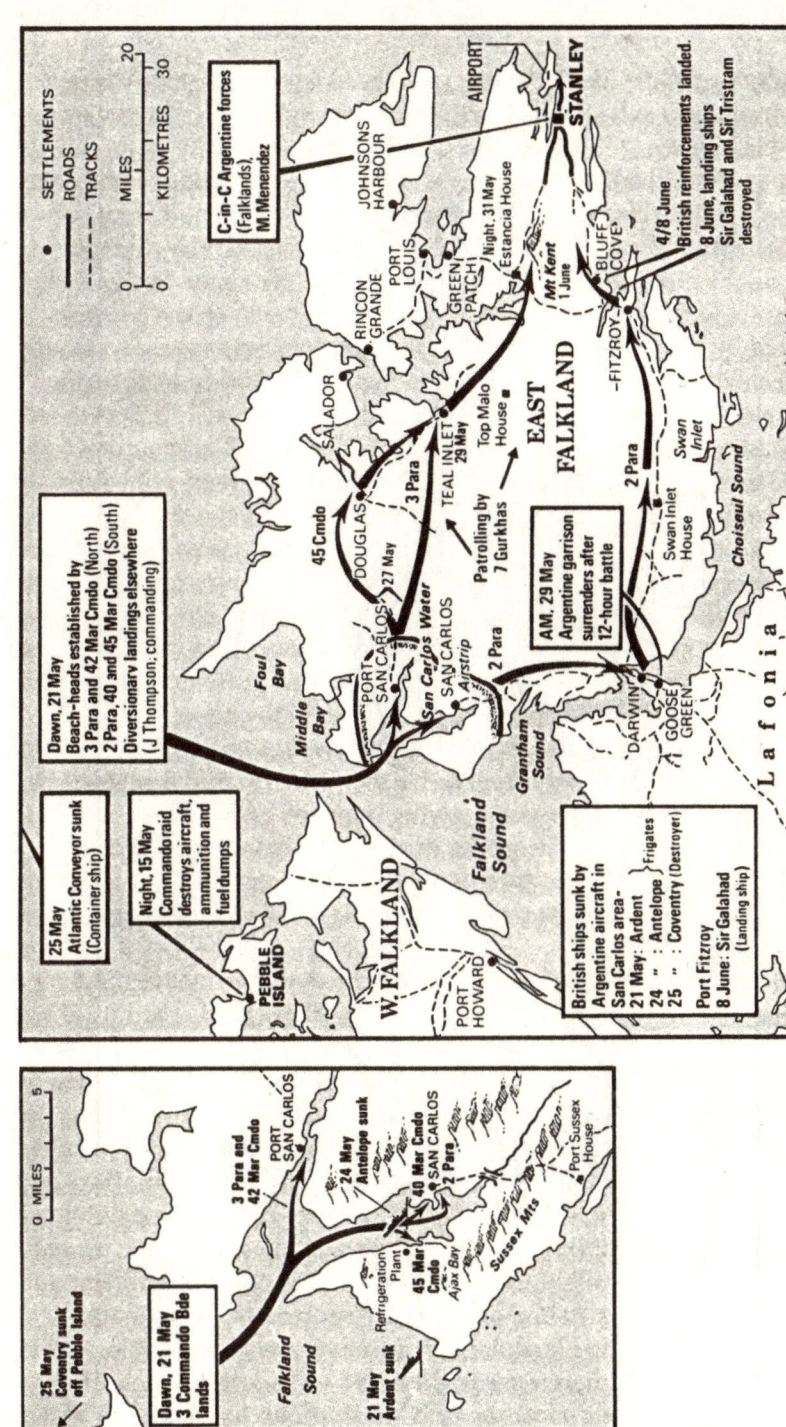

The Falklands War: (*left*) the landings at Port San Carlos, and (*right*) the two-pronged attack towards Port Stanley.

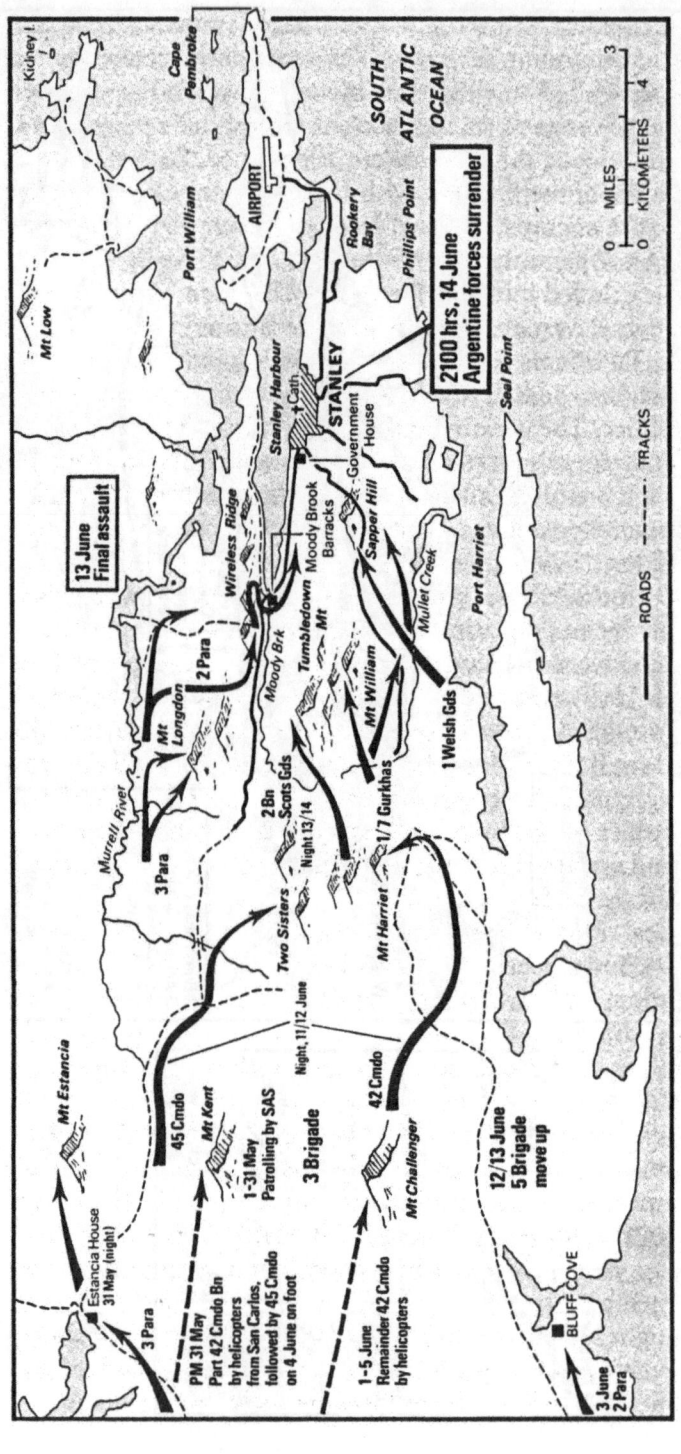

The Falklands War, the Battle for Stanley.

almost copybook manner, with the Chiefs of Staff system again justifying itself, as it had so conspicuously in World War II. Finally, if one minds about these things, as one should, and checks the criteria for a Just War, or if you prefer, 'appropriate war', first set out by Thomas Aquinas in the Middle Ages, and which are still a useful check list – self-defence, honourable intentions, proportionality, a successful and more benign outcome etc. – you would find that the Falklands campaign would get pretty high marks, unlike some more recent conflicts. Also, incidentally, (and this in no way conflicted with honourable intentions) it saved the Thatcher Government, which would have certainly fallen if, having allowed the Falklands to be captured under our very noses, we did not retake them. In fact, that campaign undoubtedly won the next General Election for Margaret Thatcher when she had been miles behind in the polls. All politicians since have tended to hanker after 'The Falklands Factor'.

There was indeed no proper warning that the Argentines were actually going to invade, and what straws there were, such as the landing of the Argentine scrap metal merchants on the island of South Georgia, about 800 miles to the south-east of the Falklands, were probably 'played down' by the Foreign Office, who were more or less in the middle of negotiations with the Argentines to do a deal over the Falklands and did not want anything to rock the boat. This is why, when the invasion actually happened, and the FCO were proved wrong and the country outraged, the Foreign Secretary (Lord Carrington) and all his ministers and his Permanent Secretary resigned, showing a commendable sense of responsibility when their Department had made a nonsense, something that rather noticeably has never been done since.

Luckily, the Royal Navy, which did at least know where the Falklands were, having fought a successful battle there against the Germans in December 1914, did smell a rat and had taken some preliminary steps to alert a Naval Task Force under Admiral Sandy Woodward, which was, by chance, exercising in the Mediterranean, that they might just be required to sail south, and Admiral Fieldhouse, Commander-in-Chief Fleet, a splendid down-to-earth Yorkshireman, who was to be the commander-in-chief of the whole subsequent operation, flew out to brief them. But the Chiefs of Staff collectively certainly had no definite information that an invasion was imminent and indeed were not ideally placed to deal with the crisis. The Chief of Defence Staff, Admiral of the Fleet Sir Terence Lewin, an absolutely first class man, was on his way to New Zealand and I think had got as far as the west coast of America. I was in Northern Ireland, which in those days was no bad place for the Chief of the General Staff to be; and when, on 31 March, it did become pretty obvious that the Argentine Navy, under the guise of an exercise, was about to invade (which they did two days later, thirty years ago to this very day, and in some strength, forcing the minute Royal Marine garrison to surrender after a token struggle) and Margaret Thatcher had called a meeting of the Secretary of State for Defence and civilian officials from the FCO and the MoD, the Chief of the Air Staff (acting CDS) was either not available, or not even invited.

Now at this meeting the Prime Minister was being told by officials on all sides, MoD and FCO, that serious as the outrage by the Argentine forces would be, after all, however much the Argentines had fantasised over the Malvinas (so dear to them) being theirs by right, we ruled them perfectly legally and the islanders were all British kith and kin. It was a clear case of aggression. It therefore justified the strongest diplomatic protests (shades of *Yes, Prime Minister* and Sir Humphrey) but, for various reasons, there was nothing we could really do about it. However, my colleague, the First Sea Lord, Admiral Sir Henry Leach, who sadly died last year, who was at the time visiting naval units in Portsmouth in uniform, heard about the meeting, rushed back to London and with some difficulty gate-crashed it.

And this is a wonderful story, the stuff of which history is made, because, as he entered the room, the Prime Minister said, 'Oh hello, Admiral, what can I do for you?'

To which Henry replied, 'Prime Minister, it is what I can do for you!'

'What can you do?' asked the Prime Minister, to which the Admiral replied most forcibly (influenced, no doubt, to some extent by his fury at what the Secretary of State, John Nott, was about to do to cut the Royal Navy in one of those periodical economic blitzes) that within four to five days we could sail a Task Force from Portsmouth, plus the Mediterranean force, to the South Atlantic and that in his opinion we should do so.

'Why do you say that?' asked the Prime Minister, to which the Admiral replied, 'Because otherwise our national name would be mud and as a country our word and power to deter would never be trusted or respected again.'

This, of course, was just what the Prime Minister wanted to hear, and she immediately agreed and Operation CORPORATE, as it was known, was to be put into operation.

It was, of course, a courageous decision of the Admiral, perhaps not even entirely in line with the advice of his own Naval Staff, but then if we wanted the Falklands back, by whatever means, we could hardly content ourselves with cajoling and complaining with high-sounding phrases from a distance; instead we had to project power and commitment into the South Atlantic. On that all the Chiefs of Staff were agreed. The question of whether we would then be in a position actually to land and successfully to recover the Islands had, of course, still to be resolved. But with the die cast, the Chiefs of Staff Committee was beholden to produce an outline plan to bring about the re-possession of the Islands. The first question I asked Henry was: can the Task Force protect itself when it gets down there? To which, with perhaps his fingers crossed, he firmly said, 'Yes!'

It was clearly going to be an immense task, with Argentine aircraft operating from fixed bases only 350 miles away, to say nothing of their aircraft carrier flagship, so the air situation would be distinctly adverse, and winning the air battle was usually an essential preliminary to any successful land battle. Indeed, no less than Field Marshal Montgomery had added a further Principle of War to the ten established ones: 'First win the air battle'. In the case of the Falklands this would have to be done, if it could be done at all, during the battle itself, with Sea Harriers (now defunct) operating from all that was available – Naval 'flat tops' *Hermes* and *Invincible*, bobbing about in the atrocious weather of the South Atlantic. The risks would have to be assessed most accurately, if humiliating mistakes were not to be made, as occurred for instance in the ill-fated invasion of the Dodecanese in 1943.

For this reason alone, serious efforts would have to be made to see whether there were not, with the help of friends in the UN and USA, other ways of getting the Argentines to withdraw their forces. Indeed, the Americans, despite their concern for human rights, were actively courting the Junta of Galtieri and wanted to do everything possible to produce a settlement which would avoid British military intervention, and at the same time ensure that Galtieri did not lose face. An impossible task as it turned out and the 'Iron Lady' was quick to appreciate. But at the insistence of President Reagan, and using his Secretary of State, General Alexander Haig, to act as a go-between, the Foreign Office, now under Francis Pym, went through the motions of trying to draw up draft proposals to which both sides could agree. Al Haig, whom I knew earlier when he was NATO Supreme Commander, made at least three visits to London and as many, if not more, to Buenos Aires, but although his efforts might have produced a sort of Argentine military withdrawal, none would have restored the *status quo ante*, instead removing the British Governor and inserting an Argentine representative on the islanders' Ruling Council. This would have been totally unacceptable to Margaret Thatcher and to Parliament, and luckily it was the Argentines who first, before us, rejected Haig's final draft which removed any blame from us; and he then gave up the struggle. After which, President Reagan, who had been dithering for nearly a month, threw the United States' support firmly and helpfully behind Great Britain's determination to get the Falklands back, under the UN's self-defence clause. But while this diplomatic to-ing and fro-ing was going on, planning, of course, had to go on at a pace for military repossession and a proper battle ahead.

The organisation for getting the Task Force away with the right things on it for a possible future (contested) battle was in itself a formidable challenge, at such very short notice, with all three Services co-operating marvellously with a sort of World War II spirit and with large-scale commandeering of merchant shipping known colloquially as STUFT (Ships Taken Up From Trade). The American base on the leased British island of Ascension, off the coast of West Africa and, at 4,000 miles, about midway to the Falklands, was put at our disposal and proved an invaluable place to get things put on the Task Force which had been forgotten when it left Portsmouth in such a hurry. Subsequently the Armed Forces won great plaudits from 'Big Business' for this impressive piece of organisation. Then there was the composition of the land forces to go with the Task Force to be decided. The initial landing force for this maritime operation was to fall, rather naturally to the Royal Marine Commando Brigade of three Commandos, but this had to be reinforced with two Parachute Battalions, the 2nd and 3rd, to make it much more formidable. I insisted on the 2nd Battalion going as well as the 3rd, although, as I was constantly reminded, it was the 'in role' Para battalion for any NATO emergency. I thought this was emergency enough! Clearly there also had to be a reserve for any subsequent eventualities on the Islands themselves. This, after a certain amount of discussion, was to be provided by my old Brigade, 5 Brigade, which included a Ghurkha battalion and to which we added in place of the two Para battalions who had been part of it, two easily accessible and proven Guards battalions, the Scots Guards and the Welsh Guards, both experienced from fairly recent tours in Northern Ireland. Although as at that moment both were on Public Duties, they were given further crash training in the Welsh mountains under the professional eye of General Frank Kitson, C-in-C UKLF. These had to follow the Task Force in the only ship capable, in terms of size and speed, to get the whole reserve down there in time to be of any use, no less than the SS *Queen Elizabeth*, and they were seen off by the Secretary of State, me and the C-in-C.

Then the chain of command and Rules of Engagement had to be settled. At the top, a War Cabinet was to be set up, chaired by the Prime Minister, who was everything a war leader should be: well informed, decisive and ready to take the key decisions exactly when they were required and prepared to take risks if the results would justify it. In this War Cabinet were the Foreign Secretary, Francis Pym, the Lord President of the Council, Willie Whitelaw, both with World War II experience (it was about this time that Margaret Thatcher made her famous remark that 'every Prime Minister needs a Willie'), the Defence Secretary, John Nott, the Senior Law Officer and various others, but no one from the Treasury (Harold Macmillan had advised her not to have one, and she didn't), and very much always in attendance, the Chief of

Defence Staff, who became, partly because of his efficiency and personality, the second strongest person in the War Cabinet. When the CDS attended, he had, as our leader, been briefed and advised daily by the other Service Chiefs of Staff, all of whom usefully had also had World War II experience and knew what proper battles were about, and who the Prime Minister saw collectively at regular intervals, quite unlike what happens today.

Once the overall strategic policy was settled in War Cabinet, the Chief of Defence Staff was in a position to give clear and firm instructions to the Commander-in-Chief who, having completed the more detailed planning for any landing, then gave his own orders to the Task Force Commander and later the Land Force Commander, who initially had himself been one of the planners. This worked very smoothly, with no second-guessing or back-seat driving from officials in the MoD as has tended to happen more recently. The War Cabinet also approved the vital Rules of Engagement, drawn up by the Chiefs of Staff, which clarified how far, particularly in the early stages of the campaign while diplomatic exchanges were going on, we were actually at war with Argentina. Clear definitions were needed for our own forces to give us the initiative and psychological superiority over the opposition. There was a very considerable potential threat from both the Argentine navy and air force, and if they struck first and, say, took out a carrier, any landing might become impossible.

The strategy evolved by the Chiefs was therefore both elegant and simple and struck a balance between giving the Task Force protection and avoiding escalating the conflict too early during the diplomatic efforts of the American Secretary of State, and it developed like this:

Phase 1. Sail the Task Force the 8,000 miles to the South Atlantic, preceded by one, then another, nuclear-powered killer submarines to act as a further deterrent to Argentine counter action. Some say they should have gone earlier.

Phase 2. Re-take South Georgia, as I said 800 miles ESE of the Falklands, which after a few fits and starts was done quickly by a small force detached from the main Task Force and consisting of Royal Marine Commandos and D Squadron SAS on HMS *Antrim*. This was helped by catching an Argentine submarine on the surface, disabling it with a missile and capturing it. It was felt that success here might help the diplomatic effort by putting further pressure on the Argentines to concede and withdraw without a fight.

Phase 3. Establish and promulgate an Exclusion Zone crucially 150 miles out from the Islands so that any Argentine forces that ventured out into it would then be 'fair game'. The responsibility would thus have been put on them; and at the same time a wider point was made about our ubiquitous power by bombing with a Vulcan bomber the runway at Stanley Airport and putting it out of action for any Argentine high performance aircraft (actually the Vulcan, flying from and returning to Ascension Island, had to be refuelled in mid-air no less than five times).

Phase 4. Position the Task Force within striking distance of the Islands but as far as possible out of range of the Argentine aircraft. The setting of the Maritime Exclusion Zone had, however, already led to an encounter with an Argentine light cruiser *Belgrano*, which had been zigzagging in and out of the zone, providing a serious threat to the Task Force. This could not be ignored when combined with the Argentine carrier threat in the north. It had, therefore, to be sunk as the opportunity occurred. This was done on the authority of the War Cabinet by the nuclear-powered submarine, HMS *Conqueror*, with, regrettably, the loss of 323 Argentine sailors (although 700 were rescued), but it showed that the War Cabinet were prepared to take the necessary tough decisions. In fact, this was quickly followed, which balanced some of the inevitable international outcry about the *Belgrano*, by the sinking of the destroyer HMS *Sheffield* by an Argentine Super Etendard aircraft flying off their carrier, armed with the French (categorised as friendly) Exocet missiles. This had confused the ship's radar defences. The chips were now really down, and clearly we were to all intents and purposes at war. The sinking of the *Belgrano* did, in fact, most importantly, force the rest of the Argentine navy to retreat into port for fear of further submarine attack and it played no further part in the campaign – a very great help.

Phase 5. If suitable conditions applied, and there had been successful preliminary raids and recces by Special Forces (which indeed happened, as at Pebble Island where the Argentines had their close support aircraft, and on the mountains west of Stanley), make a landing to reoccupy the Islands.

By the middle of May, with the negotiations to get the Argentines off the Islands by diplomatic means virtually, with the Argentines rejecting Haig's final proposals, broken down and the Task Force in position, the decision had to be taken whether to carry out the landing at an early stage. There were few windows of opportunity for tide and wind before the winter set in in earnest and then a landing might have to be abandoned *sine die*.

On 18 May all the Chiefs of Staff were summoned before the War Cabinet and each was required individually to back his judgement and say what we should do and how the battle was likely to develop, and it is doubtful if any, with hindsight, would have changed the advice he gave at the time. The gist of that advice was that we really now had no alternative but to go ahead with the landing. Attempts at a diplomatic solution (which were never, as I said, much favoured by the Prime Minister) had clearly failed; we could not keep the Task Force hanging about indefinitely or, like the Grand Old Duke of York, bring it all the way home, with the obvious dangers to British prestige, not to mention the domestic political embarrassment.

The risks were certainly high because of the air threat which could only be improved during the battle itself (as indeed it was). Although the choice of a selected landing site in San Carlos Water (not ideal because of the distance from Stanley) would at least cut those risks to a minimum, by making it very difficult for the Argentines to use any sea-skimming missiles in the close confines of the Bay itself. But there were bound to be losses in naval units in the initial approach and landing – perhaps up to seven naval and logistics ships (in fact six were sunk and a further twelve damaged but remained seaworthy). Once the troops were ashore I personally stressed to the Prime Minister that they would not be so vulnerable to the air threat, and that our 'First XI' should, I believed, be more than a match for the opposition, whose country had not had a war for a hundred years. All three Chiefs of Staff told the Prime Minister that all three Services would do their duty and press the attack home with all possible vigour (as happened). It was bound to be a bit of a gamble, but one worth taking, and given a reasonable share of luck we would triumph, with great enhancement to British prestige and status and to our deterrent credibility, while the risks of losing ships and casualties in the land battle too had to be expected and accepted.

With this balanced but generally positive and optimistic advice, the Prime Minister took the decision with the full support, I may say, of Parliament and the country, whom the Prime Minister had taken the greatest pains to keep on side – even the Leader of the Opposition, Michael Foot, supported her strongly – to land in San Carlos Water on 21 May. This went ahead with elements of both good and bad luck, as happens in life.

The first bit of good luck was the weather conditions of low cloud which persisted over the landing period and prevented the effective use of the Argentine Air Forces. Indeed, the landings themselves proved a triumph for Admiral Woodward, the Task Force commander, and the seamanship of the Royal Navy. He succeeded in putting ashore from assault ships and the P&O cruise liner SS *Canberra* some 5,000 troops with scarcely a single casualty; and this was repeated just over a week later when the 5th Brigade arrived, initially on the *Queen Elizabeth*, but they were transhipped at South Georgia so as to enter San Carlos Water in a slightly less prestigious ship. Because by this time, of course, the air battle had started in earnest, with piquet ships, logistics ships and frigates, although luckily not the *Canberra*, under attack, being hit and sometimes sunk, as well as Argentine aircraft being shot down by Harriers and Rapier ground-to-air missiles, so as gradually to win air superiority. You may well remember Brian Hanrahan's helpful comments about the performance of the Harrier and Argentine claims to have shot them down: 'I counted them all out, and I counted them all back.' One incident was in a sense both a piece of good and bad luck – good in that the configuration of the logistic ship *Atlantic Conveyor* had appeared on the Argentine radar as that of a carrier, which they thought they were attacking and claimed they had sunk (which would have been disastrous). The bad luck was that the *Atlantic Conveyor* was carrying Chinook helicopters earmarked to carry forward the landing force over the 50 miles or so from San Carlos Water to the hills above Stanley.

Immediately after the landing there was, in any case, a bit of a hiatus because Major General Moore, the Land Force Commander, had not arrived with the leading brigade (he came down on the *Queen Elizabeth*), so the Commander-in-Chief's determination, backed I may say strongly by the Chiefs of Staff, with memories of Anzio in early 1944, to push the Commando Brigade out of the bridgehead as soon as possible, had not really got down to the Brigade Commander, who, hampered and restricted by the lack of Chinook helicopters (all but one of which had gone down with the *Atlantic Conveyor*), was concentrating on consolidating the bridgehead itself against, I may say, negligible opposition, until the arrival of the reserve brigade, rather than taking the war to the heart of the enemy.

But then, after pressure from the Commander-in-Chief, two things happened more or less simultaneously. Protecting the Brigade's right flank, 2 PARA with only about 300 bayonets, and after a very tough battle on 28 May, in which their Commanding Officer won a posthumous VC, outflanked and then bluffed the whole Argentine garrison of well over a thousand at Goose Green to surrender; and then Brigadier Thompson, late awarded, and rightly, the 'Man of the Match award' 'yomped' (i.e. marched) most of the rest of his brigade across the 50 miles of soggy terrain of East Falkland to bring them right up to the mountains and Mount Kent, already occupied by Special Forces, which protected the port of Stanley and the Argentine Headquarters. So, by the second week of June, General Moore was investing the main Argentine force east of the mountains, which now had to be taken out one by one. At which point the Task Force experienced its worst piece of luck when the RFA *Sir Galahad*, helping to bring forward some of 5 Brigade (in this case the Welsh Guards) round the south of East Falklands for the final stages of the operation, went into the wrong bay and got caught in the open before the officer in charge was prepared to off-load the troops, with the result that forty-eight Welsh Guardsmen were killed and many others injured. This setback did not, however, delay the final attack. A superb and well-planned night attack by the Commandos on 11/12 June captured the Two Sisters and Mount Harriet feature, and 3 PARA seized Mount Longdon in as tough a fight as 2 PARA had at Goose Green, winning another posthumous VC. In the second phase, 2 PARA attacked Wireless Hill, immediately north-west of Stanley, and the Scots Guards went for and captured the key, formidable and rocky Mount Tumbledown, overlooking Stanley and held by experienced Argentine Marines, in another ferocious battle, and finally 1/7th Ghurkhas, with elements of the weakened Welsh Guards, drove a by now fleeing enemy off Mount William. Indeed, as the Ghurkhas, preceded no doubt by stories of their lopping off heads, approached, the Argentines turned and fled back to Port Stanley, which enabled the leading battalion, now 2 PARA, to enter the town, led rather irritatingly by Max Hastings, and take the total surrender on 14 June, with the Argentine conscripts throwing down their arms all around them. The final count of prisoners was about 11,000, mostly from the Stanley area, instead of the 6,000–7,000 which Intelligence believed were there, of which 700 lost their lives.

There are many good stories about Margaret Thatcher in relation to the Falklands, but one of the best concerns the Ghurkhas. Rather wimpish Foreign Office officials were most reluctant to allow the Ghurkhas to sail with the Task Force, although they were already part of 5 Brigade, for fear of offending the Third World, and I, helped by John Nott, himself a Ghurkha, had a battle to make sure they went as an integral part of the Brigade.

So, when at Chequers I saw the Prime Minister approaching the Foreign Secretary and his PUS, I said in front of them all, 'Prime Minister, you do know we are sending a battalion of Ghurkhas with the Task Force?'

To which she replied, with only a moment's pause, 'What, only **one**?'

Our casualties in all three Services were 253 killed in action and 450 wounded or injured. Of these eighty were lost at sea and the same number killed or wounded on the *Galahad*, but each assaulting commando or battalion lost up to seventeen or eighteen killed and forty to fifty wounded in their respective actions, which shows how tough the fighting was. These casualties are, of course, greatly to be grieved, but I think the country will always look back with pride on this unique feat of arms which did so much for British prestige in such a short time, and for which the principal credit must go, of course, to the courage and resolution of the men on the spot, but whose ultimate success was only made possible by clear and positive political direction and by the closest inter-Service co-operation at every level from Whitehall through the 8,000 mile logistic chain to the commanders, soldiers, sailors and airmen in the Task Force itself. I think the spirit and memory of that campaign cannot be better summed up than in a letter I was very proud to receive from a very distinguished predecessor of mine, Field Marshal Lord Harding of Petherton, who wrote:

> In connection with the Falklands victory a sentence from one of Winston Churchill's war-time speeches has come to my mind, as it has from time to time in the past. If my memory serves me correctly it was: 'All the great struggles of history have been won by superior willpower wresting victory in the teeth of odds or upon the narrowest of margins',[13] and it seemed to me that the greatest single factor in the Falklands campaign was that all ranks of all three Services had the will to take the risks, the will to overcome the obstacles, the will to face the dangers, and the will, if need be, to make the final sacrifice – the will to decide and the will to win – the indomitable spirit of the warrior – fully supported by the same spirit in the Prime Minister, the Government and the public.

And none of this happened by accident, but because of the way the Services had been organised, trained and led over the years, despite frequent cuts and cheeseparing. They triumphed not because they fundamentally wanted to save the government's bacon, or even because they had much interest in the future of the Falklands Islands, but because they had been handed a job to do, and no one was going to stop them doing it. That speaks volumes for morale, built on the basis of the traditional system of the Regimental and Corps loyalty. Moreover, the operation not only restored the Falklands to British sovereignty and reinforced respect for British arms but also incidentally turned out to be one of those rare episodes in history which ended with politicians and the military enjoying mutual respect for each other's contribution to victory, something not all that evident in recent years.

(b) Speech to 2nd and 3rd Battalions, The Parachute Regiment, 1982

In June 1982 Bramall flew to MV Norland off Ascension Island to greet 2nd and 3rd Battalions, The Parachute Regiment, on their return voyage home and spoke to all ranks.

Well, you're about to start your last leg home, where your Colonel-in-Chief,[14] I know, waits to greet you, and you won't want to be delayed, even for a moment, by waffle and flannel from someone who has seen the Falklands crisis through from the safety and comfort of Whitehall! But I thought the least I could do, as the professional head of the British Army and one of those who sent you to war, was to come out and thank both Battalions together for all you have done for the country, for the British Army and for your proud and splendid Regiment, in carrying out, against great odds, however difficult every task given to you and in restoring the British flag to the Falklands.

You have done an outstanding job by any standards and even that word is inadequate, and you have justified a thousand-fold the confidence we placed in you; and you can now fully take your place alongside those of the previous generation who fought with great glory at Bruneval, in North Africa, Sicily, Normandy, across the Rhine and at Arnhem. You have earned the admiration of all of us old soldiers, who may even be prepared to admit that you are probably actually fitter and more professional and just as, if not more, courageous than your fathers were (and that, for an old soldier, is no easy concession to make).

And both Battalions share equally in the glory. 2 PARA, as your Padre and others have reminded us and no doubt will continue to remind us, were the first ashore, the first to break out of the bridgehead with your most courageous and tough battle at Goose Green – almost a 'mission impossible' but you did it and it was a turning point – and the first to enter Stanley; and 3 PARA took part in that staggering 'bash' across East Falklands to surprise and unbalance the Argies and push them off the dominant high ground, and then fought the crucial and very tough engagement on Mount Longdon which made such a major contribution to the turning of and the final crumbling and collapse of the Argentine position. So, share the honour between you. And, of course, both Battalions will have seen plenty of some of the horrible aspects of battle and have lost good and brave men and fine comrades, whose death or serious injury we greatly mourn. 2 PARA has in the course of a few months lost two outstanding COs in H. Jones and Colin Thompson. You will never forget them and we must see that the country and the Army also never forgets them, or the families that some of them have left behind. I think I can reassure you on that point.

And in all of this do not forget those in the Task Force who supplied you and backed you up, and sometimes made your hard-won success possible. The Royal Navy who put you ashore under very difficult circumstances and did their level best to keep the enemy Air Force off your back. The helicopter pilots who flew you heroically in all conditions, the Gunners, the Sappers, the Doctors and Padres who helped your wounded, and the logistics organisation who went through the remarkable exercise of keeping you supplied with essential stores and ammunition 8,000 miles from home.

And perhaps a thought might not even be amiss for your own 1st Battalion (for whom no doubt your hearts bleed) sweating it out in Fermanagh, Northern Ireland. It is not their fault that they were not alongside you in these last few difficult and dangerous days, where I have no doubt they would have preferred to have been.

So now you go home to a great and well deserved welcome from your loved ones and friends and the country as a whole, who rightly rate the Falklands campaign (for which incidentally there will be a special medal) as one of the most brilliant and bravest in British military history.

Accept the praise and applause with modesty and dignity and try very hard not to do a single thing back home which will compromise that dignity or lose the respect that everyone in the land feels for you. You have, after all, nothing left to prove to yourself or to anyone else. In the armies of the world, they come no braver or tougher than those in Great Britain's Parachute Regiment, full stop. So, if anyone tries to pick a fight with you, or lure you into unwise behaviour, treat them with the contempt they deserve and tell them to get some service in! Besides, it may even make a nice change to make love, not war for a bit.

So I bring congratulations from everyone for your collective stamina, professionalism, courage and spirit and I wish you a safe and marvellous return to your families and a well-earned leave. In the years ahead and when you are old men (particularly when you are old men) you will be able to say, as they said after Waterloo, after Alamein and after Arnhem, 'I marched, and fought, and won in the Falklands, and showed to the world the incomparable quality of professionalism of the British Army and the spirit and strength of the regimental system.' No doubt you will bore successive generations of children and grandchildren into the bargain, but that is life.

So, one again, thank you very much indeed, and well done all of you.

(c) Speeches in the House of Lords on War Crimes Investigation

In 1993 and 1994 there was some discussion in the media and Parliament about possible war crimes committed by British forces during the Falklands War. Bramall spoke three times in the House of Lords on this matter, firstly on 15 December 1993.

My Lords, I am grateful to the noble Lord, Lord Campbell of Alloway,[15] for giving your Lordships' House the opportunity to debate such an important matter. I believe that most noble Lords would agree that the British Army has an enviable reputation as regards its discipline and conduct in peace and war. Wellington's Army in the Peninsula may have occasionally got off the leash; and over the years there have undoubtedly been other incidents in which the highest standards have temporarily lapsed. But in general terms and certainly in recent times, the British soldier has demonstrated again and again that he not only acquits himself with honour but that he has a capacity for compassion for those whom he has defeated, particularly the wounded, who need succour and attention when the battle has passed on. Certainly, as one who served so long in the British Army and, indeed, was its professional head during the Falklands campaign, I am very jealous of that reputation for honour and decency and would not wish innuendo and allegations, however unreliable, to go so unchecked that that reputation might become untarnished by default.

However, those of us in your Lordships' House who have had significant first-hand experience of battle know only too well that the actual battlefield is an inherently brutal place, where absolute moral values are sometimes difficult to pinpoint and where men – fundamentally decent men – not infrequently find themselves impelled or obliged to do things about which they may afterwards feel uncomfortable or even ashamed – war, at best, being only the lesser of two or more evils.

In such circumstances, there are endless opportunities for misunderstanding and for doing things spontaneously which one would not have considered doing in the cold light of day. An enemy may give the impression that he is about to surrender, yet when you drop your guard that same enemy, or another, may open fire and kill comrades in arms. A close friend may be killed or seriously wounded right beside you, and the compulsion for revenge can be very strong. On the rugby field such an instant reflex might bring a penalty or even dismissal from the field, but on the battlefield the consequences of such a reaction would be infinitely more serious. The steadier the discipline and the greater the fire control, the less likely these things are to happen. That is why, because of our traditions and regimental system, even accusations of unreasonable conduct are seldom made. But certain individuals are, by nature, more trigger-happy and nervous under pressure than others; and fighting at close quarters in a war is not an exact science or a cool and calculated business. Those who have not experienced it can have no idea of the pressures involved.

However, I should like to make it clear that what I have said applies only to the actual battlefield – and to the close combat phase. That is why, in the eyes of experienced people, there has always been a clear distinction between actions which may be attributed to an excess of aggression, or even an involuntary lapse of self-control in the heat of battle, when the adrenalin is running and the blood is up, and war crimes, whether they involve murder, torture or some other form of grievous abuse; the difference being that the latter offence is a calculated act, carried out when the enemy have not only offered their surrender but have been properly accepted (as they should be whenever possible) into the protection of the victor or occupier, who would be in complete control of the situation and of those in his care and thus able to provide all the safeguards demanded by the Geneva Convention.

Against that background, I believe that there are points related to the police investigation which merit the attentions of your Lordships' House. As noble

Lords will realise, the investigation relating to the very serious charge of murder – that is, in the context of the campaign, a war crime – was undertaken only after a lapse of ten years because certain allegations had been made in a rather lurid and sensational book by a retired and possibly disaffected member of the 3rd Parachute Battalion.[16]

However, if one goes back to the source of the allegation (on pages 189 and 190 of the book, *Excursion to Hell*) two vital factors stick out a mile. The first is that the allegations are complete hearsay. It is not an eyewitness account. In fact, the author – who is not averse to embellishing with gory details – neither claims to have seen, nor at the time to have heard, anything which could remotely be described as a war crime. It was only two or three months later, when back in Aldershot while waiting in the pay office, that he claims he met an anonymous soldier, himself badly wounded and about to be discharged, who told him yet another unnamed soldier had in the very middle of the battle pushed Argentine soldiers over a ridge at the back of his position and opened fire on them. Talk about 'I knew a man who knew a girl who danced with the Prince of Wales'. I should have thought that any defence counsel would have a field day with such unreliable evidence.

The second point is that whatever happened – if it did happen – occurred at the very epicentre of the battle, as the noble Lord, Lord Campbell of Alloway, pointed out and as the book admits. This was not the streets of Belfast; it was a bitter close-quarter battle in a proper war, just like Ypres, Gallipoli, Cassino or Imphal. The parachutists were in foxholes on the objective. They had been under observed mortar and artillery fire for the preceding 24 hours and there was direct shooting and sniper fire all around them. Men had been killed at point-blank range. The platoon sergeant had to crawl on his stomach because of the crossfire to get into the foxhole to issue a few breathless orders. The Argentine soldiers had got themselves into the same foxhole as a result of an abortive counter-attack in which other Argentine soldiers had been killed. In the book's hearsay account, there was no white flag, no formal surrender and no formal acceptance of that surrender; the whole area was in a state of flux in which at any moment any of the participants might have been killed.

No doubt Ministers, or for that matter Law Officers, with little or no knowledge of the face of battle might have hoped that they themselves would have behaved differently and offered any Argentines around tea and sympathy. We might all have hoped that. But sadly, such paragons of virtue might have felt a bit out of place at the height of the Mount Longdon battle – a desperate place if I have ever seen one – in which, as we have heard, twenty-three paratroopers had already been killed and about another forty wounded.

In any case, that is not the scenario or the conditions in which accusations of war crimes and murder can be anything but a cruel joke. Even the investigating officers must have been out of their depth in trying to picture what was happening at the time. That makes it all the more extraordinary that in the whole investigation, despite rushing off to elicit some response from the Argentines, no one has thought it necessary to interview the commanding officer.[17]

I would submit that, although I am as anxious as anyone to preserve the good name and honour of the British Army, the general unreliability of the evidence; the scenario at the epicentre of a brutal battle, with the pressure of combat all around; and the time lapse before any accusations were first made, let alone investigated, all add up to the fact that an investigation of this weight should never have been undertaken, and if it lies in the power of the Attorney-General to do so, he should stop it now. He should certainly not allow it to result in a prosecution which, when all the facts and background are exposed, I am confident would fail. But not before it had done great harm to the reputation and morale of the British armed forces who, in general terms, and as far as the conditions allowed, conducted the Falklands campaign with decency and compassion, as well, of course, with conspicuous and brilliant success, for which the whole country has the greatest cause to be grateful.

The second speech was given on 3 May 1994.

My Lords, I am sure that the House will look to the right honourable and learned gentleman the Attorney-General[18] to put the whole unfortunate investigation into proper perspective. Does the noble and learned Lord agree that the Government owed it to the armed forces – who, at their behest, went 8,000 miles to fight with great gallantry and overall discipline and decency – to have cleared up the whole matter a long time ago?

Finally, does the noble and learned Lord agree that, if any benefit of the doubt is to be given over any of the alleged incidents – as there is bound to be, taking into account the lapse of twelve years and the circumstances of intense battle prevailing at the time – that benefit should be accorded to those who risked their lives in the national interest?

He spoke again on 9 June 1994.

My Lords, there will be some relief at the reply of the noble and learned Lord, the Lord Advocate,[19] because there is considerable expectation in the House that the right honourable and learned gentleman, the Attorney-General should be involved so that any decisions on alleged incidents in the Falklands can be put into a proper perspective and with due regard to the public interest. Does the noble and learned Lord agree – I am rephrasing my question because of the noble and learned Lord the Lord Chancellor's[20] misunderstanding of it when last I put it in May – that if there is any doubt about whether a prosecution should be brought the benefit of the doubt should go to those who risked their lives in the national interest? I know that the accused receives the benefit of the doubt in a court of law but by then infinite damage may have been done. In view of the lapse of time and the intense warlike circumstances, which have recently been brought home to us in our memories of the ferocious fighting in Normandy, there is bound to be doubt. Should not the benefit of that doubt go to those who went 8,000 miles to risk their lives for our kith and kin and for the benefit of the whole nation?

Chapter 9

The First Gulf War and the Liberation of Kuwait

(a) Speeches in House of Lords
(September 1990 to February 1991)

Before the Gulf War Bramall spoke in the House of Lords about the way events might progress, and made a number of prescient suggestions. His first contribution was on 6 September 1990.

My Lords, after the magnificent speeches from such distinguished noble Lords, what hope is there for a simple soldier? Perhaps, to keep my end up, although I feel diffident about mentioning this, I should say that I reminded your Lordships' House during the debate on the Defence Estimates on 17 July that the Middle East might explode at any moment; that it was not difficult to imagine a scenario in which our armed forces might be needed in some capacity to counter or balance a pervading threat; and that if that happened, it would not be a question of meddling in affairs that did not concern us, because we would perceive that our interests were much affected and because the result of not becoming involved was likely to more serious still.

First, I should like to add my congratulations to the Government, especially the Right Honourable gentleman the Foreign Secretary,[21] on the handing to date of the Gulf crisis. Equally, I have not the slightest doubt that the Government will have been well advised on the military side by the United Kingdom Chiefs of Staff. It is a question of so far, so good, with some important achievements which should not be underestimated whatever the future holds.

Unhappily, in practice international law so often seems to be governed less by any binding set of rules, even the United Nations Charter, than by what is acceptable, particularly what one can get away with internationally. It was vital – I agree with Ministers – that someone as power-hungry as Saddam Hussein should not be allowed to get away with annexing a sovereign state of some seventy years' standing and pinching something that did not belong to him, a perception, it is important to remember, not just of the Americans and

SUMMARY OF THE OFFENSIVE GROUND CAMPAIGN

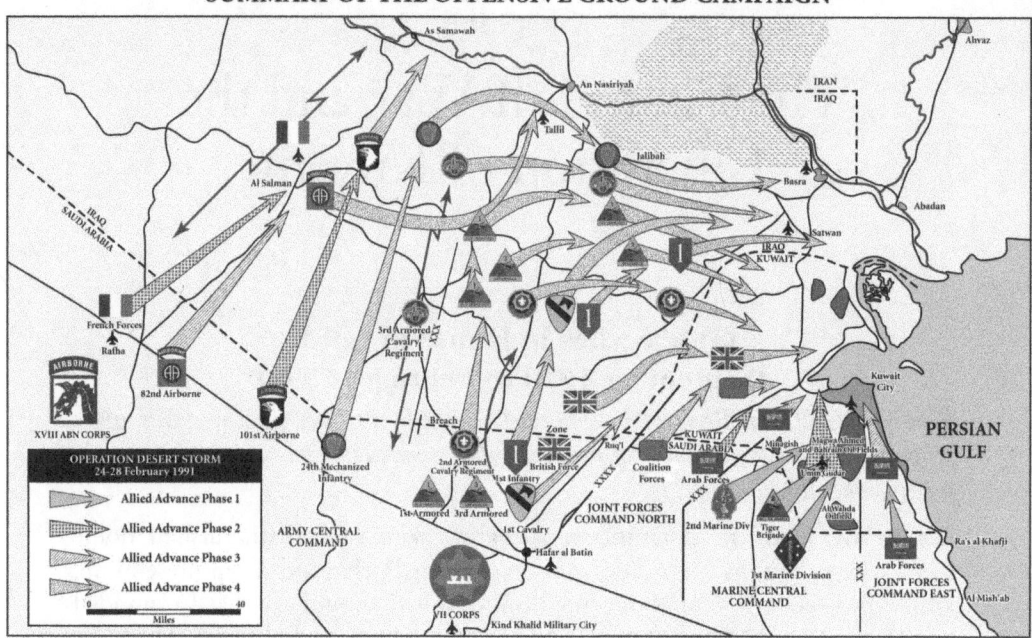

The First Gulf War, February 1991.

ourselves but of virtually the whole world (a unanimous Security Council having declared the action invalid and imposed mandatory sanctions, to which it has subsequently given teeth), the majority of the Arab League, the entire European Community and the Soviet Union, without whose co-operation our crisis management might have looked very different, as the noble Lord the Leader of the Opposition has reminded us.

After all, many of us remember all too clearly such sinister and high-handed behaviour in Europe in the 1930s, each occasion with its own similarly trumped-up excuses and justifications, and how bitterly we came to regret that we had not been in a position to blow the whistle earlier. The important thing is that as a result of this remarkable and almost unique degree of unanimity – the incredibly rapid and powerful American response to the Saudi Arabian request for help, backed by valuable contributions from ourselves, the Arab world and the Soviet Union among many others – Saddam Hussein has not got away with it, in the sense that he has been pulled up sharply in his tracks. The situation has been somewhat stabilised apart from the appalling problem of the refugees. The territorial integrity of Saudi Arabia has been secured. The blockade of Iraq's ailing economy is being made increasingly effective. Iraq is balked from moving offensively in any direction without paying a terrible price which its dictator would be most unlikely to survive.

In short, Saddam Hussein is increasingly isolated: condemned by the United Nations; alienated from other Arab leaders; rejected by his one-time ally; and manifestly worried enough to want to bargain and negotiate to some degree. Hence his posturing on television and his despicable manipulation of the hostages. Any visions that he may have had of Middle Eastern and Arab domination and of an inexorable march towards a war with Israel, have, if we continue to play our cards wisely, been thwarted, at least for the time being and perhaps for the foreseeable future. That gives a firm base, as has been said, for tough diplomacy and a chance to achieve a just and lasting solution. Saddam Hussein is weaker than when he started on his latest adventure, even though he has launched a well-conducted propaganda offensive designed to divert attention from the immediate issue and to whip up Arab nationalism against outside interference and towards the traditional Arab struggle against Israel. We would have predicted this, and it is something that we have got to learn to live with and counter as we can.

However, now we come to the difficult part because, of course, Iraq is still in Kuwait and shows no sign of handing it back unconditionally. Saddam Hussein still has numerous hostages and that is perhaps an even more worrying card in his pack because of the isolation of the males. The substance of this debate – and I agree with the noble Lord, Lord Carrington – is what we do now. Here I am sure that most noble Lords will advocate cool heads and considerable patience, for there is still much to do and some way to go to increase Iraq's isolation in the United Nations – it is still, after all, essentially their problem – in the Arab world, which has a major stake in cutting Saddam Hussein down to size, and through all possible means of diplomatic pressure, before having to decide whether any further offensive action (other than reacting to his attacking Saudi Arabia) would have to be threatened and, if necessary, taken.

I hope that we can discount the argument that because troops have been deployed they automatically have to do battle. We have grown up since the days when the younger von Moltke told the Kaiser that he had to go to war because the mobilisation plans were too far advanced to stop it. In fact, military forces play a major part in powerful diplomacy. As that great Chinese general and military theorist of over 2,000 years ago, Sun Tsu, reminded us, the best general may be the one who achieves his political and strategic objectives without having to fight.

However, in the meantime – and here I entirely agree with the noble Lord, Lord Carrington – it cannot be bad from the point of view of crisis management that Saddam Hussein has the possibility of such damaging action hanging over his head, as he is persuaded to ponder the folly of his ways. For he must realise, as General Galtieri had to learn the hard way, that in this world if something or some principle is important enough, it may have to be fought for.

If offensive action is to be considered in the light of the international scene at the time, may I as a former military man make a plea not to underestimate the scale of the task? The noble Lord, Lord Deedes reminded us in the *Daily Telegraph* on Monday of Winston Churchill's heartfelt words about never, ever, ever believing that war will be smooth or easy or precisely controllable. The situation in the Gulf has some special problems of its own, both political – on which others are more qualified to judge – and military. The desert can be a harsh environment to the unwary and those not used to operating in it or over it. The Iraqis may not be the greatest army or air force in the world and their success against Iran, at least in offensive operations, was strictly limited.

Nevertheless, we cannot sweep aside, as we have heard some Americans do with macho sentiments and expressions of contempt, the battle experience accumulated in nine years of war. For in the training of a soldier there can be no substitute for actually being shot at by modern weapons, and no greater spur than fighting with your back to your homeland. This would be in complete contrast to the Argentines, who had not had a war for a hundred years. The last people who ignored such experience were the Chinese when they failed to teach the Vietnamese a lesson in the early 1980s.

America, of course, has all the latest technology at its command. With the cloudless skies and lack of cover in the Gulf area, the battle in the air, in which the Americans are immensely strong, could be decisive. But the technology will only triumph if there is no complacency and if the tactical plan takes full account of the well-tried principles of war and the other prerequisites which make all the difference between winning and losing battles.

I have particularly in mind, apart from the early winning of the air battle, the need for up-to-date and accurate intelligence, both comforting and disquieting; for selecting and maintaining a clear-cut political aim – so lacking in the Suez operation – within which the military can work and develop their own plans. For instance, would the aim be to re-occupy Kuwait or should the release of the hostages and the toppling of Saddam Hussein be just as important? Or would we merely confine ourselves, as Dr Kissinger advocates, to the destruction of his military assets from long range, being ready to counter-punch when and if he reacted?

In an open debate like this it would be quite wrong to speculate, for an equally important principle of war is that the opposition must be kept constantly surprised and mystified, not only about future intentions but in the course of any offensive itself. None of this would be helped if the media persist in their determination to bare all possible military options to public scrutiny well in advance.

Then, if a decision is made to strike, it would have to be made with sufficient concentrated force to put fear into the hearts of the enemy and induce confusion in its leadership. This will not be pleasant, but with such battle-experienced opponents it will be the only way if casualties are to be kept to a minimum and the business completed within an acceptable period of time. Because it will not be pleasant, there is a need not only for maximum international backing, vastly preferable under the United Nations' auspices – and many noble Lords have made this point – but also for a carefully considered programme of psychological operations to support and complement the tactical plan and to combat, where possible, the inevitable propaganda reaction of Iraq. If it were to be felt that in the process the international heat would become too great, it would be better to stay out of the kitchen in the first place. I think that Suez taught us that lesson.

Finally, there will have to be a proper chain of command with a good, experienced commander-in-chief to take charge of implementing the general strategy. We cannot win battles by committees, let alone by the military committee of the United Nations. Once the political guidelines and policy on the use of force have been established at governmental level and in the United Nations, the commander-in-chief, whoever he is – and he would have to be an American – and his subordinates must be allowed their battle on land and sea and in the air with as little interference as possible, otherwise there will be chaos.

All these matters seem obvious enough, but World War II, when they were perfected and practised, is long past. More recent history has shown that they can easily be forgotten. I believe that our Chief of Defence Staff[22] or one of his chiefs of staff should be sent to satisfy himself on how much these important principles have been taken into account in any future American planning, just as was done frequently in World War II. For if they are not diligently followed, an attacker could find himself enmeshed in a longer struggle with much wider ramifications then he bargained for.

So, while hoping above hope, as I know all noble Lords do, that time is on our side, that tough diplomacy on a broad basis backed by effective sanctions and the threat of force will do the trick, the use of force cannot be ruled out for a number of reasons, always provided that the international climate can be held sufficiently tolerant. But we should be under no illusions that we shall be playing for high stakes, particularly political. That makes it all the more necessary not only that we should weigh up all the advantages and disadvantages carefully, dispassionately and objectively, but that we should do all we can and use all our influence to see that America does so as well.

Offensive action authorised by the United Nations, with a much better political climate for success, is something to which we should be bound to subscribe with all the force we could muster. But we should not at this stage commit ourselves to further offensive action outside the United Nations unless and until we are convinced that the selective aim is worth the risks and the economic costs; that the international climate is at least likely to be tolerant of such action; and that the plans – not taken at face value but vetted by our own chiefs of staff – were felt to be sound enough to ensure the achievement of the aim within a reasonable period of time. We cannot afford another Suez fiasco, when the first two criteria at least were not present. Meanwhile, I warmly support the actions of the Government.

Bramall next spoke in the House of Lords on 15 January 1991, after he had visited the Gulf region as a member of a Parliamentary delegation to see what was happening.

My Lords, as another member of your Lordships' House who has been fortunate enough recently to have visited the Gulf and the splendid and well-equipped British forces out there, perhaps I may also offer a few observations on the very serious state of affairs we are discussing today. First, it does not surprise me at all that events have taken the course they have. We were, I believe, right to halt Saddam Hussein in his tracks, to gain consensus for our actions through the Security Council and to carry out the various deployments and the military and diplomatic pressures which we have done over the past few months.

However, given the fundamentally different perception of the criminality of the invasion of Kuwait between, on the one hand, the vast majority of the international community as reflected in the various United Nations resolutions and, on the other, President Saddam Hussein and his henchmen, driven on by his own equivalent of *Mein Kampf*, supported by extremists bent on confrontation with Israel and relishing the language if not the realities of a holy war, there could be little, if any, meeting of minds. Therefore, there could be no doubt that if Saddam Hussein, by *force majeure*, withdrew at all it would be at any time before five minutes to midnight, wrong-footing the alliance as much as he possibly could. By 'midnight' I do not mean the somewhat arbitrary so-called deadline which is shortly about to expire. Still less do I mean that nebulous, quite indefinable and probably not even assessable future date when sanctions may be said to have worked. I mean when, and only when, Saddam Hussein believes that he is about to be struck by overwhelming and, in his perception, irresistible force; and he may feel he has some time to run yet.

This is why it was highly unlikely that anything would come out of the Geneva meeting or, indeed, from the Secretary General's welcome but vain initiative. This is all the more so because for other practical reasons which have been fully explained by the noble Lord, the Leader of the House[23] – reasons of foreign policy – it was not deemed to be either right or feasible to link any Iraqi withdrawal to a simultaneous, let alone a before-the-event, conference on other outstanding United Nations resolutions on the area. That would be, I suppose, the one chance of a diplomatic breakthrough.

Of course, even a withdrawal at five minutes to midnight will produce its own problems, particularly if that withdrawal were to any extent staged, or only partial. However, it should not be beyond the wit of man, with so much at stake, even at that late hour to take advantage of such an undoubted step forward and then, from a position of increased strength, still backed by the alliance's formidable military power, to press for whatever further needed to be done in the interests of long-term stability in the area. So 'five minutes to midnight' remains a possibility, provided Saddam Hussein is convinced we are in earnest.

Unfortunately, it may well be that he actually wants some sort of conflict and that he does not have it in mind to withdraw until at least five minutes past midnight, after he has been attacked in strength. That would provide him with some excuse for his own people as to why, faced by the overwhelming power of outsiders and infidels and invoking Israeli threat, real or imagined, he had been forced to throw in the towel and save his country and people from complete defeat and probable destruction. That may be the only way he feels that he can extricate himself with any honour. Therefore, we must also consider the possibility of that scenario. Of course, those 'five minutes' could themselves be a highly dangerous period.

When we study the form book and note the assembled strength of the alliance with all its latest technology, particularly in the air and at night, we should not doubt that Saddam Hussein would find it very difficult once attacked, to control, supply, manoeuvre and even protect his forces in the open desert under the usually cloudless skies. His unsupported forces pounded from the air, frightened as they are bound to be in the face of such power and somewhat weary from an earlier encounter, could quickly be written down to manageable proportions. That would be the real incentive for him, or for someone else in Iraq, to call it a day if anything was to be salvaged from the wreck.

However, technology will only triumph if there is no complacency and if it is part and parcel of an effective strategic and tactical plan based on the well-tried principles of war; particularly surprise in timing and method and sufficient concentration of force to induce continuing confusion into the hearts of the enemy and its leadership. It would thus achieve its aims with the minimum of our own casualties – the whole controlled and directed at every level by highly professional and, on occasions, heroic leadership.

It also has to be faced that air supremacy by itself did not provide a panacea in Vietnam; though there, of course, the terrain was very different from the open desert. Even over the open hillsides of Korea and before that the rolling farmland of Normandy, despite the enormous value of unchallenged air inter-diction without which victory might not have been possible, spirited ground resistance was still possible.

Therefore, although we are putting great faith in the alliance air effort, if all goes exactly according to plan – in war, of course, it never does – the sub-sequent follow-up may be a great deal easier and quicker than some pessimists fear. But one cannot be certain that the whole operation will not take some-what longer than extreme optimists may hope. As Winston Churchill once reminded us, you should never believe that war, any war, will be smooth, easily or precisely controllable.

We should therefore, as I said in this House last September, be playing for high stakes, albeit in the pursuit of a most important principle. We therefore need, and I am sure we have assembled, the very best hand possible. Certainly, one of the Cabinet's most important responsibilities to the British people before hostilities actually start is, through our own chiefs of staff, to satisfy itself that the military plans of the alliance are sound and are likely to be achievable in a reasonable, sustained period of time, and that that the tasks given particularly to our own forces are consistent with their capabilities.

Here we must remember that there is a marked difference from the Falk-lands in that instead of a clear-cut British chain of command combining the responsibilities for advice, planning and carrying out of those plans, our chain of command in the Gulf above divisional level acts largely as adviser and observer to the United States' decision-making process, with the main line of operational responsibility running from the United States headquarters in Saudi Arabia to Washington.

That is why it is more important than ever, as I suggested on 6 September, that our Chiefs of Staff and their supervisory commander-in-chief should keep in the closest touch on a personal and day-to-day basis with the United States Joint Chiefs of Staff and their Chairman, General Powell.[24] This was common practice during World War II but, perhaps more significantly it occurred in a more comparable coalition war – Korea – when a very senior member of our own Chiefs of Staff (the late Lord Tedder,[25] who had only just handed over both as Chief of the Air Staff and as chairman of the Chiefs of Staff Committee) was sent to Washington to sit with the US Joint Chiefs to represent the British view, and vice versa.

That situation could be vital in the weeks ahead and I hope that the Government, in view of the large contribution we are making to this operation, will consider something similar. After all, it would be no good in the unlikely event of things going wrong for the Government to say, 'It wasn't our fault because it wasn't our plan.' Nor could we default at the last moment if we were unhappy about certain orders given to our men. We have to get the planning and representation right in advance.

Of course, there is likely to be another important difference from the Falklands. The British people are likely to have to make more sacrifices and have the realities of war brought home to them more than they did in the Falklands, unless they, very sadly, lost relatives and loved ones in the battle. For, however long or brief the shooting war may last, there is bound to be a considerable impact on the economic life of this country, on oil process, on financial markets generally, perhaps on taxation and on the smooth pursuit of business interests worldwide.

We may also have to face up to terrorist threats and actions against British lives and property at home and abroad. But perhaps we should be satisfied that the burden of any armed struggle against tyranny, for the benefit of future collective peace and the preservation of international order and the United Nations, is borne more widely and not only by our professional fighting men far from home.

I expect that the Government will have made their appreciation of whether standing up to tyranny and blatant aggression now is better than facing it in other, perhaps worse, guises and situations in the future; whether doing just that merits the perhaps almost indefinable, but still inevitable risks; and whether indeed we have gone the last mile for peace and explored every other practical alternative.

If the answer had been 'no' to those questions, it would indeed have been right and still courageous to abandon any immediate thought of the use of force and to pursue the same objectives by some slower, less emphatic, and, of course, much less certain means, however awkward that might be. But if the Cabinet's decision – and it is only the Cabinet, knowing all the facts and having all the information, which can take it – is to say 'yes' to those questions, then I personally believe that there is now no practical alternative but to show the courage of our convictions. Then, at the proper moment, we should move up with confidence to that midnight point and, if still necessary, initiate warlike operations.

We must not flinch from the task, nor from the odd setback, as, incidentally, occurred early in the Falklands, nor in the face of a surely to be anticipated propaganda counter-attack against us and our allies perpetrated by every possible means – I hope not fuelled too much by our own media – nor from any terrorist activity aimed at British lives and property. We must be prepared to pursue our justified and military aims to a proper and reasonable conclusion. If the final decision is taken to use force to free Kuwait, the Government will be expected to show real leadership.

I hope it is not presumptuous to say that we heard a fine, fighting speech from the noble Lord the Leader of the House at the start of the debate. The nation will, not unnaturally, be extremely apprehensive and will, to a considerable extent, have to be geared up to war, however short we may hope that war will be. The nation will have to be rallied with the same sense of commitment, duty and confidence in the justice of our cause as Winston Churchill inspired the nation when power-hungry tyranny last had to be forcibly resisted, because the alternatives to not doing so were so much worse still.

I am completely certain of one thing knowing the Armed Forces as I do. I visited them recently together with the noble Lords, Lord Pym, Lord Mayhew and Lord Richard. I know that the Armed Forces when given the order – I hope that the order will be based on a plan which reduces risk and our own casualties to a minimum – will act with the greatest resolution, courage and professional skill. They do not wish for a war in any way. They are the ones who would have most to suffer and most to lose. Nevertheless, they will carry out their duty in an exemplary fashion and in a way which will make us feel immensely proud and not a little humble. In that context, I wish to pick up on a point made by the noble Lord, Lord Pym. I hope no one in Whitehall will be so remiss as to plan, let alone announce, severe future reductions in the Armed Forces while the outcome and aftermath of the Gulf crisis are still impossible to assess accurately. Not only would that be tactless and unfeeling beyond belief with so many servicemen prepared to give of their all to see us through, but with the situation in the Soviet Union also so confused, dangerous and uncertain it could also be highly irresponsible. There have in the past been too many similar instances of euphoria about peace in our time, which have so quickly proved to be false dawns, for us to be entirely comfortable about the way in which the so-called Options for Change seem to be developing. I trust that the House will receive some reassurance on that point from the Minister when he replies to the debate.

On 21 January 1991, after Operation Desert Storm had begun, Bramall spoke again in the House of Lords.

My Lords, I will be brief because I spoke at some length in the debate last week. I believe that most of what I said is still relevant and I hope not unhelpful. I also hope that the introductory remarks of my noble and gallant friend, and my erstwhile commander, Lord Carver, were not aimed directly at me, because in fact I agree with virtually everything he said, particularly about the very high media profile. I do not agree with him on the subject of Options for Change, but that is another matter which we can leave until later.

For the moment, I should like just to add my congratulations to those which I am sure other noble Lords would wish to express to everyone concerned on the most impressive start to what was never going to be an easy campaign given the numerical and equipment strengths of the Iraqis and the self-centred fanaticism of Saddam Hussein, with his refusal to see reason.

War, as I have warned more than once in your Lordships' House, is never easy and reports about events in war are often, with the best will in the world, not quite what they seem at first – neither as good nor sometimes as bad as spokesmen, commentators and speculators would have us believe. Of course, it is very early days yet. We are only five days into the conflict, although those of us who have been sitting in front of our television sets might imagine it to be nearly a month. However, even allowing for a certain amount of media hype, tinged progressively with relief, euphoria, even disappointment and the inevitable fog of war, it is clear that having achieved a most welcome measure of surprise the first phase of the operation, designed to gain air supremacy, to destroy Saddam Hussein's very centralised command of communications machinery and retaliatory capability and generally to restrict his freedom of action, while we meanwhile progressively turn our efforts by air and on land into forcing his land forces out of Kuwait, has made excellent progress and, in that well-worn phrase, is going according to plan. As the highly regrettable and provocative attacks on Israel, followed by the desperate but as yet ineffective attacks on Saudi Arabia showed, there is still work to do on his missile launchers and probably against his aircraft which escaped earlier attacks.

As one who had some misgivings earlier about a proper sense of realism and a possible underestimation of the tasks facing us, I wish to say that I have nothing but admiration for those who have masterminded and planned this intricate operation. Not of these generals could one use that hackneyed and snide taunt that they were fighting the next war with the weapons and tactics of the last. This has been a triumph for modern technology which has enabled us – I hope this will continue to be the case – not only to hit vital targets and restrict, although sadly not eliminate, our own losses, but also to retain some of that all-important moral high ground by reducing civilian casualties to the absolute minimum.

The war is also a triumph for the bravery, human spirit and intense professionalism of the Armed Forces in the alliance who have operated this new technology with such skill. We have special pride in this context in our own forces and particularly at the present time in our Tornado and Jaguar pilots of the Royal Air Force.

There is still much to do in Operation Desert Storm before the liberation of Kuwait can be assured. There will undoubtedly be setbacks to overcome. However, I think it is worth reminding ourselves from time to time that for every problem we have, Saddam Hussein must have many more still. If from this good start we keep our aim clearly in mind and our resolve firm, there is no reason why, through our certain and undoubted victory, accompanied by positive and sensitive diplomacy, we should not ultimately be able to bring about greater safety and stability to this potentially constantly volatile and dangerous area. As the noble Lord, the Leader of the House has said, that must be our paramount aim. If we achieve that, I hope it will be widely felt that any sacrifices which have had to be made will have been worth it.

Finally, Bramall spoke on 28 February 1991, after victory had been conclusively won.

My Lords, how relieved and proud we all were to hear the splendid statement from the noble Lord, the Leader of the House. Our first and overriding emotion must be one of thankfulness that an essential and honourable task has been completed with so miraculously few casualties, although our hearts do indeed go out, as the noble Lord said, to the families of those who have lost their lives in the cause of justice and who, sadly, will be unable to share in the general elation of the rest of us. That is the tragedy of war. Our second emotion is one of pride and immense congratulations to all those who have been responsible for planning and executing such a brilliant military operation which I believe will stand in history as a classic campaign to be compared with any of the great battles of the past. It was designed with the greatest skill and imagination and executed faultlessly, with flair, courage and the highest possible professionalism.

The lion's share was borne by our American friends and allies, and it is so good to see them with such an outstanding success under their belt. But we are naturally especially proud of our own Armed Forces who played such a notable part in the victory: our pilots in the Royal Air Force who bore the brunt in the early difficult and dangerous days; the ships and men of the Royal Navy who ranged the dangerous waters of the northern Gulf; and the commanders and troops of the 1st Armoured Division[26] who struck so rapidly and fearlessly deep into the heart of the Iraqi army in the true spirit of armoured forces. They more than upheld the great traditions of their proud regiments in a way that their forefathers and predecessors in the Desert Rats, of both Red and Black variety, would indeed have been immensely proud, and indeed are immensely proud, because there are still some of us still around. What great Armed Forces we have. I do hope that this will not be forgotten when the guns have gone silent.

When the parliamentary delegation, including Members of this House, was in the Gulf before Christmas the message of the Gulf States was unmistakable: 'We want Saddam Hussein out of Kuwait. We want him taught a lesson. We do not want him in a position to do it again, but we do not want Iraq destroyed as a country.' I believe that virtually all those laudable aims have been triumphantly achieved. If there are still things to do I am sure they can be done by tackling and organising the peace with the same flair, imagination and compassion that were shown by the commanders and troops in the field. I only hope that Parliament will be able to show the same unanimity over securing the peace as it has during the course of the war.

(b) 'Victory in Kuwait': Lecture to the United Services Institute, Delhi, 1992

In December 1992 Bramall was asked to address the United Services Institute, Delhi,[27] on the subject of the Gulf War.

I am greatly honoured to have been asked to address this distinguished and prestigious Institute. I only hope the subject I have chosen will prove of interest.

I must, however, ask you to bear in mind that although I did **visit** the Gulf area in December 1990, after the Iraqi invasion of Kuwait and before the shooting war started in earnest, and talked to commanders and troops on the spot, and have since had a number of discussions with the commander of the British Forces who was under the American General Schwarzkopf,[28] and indeed although I am not unused to crisis management when I was eight years a Chief of Staff, including during the Falklands Campaign, I was not an eyewitness to the battle, and for that I can but apologise.

Indeed, I have been largely dependent, as many in this audience will have been, on the copious, almost too copious, often exaggerated and sometimes contradictory reports of the media, which one has had to measure and assess against historical parallels and sometimes personal experiences of one's own.

I also, inevitably, look at the background to the campaign itself and its aftermath through Western eyes, which may not always coincide with the perspective of those situated on this side of the Middle East, who may look at the events and problems from the background of different experiences and culture.

I have tried, however, to be as objective and open-minded as I can be and I hope that I don't say anything that jars too much to Indian ears. If I do, then no doubt it will come out in questions afterwards, which will make that session all the livelier. In any case I will much look forward to that session. So, with that proviso, here goes.

My goodness, how topical this war and its aftermath still are – some even believe that somehow it was Saddam Hussein who after all came out on top, or at least not as far underneath as he ought to have been. But that it was a remarkable and notable campaign there is surely no doubt. It illustrated so many of the ingredients, some of them new, of modern war, and I will try to analyse these. It's bound to influence the world's attitude to conflict for a very long time to come and it will undoubtedly be discussed and taught at staff colleges and training establishments all over the world.

It was also in purely military terms a very famous victory, in which the Iraqi army in Kuwait was virtually destroyed, losing in the process out of its vast war machine, the fifth largest in the world, 280 of its latest aircraft, either destroyed or fled to Iran, well over 3,000 tanks, 2,000 other vehicles, 73 ships and patrol boats, and leaving behind 175,000 prisoners of war and approximately, and perhaps many more, 65,000 dead – all at a cost to the Coalition of 60 aircraft shot down, well under 200 killed, including just under 40 British, 207 wounded and a hundred or so missing or captured, and now, thankfully, all accounted for.

There are only a handful of battles throughout history in which victory has been so complete, and hardly any in which the ratio of casualties between vanquished and victor has been so great. In more recent history, one can recall Wavell's and O'Connor's destruction of the Italian Army in Libya in 1940, in which the Indian Army (4th Indian Division) played such a distinguished part, the Blitzkrieg, also in 1940, which forced the evacuation from Dunkirk and brought about the fall of France, Hindenburg and Ludendorff's encirclement and defeat of the Russians at Tannenberg in 1914 during the First World War, Kitchener's massacre of the Khalifa's army at Omdurman (1898) at the end of the last century, and before that I suppose one must go for equally inexpensive and decisive victories back to Frederick the Great against the Austrians in 1757,[29] Hannibal's destruction of the Roman Legions at Cannae in 216 BC and Alexander the Great's rout of the Persians in 331 BC at a place called Gaugamela, only just up the road from Baghdad. And it was only really at that last, and at Omdurman, where the victors' casualties were quite so low.[30]

If the Iraqis' destruction was not greater still it was only because Saddam Hussein was always more concerned about protecting his power base and fighting a political battle, rather than engaging in a last-ditch defence of Kuwait itself. Once he had lost his gamble of a cheap annexation of Kuwait (and there is no doubt he was taken by surprise by the vehemence and speed of the international reaction to what he had portrayed as the tidying up of a local dispute), he used his propaganda machine to do all he could to deter any counter reaction and to split the Coalition.

And if this failed he certainly wanted to do damage and cause casualties to any Coalition attack, but he had no intention of sacrificing his future on the altar of a fight to the finish in Kuwait which he must have known he couldn't win. With this in mind he kept much of his best troops, his Republican Guard, perhaps more than we thought at first, around or north of Basra and out of the battle altogether.

It would, however, be absolutely wrong to suppose that the battle went exactly as Saddam Hussein anticipated. In fact, he greatly misjudged the strength of the Coalition's air resources and the extraordinary accuracy of their weapon systems and the effect of these on the conduct of the land battle, particularly in severing communications with the front line and the extent to which, cut off as they would be, his troops would continue to fight. The promised 'mother of all battles' may have been largely a figment of his propaganda machine, but he certainly expected to do much better than he did, and I'll come back to all this in a moment, after we've taken a look at the background and lead-up to the war itself.

Now, the Middle East, as everyone knows, has for many years, perhaps throughout history, been an area of great potential danger. And those dangers are still there, even if the ending of the Gulf war does give us a fleeting opportunity to produce something more in the way of stability there.

Whether it will be taken is a different matter, and personally I fear the worst. There are, of course, deep conflicts of interest, particularly over the West Bank and other Israeli-occupied territories, and in the last fifty years there has been much inter-state and internal violence – three Arab-Israeli wars, an almost everlasting civil war in Lebanon and a nine-year war between Iraq and Iran, at the end of which it was virtually certain that one of the protagonists would turn their attention to making trouble elsewhere, initially in the Gulf area, and after the death of Ayatollah Khomeini the odds would have been on Saddam Hussein – an archetypical power-hungry dictator, with an appalling record of cruelty among his own people and against the Kurds, and a determination to extend his influence over the whole area, leading, I suppose, eventually to a cataclysmic conflict with Israel in the name of Arab unity and under the guise of a holy war.

Like many dictators before him he committed all this to paper, just as Hitler had done with *Mein Kampf*. So the warning signs should have been there; instead of which, many countries which should have known better armed him to the teeth. Indeed, even at the height of the Cold War, when NATO and the now defunct Warsaw Pact were glowering at each other over the inner German border, I personally, as Chief of Defence Staff (UK), never believed that the most likely threat to world peace was the Russians coming across the Elbe.

The stability of NATO and the balance of nuclear terror saw to that. But the threat was rather in the Middle East, with some sort of showdown involving Israel, Syria and Iraq and bringing in the United States on one side and the Soviet Union on the other, all of which would then, of course, later have involved NATO. Well, happily we've been spared all that, although if we had been back in the Cold War period the Kuwait situation could have looked very different and might have had to be treated very differently.

But notwithstanding all that, the crisis in the Gulf when it came owed something to a security vacuum, wrong signals perhaps being sent, and seemed still to have come as something as a surprise, at least as regards timing. And Britain's contribution of a significant number of Tornado and Jaguar aircraft and eventually a whole armoured division was, I am sure, entirely unexpected in the Ministry of Defence or at least entirely unplanned, which is perhaps why it was so successful.

It was put together because it was the political perception of the British Prime Minister (Mrs Thatcher at that time), correct as it turned out, that more than token support for the Americans was needed, and it was the military belief that this was the minimum, and, bearing in mind the distance and logistic problems, probably also the maximum viable force under the circumstances. And I must say that back in July, six weeks before it did start, in the Defence Estimates debates in our Upper House, the House of Lords, I did in fact warn that British Forces might be required to support the United States in the Middle East in containing a pervading threat in the area. But had the planners actually got down to it there would have been no political or financial support.

The planners would have been told, as they would have been told before the Falklands, that they were out of their minds, so quickly do political parameters change. All of which only underlines what the military have always claimed, and politicians, and particularly our Treasury, have never been prepared to admit – that what you plan for seldom happens, probably because you are seen to be ready, and what you don't prepare for, and make no funding for, invariably does. Unexpectedness is indeed one of the features of modern conflict as far as the British are concerned; look at Korea, Borneo and the Falklands to name but three, and it is wise for governments not to forget it.

The next characteristic of modern conflict, illustrated so well by the Gulf crisis, is its inevitable coalition nature. No one country can any longer bear the financial and political burdens of going it alone in a full-scale sophisticated conflict, except in defence of its own soil. The only way to sustain effective action, however justifiable in one's own mind, is by means of as wide a consensus in the international community as possible. And the widest and most convincing and the most legitimate of all, of course, is through the

United Nations Security Council, however the military force emanating from that consensus is actually controlled on the field of battle.

The financial burdens are pretty obvious, but the wider the consensus the easier it is at home and abroad to stand up to the various political pressures that ensue, for example those of sustaining casualties, in this war, as I said, miraculously light, of inflicting civilian casualties on one's opponent, of indirect reactive violence through terrorism of one sort or another, of real issues getting clouded and distorted and of ecological disasters, which are yet another characteristic of modern war.

Finally, and while we are still on the characteristics of modern war rather than the way it, in this case, unfolded, it is clear that in moving in that direction over the last few years, the Gulf War represents something of a sea change in the technology of war; perhaps as great as was experienced in the fourteenth century, with the introduction of gunpowder, in 1860 with the industrially supported American Civil War, in 1904–5 with the trench warfare and machine guns of the Russo-Japanese War and in 1940 with Blitz-krieg. And certainly no one can accuse General Schwarzkopf and his team, as generals sometimes get accused, of fighting this war with the tactics and the weapons of the last. Indeed, they conducted a brilliant and innovative campaign, based on the old principles of war but using the latest technology to the maximum, and with the most imaginative end game, of which I will remind you in a minute.

And there is also a sea change in the way war has to be publicly conducted, with every strategy, tactic, disposition, and nuance now crawled over in the public eye and with the enemy's propaganda priorities (Saddam Hussein's threats of the 'mother of all battles', chemical warfare, ghastly unspecified surprises, civilian casualties, etc., etc.) often boosted and disseminated by one's own media.

Now, in the restless seeking by the media of all the facts, from which the truth may, or may not, emerge, this may be unavoidable. But it can, on occasions, seem a bit odd and it would have made life undoubtedly very difficult to both our political leaders and military commanders alike if, during this war, the coalition had to go through some really difficult fighting as in earlier wars. And the extent to which the West did some of Saddam Hussein's job for him can best be judged by the enthusiasm with which he received Western media representatives while the war was on and how little he wanted them when the war was over.

But the main change was the high technology of what may be described as SMART weapons – those that can be delivered from a great distance away, find their targets by laser guidance or other means with the very greatest accuracy, like the Tomahawk cruise missile, fired from the battleship *Missouri*, which could virtually fly up a street in Baghdad, turn right at the traffic lights and go straight down the well on the inside of a building of a strategic military target, with very little damage or casualties outside at all.

Also, weapons to attack enemy radar and other early warning systems. Equipment – thermal imaging, to enable military formations to fight at night and in virtually all weathers, which gave General Schwarzkopf's armour an enormous advantage over that of the Iraqis. Navigation systems which told the forward troops **exactly** where they were in the wide-open desert, a most unusual experience for any desert warrior of the past, as any member of the Indian Divisions who fought in Libya in the early 1940s will know.

And also, anti-tank missiles like Patriot, with a great success rate (at a cost of about $500,000 a shot) against relatively first-generation missiles like SCUD. And in the horrible business of war, this high technology has done those who possess it and enjoy the advantages it bestows a double service in that it not only increased lethality against vital targets and reduced our casualties, but by such selective targeting reduced the loss of civilian life to the minimum.

And if ever in the future we are to use the military option to prevent still worse evils occurring and to maintain international order, both of which aims made this war, I believe, utterly justified, all who use it must try to maintain the high moral ground both for their own peace of mind and to retain public and international support. Unfortunately, at the end of World War II Britain did not have that technology to do this and I believe we lost some of that moral authority in what was so undoubtedly a just war by fairly indiscriminate mass destruction of German cities, even if, for a time, this was the only means we had to fight back.

But turning now to the way the Gulf War actually developed, two things happened immediately after Saddam Hussein had moved in and claimed the annexation of Kuwait. First, it became the perception of virtually the whole world that he had pinched something – in this case a sovereign state of some seventy years standing – which didn't belong to him, and he shouldn't be allowed to get away with it. And, secondly, the immediate priority was to ensure that he could not exploit his surprise attack into the oil fields and refineries of Saudi Arabia, which he might well have done if he had found only light opposition.

So against this background, and in answer to requests from Saudi Arabia as well as Kuwait for help, the United States with as much international support and as many allies as it could muster, fortified by a Security Council condemnation of Iraq, put together in August under the code name Desert Shield a formidable array of defensive power which could simultaneously demonstrate that the international community was in earnest about Saddam Hussein leaving Kuwait, put real, albeit slow moving, pressure on him by enforcing a near total economic blockade, agreed by the United Nations, and guarantee the safety of the Saudi oil installations.

Now initially the American contribution was non-mechanised airborne troops, and at this point Britain offered both what was needed and, at the time, most readily available – Tornado aircraft both for air defence and airfield destruction if Saddam Hussein was to attack Saudi Arabia, ships to enforce the blockade and later, with more difficulty because the British Army of the Rhine had to be virtually grounded, an armoured brigade of main battle tanks and mechanised infantry, of which the Americans were short. And, of course, we can detect Mrs Thatcher's hand both in President Bush's initial resolution and in the speed and comparative strength of Britain's support.

The next few weeks were then taken up by the American administration in consolidating that consensus and support: in Congress, amongst their own people, throughout the Coalition and at the United Nations, and the British kept very much in line with this. The aim was to legitimise both the American defensive deployment and also any possible subsequent offensive operations, if Saddam Hussein would not go of his own accord, ranging from the initial condemnation and the agreement to sanctions to the ultimate authorisation of any force that might be necessary after a final ultimatum to enforce compliance with all the United Nations Resolutions.

Now Mrs Thatcher had worked in a very similar manner during the Falklands crisis, which gave a fair wind to that operation. But at Suez in 1956, admittedly with a less good case, the British and French were unable to get the United States and world opinion behind them, which meant that the military operations were doomed if not to failure then at least to a most unsatisfactory outcome.

Now at this stage anyone else but Saddam Hussein, I suppose, might have taken the hint and cut his losses when he saw what he had let himself in for. But as many here will realise, he is obviously a clever as well as a tyrannical man and, not without reason, felt that he could extract a great deal more advantage out of the crisis and still stay in power, perhaps even with increased prestige in the Arab world. Because he just did not believe that President Bush after Vietnam, and Britain, possibly after Mrs Thatcher, and the Arab countries in the Coalition with the Palestine problem still unresolved, really had it in them to take what might amount to bloody action – to have it in them to do anything other, perhaps, than impose sanctions, which he may have thought he could ride out, or circumvent. He still thought they were bluffing. So he relied on his propaganda machine, promising body bags, a holy war, other unspeakable horrors, to weaken their resolve and to encourage the doubters in the peace movements and the purveyors of other courses of action, which would have left him still in possession of his prize.

Moreover, since he had an air force, although not of such high quality as those of the Coalition, and ground forces said to number in Kuwait alone 500,000 men, considerably at that time outnumbering the allies and with plenty of operational experience under their belt, he was, perhaps not surprisingly, quite confident that not only might he deter attack, but that, if attacked, his troops, fighting with their backs to their country, supported by many SCUD missiles and a potential chemical capability, could cause the Coalition enough casualties for either nervous public opinion to force them to break off the battle; or he himself would be able to withdraw gracefully under pressure and retain his power base with his prestige as an Arab hero enhanced.

So there was no way, despite the Resolutions and the sanctions, that Saddam Hussein was going to back down before what I described in the House of Lords in early January, before the battle started, as 'five minutes past midnight' – midnight being the time when the talking stopped and when he was actually attacked from the air or, more probably, because he would use the airborne bombardment on him, linked, as he imagined, to high civilian casualties, as further opportunity for a propaganda offensive against the Coalition, from the ground.

So in mid-November, shortly before I myself visited the Gulf with a UK Parliamentary delegation, and with all this becoming fairly evident, the decision was taken, sensibly, courageously, and I detect the senior military commanders behind this, massively, to reinforce the Coalition forces so that the offensive operation could now become a feasible option without the probability of disastrous Coalition casualties.

The numerical disparity alone had to be redressed and so the number of US ground troops was therefore doubled, including two US armoured divisions, a cavalry division and two mechanised divisions, with all the supplies, the ammunition, medical facilities, and the general logistic backing, and, even more significantly, the air power was nearly quadrupled, to take it way above the Iraqis' 700 aircraft.

It was a formidable logistics and movement operation, which in its scope could only have been tackled by the United States, although Britain more than pulled its weight by sending more Tornado and Jaguar aircraft and another mechanised brigade to bring our ground forces up to a complete division, with all its backing. General de la Billière told me that the logistic support sent out by the British Chiefs of Staff was absolutely superb and made all the subsequent and very complicated manoeuvres, which we'll go into in a moment, possible.

The Coalition was now in business, and by mid-January had also assembled about 500,000 men, around 2,000 up-to-date aircraft, ranging from massive B52 bombers to tank-busting helicopters, and was keen to get on with it for, as the Arab leaders we met put it to us so succinctly when we were out there: 'One: we want Saddam Hussein out of Kuwait, and the sooner the better. Two: we want him taught a lesson. Three: we don't want him in a position to do it again, and Four: we don't want Iraq destroyed as a country, otherwise the balance in the Middle East will be disrupted.'

Now, please notice the wording, because in the light of what happened at the end of the war it is important – no mention at that stage, rightly or wrongly, of invading Iraq or removing Saddam Hussein. And important, too, because these points more or less became the political aim of Desert Storm, the code name of the land/air battle, no doubt with the nickname of 'Stormin' Norman' in mind. This was to start after the final ultimatum expired in mid-January.

Every operation has to have a clear aim; indeed, its selection and maintenance is the first principle of war, and those points I've set out undoubtedly influenced the whole planning of the Desert Storm operation.

Now apart from a clear aim, there are, as all the staff-trained people in the audience know, traditionally nine other principles of war, although the British Field Marshal Montgomery wisely after World War II added a tenth as a pre-requisite of any operation: 'winning the air battle'. And never was that tenth principle more important than in this war, because with the strength of the whole Iraqi war machine, which had to be written down very considerably if the land forces were to stand a chance, and now with the great superiority of the Coalition's air forces, both in numbers and technology, the air battle was going to be absolutely critical, and the whole operation was going to therefore have to be conducted in three phases.

The first phase, which started on 17 January, was to use the full Coalition air power and its technology to attack and destroy Iraq's infrastructure, its very centralised command and control communications, cutting off Baghdad from the battle area, its retaliatory capability, such as its airfields and aircraft dispersal areas and generally winning air superiority, becoming air supremacy, and, of course, the SCUD missiles, and for good measure dealing with any nuclear and chemical production plants or local dumps of these weapons.

Now this, I have from General de la Billière[31] himself, was brilliantly planned and most bravely and expertly conducted. The attention to detail was fantastic, each daily air-tasking order being about ninety foolscap pages in length, and it was this careful strategic targeting, combined with the extraordinary accuracy of the weapon delivery systems, which caused Saddam

Hussein so to misjudge the strength and duration of our air resources and the effect it would have on his subsequent control of his forward land formations.

Saddam Hussein apparently planned to hold back his own air effort on the assumption that ours would be spent within three or four days. The land battle would then, he thought, be immediately engaged, in which case his air force would then intervene with effect. But of course, having failed to deploy his air force in the early stages he was then denied the opportunity to do so, because most of the strategic targeting was, as I said, directed specifically to destroying his capability to launch and control his aircraft and in this business the United Kingdom's Tornados played a formidable and very brave part, having the only weapon, the JP 233, specifically designed for airfield runway destruction, but which could be very hazardous to deliver because there was no alternative but for the pilot to fly straight down the runway at very low altitude.

However, and this surprised me, I have been assured by the UK Chief of the Air Staff,[32] that in fact only one of the six Tornados lost was actually shot down on a low-level run. Anyhow, the result was that the Iraqi air force was never able to get in the air battle, and eventually to save itself, and possibly to preserve Saddam Hussein's future power base, 140 of its best aircraft abandoned Iraqi ground forces and fled to Iran, where I sincerely hope they still are.

Now, the chief agents of the air assaults, apart from the Tornados, were Stealth bombers, launching laser-directed bombs, and those Tomahawk cruise missiles I mentioned earlier, the F111s and later the B52 bombers, the latter because of their greater spread and destruction on troop targeting in the open desert. SCUD missile sites, both fixed and mobile, were also attacked, and in this as well as in other important information-gathering roles our Special Forces, particularly the SAS, played a notable and gallant role in the wide-open spaces of south-western Iraq.

Some of the first reports of the air assault were both inaccurate and over-euphoric. In war, as most of us know, nothing is ever as it first seems, neither as good, nor as bad, and this led to some initial disappointment when everything seemed to be taking longer than some expected and there were some casualties to our aircraft. For a short period we were losing a Tornado a day, and ultimately, as I said, the total loss did reach sixty Coalition aircraft, which is certainly not negligible, shot down throughout the whole war.

But the battle had achieved a large element of surprise, and it had got off to an excellent start, while Saddam Hussein's only response was to fire off, rather irregularly, any SCUDs he could, using mostly the mobile sites, as most of his fixed sites had been destroyed early on, and firing them off not very effectively and not, until the last fluke shot on the United States Marines' barracks, near Dahrain, really causing very many casualties; but cunningly and predictably he included Israel in his targeting, hoping they could be provoked to enter the war in a way that would split the Coalition. He certainly kept everyone on their toes with the threat of chemical attack on congested population areas, although there was no evidence that he actually had the capability to arm SCUDs with chemical warheads.

Fortunately, Israel, fortified with US Patriot anti-missile missiles, and maybe exacting some political price of which we are not yet aware, showed restraint, and the world stood by, largely contentedly, even the Arab world, while Saddam Hussein took his punishment.

Now the second phase, also an air phase, was using the Coalition's unchallenged air supremacy to turn the weight of its attack on to the Iraqi ground forces, destroying their more local communications, particularly bridges, their supply dumps, soft-skinned transport, forward strong points and progressively their artillery positions, their tanks and personnel carriers, both of the more immediate reserve, notably the Republican Guard, with its better equipment and its T72 tanks, many of which were bound to be dispersed and dug in in the desert, with a wide assortment of dummies and decoys.

The aim of this phase was to write down by perhaps as much as 40–50 per cent the morale and fighting effectiveness and numbers of the Iraqi army, so as to make a land assault, even through the fixed defences and minefields on the Kuwaiti border, feasible and comparatively inexpensive to our own troops; and very effective all this turned out to be, as was proved later.

The third phase was going to be the land offensive, because whatever the overwhelming success and power of the air battle, which as I say was critical to the whole operation, air power could only, and can only ever, do so much. The full Coalition aims could only be met if Saddam Hussein was actually driven out of Kuwait and it was re-possessed by land forces.

Now these three phases did, of course, go on to some extent concurrently, but the second and third phases couldn't proceed until the previous phase had achieved a satisfactory position. In fact, the first two phases took a good deal longer than was originally anticipated, largely, I think, because after the ultimatum expired there was very considerable political pressure to get on with it and start something early. So the time between the start of Phase 1, the air bombardment, and being completely ready for Phase 3, the land phase, which wasn't going to really be until the middle of February, was longer than originally planned – about five and a half weeks.

But this had the advantage of putting greater and more devastating pressure on Iraq's war machine, and as long as the international political front held (and keeping civilian casualties down was critical in this) and that, of course, was the one danger of prolonging the air bombardment too long – but as long as it held it was actually a bonus. There were also some problems with the weather and the difficulty in getting confirmation that certain critical strategic and tactical targets had in fact been destroyed. So it all added up to a prolonged first and second phase.

But by mid-February the land forces had made all their plans, they had completed their deployment, tactical and logistic, and the air bombardment had probably achieved as much as it ever could, both strategically and tactically, without getting the Republican Guard up in the north out into the open, and this would only happen when they were about to combat an actual attack. Then continuing the bombardment would be able to do them a very great deal of damage. In any case, because of the atrocities and ecological devastation being caused in Kuwait, that attack could now no longer be delayed.

General Schwarzkopf was therefore now in a proper position, five and a half weeks after Desert Storm started, to launch his ground offensive, prepared, no doubt, as indeed I knew he was, for a tough encounter, at least for a few days, while we, watching at home once D Day came, were able to appreciate the brilliance of his design for battle, which kept faithfully to the well-established principles of war and had as its military aim to meet the political one I mentioned earlier: the encirclement and complete destruction of the entire Iraqi army south of the Euphrates, or – as General Colin Powell, Chief of the United States Combined Chiefs of Staff put it more succinctly: 'We're going to cut him off and kill him.'

Now, I think of all the principles of war, and all came into it in some form, I suspect most of the experts in the audience would agree, surprise is probably the most effective. There has scarcely been any great victorious battle or campaign in history in which the element of surprise has not been employed to seize the initiative, reduce own casualties while threatening an enemy's morale and generally achieve material advantages consistent with a much larger force. All great commanders have consistently sought ways to mystify and mislead the enemy as to their true intentions so as to achieve their aims more easily, and this 100-hour battle was no exception. Indeed, Mao Tse-Tung's dictum of 'make a noise in the east and attack in the west' could never have been more apt.

The Americans had a formidable amphibious capability, which the United States Marines were dying to use (no doubt with an eye on the long-term costings in the United States defence budget), and the Iraqis certainly expected them to use it. Yet to do so, up at the northern end of the Persian Gulf, would have inevitably, because of mines, coastal obstacles and the concentration of Iraqi troops on either side of Kuwait City, been costly in casualties and heavy in destruction of property around Kuwait City from suppressive supporting fire, designed to reduce those casualties to a minimum.

So the grand design started, not with a landing but with a major feint, deploying selective suppressive fire from the battleship USS *Missouri*[33] in the build-up period, increasing attacks on what had been left of Iraq's coastal navy, and carrying out the full deployment and final run-up of the amphibious shipping to some miles off-shore. It was even reported that the Marines had landed on an off-shore island near Kuwait City, when in fact they were prepared to go ashore much further south actually behind the troops attacking from the south.

All this helped keep Iraq's divisions tied down on the coast and facing the wrong way. At the same time, the first effective arm of the envelopment got under way well out to the west, in Iraq itself, with the French (largely Foreign Legion) and the American 82nd Airborne Division striking across the desert, first to seize a forward airfield, to be used for re-supply and reinforcement, and then to push on to the nearest point in the valley of the Euphrates, this shortly afterwards to cut off one of Saddam Hussein's main escape and supply routes to and from Baghdad, as well as, of course, providing flank protection for the whole operation.

Then, with the preliminary moves completed, under the cover of artillery fire, to remove and fill in the forward minefields and obstacles, an assault echelon progressively from the east was launched by the Kuwaitis, the US Marine Corps, the Saudis and the Egyptians and other Arab forces on the fixed defences along the southern border of Kuwait and on the shortest route due north to Kuwait City.

This was an operation that could have been most dangerous and expensive, because it was the one area where Saddam Hussein might have used chemical weapons fired from artillery at the moment when the assaulting troops were concentrated, crossing the minefields and obstacles. In fact, no chemical weapons were found deployed with the forward artillery at all. He had no doubt been deterred, partly by realising that with the prevailing wind blowing the wrong way they really wouldn't do a great deal of damage, but partly also, perhaps, by the fear of nuclear retaliation by the Americans against him, however unlikely that might be.

But nobody knew, then, that chemical weapons would not be used, and all precautions had to be taken, which were considerably burdensome to the forward troops. But thanks to superb intelligence from numerous sources, the pounding the Iraqis had taken from the air over several days and supporting artillery, which produced a disastrous deterioration to their morale, which their disrupted propaganda machine and chain of command were quite unable to stem, and the skill and professionalism of the assaulting engineers prior to and after H-Hour, the break-in, which quickly became a breakthrough, was quickly achieved with minimum casualties, which must have been a great relief to the commanders.

Finally, with their frontal and direct threat to Kuwait City going well, General Schwarzkopf – again calling on the element of surprise – delivered the *coup de grace*. Having kept his two United States Army Corps, the 18th and the 7th, well behind the front line in the east, the British Armoured Division ostentatiously linked in with the US Marines in the coastal sector, he moved them all at the eleventh hour in a wide sweeping approach march, which must have stretched his logistics resources to the limit – the British Armoured Division alone did about a 500-mile approach march, to the open flank to the west of the Iraqi-Kuwait border – and using them in the traditional way, he struck where the extended fortified defences were weakest, and drove north-wards and eastwards deep into Iraq and Kuwait respectively.

The eastern thrust, consisting of the two United States armoured divisions and a cavalry division, with the 1st British Armoured Division on their right, using the 1st US Infantry Division to break through the fixed defences, cut a swathe between the more immediate armoured reserves, supporting the forti-fied positions to the south, and the main Republican Guard reserve divisions, with their T72s in the northern part of Kuwait and over its northern border, and then pressed on directly to cut the main road from Kuwait City to Basra.

It was indeed a classic armoured action, delivered with great speed and boldness by, as far as the British were concerned, two brigades abreast, and thrusting deep into the enemy vitals, and it achieved almost complete sur-prise. Saddam and his generals, strange as it may seem, completely failed to identify the threat from the flank, being convinced that the only one they would have to worry about would be the frontal attack, combined with the marine amphibious assault, a view that all the Coalition deception plans would have been designed to foster. As a result, they were facing the wrong way and, due to the disruption to their command and control system, they were quite incapable of redeploying at the speed necessary to counter the extraordinarily rapid advance of the armour, which in the final phase to the Kuwait road covered 45 miles in little over an hour. In World War II we thought we were doing very well if we were doing 50 miles in a day.

The old Desert Warriors of World War II, both of the red (7th Armoured Division) and of the black (4th Armoured Brigade) varieties, would have approved of the élan and panache of the Royal Scots Dragoon Guards, the Queen's Own Irish Hussars, the 14th/20th Hussars and their supporting infantry, to name but a few of these, and how they would have enjoyed the better equipment of today – the tanks, the Challengers, which despite having to cover that 500-mile approach march after intense training, showed an over 95 per cent serviceability rate at the end of the battle and were well able to stand up to anything the Iraqis could throw at them and could, of course, knock out anything that was in their way, which only shows what can be dome when there is no cheeseparing of spare parts, track mileage and things like that.

The infantry personnel carriers, the Warriors, were equally effective. The navigation equipment I have mentioned in most of the vehicles told them exactly where they were in the wide-open desert which, as I said, would have been a rare experience for the Desert Rats of the 1940s. Then there was the infinitely more effective artillery support with accurate, effective position-fixing, and the greatly improved equipment, including the multi-launcher rocket system with its terrifying airburst over a wide area and its release of hundreds of bomblets to destroy targets from on top; and of course, the thermal imaging sights, which enabled our tanks and 30mm cannon to engage the enemy targets at night and in bad weather before they could see us.

To give some idea of the power of the artillery, one Iraqi brigade entered the war with a hundred tanks, and after the air bombardment had done its worst for many, many days against its dispersed tanks, was down to eighty. But after the artillery concentrations, which preceded the armoured thrust on each objective, had lifted, he was down to a mere seventeen.

This shock action by the Coalition armies, coming after the days of softening up, was indeed formidable, and as a result all resistance quickly collapsed. The back end of the forward reserves, with their T55s, were either destroyed or abandoned their equipment and surrendered with their outflanked comrades in droves, thus opening up the way to Kuwait City. And the Republican Guard not taken on by the United States armoured divisions retreated northwards towards and beyond the border, only to be destroyed by tank-busting helicopters and other forms of air-power, using cluster bombs. The same happened on the road north from Kuwait City to Basra, where, sadly, a lot of escaping civilians, or hostages, got killed as well, all to be cut off and hemmed in and forced to abandon their equipment by the other US corps' outflanking movement.

So it became a most decisive military victory, in which forty out of the Iraqis' forty-one divisions actually in Kuwait had been rendered ineffective and only 250 out of their 4,000 tanks had escaped, and although it is all too simple to consider that the campaign was a walkover, certainly both the land and air battles were executed with much greater ease and far, far lower casualties, than even the most optimistic of us armchair strategists or, far more importantly, the commanders on the spot had expected. All of the planning and mounting had been done, rightly, on the basis that in the early days of the execution the enemy would be an altogether tougher nut to deal with; if there was some over-insurance, it was better to be safe than sorry. Certainly,

General Schwarzkopf can't be blamed for winning with so few casualties to his own side; in fact, just the reverse. Because, as the Chinese General Sun reminded us many centuries ago, the best general of all may be the one who wins his victories without having to fight at all.

General Schwarzkopf proved himself not only the master of strategy, in the mode of Hannibal (whom he is said much to admire) but also a consummate manager and orchestrator of the battle and all that goes to make it up, as were Montgomery and Wellington, to cite two British generals, amongst, no doubt, many others. The scope and technical complications of this one must have been immense, particularly when you think that he was doing the job of commander-in-chief and army commander at the same time, although I have no doubt that he was extremely well advised by our own General Peter de la Billière, who tells us that General Schwarzkopf did it, as did Monty and Wellington before him, by standing no nonsense, tolerating no 'bellyaching' and being bloody rude to people if necessary.

Should we have stopped where we did? Well, had we known exactly the terrible things which were going to happen to the Kurds in particular, which could, I suppose, be looked on, at least in part, and whether intended or not, as connected with President Bush's invitation to the Iraqi people to remove Saddam Hussein, things might have looked a bit different. But in general terms, without hindsight, and bearing in mind the aims of the operation, which I have spelt out in some detail, and which included keeping Iraq as an entity, I am sure we did the right thing.

As General Schwarzkopf confirmed, south of the Euphrates there was nothing left to fight, and to continue would have involved more fighting through Basra and even up to Baghdad, more casualties, more destruction on all sides and perhaps getting involved in an open-ended commitment and a civil war. All way outside the United Nations' remit and, I suspect, inter-national and national tolerance. Saddam Hussein has been taught a lesson; he isn't in a position to do it again and, indeed, was in no position to interfere in what we subsequently decided to do. It was much better [for] contributions to come in from NATO and Turkey, in a purely humanitarian capacity, which hopefully will lead to United Nations monitoring and Kurdish autonomy within Iraq, than to blunder forward into a continuing and unpredictable battle.

Saddam Hussein, of course, remains a problem, but his international clout is nil, the international community still has considerable hold over him in the way of reparations and sanctions if he fails to comply, and his prestige with his own people must be a wasting asset. If everyone keeps to their word, includ-ing the Commonwealth of Independent States, as successor to the defunct

Soviet Union, then Iraq will be an international pariah until Saddam Hussein stands down. I should have thought his days are numbered.

But then winning the peace is often much more difficult than winning the war. War, however necessary and just, seldom settles anything properly. In this case so much remains to be done to take the fleeting opportunities there may be still in the Middle East to make it a safer and less dangerous touch-point for world conflagration.

The other lessons? Well, the two main ones, apparently contradictory but complementary, I think, are: first, because of the appalling cost of making war in both human and financial terms, and its ecological repercussions, we've got to do all we can by diplomacy to see if we can in future maintain international order, national honour and justice by peaceful and not warlike means. This, of course, means maintaining adequate security arrangements in areas where these have already been successful as, for instance in NATO for forty years, and then helping to establish them where hitherto they have not existed, or proved inadequate, inadequate because often, and both the Falklands and, to some extent, the Gulf were examples of this, there has been no credible *in situ* deterrent and the wrong signals have been sent to potential aggressors. But when this state of affairs is achieved, and it's sometimes easier said than done, the chief value of military forces in the area, or ready to come to the area, becomes the expression of interest, determination to maintain a proper balance of power and act as a deterrent to any military option being used for aggressive purposes. You will have many parallels in this part of the world.

The second lesson is that if this stability cannot be achieved, and even if it can only be achieved with difficulty, the world remains a dangerous and uncertain place, in which those who have it in mind to extend their power and threaten international order are still prepared to use military force, which may affect our kith and kin, our economic interests or our international responsibilities. In both instances this calls for a continuing, adequate and flexible insurance policy for our country, which is what defence spending amounts to, and armed forces which are flexible in thought and organisation and have both the modern operational capability and mobility to react to the unexpected, which always turns up, and to support our foreign policy as the government of the day thinks fit, which politics sometimes requires to be done at very short notice.

It is also well to remember that quality in men and equipment is not something which can be manufactured overnight. It can't be turned off for long periods and then turned on again at a drop of a hat. Britain should have learned that lesson in the 1920s, when after the Treasury cuts at the end of the First World War they nearly lost the Second.

These things have to be nurtured and need a certain amount of stability, tradition and *esprit de corps*. They need the confidence and professionalism that come from a credible operational capability and the self-respect of those who know they are appreciated. For the last forty years, the Armed Forces of the British Crown have been needed in one form or another a remarkable number of times, and they are still needed in Europe, in the Middle East, in the aftermath of the Gulf War and indeed in other places in the world. Moreover, there can be few national institutions, and I am sure this goes for your armed forces as well, which have so well preserved their reputation and integrity in the eyes of the public and, after this latest example of their value, it is important that they should not be forgotten and stinted on, as so often in the past.

No one, in any country, likes paying insurance premiums. When everything is quiet, we bitterly resent doing so. But my goodness, when the wind blows and the floods come, and we find ourselves in the worst winter or monsoon or whatever for five years, how glad we are that we didn't suspend paying those premiums, and I should have thought that money is worth spending on defence in this most uncertain of worlds, with its record in peace as well as in the happily only occasional periods of war, and the impact that defence has on employment and industrial expansion. I think those insurance premiums are worth paying more than ever.

Chapter 10

Intervention in the Balkans

Background

The Balkans holds an important position between central and south Europe and between the Adriatic and Black Seas. Much of it was part of Yugoslavia until that state started to collapse following the death of Josef Tito in May 1980. Its population consists of both Christians and Muslims. In the 1980s there were frequent demands that many areas become independent, with ethnic tensions spilling over in frequent violent outbursts against the Yugoslav state authorities. In 1989 Serbian President Slobodan Milošević employing a mix of intimidation and political manoeuvring, drastically increased Serbia's control, and started cultural oppression of the ethnic Albanian population. Bosnia, Kosovo and Croatia, particularly, responded with a non-violent separatist movement, employing widespread civil disobedience. In July 1990, the Kosovo Albanians proclaimed the existence of the Republic of Kosovo. This was rejected by the political representatives of the Bosnian Serbs, and following Bosnia and Herzegovina's declaration of independence, the Bosnian Serbs, led by Radovan Karadzic, supported by the Serbian government and the Yugoslav Peoples' Army, mobilised their forces in order to secure Serb territory. The war soon spread across the country, accompanied by the ethnic cleansing of the Bosnian and Croat population, especially in eastern Bosnia, notably at Srebrenica in July 1995.

After popular pressure, NATO was asked by the UN to intervene in the Bosnian War after allegations of war crimes against civilians were made. In response to the refugee and humanitarian crisis in Bosnia, the United Nations Security Council passed Resolution 743 on 21 February 1992, creating the United Nations Protection Force (UNPROFOR), whose mandate was to keep the population alive and deliver humanitarian aid to refugees in Bosnia. Initially this was confined to enforcing a no-fly zone over Bosnia. However, Serb forces continued to attack UN 'safe areas' in Bosnia and UN peacekeepers were unable to fight back as the mandate did not give them authority to do so. This was authorised on 4 June 1993. Air operations to protect the 'safe areas' started in February 1994, and air strikes were made to protect UNPROFOR positions. On 25–26 May 1995, after violations of the exclusion zones and the shelling of 'safe areas', NATO aircraft carried out air strikes against Bosnian Serbs tanks, stores and command and control infrastructure. Some 370 UN peacekeepers in Bosnia were taken hostage and subsequently used as human shields of potential targets in a successful bid to prevent further air strikes. However, there were no NATO ground troops to secure what was needed to stop the ethnic cleansing by the Serbs. The only troops were strictly there as UN peacekeepers and had no rules of engagement to allow them to stop humanitarian disasters.

On 31 May 1995 Bramall spoke in the House of Lords about Britain's involvement in Kosovo.

My Lords, I wish to add my congratulations to the noble Lord, Lord Owen,[34] on his brilliant maiden speech. As one would expect from a distinguished statesman who has been in the thick of it, the speech contained all the wisdom, realism and perception that we anticipated, and obviously at this juncture in our affairs it was a vital contribution to the debate.

The speech also reminded me that lacking, as I do, any detailed first-hand knowledge such as is possessed by the noble Lord, Lord Owen, any observations I make will be of much less value. However, with the indulgence of the House, I must remind noble Lords that some months ago in a debate in the House on Bosnia, I said that if air bombing – and under the circumstances in which we found ourselves I had always been so strongly against it – had to be carried out, because we had threatened tough action so often that we had to be seen as being as good as our word, I hoped that all possible moves and counter-moves would be thought through in depth. I hoped that contingency plans would be made well in advance while we still had the flexibility. I said that indulging in such a highly dangerous course of action merely with our fingers crossed would lead us into a very serious situation indeed. I cited as examples of what we must be prepared to do, in advance, the temporary suspension of humanitarian operations, the need to give our troops on the ground more fire power, helicopter support and, temporarily at any rate, to increase their numbers.

For various reasons, we have yet again allowed ourselves or been forced to engage in a half-hearted war-fighting action, with still only peacekeeping capability deployment and rules of engagement on the ground. Thus, we have been unprepared for any warlike counter-measures being taken against us. We have, therefore, at short notice to provide those very reinforcements in size and strength which, had they arrived earlier, might have prevented our present predicament.

I wholeheartedly agree that recrimination – even if desired – is not at all helpful at this stage. The question is what to do in the immediate future to extricate ourselves from one of the most serious crises facing Western Europe probably since the Berlin airlift.

This is where the collective advice of the Chiefs of Staff will be so invaluable to the Government. But the first thing, of course, is to get the troops being held hostage freed. It is easy to say that from a safe distance, but I do not believe they are in great personal danger. Not even the Bosnian Serbs would want for long to assume the mantle of Saddam Hussein, although he had the good sense to realise that he should release his hostages fairly soon. The wrath of the entire international community which would fall on them and on the Serbs if anything were to happen to the hostages would and should be terrible to behold. The perpetrators of that act of terrorism must be encouraged to remember that.

At the same time, obviously, we cannot take any chances. It would seem wise, at least, as the noble Lord, Lord Callaghan,[35] said, to suspend aerial bombing. In any case, its value has often been highly doubtful and we should suspend it while at the same time using every other means – diplomatic, international, economic and the positioning on the ground of greater military strength and power to defend ourselves from further military attacks – to put pressure on the Bosnian Serbs and the Serb leadership to effect the hostages' release. Like my noble and gallant friend, Lord Carver, I warmly welcome the reinforcement by the brigade group which has been announced, because without pressure and threats and promises which can be fulfilled, one usually gets nowhere in negotiations like this. I was interested to hear from the noble Viscount, the Leader of the House that it would form part of the UN command under General Smith.

All that may take some time and we must be prepared for the Bosnian Serbs to try, however outrageously, to extract territorial concessions from the holding of the captives. But if cool heads are kept all round and we show firmness, I hope that their freedom could be achieved by negotiation. I was interested to hear the noble Lord, Lord Owen, say that he thought there was still a chance and I still hope that, with the warring parties not that far apart in geographical terms, a political settlement might be reached in the not too distant future. Indeed, this latest crisis may be a good window of opportunity to pull out all the stops and make a last effort to achieve that.

However, if neither is achieved or if only the first suggestion is achieved and the fighting goes on, if anything with increased intensity, we really must come to terms with whatever options are now open to us in a way which we have largely skated over in the past, surviving for a time quite largely, I believe, on the intrepid and charismatic leadership of General Rose and the superb professionalism of our forces, to which all noble Lords have given credit. As is generally recognised, the trouble is that all the options carry considerable risks, the net consequences of which can be measured and accurately assessed only when one considers the consequences of adopting another course.

Doing what we are doing now, half in and half out of the battle, sometimes called 'muddling through' – although as has been expressed on many sides, the benefit it has brought to many people in saving lives and in humanitarian terms has been immense and should never be understated – carries the risk of further humiliation and denigration of the whole status and authority of the United Nations. We have had a dramatic example of that recently demonstrated. That applies particularly if we persist in a largely passive identification with the so-called 'safe', but now manifestly unsafe, areas. Here we can only raise expectations which we cannot deliver and expose ourselves to considerable risk into the bargain.

As an increasing number of people in the media and elsewhere seem to urge the Government to do, we could get shot of the whole wretched business. The extrication would not be easy and, so we are told, would require many more troops to achieve it without interruption and casualties. However, the proposed reinforcements now being sent would certainly help in that respect, give us flexibility and allow us to make some adjustments. In any case, we should not persist with a policy which may lead us God knows where, merely because it is dangerous and expensive to stop it, if to get out is, on the best advice, the wisest course.

But if we were to cut and run, together presumably with everyone else, could any of us who believe in international order hold up our heads again? Such an act would result, as has been said, in grave humiliation for the United Nations. It would presage a fierce intensification and possibly a widening of the war; and it would probably create the conditions for a Serb victory. Given that – however absurdly Bosnia was recognised as an independent sovereign state – it would be embarrassing to say the least. The outcome would have repercussions for the stability of the southern flank of NATO, as well as compromising the United Nations' efforts at peace keeping and mediation for perhaps decades to come.

Finally, we could grasp the bull by the horns and try, in conjunction with others if they would come with us, to impose our will on the transgressors by indulging in war fighting, which so far, with a few unsuccessful exceptions, we have done our very best to avoid. Here the risks are more obvious still. Still more troops would be required; and in that terrain, with an implacable foe, we could so easily become sucked in and bogged down, as the Germans were in this very area in World War II, as the Americans were in Vietnam and the Russians in Afghanistan.

Such action, even accepting that vital interests could be held to be at stake, could only remotely work in a NATO context with a strong, effective, well-balanced NATO corps employed and operating away from white vehicles, as the noble Lord, Lord Mayhew, said. It could work only if we made up our minds as to whom we were fighting. We could not fight two sides at the same time. It could work only if the objectives were strictly limited; that is to say, if we did not try to enforce arbitrary boundaries and acquire territory but tried to make safe areas truly safe, and also demilitarised, to be used as a springboard for negotiations from a position of strength. It would work only if the governments concerned were confident that, despite the undoubted casualties that would accrue, even in the pursuit of limited objectives, they could count on the support of their own public opinion.

Although from this new position of strength all efforts would be made to keep negotiations for a political settlement going, there could be no guarantee that the one would lead to the other or that the military objectives, however limited, could be achieved and sustained before the winter set in. Judgements on these difficult decisions can be made only with the best possible military advice as provided by the Chiefs of Staff, and in close conjunction with commanders on the ground and other close allies.

In conclusion, I make three points. If, and wherever, we do maintain troops on the ground, they must have the strength and authority properly to defend themselves. The reinforcement gives us a chance to do that. Secondly, it is no good raising the expectations of the local population in areas where we have neither the strength nor the will to deliver them. Thirdly, whatever we decide, let it be with due recognition of the long-term consequences and repercussions on the future stability of Western Europe and the future maintenance of international order world-wide. And let us not be prepared, despite the pain and the grief that we may have to suffer, to put those principles in jeopardy for the sake of short-term convenience. If that is also the philosophy of Her Majesty's Government – as I believe it is – then I wholeheartedly support it.

Afterword

The Dayton Peace Accords were signed in Paris on 14 December 1995. The Implementation Force (IFOR) replaced UNPROFOR, and 60,000 NATO soldiers, in addition to forces from non-NATO countries were deployed to Bosnia. The Allied Rapid Reaction Corps, commanded by Lt. Gen. Sir Michael Walker was deployed, and this was the first NATO out-of-area land operation. At its height IFOR involved troops from thirty-two countries, and consisted of three Multi-National Divisions. It served for a year and was replaced by SFOR (Stabilisation Force) until 2004. IFOR was heavily armed and mandated to fire at will when necessary to carry out its mission.

Chapter 11

The Second Gulf War and Iraq

In 1998 Bramall spoke many times in the House of Lords, and wrote often to The Times, *about the invasion of Iraq and the subsequent campaign there. There follows a selection of those speeches and letters.*

Speech to the House of Lords, 17 February 1998.

My Lords, first I must apologise and crave the indulgence of your Lordships for not being present during the earlier part of the debate. Therefore, apart from anything else, I lay myself open to being guilty of repeating what other noble Lords have said already. But I was in Yorkshire attending the funeral of my World War II commanding officer,[36] and I know that no noble Lord would wish to dissuade or deter me from that.

The last thing I want to do is to weaken in any way support for Her Majesty's Government in their determination that Saddam Hussein should not be allowed to go on producing and stockpiling NBC [nuclear, biological or chemical] weapons and must comply with the Security Council resolution on free inspection which makes possible that prohibition. With so many imponderables, difficulties and dangers, it is not at all easy to arrive at the best solution. But clearly if diplomacy is to work, as is to be hoped, Saddam Hussein must have a threat of very dire and effective consequences hanging over him. Any suggestion that the United States and ourselves and those who stand with us do not somehow mean business would therefore be most unhelpful.

But when it comes to the actual use of force, if and when that becomes necessary, then I believe from my experience and what I might call informed memory of such matters – which I share with other noble Lords going back a long way, far further than many in Whitehall today – I am entitled to ask three questions. First, as with any military operation anywhere, at any time, what is the aim of the exercise? Field Marshal Montgomery, if no one else, impressed on us all how vital is the selection and maintenance of the aim as a first principle of war.

In the [First] Gulf War the aim was clear. In some people's minds, it was not exactly the right one but it was clear enough: to get the Iraqis out of

Kuwait as soon as possible and teach Saddam Hussein a lesson. Perhaps he was not taught a sufficient lesson, but the American coalition, under the clear authority of the Security Council, had assembled enough military resources on the ground, in the air and at sea, to be able to do the job properly, come what may.

I remember well that, after the attack on Kuwait, I went out with a parliamentary delegation under the leadership of the noble Lord, Lord Pym,[37] which included the present Leader of the House.[38] I came back convinced that the combination of most precisely targeted and disruptive air attacks and, in due course concentrated armoured assault, would achieve the aim; and it did, or more or less did, in a very short time.

This time the aim is much more obscure. Is it just to destroy the NBC weaponry which exists and Saddam Hussein's present capacity to improve and increase it – that is, if we know where those sites are and will continue to be? Is it to reduce Iraq to such a stone-age condition that never in the future will it be possible for Saddam Hussein to recreate the capacity to make such weapons? Is it, as has just been said by the noble Lord, Lord Marlesford,[39] to ensure the removal of the dictator, either by death or by other unspecified means? I do not ask the Minister for highly sensitive answers, but I beg the Government, with the advice of the Chiefs of Staff, to get the aim absolutely clear and to stick to it.

My second question is whether the Government consider – nay, believe – that sufficient and correct forces have been or will have been assembled to do the job? I say this because I can think of no case where military aims and objectives have been achieved by air attacks alone. Massive destruction of German cities was not sufficient to remove Hitler in World War II, nor did President Nasser throw in the towel, as was confidently predicted in 1956, when the Royal Air Force destroyed the Egyptian air force on the ground and bombed Cairo. It might not be a bad thing for Ministers to re-read the history of the Suez crisis, where there was little international authority for what we did.

Even the high-tech and very smart weapons which did so much damage to Iraq in the Gulf War were not sufficient by themselves to recapture Kuwait, let alone remove Saddam Hussein. Even if one feels disposed to quote the two atomic bombs on Hiroshima and Nagasaki – and I do not imagine that the Government have such things in mind – their aftermath required the early arrival of an occupation force. Yet there seems to be little sign of a land back up to support and, if necessary exploit, air- and sea-based strike forces – a land element which, of course, as far as this country is concerned, becomes, as a result of the endless defence studies and reviews over the past ten years, ever more difficult to provide.

Finally, I turn to my third and last question. Has any proposed operation been thought through to the bitter end, which is the hallmark of good generalship? Have we, at the Chiefs of Staff level, clawed through every detail of the American plan, because undoubtedly it has to be an American one? I do not see, as there was in the Gulf War, a de la Billière to stand alongside the American Commander-in-Chief on the spot and, where necessary, give him wise advice.

Further, what if, after the air and missile strike, the NBC weapons have still not been destroyed, or only partly so – and, of course, we may never know because all ground inspection will by then have ceased? Do we go on and, if so, what are the targets? What if after devastating destruction in Iraq, Saddam Hussein is still there? Again, do we go on and on, and, if so, in what way? If as a result of an Anglo-American attack, Saddam Hussein retaliates with his own Scud missiles from mobile launchers, which he may still possess, targeted on Kuwait, on Saudi Arabia but, above all, on Israel, who this time, without perhaps the assurances provided by the desperate efforts of special forces, hits back at Iraq? Have we considered the consequences for the stability of the whole Middle East? There is also the possibility, I suppose, that Saddam Hussein may introduce bacterial agents into, say, water supplies around the world or indulge in other forms of terrorism. Have we made all the necessary counter-preparations for that situation?

Again, I am not asking for answers which might be embarrassing. I only ask for the deepest possible reflection and thought in depth. If, after weighing up the balance of advantage and disadvantage, of good versus evil, and of success versus failure, a war option is decided upon, and under the circumstances is considered morally justified, it must, as I am sure other noble Lords have said, be done properly.

In modern war there are seldom any soft options; no quick fixes which give pain and grief only to your opponent and no body bags for yourself. In the Falklands crisis, the whole thing was thought through and the risks weighed up carefully – and, as it happens, accurately. The aim was clear. It was thought worth it. It was morally justified and it was done properly. The same could be said of the Gulf War in 1990. I only hope that the same rigorous thought processes are being applied this time.

My Lords, I apologise for interrupting the Minister, but can he inform the House whether a Commander British Forces Gulf has been appointed, like General de la Billière? If that were done I believe that it would give this House confidence that there was wise advice on the spot alongside the American commander and that British forces would be used in the correct manner.

Speech, 17 December 1998.

My Lords, like many other noble Lords, I get no great satisfaction from the events unfolding in Iraq, but many of us must feel that we have no alternative but to support selective military action by the Americans at this time. You cannot go on making threats and giving final warnings and not be as good as your word . . .

Is it not high time that we tried to introduce a more positive side to our policy towards Iraq and the Iraqi people, as opposed to the clearly negative side of the necessary present air offensive? You cannot go on making a desert and calling it peace. Our military offensive may succeed in doing irreparable and irretrievable damage to Saddam Hussein's capacity to make weapons of mass destruction and then to employ them, but if with all the intelligence at our disposal we cannot do this, I cannot see much point in attempting it at all. Would this not be a good moment, having administered the stick and from a position of strength, to offer some carrot to the Iraqi people, with whom, as the noble Baroness said, we have no quarrel? This could be in the form of a pan-Arabian Marshall Plan or the full, partial or gradual withdrawal of sanctions. Yes, of course, this may, at least for the time being, confirm Saddam Hussein's position; although no more, I suspect than a stronger, non-Arab power with little risk to itself knocking hell out of a weaker Arab one with as yet little capacity to hit back.

I am quite convinced that, eventually, destiny and retribution will catch up with him. But at least such a move would give our policy in that part of the world some constructive end gain which I believe would be increasingly widely welcomed by Arab countries, by the Third World, by some of our European partners and, above all, by the United Nations.

I remember so well, when I went out to the Middle East with a Parliamentary delegation under the noble Lord, Lord Pym, soon after Iraq invaded Kuwait, how all the Arab governments were adamant that, however much they wanted Saddam Hussein out of Kuwait and taught a lesson, they did not want Iraq broken up as a country. That for the moment meant, and may still mean, Saddam for a little longer. So I do hope that the Government can come up with some constructive thoughts about the future as opposed to merely having to justify what we have to do at this particular moment.

Speech, 10 April 2002.

My Lords, I too am most grateful to the noble Baroness, Lady Williams of Crosby.[40] It is always better to discuss such matters as peace or war early on in a calm atmosphere when the Government have made no commitment, rather than wait until British forces are about to be deployed, when you feel that you must give them full support and encouragement for whatever hazards may lie ahead.

At the moment, I doubt whether there are many in your Lordships' House who do not feel concern over what may happen in or over Iraq. As one who is still supporting our commitment to Afghanistan, where we are reinforcing comparative success and have a clear strategy and end plan, I feel that a distinction should be drawn between that particular action against proven supporters of terrorism and taking on the so-called 'axis of evil', which raises altogether different issues.

Unlike many in Whitehall, I was once upon a time swept up in the Suez crisis. Although it was over forty-five years ago, I remember all the details of that extraordinary period as if it was yesterday. Although no doubt we shall be told, with mutterings about '11 September', 'war against terrorism', 'weapons of mass destruction', 'evil people with evil intent', that the circumstances are this time different, there are some ominous similarities between the two scenarios.

Then there was no clearly defined political aim. Were we just aiming to topple a dictator, or temporarily take over the whole country, remembering that the original plan was for a D-Day-like operation against Alexandria and a march on Cairo? Or, as later emerged after collusion with Israel, were we merely intent on reoccupying the Canal Zone? Certainly, a clear-cut political aim and end plan are essential for any successful military operation. Then one of the incentives for repossession was that Egypt would be incapable of running the Canal on its own. That was clearly a flawed parameter and intelligence at the time proved faulty in other respects as well.

Above all it was a British Prime Minister[41] who convinced himself that the President of Egypt was an 'incarnation of evil', a re-run of Hitler, who could not and should not be appeased and, if not dealt with and removed, the world would be on a totally unacceptable and dangerous slippery slope. Looking back these forty-five years, all that sounds rather absurd, but one has heard similar arguments being advanced at the moment and in the event taking action was more damaging to our interests than not doing so.

Now I, and I imagine others in your Lordships' House, have no brief whatever for Saddam Hussein. He has done some terrible things in his own country. He has illegally attacked Kuwait and Iran. He has defied UN resolutions – as, of course, manifestly, have others – and he appears to be trying to get together weapons of terror and mass destruction as, sadly others have done. Sadly, one of the many casualties of the outrageous attack of 11 September is that strategic thinking about balance of power and deterrent seem to have gone out of the window. In the past, any such potential threat has been met by manning at instant readiness an overwhelming deterrent, nuclear or conventional, which would largely invalidate the threat by posing such dire consequences if it was ever to be implemented. I can see no compelling reason why Saddam Hussein could not be similarly deterred.

Moreover, it could be argued, and argued pretty cogently, that Iraq would be far more likely to use some of those weapons if overwhelmingly attacked and with nothing to lose, than if it had been contained more sensibly and constructively by other means. In that respect, I like the phrase attributed, whether correctly or not, to the Foreign Office of 'aggressive containment'. I do not know exactly what it means, and I doubt whether they do either, but it seems to put the emphasis in rather a better place.

So I hope that when trying to maintain our proper support for America, the Government will analyse and cross-check most carefully all the intelligence; try to get the United Nations observers back into Iraq and try to establish a dialogue with other Arab neighbours so that they too can put pressure on Iraq to allow that to happen and not to do anything which would bring further discredit to the area. As a loyal partner of America, I hope that the Government will make certain that our views are strongly represented, rather than following in its wake whatever the circumstances. Forty-five years ago, it was the Americans who perhaps not surprisingly pulled the rug out from under us, as perhaps they ought to do to Israel now, as was suggested by the noble Lord, Lord Hurd. How much better for us, however, to counsel them wisely, well in advance, so that no misunderstanding can occur later.

In your Lordships' House we are not naturally privy to the very latest intelligence or to future plans. However, one thing, which has been said over and over again, is certain; that is, that if a land invasion on any scale took place against Iraq, there would be no support – and possibly considerable hostility – from all Arab countries in the area. They have never been that keen on Iraq being broken up as a country; and certainly, no such action could be countenanced unless and until there was far more positive and sustained American backing to bring about a peaceful and just solution to the Palestinian problem.

These terrible suicide bombers have inflicted death and anguish on many innocent civilians, to whom our hearts go out – we should think about what it would be like if that happened in this country. Because those bombers are more specifically motivated and of a different ilk from those who carried out the 11 September outrage, the crisis in Palestine cannot be looked on simply as an integral part or an extension of the wider war against terrorism. The problem is in Palestine itself. If Israel is ever to win back the moral high ground and the respect of the world, she must withdraw from the West Bank.

When I gave the Balfour Memorial Lecture not long ago in Tel Aviv – my opposite number was Ehud Barak[42] – I reminded the audience of Milton's famous line that peace has its victories no less renowned than war. In Israel's case, I genuinely believe, as do others who have much closer knowledge of the problem than I do, that peace would not only bring it much more credit but would be far more productive than its present policy in terms of achieving its goals – our goal and everybody's goal – of a safer, securer and permanent Israel to which the entire world could give its good will and support, both military and moral.

I certainly hope that in the months to come, statesmanship and clear-headedness will continue to prevail over any emotion of revenge. But when you get any whiff of that over-simplistic philosophy that we are the 'goodies' and those out there are the 'baddies', and that whatever the goodies do to the baddies must be right, that attitude has a habit of generating its own momentum. And my Lords, as other noble Lords have said, we all know that in this modern world life is considerably more complicated than that.

On 29 July 2002 Bramall wrote to The Times *about a possible invasion of Iraq by the United States.*

Sir,

The question we should be asking ourselves is not whether the Americans can invade Iraq, or indeed whether they will invade, but whether they should do so; and of course, whether we should follow in their wake.

Apart from the difficult moral question of lesser or greater evils, there seem to be two distinct but tenable schools of thought on what the outcome of such action would be.

The first is that if Iraq is successfully attacked, by whatever means, and as a result, Saddam Hussein is removed, preferably with the help of a popular uprising, the terrorist-ridden, war-torn Middle East would unravel beneficially. It would then become a more benign, tolerant area in which moderate Muslim governments would take heart, a Palestine solution would become possible and the ability of terrorists to strike another blow at the US (or indeed Europe), with or without weapons of mass destruction, could be effectively neutralised. The flames of resentment and protest which exist in the area today would have then, at least, been doused, and the 'war against terrorism' would have achieved a major victory.

The second viewpoint is that conflict with Iraq would produce, in that area, the very display of massive, dynamic United States activity which provides one of the mainsprings of motivation for terrorist action in the region, and indeed over a wider area. Far from calming things down, enhancing any peace process and advancing the 'war against terrorism', which could and should be conducted internationally by other means, it would make things infinitely worse. Petrol, rather than water would have been poured on the flames and al-Qaeda would have gained more recruits.

It would be interesting to know to which of these two points of view the British Government is more inclined.

America, with all the power at its disposal, and with no other super-power to gainsay it, can presumably and eventually achieve any military objective it wishes. I cannot help, however, but be reminded of that remark by a notably 'hawkish' General (later Field Marshal) Sir Gerald Templer,[43] who when, during the Suez crisis of 1956, Britain was planning a massive invasion of Egypt through Alexandria, said something to the effect of 'Of course we can get to Cairo but what I want to know is this. What the bloody hell do we do when we get there?'

Yours faithfully,

BRAMALL FM

He spoke again in the House of Lords on 24 September 2002.

My Lords, we have heard some excellent speeches, not least those of the noble Lords, Lord Phillips of Sudbury[44] and Lord Grenfell.[45] I agree with much of what they said.

The priorities in the Middle East must surely be, first, however difficult it may seem at the moment, to obtain a just and guaranteed solution to the Israel/Palestine question; to build up the economic and political stability of Afghanistan; to encourage Pakistan and other countries to deal with any Al Qaeda on their territory; and, most urgent of all, to get the UN inspectors back into Iraq.

Saddam Hussein is indeed in breach of innumerable UN resolutions and the Security Council has every right, indeed an obligation, to insist on compliance and even to authorise the use of any force it believes necessary to ensure that happens. There can be no doubt that some degree of credible sabre rattling and psychological warfare has been necessary and could still be essential right up to the wire to bring about that compliance.

I therefore back the Government in their support of America in its diplomatic offensive with heavy military overtones and congratulate the Prime Minister in steering it through the United Nations, which is obviously the answer. That is the easy part. It is now up to the UN with our full support to enforce and maintain the unconditional return of the observers, backed, I hope, by a strong Security Council resolution holding Saddam Hussein personally to account for that compliance.

I presume that the Government consider it important that time is now given for the observers to assess that task and report back before any further action is decided on. Here we come to the difficult part. If, in addition to all those priorities, irrespective of how the observers were making out, and without any further authority from the United Nations, British forces were to be committed to a large scale United States military action, primarily to effect a regime change, the British people – not unreasonably – would expect satisfactory and reassuring answers to some searching questions, some of which have hardly been touched on before this debate, to be sure that they had been thought through.

First, would such action really be necessary? Plenty of evidence is pouring in of the threat of Iraq developing and possessing weapons of mass destruction and delivery means. But surely the key question is whether, survivor that he is, Saddam would ever want or be in a position to use those weapons offensively when all the eyes of the world are on him and he must know that retribution would be terrible and swift. Could he still not be deterred, as to some extent he was during the Gulf War *vis à vis* Israel?

Iraq has not been appeased, as some claim it would be if it were not attacked. Sanctions are in place; there are no-fly zones at either end of the country. Selected sites in those zones have been taken out by air with impunity. Saddam must realise that other sites related to the production of weapons of mass destruction could be treated in the same way. Forces are at hand in the area ready to be used if so authorised. That is hardly appeasement. Observers able to do their job would greatly further inhibit him.

For fifty years we have based our defence policy on deterring, with heavy large-scale weapons of our own, those with more serious and numerous weapons of mass destruction. I wonder why the government are so adamant that Saddam cannot be kept in place by similar methods; what the Foreign Office once in its wisdom described as 'aggressive containment'.

Secondly, would such action be morally justified? It is reasonable that the people of this country not only speculate whether the Americans can and will attack Iraq but whether they should. Unfortunately, one cannot always base a country's foreign policy on morality. The instinct of self-interest, and, even more, self-preservation, is always more compelling both for governments and those who elect them.

But the weaker the case for necessity, the more the moral question has to be taken into account, particularly at times when pre-emptive action, largely to effect a change of ruler or implant a more favourable type of government, would not by itself be considered suitable justification for war – consider the case of the Soviet Union's invasion of Afghanistan. When such strong efforts are made to link military force to the authority of the United Nations the moral high ground is important, and this country is supposed to take a lead in such matters.

Thirdly, would an attack on Iraq to topple Saddam Hussein work? The advice of the Chiefs of Staff will be crucial; I hope that the Government are listening to them. With all the power at its disposal and no other power to gainsay it as occurred in the past, America can, I presume, eventually achieve any military objective it wishes, although historical precedent indicates that attack on a homeland as distinct from captured territory can be messy and prolonged.

Getting into Iraq may not present too many problems, but, as many noble Lords have asked, have we really thought through what to do when we get there and how we put together a fragmented and disparate Iraq that its Arab neighbours have never wanted broken up as a country? My noble and gallant friend Lord Vincent[46] talked of the need for a clear political aim. Others have talked about any attack being only the beginning and not an end. A lot more work needs to be done on that.

Fourthly, will the wider aftermath of such an attack be beneficial or the reverse? There are two conflicting schools of thought. One, for which the support is slightly weakening, is that, as a result of a successful attack, with Saddam Hussein being removed, preferably with the help of a popular uprising, the terrorist-ridden, war-torn Middle East would somehow start to unravel beneficially, moderate Muslim governments would take heart and thus take more effective action against their dissident elements, the situation in Palestine would become more possible and the ability of the terrorists to strike another disastrous blow at the United States or Europe, with or without weapons of mass destruction, could be effectively reduced or even removed.

However, the other school of thought is that all-out war with Iraq, as distinct from 'aggressive containment', would produce in the area the display of massive, dynamic western military activity that is one of the mainsprings of motivation for terrorist action and outrages in the region and over a wider area. Far from advancing the war against terrorism – which could and should be conducted internationally by other means – and enhancing the peace process around Israel's borders, it would make things infinitely worse. Petrol, not water, would be poured on the flames. Those who subscribe to this latter view might well consider that even if a *prima facie* case could be made for attacking Iraq unilaterally, the disadvantages might well outweigh the advantages and produce more pain and grief than they solved.

All this is a matter of judgement as to which scenario is more likely, which is difficult to make unless you are in possession of all the facts. I am not too certain of the answer, but it is a judgement that the Government, with all the intelligence and diplomatic channels at their disposal, can and should make on behalf of the British people. If the first point of view commends itself to them, they should stake their reputation on it and communicate it to the

British people with all the conviction and vehemence that the Government can muster so that they can get a full consensus in the country, which our forces would need. If the second point of view prevails and they more or less say that come what may, right or wrong, the special relationship is so important that it must be supported at all costs, that viewpoint should be tested as well.

Many of us – including the British Government, I am sure – hope that the authority of the United Nations and the influence of other Arab and Muslim states will be sufficient to get Iraq to accept certainly no less than all the points in the previous United Nations resolutions. Then the case for further military action will have been weakened and an opportunity will exist to pull back or pull back with honour. If not, then the Government will face a very serious situation. Going to war, which is what it would be, is a very serious step – particularly a war that, whatever the outcome, is bound to antagonise large sections of the Muslim world and cause a great many innocent casualties. If then, I, like the noble Lord, Lord Grenfell, would fear for the future and hold a pessimistic point of view, which I certainly did not at the time of the Falklands War, when I held office, or at the time of the Gulf War, when I visited the area in a Parliamentary delegation – on both occasions, I was convinced that whatever risks there were should be taken and that we would win – it is because I feel in my heart of hearts – I believe that many who know the Middle East better than I do would agree – that the peace and stability of the world would best be served by less, not more, Western military action in the Middle East, following the pattern successfully set in the last quarter of the twentieth century in South-East Asia.

The West, led by America, must remain strong, alert and ever-vigilant, with improved missile defence and constantly improving and better-funded intelligence. It must be ready, too, to adapt the laws in a democratic society so that terrorist cells cannot so easily be planted and prosper. The much-needed bridges which will have to be built in the future between the affluent West and the less secure and resentful Muslim world would then be on the basis of mutual trade, aid, where it was needed and asked for, and, above all, mutual respect. Under those circumstances – again I look at South-East Asia – I believe that Al Qaeda would wither on the vine or that its members would be properly treated as criminals, as has so often happened in the years gone by.

He spoke again on 28 November 2002.

My Lords, I must first ask the indulgence of your Lordships' House as I was unavoidably detained and unable to attend the opening of this important debate. Nevertheless, I feel it my duty to try to make some modest and short contribution despite my waywardness in respect of the rules of your Lordships' House. I hope that noble Lords will accept my apology.

The unanimous resolution of the United Nations Security Council to get their observers back into Iraq while threatening Saddam Hussein with serious consequences if he obstructed them was a diplomatic triumph, as the noble Lord, Lord Thomas of Swynnerton,[47] said in his powerful speech. All concerned, not least the Prime Minster and the Foreign Secretary,[48] deserve heartfelt congratulation and thanks. It must be recognised, however, that this could not have come about, let alone been accepted by Iraq, without a credible and continuing threat of force by the Americans.

But surely we now need to build on that consensus, which must be the only right way of handling international relations in the modern world, and not deviate from the Security Council unless it becomes literally the only way to achieve the indisputable aim of destroying or disarming Iraq's weapons of mass destruction, as required and demanded by the Security Council itself. That objective must somehow be brought about.

However, the date of 8 December, by which time Saddam Hussein is required under the resolution to disclose and list any such weapons in his possession, may, if he prevaricates, provide a flashpoint for military action. That causes me some concern. It must be better for the observers, armed with all the intelligence at their disposal from the United States and others, which must be considerable and detailed, to find whatever weapons exist and destroy them rather than that we should use a quibble over paperwork as an excuse for going to war prematurely and without further UN sanction.

There are, after all, to coin a phrase, more ways of killing a cat. However much the British Government may want, quite understandably, to be seen to be supporting the United States, I hope that the Prime Minister will not forget that wise observation of the renowned Chinese general of 500 BC, General Sun Tsu, who said that the supreme art of war is to subdue the enemy – notice the phrase 'subdue the enemy' – without fighting. Incidentally, that is a philosophy which seemed to suit the Americans at Yorktown.

Finally, I hope that war will not become inevitable. Whatever success there may be early on, any – even temporary – occupation of Iraq will, I believe, create more problems than it solves. But, if it does become inevitable, can the Government assure us flat that the British forces that they send to participate in any American action – if, indeed, that is the intention – will, in every sense, be properly prepared for whatever lies ahead of them?

Will they, for instance, be properly equipped? That has been mentioned previously. There have been some ominous rumours about equipment. Much work needs to be done in that area. Will they be properly supported, particularly in the medical field, given that the medical services are struggling to keep their heads above water? In view of the pressures on them and the over-stretch highlighted by the Chief of Defence Staff,[49] will they be properly trained? Can we be reassured that the views of the Chiefs of Staff will be listened to and respected and that, as a result, our forces will have clear-cut, attainable objectives, both in the short and longer terms? Judging by Afghanistan, they could be there for a while.

In short, can we be assured that our forces are not being asked to take unnecessary risks? All armed forces take risks and they do it willingly and consciously. But we want to be assured that they are not taking unnecessary risks. It is absolutely ludicrous to think that war can somehow be cash-limited. Either something is worth fighting and making sacrifices for or it is not.

I hope that the Minister will try to give assurances on the points I have raised. At least my contribution, which comes so close to his winding-up speech, should be comparatively fresh in his memory. After all, we would be asking men and women to risk their lives for reasons which, to say the least, are more obscure and contentious than those which prevailed in World War II, the Falklands or the Gulf. So, the Government had better get it right.

A further contribution came on 6 February 2003.

My Lords, I assume that all these deployments have the full support of the Chiefs of Staff. If war is inevitable, as sadly now seems likely, can the Minister assure the House that British troops will not be committed to battle without the clearest of national political aims? Those must include not only the initial objectives but also, once the battle is won, the interim political arrangements in Iraq itself in view of the great risks of internal strife. There must also be a clear exit strategy. The last two will always be much more difficult than the first.

On 26 February 2003 he spoke again, at more length.

My Lords, this very important debate may be the last time that some of us can allow ourselves to be critical or cautionary about our readiness to take part in military action without a resolution specifically authorising it. Once our armed forces are committed, I, and I am sure others, would want to give full support to what the Government required them to do and to wish them God speed.

Nor would I want to make it harder for the Prime Minister to secure the nation's support for those forces were they to be committed to battle. But I think it is very important that everyone is quite clear what we are likely to be letting ourselves in for if we go down the military path.

Even now – and I agree with my noble and gallant friend – involving this country may, sadly, be inevitable – and I imagine the Government, despite statements to the contrary, must be resigned to this – with the removal of Saddam Hussein being the 'nature of the game'.

History has shown that when land forces are deployed to battle positions, as ours soon will be, it becomes difficult to reverse the process. And having so overtly supported the Americans on the possible need for military action, the Prime Minister can hardly withdraw that support now; while, unless there is absolute proof – always very difficult to obtain – that no nuclear, chemical and biological weapons remain in Saddam Hussein's grasp, and probably without him opting, in advance, for exile, it is difficult to see how the President of the United States, after all the rhetoric, can pull back without very serious political consequences, both domestic and further afield, however well or badly the case for imminent action has been made.

Of course, should Saddam Hussein pre-empt it by voluntarily seeking asylum, there would be general rejoicing and an understandable rush to praise the statesmanship of the President and our own Prime Minister. It seems so unlikely, however, that all necessary conditions would be met, and I think our most fervent hope must be that the Security Council can, despite the turmoil within NATO and Europe, be persuaded that military action is the only way to uphold its vital authority.

This does not necessarily mean that war is the best thing for the region – far from it – but most of us who have been critical would feel obliged to accept specific authorisation as being the proper way to deal with international problems in the twenty-first century.

Over six months ago – and for the moment putting on one side the difficult moral question of the greater or lesser of two evils – I set out in a letter to *The Times* differing views as to what the aftermath of military action might be. The first was that if Iraq was successfully attacked and Saddam Hussein was removed, preferably with the help of a popular uprising, the terrorist-ridden, war-torn Middle East would somehow unravel beneficially. It would become a more benign and tolerant area in which moderate Muslim governments could take heart; a Palestinian solution might even become possible; and the ability of the terrorists to strike another blow at the United States, or indeed at Europe, would be neutralised.

The second was quite the opposite, with a conflict in Iraq producing in that 'cauldron of anti-Western feeling', as Secretary of State Powell described it, the sort of display of massive United States activity which has for some time provided one of the mainsprings for terrorist motivation. Far from calming things down, making the Middle East, or the world, a safer place, enhancing any peace process and advancing the war against terrorism, it would make things infinitely worse.

To some extent, you pays your money and you takes your choice, although I did point out strongly that, even with all America's military power and the high technology, getting into Iraq to implement a political aim – whatever that may turn out to be – was always going to be easier than handling what you did when you got there and being able to extricate yourself after the battle was over.

Well, either of these two scenarios, I suppose, remains a possibility, and should the first one happily be more accurate, one good thing that could result would be that the Americans, from a position of apparent strength and should they be so disposed, could enforce as only they can a fair and just solution to the Israel/Palestine problem. Indeed, any odium in the Muslim world which the Americans and ourselves would be bound to incur over coalition military action might be reduced if that action were to be linked to solving and underwriting the Palestine problem.

But the downside of the more likely second scenario, and to some extent of the first, has also to be appreciated and thought through. Winston Churchill once wrote, 'Never, never, never believe any war will be smooth and easy, or that anyone who embarks on that strange voyage can measure the tides and hurricanes he will encounter.'[50] Well, there are bound to be risks in terms of casualties both to innocent civilians and to Anglo-American forces, and over a longer than anticipated duration, bearing in mind the possibility of fighting in built-up areas where the effect of fire power would be greatly reduced.

After all, in Kosovo it took NATO warplanes – admittedly without ground force action – seventy-one days to bring the Yugoslav dictator to his knees, and then it was only the intervention of the Russians that clinched the capitulation; and the Yugoslav ground troops had hardly been weakened at all. Although it took only 100 hours to kick the Iraqis out of Kuwait, the Republican Guard was able to extricate itself back into its homeland without too much difficulty. With these sorts of risks, the moral justification and the threat have to be particularly strong, as they were in Korea, in the Falklands and in the first Gulf War.

Then it must be recognised that such a largely American military action would constitute, whether intended or not, a massive piece of imperial policing in an area where it is probably less, not more, western intervention that is needed. Any satisfactory rearrangement of Iraq is bound to require quite a lengthy occupation; and like imperial interventions in the past, it is often difficult to know when and where to stop and all too easy to get drawn forward to yet more rearrangements in other areas. After all, Afghanistan is still an ongoing and tense issue.

So the burdens of this sort of policing are often of long duration, very expensive and ultimately dangerous, and democracies soon become impatient of such burdens; and this time, I suspect, even more quickly. And of course, by then the funding and resources of our already greatly over-stretched Armed Forces will have been woefully and totally inadequate because of their under-funding during the past decade.

From the outset, when he took the view that the Americans should not be left to deal with the difficult problem on its own, the Right Honourable gentleman the Prime Minister has been a key player and a major influence in steering the whole question into the UN arena and securing that diplomatic triumph of a unanimous vote in the Security Council. For that, I believe the country should be very grateful to him. I would like to think also that our hearts are with him at this very difficult time in the nation's affairs.

So what is it that we should reasonably and constructively ask of him even at this late hour? There are four things. First, that he sees that the United Nations inspectors are given all possible intelligence of the sort that has convinced him and the President that Iraq still has these weapons and that they still pose a threat, so that they can seek them out and get rid of them. That is by far the most painless and easy way to disarmament. If they can do so, they should be allowed to continue to do so. They will of course need more time and one has to accept that the longer they have the less credible and immediately practicable any fall-back military option becomes.

Secondly, the Right Honourable gentleman must continue to do all in his power to build on that earlier UN consensus to secure an agreed, positive and effective course of action, not ruling out a permanent United Nations inspectors' presence, and perhaps trying to bring together the two resolutions in order to ensure complete disarmament, on which everyone agrees, or a resolution specifically authorising force in certain circumstances. A successful outcome will of course be influenced by how Dr Hans Blix and Mohammed El Baradei[51] report and what they feel they can do subsequently.

Then, like the noble and learned Lord, Lord Howe,[52] I believe that the Prime Minister and his Ministers must do more to get the nation's support. So far, some of their efforts, including that absurd dossier, have not done them justice. Despite – perhaps because of – the continual changes of direction in justification for various actions, they have failed to convince.

A national consensus affects their standing but, even more important, it is essential for the morale and motivation of the men and women of the Armed Forces who will put their lives on the line. Before going into battle, they need to know that the country is behind them. Convincing the country that there is a good, constructive case for such action will largely depend on the progress that the Prime Minister makes on the first two tasks.

Finally – this point has already been extremely well dealt with – there must be a proper political aim at every stage of the operation, so that the military objectives and plan can fit into it. The wider implications of war must also be thought through, so that any damage limitation exercise can be in place from the outset.

If all those matters are handled well, I suppose that there is just the possibility that a damaging war could be averted or, if not, at least that military operations will be conducted as quickly and intelligently as possible. By that I mean a land battle of fourteen days at the outside, otherwise we are in deep trouble.

If anything goes wrong, certainly in the short term but probably in the longer term, serious questions will undoubtedly be asked about why the Government, with Her Majesty's Opposition close in their wake, went down that road in the first place, instead of that of continued containment of Iraq and concentrating on the more imminent threat posed by Al Qaeda and other terrorist organisations – which, after 11 September, continue to be the real and most pressing threat.

After the invasion of Iraq he spoke again, on 8 September 2003.

My Lords, for a number of reasons, some of them apparent, I was against the war, brilliantly as the initial military campaign was conducted. However, I fully recognise now that we must do what we can to finish what the coalition has started. That, as the Minister said, will require more of our own forces. Indeed, reconstruction apart, the coalition seems to have embarked consciously on the vital war against terrorism on a definite strategy, which can only be described as a Dien Bien Phu[53] strategy. Having forced Al Qaeda rather incongruously into cahoots with Saddam's loyalists, it intends to take on the terrorists head-on, on ground of its own choosing – that is Iraq – and to destroy them with superior force.

There were other ways, but that can be said to be one coherent strategy, which, although the name which I have given it implies risk, could be successful. I sincerely hope that it will be. Those supporting it – and judging by his latest press conference, that includes our Prime Minister – will claim that it will pre-empt later, less manageable terrorist activity, which could then be encountered only over a wider area and in much more inaccessible places. However, successful or not, it will require many troops over a prolonged period at a prodigious cost, and a very steady nerve, not only in government but in the country. Democracies sometimes soon get tired of such demanding adventures.

The question that I put to the Minister is how the Government will reconcile that prospect with the state of our long-term over-stretched and underfunded Armed Forces, whom the last Chief of Defence Staff, my noble and gallant friend Lord Boyce, clearly warned could not undertake another commitment on the scale of the Iraq invasion, to which the impending force levels are rapidly returning, for another one or two years. When will the Government – which of course means the Treasury – match resources in manpower, material and money to commitments? Alternatively, when will the Government deal with our far-flung commitments more circumspectly?

In a letter to The Times *on 17 March 2004 Bramall reflected on the Iraq invasion and its aftermath.*

Sir,
Let it be quite clear, whatever anyone may have thought of the war in Iraq, we must now see it through to a conclusion. This means handing over political power to an Iraqi government as soon as it is possible to do so, and leaving enough troops there to control the security situation until such time as the Iraqis can cope with their own resources. We can only then 'keep our fingers crossed' and hope for the best.

At the same time, we should intellectually reject the largely political argument that those who have been less than enthusiastic, particularly over the reasons behind going to war in the first place, are somehow being pusillanimous about the so-called 'War against Terrorism' which is a separate issue, but which must remain the highest international priority at the moment.

Indeed, one of the main reasons that so many of us were against the attack on Iraq was that we did not think it was the best way to fight and beat that particular brand of terrorism emanating from the Middle East. Far from putting Al-Qaeda 'onto the back foot', we thought it would make matters infinitely worse; encourage Al-Qaeda recruitment; spread the threat (as it has in Iraq) and, inasmuch as those sorts of attacks on innocent people can ever be justified, provide some faint justification for this retaliatory action when none existed hitherto.

The Afghanistan operation was an entirely different matter. It was directly related to the threat and to the major concentrations of terrorists and their training; and produced a major step forward in gaining vital intelligence on the whole Al-Qaeda organisation. This is why I, for one, and so many others who had doubts about the Iraq War, so strongly supported it.

I am Sir,
Bramall FM

Chapter 12

Afghanistan

Throughout 2001 Bramall also spoke regularly in the House of Lords on the subject of Afghanistan. The following speeches are representative of what he said.

5 November 2001.

My Lords, once this country becomes involved in active operations, those of us with some military expertise – albeit a bit out of date – have to be careful over what we say so as not in any way to weaken resolve or, however unintentionally, to compromise what may turn out to be actual military plans or train of events.

However, in the context of this infinitely complicated and politically weighted operation now going on in Afghanistan, I make three largely military points, First, from a military point of view, I am much happier about the comparatively slow tempo of operations than I would be rushing in where angels and wise men fear to tread.

The early political hype, much of it for domestic consumption after the horrors of 11 September which so demanded action, quickly picked up and, embellished by some of the media looking for compelling eye-catching stories, encouraged the expectation of 'heads on chargers' within a reasonable period of time, whereas anyone who knew Afghanistan and the Afghan people and had studied Afghan history would have realised that the task was going to be very difficult and lengthy.

How much better, from a military point of view and bearing in mind the vital importance of surprise as a principle of war, if perhaps we could have had fewer optimistic statements of intent, raising immediate expectations, so that the opposition could have been kept ominously guessing for rather longer. But we are where we are and the long haul is before us, perhaps through the whole winter and even beyond. During that time, it will be most important to put in order our security affairs at home, while within the framework of the overall aim and based on ever-improving intelligence, we – that is, the Americans with ourselves at their side – should look for opportunities for relevant and profitable operations in the ground/air field. That would be a sensible way of going about it. Furthermore, as has already been said, it is most important that any such operations must end in success and not in failure.

Operation Overlord: the High Command

1. The senior commanders planning D Day, 1 February 1944. (*L to R*): Lieutenant General Omar Bradley, Admiral Sir Bertram Ramsay, Air Chief Marshal Sir Arthur Tedder, General Dwight D. Eisenhower, General Sir Bernard Montgomery, Air Chief Marshal Sir Trafford Leigh-Mallory, Lieutenant General Walter Bedell Smith. Bramall's analysis of their strengths and weaknesses is in Chapter 1 (a).

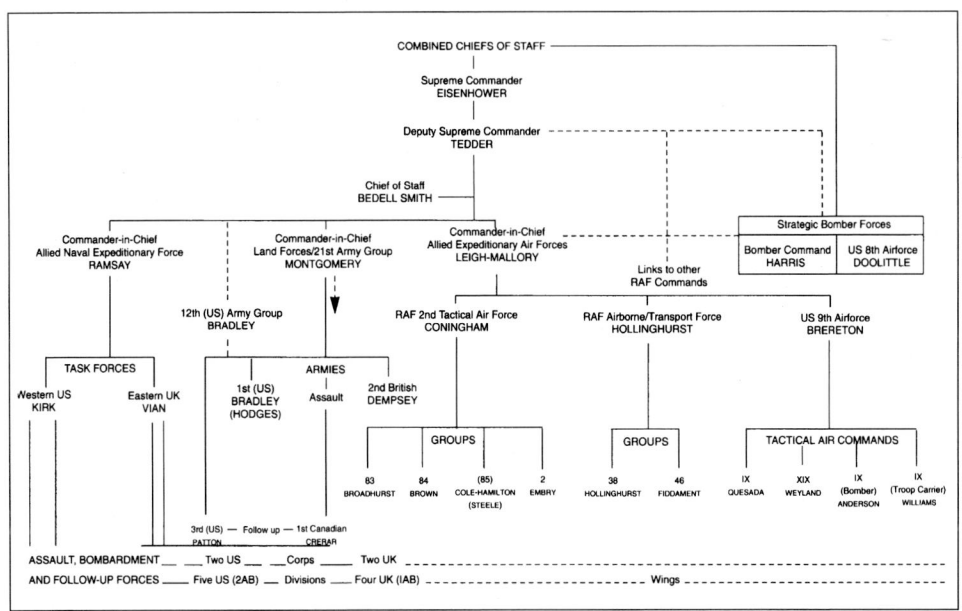

2. The chain of command.

Normandy, 1944

3. Operation Overlord. D Day+3 and British troops come ashore past a Royal Naval beach party, flying the White Ensign. Bramall landed on D+1.

4. Operation Epsom. British infantry – 6 Royal Scots Fusiliers of 15th (Scottish) Division – move forward through waist-high corn in the dawn light, with a Churchill tank in support, 26 June 1944. Bramall's experiences and appreciation of this are in Chapter 1. (IWM B5956)

Operation Varsity, March 1945

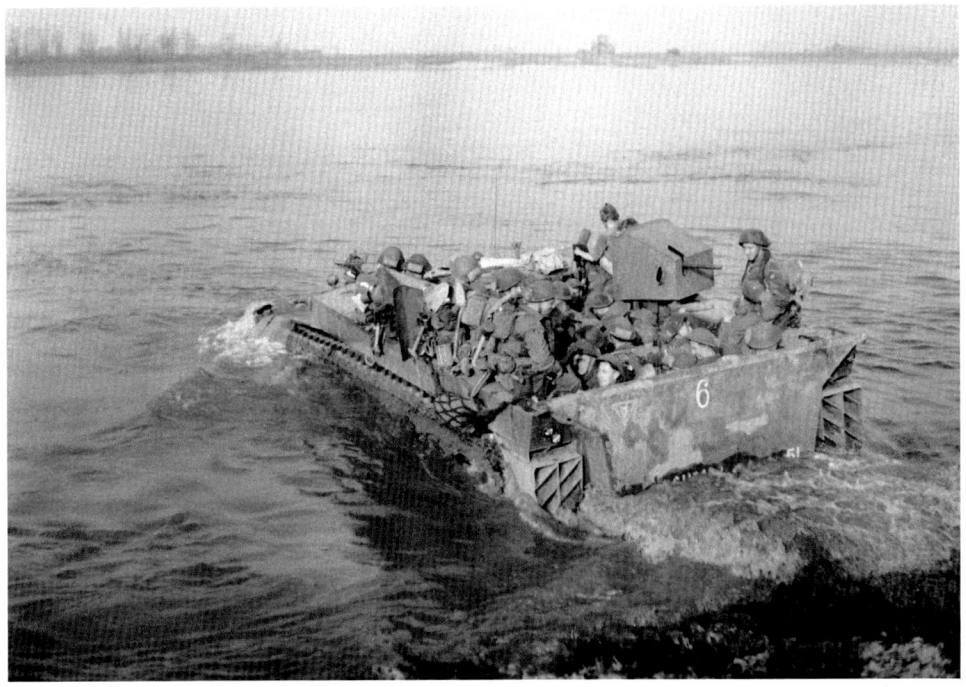

5. Troops crossing the Rhine in a Buffalo vehicle. (IWM BU2449)

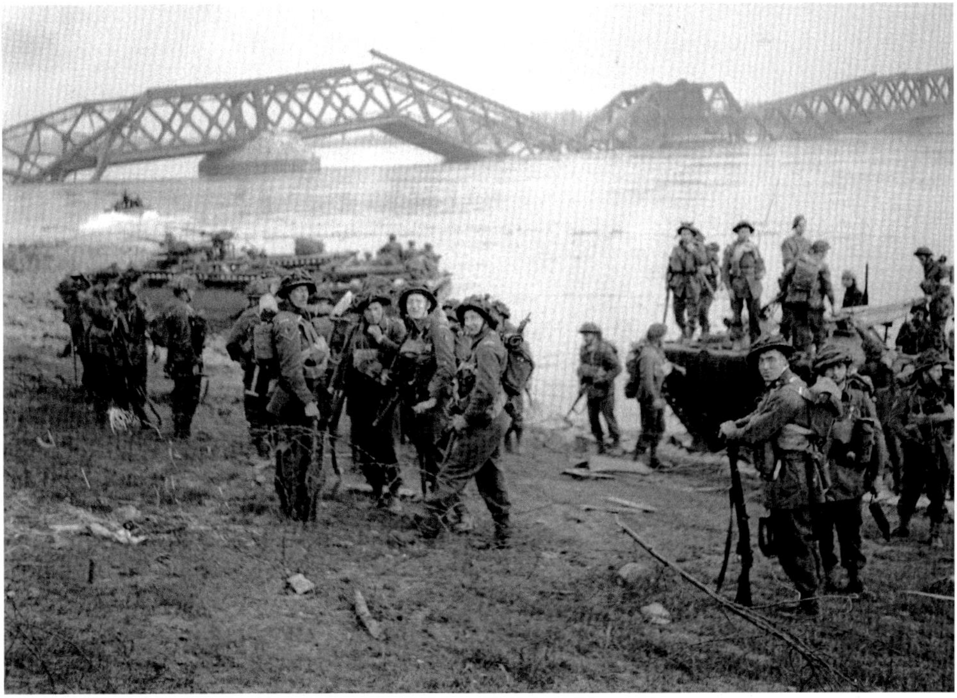

6. Regrouping on the river bank. (IWM BU2336)

War Devastation

7. Hamburg suffered grievously by conventional bombing. (IWM CL3400)

8. Hiroshima after the dropping of the first atomic bomb. Bramall was almost unique in observing both Hamburg and Hiroshima in 1945. (IWM MH29437)

9. Bramall was stationed in Berlin when the Wall was erected in 1961. This view of the Brandenburg Gate was taken from the KRRC observation post.

10. As Commanding Officer of 2nd Green Jackets (KRRC) in Borneo with his own Sioux helicopter. The Battalion had its own helicopter flight, piloted by Green Jacket officers.

Bramall as a Formation Commander

11. Commanding 5th Airportable Brigade, with the Russian military attaché, on Exercise Iron Duke, summer 1968.

12. As GOC 1st Armoured Division on exercise in Germany, 1972.

13. The Chiefs of Staff during the Falklands War. (*L to R*): Air Chief Marshal Sir Michael Beetham (CAS), Admiral Sir Henry Leach (CNS), Admiral of the Fleet Sir Terence Lewin (CDS), General Sir Edwin Bramall (CGS). A team that worked together excellently under the CDS.

14. Seeing off the Task Force on the QE2 are (*from left*) General Sir Frank Kitson, C-in-C UK Land Forces, his ADC, Captain (later Major General) James Gordon, General Bramall (CGS) and Sir John Nott MP, the Secretary of State for Defence. Bramall's account of the Falklands War is in Chapter 8.

Liberation of Kuwait, 1991

15. General Norman Schwarzkopf (Commander Coalition Forces) and his British deputy, General Sir Peter de la Billière, who in an outstanding example of Allied cooperation conceived and directed the military operations to reoccupy Kuwait.

16. Saddam Hussein, whose illegal invasion of Kuwait prompted the Allied operation, is seen here dictating strategy to his cabinet, who would not have been allowed to make any contribution to the discussion.

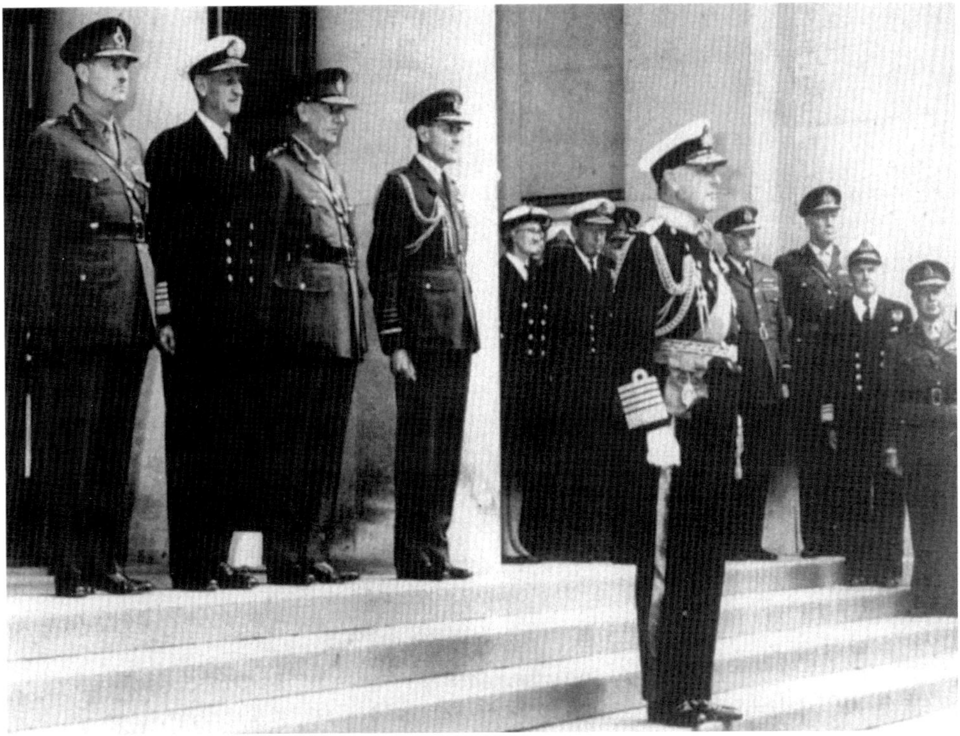

17. Admiral of the Fleet Lord Mountbatten of Burma, the architect of both the unified MoD and our nuclear submarine force, departs from the MoD main building on his final day as CDS. Behind him stand (*from left*) his successor as CDS, Field Marshal Sir Richard Hull, and the Chiefs of Staff: Admiral Sir David Luce, General Sir James Cassels and Air Chief Marshal Sir Charles Elworthy.

18. Mountbatten's conversations with the US Admiral Rickover allowed Britain to construct Polaris and later Trident submarines. Bramall discusses the nuclear issue in Book 4 and the unified MoD in Book 5.

19. Haig and his generals savouring the moment: 11.00 am on 11 November 1918 at Cambrai. Haig (*front centre*) is flanked by (*left*) Plumer and (*right*) Rawlinson. In the row behind (*from left*) are Byng, Birdwood and Horne. Behind them are a collection of senior staff officers. (IWM Q9689)

20. 'Compare and contrast'. Montgomery addresses troops before D Day in England: a very different form of leadership. (IWM H38647)

Lord Bramall of Bushfield

21. Taking his seat in the House of Lords, with (*left*) Field Marshal Lord Carver (his Brigade Commander in Normandy, and very much his mentor in high command) and (*right*) Admiral of the Fleet Lord Lewin (not just CDS during the Falklands War, but a real friend).

22. A bevy of Field Marshals and politicians, with the latter taking a back row, at the Army Benevolent Fund 60th Anniversary Dinner, Royal Hospital Chelsea, 2004. Front row (*L to R*): Field Marshals Lord Bramall, Lord Carver, HRH the Duke of Edinburgh and Sir Roly Gibbs. Back row includes: ex-Defence Secretaries Michael Portillo, Lord Roy Mason, Michael Heseltine, Lord Carrington, Lord Gilmore and Sir John Nott, as well as Prime Minister John Major, Richard Moon and Ron Gerard.

23. The aftermath of the liberation of Belsen concentration camp: a mass grave with former SS guards being put to work. (IWM BU4260)

24. The Queen opening the new Holocaust Gallery at the Imperial War Museum on 6 June 2000, here talking to historian Sir Martin Gilbert.

25. Lord Bramall receiving the Inter-Faith Gold Medal from the International Council of Christians and Jews, 2001. (*L to R*): Baroness Boothroyd, Alexander Bramall (grandson), Sir Sigmund Sternberg, Lord and Lady Bramall, Dr Rudy Vis MP and Nicolas Bramall (son).

26. Charles Upham VC and bar being congratulated by New Zealand soldiers. Bramall's eulogy to Upham is in chapter 26.

27. As CGS, meeting members of 3 Para on board MV *Norland* in June 1982. The Commanding Officer of 3 Para, Lieutenant Colonel (later Lieutenant General Sir) Hew Pike stands to Bramall's right. Bramall's speech of congratulation is in Chapter 8.

28. The Sovereign's Parade, RMA Sandhurst, August 1985. Field Marshal Lord Bramall inspects cadets, accompanied by the Commandant, Major General Richard Keightley, and the Academy Sergeant Major.

29. The 2 Rifles Medal Parade on a day of very mixed weather at Ballykinler, 2010. The last occasion on which Bramall appeared in uniform. Both his speeches are reproduced in Chapter 26.

30. Lord Bramall, as Lord Lieutenant of Greater London, with Her Majesty the Queen at the Parade of Veterans in the Mall to mark the 50th anniversary of D Day.

31. The Garter Procession to St George's Chapel after the Garter Lunch in Windsor Castle.

32. At their Hampshire home, Dwin and Avril reflect together in the evening of a long and very happy marriage, in which Avril contributed so much to support and enhance Dwin's varied and eventful career.

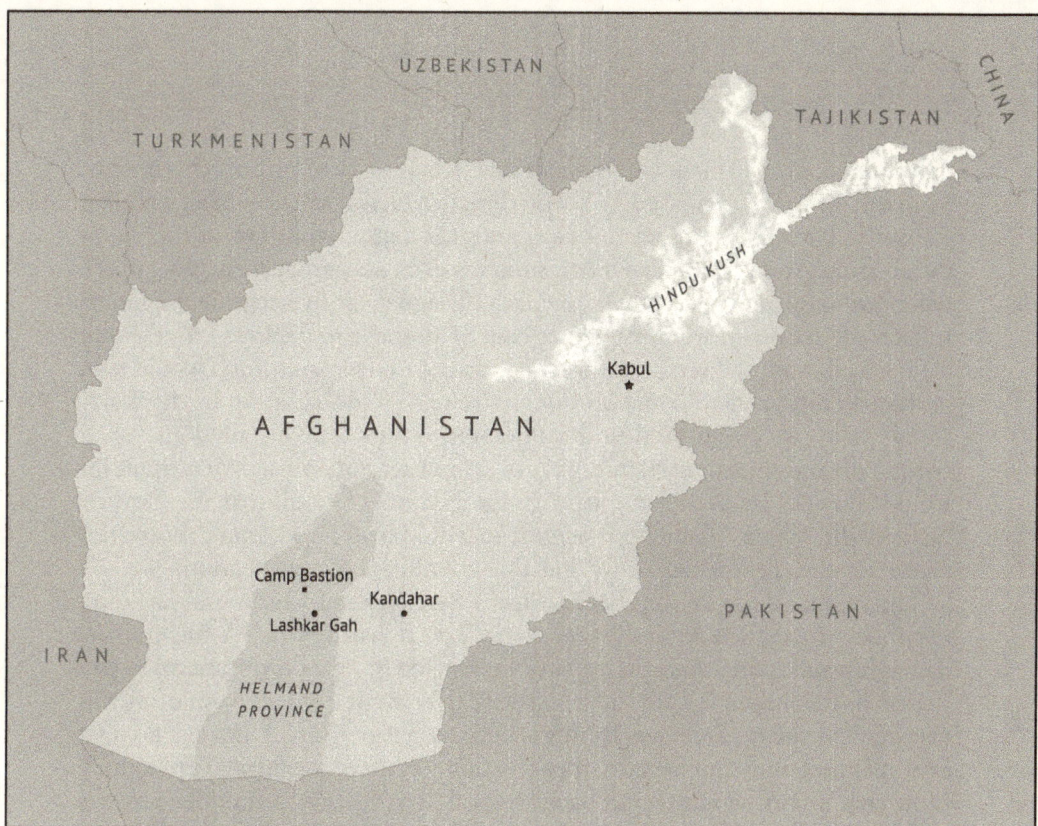

Afghanistan, Helmand Province.

It is my earnest hope that very soon the Americans will be able, and will feel strong enough, to select and undertake operations other than merely continuing with high-level bombing. Undoubtedly the latter will have inflicted damage and caused disruption to the Taliban, as noble Lords have heard. But an indefinite continuation of that type of bombing – sadly and inevitably causing further casualties among non-combatants – not only risks losing some of the moral high ground in the propaganda war; it also puts the coalition, already affected by the situation in Palestine, under increased pressure. Moreover, experience in World War II, in Vietnam and in Kosovo throws doubt on whether this kind of bombing does write down the military forces of the opposition nearly as much as initially it is always expected to do. To achieve that, it is necessary to get down to low-level, if not ground-level tactics. In World War II, whether in Italy or Normandy, when they were about to be carpet-bombed the Germans were adept at moving out of the area. When the bombing was finished, they would more back in. I am quite certain that the Afghans will not have been slow in developing some kind of similar technique.

My second point concerns an equally important part of the entire exercise: the home front. Security is also a vital principle of war. If the Government are determined, as they must be, to do all that is necessary to protect this country from any possible increased terrorist threat, which it is clear must be taken seriously, I would ask them not to ignore the potential utility of the Territorial Army. Many individual TA volunteers even now are serving, on a purely voluntary basis, alongside their regular colleagues on overseas deployments. In fact, they constitute almost 10 per cent of all those so deployed. But should it look as though the terrorist threat continues to develop, which would soon persuade employers to come on side, some partial mobilisation of the Territorial Army to guard vital and vulnerable points and installations, or to cordon off and protect certain key areas, would act not only as a deterrent, but would show, as it has in America with the National Guard, that the Government really means business. I suggest it would also be a strong motivating factor for the Territorial Army and thus would encourage recruitment.

The regular Army, going back to Lord Kitchener of Khartoum, has often been slow to recognise the value of the TA. It hardly lifted a finger when damaging and quite unnecessary cuts were made by this Government, in particular to the infantry. I am sad to observe that in the context of an otherwise excellent Strategic Defence Review. But whenever the TA has been called out, in peacetime and in war, those volunteers have performed splendidly. Now that attention is turning back to the home front in a number of ways, and with the regular Army still significantly under strength, it is only right that we should consider urgently how best to use the Territorial Army in the present circumstances.

Finally, with our Armed Forces possibly having to face – according to the Chief of Defence Staff, who from now on I shall refer to as the CDS – the most difficult and prolonged operation since the Korean War, I hope that the Prime Minister will ensure that he sets aside the time to consult the Chiefs of Staff collectively. It is perfectly proper that the CDS, as the principal military adviser to the Government, should be the sole representative of the Armed Forces in a small War Cabinet. However, experience has shown that, quite apart from four minds – or five with the vice-CDS – being better than one when military arguments and judgements on risks are finely balanced, as is invariably the case, it is invaluable for the Prime Minister to have a measure of direct contact with the professional heads of the individual Services which are, or shortly are likely to be, primarily involved.

During World War II the Chiefs of Staff as a body were recognised as making a major contribution to victory, including setting the scene for the greatest combined operation of all time. The then Prime Minister, Winston Churchill, consulted and articulated with all the Chiefs of Staff, as well as with their forceful and highly competent chairman, the then General Sir Alan Brooke.[54]

During the Falklands campaign, in some ways a model of political and military co-operation and when again there was a most distinguished and respected naval CDS with the same powers as exist today, the then Prime Minister, now the noble Baroness, Lady Thatcher, met frequently with all the Chiefs, both in Downing Street and at Chequers. Indeed, before the key decision was taken on whether the landing on the Falklands should go ahead, all the Chiefs were arraigned individually to give their appreciation of the situation and their forecast of what would happen.[55]

However professional the CDS may be, when active operations are imminent there can be no substitute for the depth of expert knowledge as regards operational detail which the professional head of the services particularly involved at the time are in the best possible position to impart. That observation is based on a lifetime of experience in that environment, and on their constitutional responsibility to the men and women of their services, who will be laying their lives on the line and who, I know, we shall all be wishing God speed.

On 17 December 2001 he spoke again.

My Lords, it was good to hear my noble and gallant friend, Lord Guthrie,[56] make his most excellent and wise maiden speech. He has had much recent experience in troubled times. No one knows better the delicate balance and interrelationship between the political and military imperatives that exist in any crisis situation. He will have much to contribute in your Lordships' House.

I want to make three points. First, as has been said, the military campaign in Afghanistan has so far gone extremely well. All concerned deserve congratulations, in particular, the Commander-in-Chief of the US Central Command, General Franks,[57] who has organised and co-ordinated the land/air battle with skill and a strong degree of sensitivity. His success has been due, first, to the fact that, as my noble and gallant friend said, he was initially patient and did not rush in before he had gathered intelligence and could be selective in his targeting; secondly, because he increasingly related the air bombardment to the ground action undertaken, largely and sensibly by indigenous forces; and thirdly, because the United States was presumably prepared to provide sufficient gold to enable field commanders to persuade large numbers of the opposition to give themselves up and even change sides without too prolonged and costly fighting, although I imagine that the going became a little rougher as the Al Qaeda were cornered. Anyhow, that famous Chinese general and tactician of 500 BC, Sun Tsu, would no doubt have approved.

As a result, the most impressive results in destroying the power of the Taliban have been achieved far quicker than many of us dared hope. In all this the American marines and special forces and our own special forces have clearly played a significant part in advising local forces of the Northern Alliance and other factions and specifically in directing the air effort to both Taliban and Al Qaeda targets and also by providing maximum fire support to friendly forces on the ground. As has been said, the Royal Air Force has played a big role in photo-reconnaissance and air-refuelling. We should be grateful to them all and very proud or our country's contribution.

Now the remaining Al Qaeda bases, hideaways and training camps must be destroyed. Osama bin Laden may well, for all we know, now be in Pakistan, and must be isolated from any network in that area or anywhere else, and, if possible, put out of action for good. But I have always felt that the network, much of which lies elsewhere than in Afghanistan, and some of it much nearer to home, has always in some ways been a more important target than the figurehead himself, whose mantle could so easily, while various issues remain unresolved, be assumed by others.

My second point is that having been so successful so far, I, too, like my noble and gallant friend, Lord Inge,[58] hope that we do not spoil it by forcing formed bodies of British troops on to the reluctant Afghans, to do heaven knows what for heaven knows how long. It would surely be tactless to those who have done the lion's share of the fighting; their precise task would seem still to be obscure; and as the realities of non-Muslim forces getting involved in internal domestic power struggles and squabbles sinks in, their safety could become increasingly precarious.

Such deployment would also significantly increase overstretch and it is highly doubtful whether the necessary support services, not least the medical services, could be provided without irreparable damage being done elsewhere. For all these reasons, it must be contrary to military advice. But if I am wrong about that, no doubt the Minister will correct me. Only in the context of humanitarian aid under UN mandate could an intervention such as this be seen to be justified.

I would therefore plead for the most thorough consultation with the people on the ground and not just in a European form, as to what kind of force or organisation is needed. Also, like my noble and gallant friend, I hope that the general officer what has been sent out there, when he comes back will be listened to carefully as to what he thinks will and will not work, and that there will not be some preconceived idea which does not fit in to his report. I also hope that we shall not be contriving to create a democratic Afghanistan with full human rights, long after the military aims have been fully met. That must surely be left to the Afghans with the maximum encouragement and financial aid from outside.

My third and last point – this has already been touched on – is that I wonder, when our Armed Forces are needed as much as they are respected, what possessed the Right Honourable gentleman the Secretary of State for Defence[59] to raise in a very long speech delivered to a seminar at King's College, London, the spectre of yet another Defence Review, albeit dressed up as a new chapter of the last one. Of course, the JIC should be making an up-to-date assessment of the relevant threats post-11 September. That is its job. An intelligence effort should be strengthened. After all, the only sensible way to deal with terrorism is to be forewarned.

In the light of that assessment, the Chiefs of Staff should be revising organisation and deployment of forces at home and overseas; and the home commands, in consultation with the home department, should, if necessary, be revising plans to deal with a variety of crisis situations, in particular, how to make best use of our splendid reserve forces, as has already been said. All that is their job, but it should be part of an ongoing process in any efficient and flexible organisation.

But to announce in public in a speech – much of which admitted, not unreasonably, that the situation may not have changed that much and that there are no obvious reasons why the presently organised Armed Forces should not be capable of reacting efficiently to any new situation – that now there would be a formal review, a new chapter, run by a small caucus of the central staff, and which proudly boasted that the Treasury were in from the outset, can only set alarm bells ringing among those desperately trying to see that the last review – which incidentally fully took into account international terrorism and the threat of religious fundamentalism – was fully implemented in terms of manpower, equipment and money.

For however it is dressed up, however the approach to this chapter is paved with good intentions, anyone with any experience of Whitehall will see this as a golden opportunity for the Treasury to question the sensible and fully agreed parameters of the Strategic Defence Review and reduce still further in cash flow terms the already underfunded and overstretched defence programme. This can of course only reproduce the uncertainty which was so powerful in the past among middle grade officers and senior non-commissioned officers, all of whom are so vital for retention and manning.

The organisation and speed of reaction of our forces' work [has been] manifest over and over again. After all, we sent a task force to the Falklands with four days' notice; we have long had a spearhead battalion at immediate readiness; we have Special Forces grouped for quick reaction, a Marine Commando Brigade, an Air Assault Brigade, a Strategic Reserve Division, and a

Rapid Reaction Corps, all designed for rapid deployment anywhere in the world. If it works, why try to fix it? No two crisis situations will ever be exactly the same – as my noble and gallant friend, Lord Guthrie of Craigiebank has said. What is needed is a general combat capability over a wide spectrum of threats and great flexibility in its usage. Of course, that is exactly what the Strategic Defence Review provides.

Finally, with your Lordships' indulgence, I should like to pay a short tribute to the late Lord Carver. Over the years, he was a most regular attendee of your Lordships' House and often a committee chairman. His speeches in debates such as this were keenly looked forward to, as he was a brilliant and erudite speaker with great experience behind him.

Although his obituaries may to some extent have dwelt on his brusqueness and intellectual self-confidence, noble Lords will have experienced nothing but courtesy and kindness from him in his dealings in your Lordships' House. As someone who served under him in Normandy and North-West Europe, I can vouch for his excellence as a commander in war. Clear headed and calm under fire, he was always, like the great Duke of Wellington, to whom he was related through his mother, where he was most needed in battle. He was ready to take clear-cut decisions, however tough, and to seize tactical opportunities as they occurred, while at the same time being considerate of the lives of the soldiers under him. In this, he was everything that a soldier should be.

Michael Carver was also, in peace time, a highly civilised human being – a man of letters and of culture. Those who knew him well – and I count a great number in your Lordships' House – will miss him very much indeed.

Chapter 13

Northern Ireland

In a speech in the House of Lords in March 2010 Bramall reflected on the Saville Inquiry, which had just reported (at considerable length, and after even more considerable time and cost) on the events of 'Bloody Sunday'.

My Lords,

As the Inquiry by the noble and learned Lord, Lord Saville,[60] so aptly summarised it, the events of the afternoon of 30 January 1972 (generally known as 'Bloody Sunday') were a tragedy. They were, of course, a tragedy for the thirteen civilians who, in the course of a civil rights march, lost their lives when they themselves had done nothing that could have justified their shooting, and for the wounded and bereaved. They were also a tragedy for the British Army in that, albeit in but one small area, some soldiers of one company of one battalion failed to come up to the highest standards of discipline and restraint for which the British Army is so rightly and consistently admired, greatly increasing Nationalist resentment and hostility towards it, and making its difficult job even harder. And, indeed, it was a tragedy for the people of Northern Ireland as a whole, in that [it] significantly strengthened the Provisional IRA and exacerbated the violent conflict in the years that followed.

Yet as far as the basic facts are concerned, this Inquiry, despite the time it took and the copious detail it went into retrospectively, really threw little more light on them than could have been gleaned from the much earlier and contemporary Widgery Inquiry, which was bound to be more directly in tune with the threats and dangers of the time.

Neither Inquiry had any truck with the suggestion that there might have been a sinister pre-designed plot actually to cause casualties amongst rioters and any, as Lord Saville described them, para-militaries – '*pour encourager les autres*'. Indeed, the Saville Inquiry specifically rejects this.

Both Inquiries accepted the right of the Chain of Command to order, if it thought appropriate, arrests of trouble-makers during the march which, although organised as a civil rights one protesting against internment, had in fact been banned and was involving rioting. Both, however, thought it was unfortunate that, because it was the only reserve, the Parachute Regiment had to be used to make the arrests, not least because it had to be brought in from outside and was unfamiliar with the highly significant and emotive areas of Londonderry.[61]

Both Inquiries considered that there had been no general breakdown of discipline and that most soldiers throughout the area behaved with a high degree of responsibility and in accordance with the Yellow Card.[62] I am glad to say that the battalion which I once had the honour to command, the 2nd Bn. The Royal Green Jackets, positioned at Barrier 14 to prevent the march reaching the heart of the City in Guildhall Square, was particularly singled out for praise for the restraint and proportionality of the force it used in dealing with intense rioting.

And both Inquiries, and this of course is the nub of the whole business, came to the conclusion that once the vehicles and men of Support Company of the 1st Parachute Battalion[63] appeared on Rossville Street, things started to go seriously wrong. The Commanding Officer of the battalion[64] had already, according to the Saville Inquiry but not to Widgery, exceeded his orders in sending the Support Company into the march from the north to make arrests (as well as one ordered by his Brigadier[65] from the east through Barrier 14) and also in allowing the Support Company to follow the march down its revised route, virtually chasing the marchers and the rioters into the Bogside and making it difficult to separate one from the other. This apparently he had been expressly ordered by his Brigadier to avoid. So it was at that point at 4.30pm, as both Inquiries agreed, that that arrest operation (although six arrests had been made) took second place for that company, if it was not forgotten about altogether, and the soldiers, believing they were under fire, turned their attention to engage their imagined assailants, firing 'recklessly' as Lord Widgery described it, and with a serious loss of fire discipline and control (i.e. 'indiscriminately') as Lord Saville put it, with the tragic outcome we now know.

Although the first shots in this particular area (there had been other shots from both sides in other areas and these were to continue) were probably, as Lord Saville pointed out, fired for rather obscure reasons by an officer in the Support Company, this would in no way have prevented other members of his company believing that that shot and others that followed might be being directed at them. In street fighting, as I can confirm from very personal experience, because of the echoes, ricochets, the small time-lag between the crack of the bullet and the thump of the gun firing, it is extremely hard to differentiate between fire that is going and that which is coming your way. And this would particularly be the case on the edge of the Bogside, where the expectations of hostile fire would be great.

In his earlier Inquiry, Lord Widgery tended to take the view that under the circumstances and noisy confusion prevailing at the time, in which security forces were clashing directly with demonstrators in a highly emotive area, some error of judgement by individuals as to which targets should be engaged, when intent on protecting themselves and their comrades, was almost inevitable. Lord Saville, who with the benefit of hindsight and no doubt feeling that it was in the national interest to be more explicit and less ambivalent and at least give an overall assessment which could be accepted by those who had pressured the United Kingdom Government into holding such a costly and lengthy Inquiry so many years after the event, considered that the failure of certain soldiers in that one company properly and beyond all doubt to identify the targets being engaged as those posing a direct threat of death or serious injury to themselves or their comrades, (*à la* Yellow Card) rather than merely being in a possible position to do so, was so serious as to constitute a totally unjustified, and therefore unjustifiable, use of force.

This assessment was fully accepted by the Right Honourable gentleman, the Prime Minister,[66] on behalf of the Government, the Army and indeed the whole country in a masterly statement he made in another place, and he gave a fulsome and heartfelt apology to those who had suffered and to the bereaved. To this all who mind about the rule of law and, just as much, the high reputation of the Army would wish to subscribe.

And there, My Lords, I hope we can leave the matter because to my mind there are many good reasons in the interest of justice and fair play why it should indeed rest there.

The Yellow Card was, and still is, a good guide as to what military force can be justified under a given (fairly tidy) set of circumstances, not perhaps to the extent of being Holy Writ, as the Saville Inquiry seems to imply, but at least in the nature of the Highway Code, and in any case requiring judgements, sometimes split-second judgements, before putting it into practice. These in turn could not fail to be influenced by the threat and risk climate prevailing at the time; and it has to be remembered just how different that was in 1972 from anything that can even be imagined today.

We were, after all, in the middle of an intense insurrection which had every intention of toppling the structure of government, and with 'no go' areas, massive destruction of property and numerous assassinations of security forces and civilians to give expression to that policy, with certain areas of West Belfast and Londonderry and particularly the Bogside being highly dangerous, and ones in which security forces could invariably expect resistance of one sort or another. This knowledge would be quite enough on the occasion of this noisy and sometimes violent march to induce at least a high level of apprehension even in hardened (and the Paras were certainly hardened) troops, particularly since they were unfamiliar with the area.

Under such circumstances the temptation must have been great, when trying to interpret the Yellow Card, to see any figures who might be hiding or sheltering behind suspicious areas, like barricades, as some were, or on the balconies of the Bogside flats (indeed acid was thrown down from one of these) or were throwing things which could be loosely imagined to be nail-bombs (one of the casualties was found to have had a nail-bomb on his person) or crawling purposefully holding something which could conceivably be thought to be a rifle, as all posing some sort of future threat and therefore a target to be engaged legitimately before worse fears could be realised. These could even have justified in their minds some sort of prophylactic fire into potential ambush areas to deter hostile and perhaps lethal resistance – absolutely common practice in normal street fighting. Not all casualties were caused by these more jittery initiatives but some undoubtedly were.

In part of the United Kingdom particularly it is not possible to condone such judgements when closer adherence to the Yellow Card could have prevented them, but in a thoroughly stressful, untidy situation it should be possible for open-minded people to appreciate why this lapse in fire discipline occurred.

The Saville Inquiry did not consider that anyone higher than those personnel in the Support Company who actually fired shots had any attributable responsibility for the tragic deaths, other than, perhaps, the Commanding Officer for exceeding his orders because he felt this was the only way to make arrests. Hardly an indictable offence. Moreover, when you consider the 651 service personnel killed and the 6,307 wounded since the Troubles started (not to mention the grievous police and civilian losses incurred) many of them inflicted in cold blood; and the leniency in terms of early release and pardons and amnesties, etc. extended subsequently to the perpetrators of these crimes, it would be a great abuse of fair play, justice and even-handedness to single out those hapless soldiers of this one company who should not have been in that area in the first place and who, whatever their shortcomings, were at least trying to do their duty as they thought fit in support of the civil power and the interests of law and order.

If this Inquiry by the noble and learned Lord can at last bring the whole tragic incident to a decent conclusion, the time it took to produce and the inordinate amount of public money spent on it, it may at least be said to have been worth it in the national interest.

Book 4

Evolving Future Strategy: Constraints on Violence, Dynamic Diplomacy and Intervention Operations

Introduction

Bramall was in a unique position to give deep and penetrating thought to the way Great Britain's military strategy ought to evolve and to offer some guidance on the methods and tactics which would need to be used to ensure that the country's political aims were fully met. Quite apart from being closely involved in a wide spectrum of conflict situations from Total War to dynamic diplomacy and peace keeping, Bramall had taught all arms tactics at both the Army's School of Infantry and Staff College, and in 1968 had been especially picked by the Chief of the General Staff[67] to write the British Army's first post-war Doctrine.

In 1970 Bramall, then a Brigadier, attended the last course at the Imperial Defence College (later renamed as the Royal College of Defence Studies) and wrote a much-acclaimed thesis entitled 'The Application of Force in the Future'. He concentrated his analysis on the immediate past and likely developments within the next decade, but it has an acute, one might even say uncanny, relevance to the later decades of the twentieth century and even to the start of the twenty-first. This saw the collapse of the Soviet Union and the emergence of the single super-power situation, various interventions in the Falklands, Kuwait, Iraq and Afghanistan, the spread of weapons of mass destruction, and a general heightening of international tension through fanatical Muslim opposition to Israel and the nations of the West, the rise of Al-Qaeda and ISIS and the invasion of Iraq.

Bramall was to continue to make contributions to higher military thought when immediately after the Falklands War he took over as C.D.S. in October 1982. He inherited Armed Forces and a Defence Programme which were in good shape. The former were immensely respected throughout the country for their fighting qualities and the organisational abilities which had enabled them to win a taxing campaign so far from home in the Falklands; although the latter was no longer sufficient to give an expectation of correcting some alarming equipment weaknesses and by the end of the decade restoring operational balance. The Falklands War had started to make people realize that our defence needs and spending could not be confined to what were still the only four pillars of our strategy – nuclear deterrence, the Central Front in NATO, the North Atlantic and Home Defence. The world, and the nature of the threats we faced, was changing, and this would put a premium on dynamic, hopefully pre-emptive diplomacy and the closest co-ordination between the FCO and the MoD, often lacking in recent times, improved intelligence gathering, high grade and better briefed defence attachés, loan service attachments and training courses and economic and/or military assistance, all designed primarily to help friends help themselves and impose constraints on those that threatened them. In the background, to support that diplomacy, there must be flexible, strategically mobile military forces capable, usually with others, of imposing an ambiguous threat or a short, sharp corrective or punitive action with a view to containment and conflict resolution, without mission creep.

Bramall considered it his principal duty, as Chairman of the Chiefs of Staff Committee and with increased powers as the Government's principal adviser on Defence, to lead his colleagues into this changed (and historically more traditional) strategic balance. In order to get more appropriate funding for these increasingly useful military instruments of softer power (still virtually confined by the Treasury to the four old pillars), he says, 'I swept them all up under one heading, "A fifth pillar of our strategy", and put a paper up to the Secretary of State to get formal political approval, always a hard thing to achieve!'

Much later, in 2013, amidst the still ongoing consideration and development of future strategy, Bramall used his valedictory speech before retiring from the House of Lords to question the need, in such a fast-changing world, for a like-for-like replacement of Trident as our own deterrent. This was preceded by a discussion paper for general debate entitled 'Getting off the Nuclear Hook', suggesting we should be looking for different ways of deterring any likely or even possible threats to our homeland.

Chapter 14

The Application of Force in the Future

Bramall's 1970 I.D.C. thesis (with the addition of some later notes).

Force has been defined in a variety of ways – as a revelation of strength and power, as coercion and compulsion, and simply as influence. It has often been considered as synonymous with military power or organised violence in some form. Undoubtedly force contains elements of all these things, but it is best equated with a form of strategy which comes into play whenever there is a clash of wills and interests. As such it covers all those measures which nations and communities can take either to compel others to do or accept something they would not do voluntarily, or to protect themselves or their property from the unacceptable influence of others. It also invariably confronts an opponent with a more disagreeable alternative in terms of loss, pain or grief than the compliance, acceptance or restraint which it seeks to impose.

In resolving a conflict of interest by the use of force it has not always been necessary to rely on directly applied violence; although violence is one important element of force. The threat of violence, on strength of evidence, has sometimes been quite sufficient, and even actual violence can be used highly selectively to illustrate and amplify a still greater threat to come. There are also a number of non-violent ways of exerting pressure and restraint which have been traditionally used by individuals and communities and are being increasingly used by nations and these should be properly be considered to be part of force, because the pressure they can apply and the influence they can exert is often just as compelling. **Force must be considered a strategy for peace quite as much as it has always been for war.**

In past decades, violence has been a commonly accepted way of resolving international disputes once normal diplomacy has failed to produce a satisfactory answer. In attempting, therefore, to analyse the pattern and character of force in the future, the first problem to be resolved is whether this state of affairs has in some way radically altered. Is it possible, for instance, that within the present century the seeds of conflict itself will have so diminished that there will be no means left for using conflict at all? Or could it be that the material, economic and moral costs of using violence will have become so great that no nation state will be able to use it, however much it might be tempted to do so, and that if force is to be applied at all it will have to be in a rather different form?

A study of the current world scene and of recent experience gives little support to the first suggestion; recent years have seen the highest incidence of significant conflict of all types since the end of the Second World War. It is true that some of the more traditional seeds of conflict, notably the desire for territorial conquest for reasons of economic gain, scarce raw materials or missionary zeal, are no longer significant. It can also be argued that some of the instability and internal violence in the developing world can be directly attributed to ideological and ethnic differences, and rivalries have continued and in some cases, have become accentuated, and these have created potential flashpoints where the problems involved seem insoluble except by violence or an uneasy armed truce.

Perhaps most disturbing of all, a pattern of revolution is developing which transcends national boundaries and at times even ideological barriers. This manifests itself in local revolutionary movements which will gladly accept outside support from those who are interested in maintaining tension and struggle. But the common and underlying theme running through most of the revolutionary situations is undoubtedly 'anti-imperialism' which, in practical terms, simply means the disruption and turning upside down of the established world order and particularly of the status and position of the developed Western powers in that order. In the long term, such a movement probably poses as much a threat to a large and developed communist country such as the Soviet Union, as it does to the Western democracies. It may therefore be assumed that the world will remain a savage and unstable place and it seems certain that the ability to employ force will continue to circumscribe international relations for the foreseeable future.

[Note 1. Since this section was written, the Soviet Union has fragmented with the loss of its superpower status. In parallel, there has been an increase in the practice of revolutionary movements or nihilist cults seeking outside assistance and even 'fighters' to bring about such a degree of chaos in a state over which they wish to have control that the use of force, as an attempt at pacification, has become but counter-productive and played into the insurgents' hands.]

Major constraints on violence

The circumstances under which it will be possible to apply force, however, and the form it will take, have been changing. Despite any impression given by statistics of conflict, the moral and economic costs of using organised violence have risen significantly since the end of the Second World War and there are now an increasing number of constraints on the use of military power for inter-state conflict.

[Note 2. Of the many conflicts since 1945, only the Korean War, Vietnam, the war between India and Pakistan in 1965, the Iran-Iraq War and the two wars against Saddam Husain may genuinely be classified as inter-state conflicts.]

Some of these constraints are new, some stem from the unprecedented destructiveness of nuclear weapons and some are even older in origin. All are proving instrumental in channelling violence away from direct, prolonged and distinct military action at governmental level and into internal conflict in which the threat is altogether more subtle.

Still the most significant of these constraints is the possession of nuclear weapons by a growing number of powers. Because of the destructiveness and after effects of these weapons, no nation, however strong and dedicated, can afford to be subjected to them. Similarly, as the stigma attached to initiating nuclear war would be so great, the consequences of doing so, so unpredictable, and retaliation in kind from some direction so likely, the problems of using them seem insurmountable. This state of affairs makes it inconceivable that direct conflict between nuclear powers could break out by design, for no prize would be worth the risk of certain destruction of the homeland. It also imposes great restraint and caution on nuclear powers in all their dealings with one another; because as long as nuclear weapons are held ready to be used, there is always a faint risk that a miscalculation of their own policies or of their opponents' determination might lead these countries into a spiral of nuclear escalation over which they had incomplete control. Indeed, it is on the prospect that, under certain circumstances, this could actually happen that the philosophy of the graduated deterrent is based.

Nuclear weapons may be virtually useless as agents of violence, but as a deterrent they still have a number of significant advantages over any conventional counterpart. They can provide a deterrent which not only super but all significant powers can afford; they impose as much self-restraint as they do enforced restraint on an opponent; and to some degree their restraining influence can be extended into areas where it would not be possible to retain or introduce a formidable military presence.

[Note 3. The most daunting development in this area is the acquisition or planned acquisition of nuclear weapons by powers with irrational foreign policies, of which North Korea is an example, or so factionalised internally, for example Iran, that there is a possibility of nuclear weapons being acquired by one faction to dominate another by threat of external use. In either case, the risk of accidental use is much greater than during the Cold War.]

There will continue to be arguments on how credible a deterrent can be which palpably should never and, perhaps, could never be used. In the near future, however, the fear and uncertainty caused by a balance of nuclear weapons should continue to be the key factor in preserving the *status quo* in areas, such as Europe, where the vital interests of the super-powers are seen to be directly affected, and where fear of escalation carries most conviction. Indeed, in Europe with the realities of mutual suicide conveniently forgotten, and with the nuclear threshold set at a plausible level, the avoidance by the super-powers of direct conflict with one another has taken priority over all other national interests.

The nuclear balance will also continue to produce prudence and caution in international relations throughout the world. Berlin in 1961, Cuba in 1963 and the conflicts in Korea, Indo-China and the Middle East are all examples of where the existence of nuclear weapons has exercised a degree of restraint and limitation of conflict which probably would not have been present without them; and in future it is not difficult to envisage some degree of nuclear stabilisation dominating any confrontation between the Soviet Union and China. Although the possession of these weapons has in no way prevented organised violence, it has undoubtedly limited its scope and the geographical areas in which it can be used between nations at governmental level. It has also reduced the extent to which nuclear powers are prepared to intervene, in competition with one another, in areas outside their immediate spheres of influence.

[Note 4. The increased risk of nuclear weapons being used, either deliberately or accidentally, by what are now regarded as 'rogue' nuclear powers has so heightened the dangers that it has brought about co-operation between major powers likely to be affected in concerted efforts to avoid nuclear proliferation and to moderate the causes of conflict likely to lead to a nuclear exchange, e.g. the India-Pakistan dispute over Kashmir.]

Enthusiasm for armed conflict between nations has also been steadily declining with only minor variations, since the First World War. One of the main reasons for this is the cost of any conflict has escalated out of all proportion over the last fifty years, with each generation of weapons and equipment liable to cost double that of the previous generation. With the equipment costs of today running into many millions of pounds, the military stakes have to be very high indeed before any risks are taken. The nations of the world have also seen it established beyond doubt that the road to national wealth and economic power lies through education and investment and not through territorial conquest or military victory.

[Note 5. Comparison of capital equipment costs in the 1970s and immediately past generations of some British Army equipment.
Armoured regiment £8.5m (compared to £4.7m)
Armoured Reconnaissance Regiment £5m (compared to £2.7m)
Medium Artillery Regiment £4m (compared to £1.2m)
Light Air Defence Regiment £7.8m (compared to £3m)]

We have witnessed the impact that the threatened withdrawal of US financial support had on Britain's last attempt at large scale military operations at Suez in 1956. While Vietnam presented the world with the pathetic spectacle of the richest nation on earth finding the level of expenditure, even in counter-revolutionary operations, unacceptable in the light of higher national priorities. Moreover, while this has been happening, other nations, which have avoided war or been able to limit their military expenditure, have significantly increased their prosperity and standards of living, especially the Federal German Republic and Japan.

Today few nations can afford to spend more than 9 or 10 per cent of their Gross National Product on prolonged military expenditure and still draw on political and public support, and the great majority wish to spend less than half this amount.

[Note 6. In 1970 only the Soviet Union, Egypt, Israel and Iraq exceeded this percentage.]

Expenditure at this lower figure may be adequate for self-defence and internal security, but it would certainly not be sufficient for the prosecution of an inter-state conflict on any appreciable scale.

Moreover, the more industrialised and wealthy the state, the higher its standard of living and the more it has to lose, the more preoccupied it becomes with the pursuit of domestic issues and with progressive and costly social programmes, and the more reluctant it becomes to embark on a foreign policy which puts capital investment involved at risk.

The second reason for the lack of enthusiasm for military adventures is the considerable moral repugnance for violence at government level. Not only are most governments inhibited from using substantial violence by the fear of the military and economic damage they will incur, but the actual legitimacy of doing so, even if they themselves consider the cause is just, is now subject to the most penetrating scrutiny both internationally and within their own countries. The moral and economic pressures which can be put on a country which flagrantly breaks international law and incurs international censure although by no means binding, can be very embarrassing, inconvenient and irksome, and can never be ignored altogether. Far more serious, for those who do defy this censure, is the critical public opinion which can permeate within the offending country itself and among its allies, particularly if the scale of violence is thought to be in excess of what the situation strictly requires. No country can fly forever in the face of these sorts of pressures.

[Note 7. The most obvious example of this is the American and British invasion of Iraq in 2003 which, in the absence of a more specific Security Council Resolution than 1441 and in the face of opposition of three of the five veto bearing permanent members of the Council, was of extremely doubtful validity in international law. Quite aside from the increased focus for acts of terror that the invasion provided, serious damage was done to the prestige and authority of the United Nations as an organisation to preserve world peace.)

Nowhere are these scruples of the popular conscience more marked than in the modern attitude towards territorial conquest. The right to deploy forces into neighbouring territory when truly vital interests of security are threatened can still be a compelling military requirement, as has been demonstrated by Israel and by the South Vietnamese in Cambodia and Laos; but nation states now have little interest in acquiring additional territorial possessions. The moral and economic costs of forcibly policing subject territory make it economically unprofitable and unrewarding, and there is also much less incentive and opportunity for conquest than there was in the 1930s when Mussolini was carving out an African empire and Germany and Japan were demanding room to expand. Large populations are now considered an asset for economic expansion, not a liability. Overt aggression has, therefore, to take into account not only physical frontiers, but also considerable psychological ones which few governments in their right mind would feel they had the nerve or capacity to cross.

Public opinion will be particularly significant in the future because it can now be developed around the catalyst of the mass communication media of television, enhanced by satellites and transistor radios. These possess the capability of not only making all conflict and diplomacy public, however desirable it may be to keep them secret, but also of actually creating opinion, sympathy, anger and protest as well as reflecting these things. All the natural misgivings about war and its horrors can now be identified and diffused through this media, and those who report and commentate on violence throughout the world are not slow to exploit these capabilities.

The result of this is that emotion and protest are stimulated, particularly, but by no means exclusively, amongst the young and uncommitted, and the media then magnifies and re-diffuses this protest in such a way that the whole community feels implicated and involved and, very often, not a little guilty as well. When this occurs, democratic governments may feel obliged, because of the depth and persistence of the outcry, to take account of this public opinion, even when the normal processes of democratic government have been short-circuited. It can for instance be argued that it was largely because of public opinion that the President of the United States had to limit the depth and duration of the American sortie into Cambodia, irrespective of the military advice he received at the time.

For any nation which can get itself internationally recognised and accepted as the aggrieved party or 'underdog', international public opinion can be a powerful ally. If properly exploited, it can enable a small nation or minority faction to win a considerable psychological victory and restrict the options and the use of force by more powerful adversaries. It is not a new phenomenon for commanders and governments to suffer a psychological defeat in the mind when neither the strategic nor the tactical position really demanded it, but the unrelenting pressure of public opinion makes this failure of will-power even more likely to occur.

But if public opinion in most developed countries acts as a restraining influence on organised violence at governmental level, it will not invariably do so.

[Note 8. An example of the failure of public opinion to influence government policy was that in Britain against the invasion of Iraq in 2003, when thousands marched in London against the war, reflecting widespread views across the country as a whole. The more muted opposition in the United States may be attributed to the belief there that Saddam Hussein was in some way at least associated with the al-Qaeda attacks on the World Trade Centre in 2001.]

If a cause has the approval of local or international revolutionary movements, or indeed of a strong sectional interest, a section of public opinion may try to urge even greater violence on their governments, or at least to get them to support others who are prepared to use it. The attitude of the 'New Left' to the activities of North Vietnam, to the using of organised violence against Rhodesia, to the Biafran rebellion and to rebel activity against Portugal and South Africa are all examples of this; as could be considered the approval of the use of violence in punitive operations between Israel and the Arab world by those who are emotionally involved in the Zionist or Arab causes. Moreover, because the mass media can transmit the challenge and record of emotion, protest and violence from one country to another, from one campus to another and from one revolutionary situation to another, public opinion may also encourage and stimulate internal violence at the lower end of the scale.

The constraint of public opinion can be reduced, as the Israelis illustrated in the Six Days War in 1967, by the speed with which violence can be initiated at government level and completed. It will also often be increased by the remoteness of any violence from the homeland of the perpetrator.

Impact of other constraints in areas of marginal concern to the superpowers

The constraints already mentioned do not have equal impact in every geographical area. In areas of the world which are in some way linked to the East-West power rivalry but where the interests of the superpowers are less than vital, the situation is clearly less stable than in Central Europe. In certain respects, however, the relevance and influence of nuclear weapons has been extended. On the flanks of NATO, the multi-national mobile force has been formed to identify threats and to accept them on behalf of the Alliance as a whole, with all the nuclear constraint which this implies. In the Middle East, the Soviet support of Egypt, Syria and Iraq and the introduction of Soviet ships into the Eastern Mediterranean has virtually balanced the presence of the US 6th Fleet and the ultimate underpinning of Israel by the United States.

While in the Far East, the United States involvement in South East Asia and the economic strength of Japan have to some extent been matched by the emergence of China as a nuclear power. All these developments tend to communicate to these areas some of the caution existing in central Europe, and to ensure a degree of compromise and limitation of local conflict should it occur.

In due course, some limited proliferation of nuclear weapons to as yet non-nuclear powers, for the purpose of local deterrent, may be inevitable. Whether this will be stabilising or non-stabilising will depend largely on the reciprocal balance of power which can be achieved and on the sense of responsibility amongst the local leaders at the time. For the moment, the best constraints on inter-state violence in these marginal areas will be very largely economic ones.

None of the constraints mentioned makes violence impossible, certainly not internal violence; nor are they utterly dependent on the nuclear influence to make themselves felt. But the constraints have collectively diminished the utility of inter-state war and they are that much more effective because of the continued existence of nuclear weapons. Together, they significantly limit the options of the great powers in international relations, and they have reduced the extent to which chance, prestige, emotion and the corruption of power can govern the initiation and spread of conflict in the name of national interest.

Future patterns of force and violence
The major powers which have most to fear from escalation and the cost of conflict, and who often find their military superiority at a discount when confronting smaller nations, have become less and less inclined to get involved in any inter-state violence. They prefer the role of bystander or that of 'honest broker' to that of participant and, as a result, are carrying out critical re-appraisals of their own hitherto vital interests. For these countries, inter-state war, in the distinct clear cut decisive pattern of earlier decades, will virtually cease to be an instrument of policy, and the avoidance of war will assume the same high priority as territorial integrity among their national interests.

The smaller and developing countries will also be subject to constraints, although perhaps to a lesser extent. There may still be some opportunities for limited inter-state violence between them; while the likelihood of internal violence will, if anything, increase. This state of affairs is partly because of the nature of the international problems themselves; partly because of the greater permissiveness in the international scene; and partly because it is in the field of internal violence that those who wish to get their own way, maintain struggle and discredit the international order can do so without undue risk to themselves.

When force has to be used, the initiator will not only have to take account of the various constraints on violence but must also try to use them positively to his advantage. As far as possible, he will exert pressure or impose restraint by active diplomacy and other non-violent methods of force. Under certain circumstances, he may imply a threat of violence but will be careful not to place himself in a position where he automatically has to use it. If he feels he must resort to actual violence to achieve a particular aim, he is likely either to exploit opportunities for subversion, terrorism and even insurgency inside his opponent's country – the indirect approach; or he will concentrate on a more direct military 'confrontation' in which he initiates a series of punitive operations each with a precise and limited military or political aim; or he may attempt a combination of the direct and indirect. If his punitive operations are to be of any scope and intensity, he is likely to try to complete his military action so quickly that he can, as the Israelis have done so effectively in the past, present the world with a *fait accompli* and, at the same time, so limit and localise conflict as to transfer the main burden of constraints on to any outside power which may feel tempted to intervene. The victim, on the other hand, will naturally try to embroil others in the conflict from the outset, at least emotionally, so as to bring the maximum pressure of public opinion to his aid.

Should a major power require to intervene militarily in someone else's internal or external dispute, it should only be on the grounds that the alternative to refusing assistance would only create still greater risks in terms of the balance of power. Any military effort would then take place in conjunction with allies so as to broaden the base of military, financial and moral support, and would try to avoid too deep an involvement on the ground. Instead it would concentrate on building up the national organisation, military strength and morale of the country being assisted and on deterring any enlargement or escalation of the violence. It could do this with the help of military aid, such as arms sales, token and Special Forces, training teams and advisers, and by ostentatiously deploying, but trying to keep uncommitted, some superior element of military power which threatened a greater scale of violence than had hitherto been used.

[Note 9. There can be no more cautionary example of creating greater risks, in this case in the international war against terror, of not gathering a broad base of military, financial and, above all, moral support and not avoiding too deep an involvement on the ground than the US-British invasion of Iraq.]

It will, however, be internal violence which is likely to prove the greatest threat to the nation states in the future. This will arise from three basic causes. First, it may occur as a forceful protest against an internal or external political issue. Although this violence will be revolutionary in character, be in sympathy with the pattern of world revolution and be decidedly tiresome for governments and security forces, it is unlikely to be pushed to the point of armed rebellion or insurrection.

Secondly, internal violence may be provoked by racial or religious rivalry and fear, or by deep social unrest brought about by labour disputes, mal-administration or corruption. These, although local issues, are liable to have much deeper political undertones and support, and are capable of being exploited both for internal rebellion or civil war and to assist the hostile intentions of neighbouring states.

Finally, internal violence may be introduced as a principal element in the strategy of force, wherever there is an acute conflict of interests or the balance of power is in the process of adjustment. This revolutionary violence may still take some of its inspiration from ideological conflict; or, and even more likely, from ethnic conflict between black and white or Arab and Jew, or it may simply and blatantly be inspired by dissatisfaction with the existing world order, with the emerging states wanting to cause the downfall of those more inclined to be associated and aligned with that order. But whatever the guise, the internal violence in this third category is likely to be sponsored and directed from outside the threatened country.

Strategy of force
From this analysis of the pattern of international force and its constraints, it is possible to distinguish six ways in which a strategy of force can be applied which are infinitely more significant than the conventional and sustained use of military power. These can be described as pre-emptive diplomacy, psycho-logical operations, threatened violence, revolutionary violence, punitive violence and peace-keeping. Each of these methods, with the exception of peace-keeping, has both an offensive and defensive aspect and each, depend-ing on the aim of using force in the first place, may be either an alternative or complementary to one of the others. Indeed, it will usually not be possible to keep them in water-tight compartments.

Pre-emptive diplomacy. With many constraints on the use of violence between states, there is both a greater tendency and need for the nations of the world to safeguard their interests and achieve an acceptable balance of power in a particular area by means of diplomacy. As with other forms of force, the aim of this diplomacy may be to impose restraint on expansion; to exert pres-sure and influence on adversaries, rivals or non-aligned countries without incurring the risks of armed conflict; or it may be to maintain influence when others are trying to threaten it and substitute their own. Where possible this diplomacy should be pre-emptive so the onus of trying to change the *status quo* is placed firmly on an opponent.

Two of the main elements in this diplomacy will be economic aid and preferential trade, and military aid in the form of advice and supply of arms. The economic aid provides an opportunity to reduce poverty and economic disparity, which so often provide the conditions for internal and external instability. Moreover, an acceptable local balance of power, which it is to be hoped will secure stability, will need some sort of economic equilibrium if it is to have a proper military and political balance. Although this aid will have definite links with the strategic and political interests of the donor, the humanitarian aspect may play an important part. The military aid can, if properly handled, produce an even greater and more direct incentive for recipient countries to follow policies compatible with those of the donor, and also to provide those donor countries with facilities and opportunities for strategic and economic expansion.

These two together, therefore, play a part in creating, consolidating and extending regional defence arrangements without the embarrassment or cost of an excessive military presence. They can also help to spread affluence, self-esteem and sophistication, with a corresponding reluctance to lose this new wealth, to hitherto unstable areas. Using economic and military aid to create the right political climate for friendly and anti-communist governments to flourish, has been a feature of United States policy since the Marshall Plan brought resuscitation to Europe after the Second World War. The application of force will always require sacrifice, but the sacrifices involved in reverting to the more traditional methods of having a large military presence and indulging in active military operations are likely to be far greater still.

By responsible behaviour in the trade of arms, the powers which have the virtual monopoly of manufacture have a real opportunity to use force in the interests of stability. If done scrupulously, the sale of arms can help developing nations achieve internal stability and a high morale; it can deter aggression, by giving small nations an adequate defence capability; and it can achieve a solidifying balance of power in various regions. It is when armaments manifestly exceed these requirements, or when conflict has occurred and escalation is imminent, that the suppliers have an opportunity to contributing towards preventing violence spreading further. Differentiating between offensive and defensive weapons, or disassociating the actual supply or limitation of arms from a political alignment and encouragement to one country or another, will never be easy; and agreements between the suppliers will still be influenced by a conflict of aims and interests.

Other forms of pre-emptive diplomacy are support and encouragement for ruling parties, and the non-violent use of military forces for making a political point rather more strongly than it can be made by purely diplomatic means. If, for instance, a nation's military forces are retained in a particular area of traditional concern, or are moved into an area where they have not been previously, they may or may not pose a plausible threat of violence and be of some military value if put to the test. This will depend on their size, striking power, logistic support, and ability to be reinforced These forces can, however, without necessarily being used, give a measure of moral support to the host nation. They can show either a continuing or a novel interest and concern in local politics and trade, and can confirm or establish their nation as a factor to be taken into account; and they can start to balance the excessive influence of others, whether that influence is expressed in political, economic or military terms. They can, as the deployment of Soviet naval forces in the Eastern Mediterranean has indicated, play a significant part in adjusting the balance of power without violence.

Psychological Operations. One of the most important ways of applying pressure and restraint without resorting to violence, or as a supplement to that violence, will be through the medium of psychological operations which fall outside normal diplomacy. These cover the planned use of the whole range of the communications media to influence, to the initiator's advantage, the opinions, emotions, attitudes and behaviour of opponents, neutrals and allies. The ultimate aim of psychological operations is invariably to discredit an opponent's commitments and reduce his options, and thus force him into an attitude and line of action compatible with one's own. This can be done either by sowing doubt and dissension in the opponent's own ranks or by getting other influential countries to condemn him and thus put indirect pressure on him.

Propaganda designed to prepare the way for violence and justify it subsequently has long been an instrument of conflict, and has been fully used by totalitarian regimes both for internal and external consumption. Nowadays, however, direct propaganda has an increasingly limited impact, because of the credibility gap which invariably develops, and as audiences both at home and abroad become more sophisticated and discerning. Direct propaganda can normally only be initiated by totalitarian countries with a controlled press and radio.

The emphasis in psychological operations today should be on getting the recipient nation, whether they are an actual opponent or other nations capable of influencing or discrediting that opponent, to implant and generate their own seeds of sympathy, anger and protest. In a free and democratic country, it is comparatively easy to find the necessary sympathisers with any cause, particularly if that cause fits into a general pattern of 'anti-imperialism'. These sympathisers may be drawn from those who are politically involved, from those who are morally motivated and support the under-privileged and oppressed, or from those who prefer sensation to responsibility; or they may come from one of the religious or ethnic groups who may be identified with a particular struggle. Provided the cause they support has some substance, and provided the sympathisers can be properly organised to make full use of the mass media, they can play a part in any psychological operations directed at their country or at the world at large.

In circumstances which are less favourable for psychological operations, the initiator can inject professionals in subversion using both traditional methods and modern methods of public relations. By these means, it is proving possible for small nations or dissident groups to restrict or stop altogether superior force being used against them. Successful psychological operations have been mounted by North Vietnam against the United States, by black Africa against South Africa, and by the Arab world against the British and the French. An example was Biafra, where a small break-away province, with a plausible but none too sound cause, was able, through the medium of a dynamic and well-planned public relations campaign to create such a favourable public opinion throughout the world that it very nearly achieved its aim of international recognition.

The more totalitarian a regime, and the more a nation's territorial integrity is seen to be directly threatened, the greater will be its immunity to psychological operations. Psychological operations are therefore most likely to succeed when directed through countries where there is freedom of expression, and when conducted in opposition to policies which involve inter-state violence by a strong nation or group against a weak one.

How deeply damaging psychological operations will prove to nations who are particularly vulnerable to them, and who perhaps ignore their potential, is a matter of conjecture. It seems certain, however, that they will play a significant role in the strategy of force in the future and undoubtedly offer a rewarding field for clandestine diplomacy and subversion.

Threatened Violence. No fully-fledged state is as yet prepared to submit to a world body such as the United Nations, wholly and in advance, its security or indeed any other of its more vital interests. In any case UN intervention usually has to follow violence not pre-empt it. As a basis for international order, therefore, all countries will continue to require military forces which can help deter any limited external aggression, or intimidation by threats of violence, or outside support for internal revolt.

A deterrent may take the form of a credible or at least plausible defensive capability (as in the case of Sweden), or it may be more appropriate and cheaper to base it on a nuclear counter threat. Precisely what constitutes a credible deterrent, and how much a potential aggressor is deterred by it, as opposed to being held back by other constraints, must remain a matter of speculation. A deterrent is clearly all the more credible if the vital interests of the deterring state and its capacity and will to defend them are seen to be clearly linked; but its effectiveness will also depend on the potential aggressors' intentions and resolve as well as his capabilities. The self-confidence which a deterrent gives one's own side that it can exact an unacceptable toll from any potential aggressor is, in reality, just as important as the effect it has over an opponent.

For the time being, collective security based on an alliance of like interests, with some ultimate call on an effective strike capability, seems to offer the best method of deterring external threats; of maintaining confidence and stability where tension between states still exist; and of encouraging self-restraint by subordinating any local disputes to the needs of an alliance as a whole. This particularly applies to Europe, but it may be equally desirable for countries which lie outside Europe and in areas where tensions exist but where super-power interest is not deeply involved, to adopt some form of collective security. In these areas, the main threat will probably be an internal one, and the main requirement for enlightened and unprejudiced government with progressive social policies and practical plans for regional economic development. In these conditions, the deterrent value of any outside powers who, for reasons of traditional ties, might be persuaded to be associated with the local security arrangements, would be limited, and the capacity of any outside power to intervene in internal violence would be considerably curtailed by political and moral considerations.

If, in spite of local solidarity, hostilities broke out which could actually be attributed to outside aggression or frontier violation, as occurred in Korea, East Malaysia and on India's northern border; or if a super-power or nuclear power such as China started to indulge in intimidation and blackmail, and the balance of power looked like becoming seriously disturbed; then another super-power, with such allies as it could muster, could still feel obliged to intervene. It would then have to do so largely in a supplementary or extended deterrent role by moving to the threatened area, but trying to keep uncommitted, some superior element of military power, as for example a naval task force, or strategic bombers or long range missiles; all with a real or imagined nuclear capability.

With these a super-power might safely be able to restrict the level of violence by the aggressor, to deter any widening or enlargement to counter any blackmail or intimidation, and to prevent any of the sponsors from intervening. Indeed, it might succeed in extending to that area a depth of constraint to that which exists where the super-powers normally confront each other directly. If attacked, such forces would have to defend themselves with minimum use of force. This was the strategic philosophy which lay behind the stationing of part of the RAF Strategic Bomber force at Singapore during the Indonesian confrontation, and it was seen in its most classic form in Soviet support for Egypt in the area of the Suez Canal.

The most difficult task which would face deterrent forces in the Middle East, Asia, or indeed Europe would be if an aggressor, for punitive reasons or political blackmail, seized some limited objective which manifestly did not justify massive retaliation but which, both on the grounds of principle and counter-action did require some counter-action. To re-establish the credibility of the deterrent which had previously been ignored would require intense diplomatic activity backed by psychological operations, and also the ostentatious deployment of fresh forces, preferably those appropriate to an enlargement of the conflict, to key areas close to the point of aggression.

Today the strategy of force is not deployment and organisation of military power to ensure tactical advantage at a critical point and something approaching victory on a battlefield, but more the complicated and devious art of producing a constraining influence and a deterrent, of threat and counter-threat and counter-bluff. In this strategy, military forces which are deployed and threatened are often quite as valuable, as if they actually had to be used; for as long as they are uncommitted they provide their governments with some degree of freedom of action in handling a crisis. That there must be some credibility gap and some disbelief that threatened violence will never be used, is inevitable, but with stakes so high and the consequences of guessing wrong so serious, this need not be significant. Provided the power and the capability are there, uncertainty may well do the rest.

Revolutionary violence. The next method of applying force is by means of internal or revolutionary violence. It includes civil disturbances and civil disobedience, as well as those acts of violence which militant revolutionaries employ, both inside and outside their country, to harass, weaken and ultimately overthrow a government of which they disapprove and to put an alternative one in its place.

Revolutionary violence is a particular phenomenon of the era, but because of its emphasis on taking over states from within by internal upheaval rather than by direct aggression, it can also be a formidable way of applying the strategy of force. It can often circumvent international conflict with its risks of escalation; it can blur the distinction between spontaneous civil disobedience by a majority with a mandate for change, and a calculated campaign by a hard-line minority, often with outside support; and it can reduce the censure normally reserved for aggression and make it difficult for more powerful military forces to intervene because on no single occasion will the threat seem larger enough to justify it.

The most economic use of violence in effecting revolutionary change is the *coup d'état*. This differs from insurgency or revolutionary war in that it tends to draw support from a different section of the community. It is quick, tidy and involves no one else and usually produces firm and comparatively capable and incorruptible administration. *Coups d'état* have been carried out effectively in the last twenty years in over twenty different countries, among them Brazil, Greece, Indonesia, Cambodia and South Vietnam, Pakistan, Egypt and Nigeria. *Coups d'état* have their limitations. They can only be effectively organised with the active assistance of the armed forces. They tend to be autocratic, and are bound to be anathema to many intellectuals, liberals and all those who look on freedom as more important than any other aspect of government and society, and on political struggle as an end in itself. Yet in a developing world many of the better educated citizens serve in the armed forces, and political acumen and a desire for modernisation and technological advance are as likely to be found there as elsewhere. Moreover, where education and living standards are abysmally low, the first priority would seem to be firm and good government rather than plurality of choice and free debate and protest.

How long this state of affairs can exist is debatable. Power corrupts and military revolutionary regimes, like all excessively autocratic regimes with a tendency to perpetuate themselves, are liable to become increasingly vulnerable to alternative revolutionary movements with international support. For the next decade, however, the *coup d'état* is likely to remain the most easily controlled instrument for change in the developing world.

The more infectious threat to international order will come from armed rebellion or insurgency, often with outside support, conducted against an established government which is fully backed by its security forces; and here again the pattern of revolutionary violence may be changing with increasing implications for the world at large.

As Che Guevara has pointed out, the right conditions for revolution may now have to be created rather than being inherited readymade, as envisaged by Mao Tse Tung.

[Note 10. Mao Tse Tung and Che Guevara, *Guerrilla Warfare*, London, 1962.]

As a result, old methods may prove too cumbersome for the somewhat more sophisticated and perhaps less dedicated revolutionary of today, who may prefer more dramatic and quicker results. Moreover, with improving communications, it is becoming increasingly difficult to find remote and inaccessible areas which provide a physical obstacle to security forces and a refuge for guerrillas in any full-scale revolution.

In the future there is likely, therefore, to be a significant shift of emphasis away from the steady progression of Mao Tse Tung's revolutionary war towards four particular areas of threat and violence, some of which will be directed through an outside party selected for its ability to publicise and help the revolutionary cause.

The first of these is likely to be urban violence. This has the potential for making a faster and more dramatic impact on a nation's stability and confidence, and since it can actively involve large numbers of comparatively innocent people, requires less personal sacrifice and hardship from the hard-core insurgents. It is also likely to provoke the authorities and security forces into an excessive reaction and thus can quickly rally liberal and moderate support to the revolutionary cause.

[Note 11. There can be little doubt that the British Army allowed itself to be unduly provoked into excessive reaction against the original IRA in Belfast in 1968 and this, indirectly, led to the formation of the more aggressive Provisional IRA, when the originals backed down, and the subsequent large-scale alienation of the Catholic and Republican elements of society.]

The second will cover such activities as kidnapping, intimidation and assassination. These have always had a traditional place in insurgency, but now they will be directed not only against the usual key officials in the revolutionaries' own country, but also against carefully selected foreign diplomats and national personalities, who may be used as hostages to blackmail a larger country into bringing its influence to bear in the revolutionary interest.

The third type will concentrate on attacks on property, economy and the overseas trade both of the threatened country and of other influential powers. Aircraft, ships, oil installations and commercial premises may all be vulnerable. These tactics can be used offensively to draw attention to the cause, but will be particularly useful in trying to prevent retaliation and reaction to other forms of violence.

The final area of activity will be psychological operations, designed both to obtain the willing support of indigenous populations and to harness world opinion to a massive psychological offensive against the government concerned. Psychological operations have always been an important element in insurgency, but now there will be considerable emphasis on the subtle and often imperceptible subversion of those with influence on the mass communication media, inside the country and in the world at large.

These methods will be aimed at rallying the population to anti-government causes; to giving the widest publicity to popular dissent; and to subjecting the government to such intolerable harassment that it becomes impossible, either economically or politically, for it to continue resistance. They may be infinitely more difficult to counter than mere military threats posed by guerrilla warfare in rural areas. To deal with this type of violence a nation must make it clear that it will not succumb to exploitation and blackmail. It may have to mobilise its civil and military resources, to abandon some hostages to their fate, to amend its laws and to redesign and re-deploy its security forces. But unless this new style of revolutionary violence can be curbed effectively, international anarchy, in which both economic and military strength will be powerless, could result.

Punitive violence. Most nation states will wish to retain the capability to carry out and resist punitive operations. These will be designed to hurt and humiliate an opponent, usually a neighbour, without too much of a risk of getting involved in an unacceptable scale of conflict. A good example of this is China's attack on India in 1962. Punitive operations can also act as a more emphatic deterrent against future acts of violence.

Punitive operations may be part of a broad confrontation designed to bring about the eventual collapse of neighbouring regimes, or alliances, as in the case of Indonesia's confrontation against Malaysia in 1963–66; or they may be intended to force an opponent either to make specific concessions or to negotiate, as in the case of Israel's activities along the Suez Canal. If threatened violence fails, or looks like failing, punitive operations might be considered to be the best way to bring home to an aggressor that aggressive policies will not succeed. Alternatively, punitive operations could simply be retaliatory for some hurt received earlier, and be used to register disapproval and maintain tension in an area of traditional dispute. Lastly, these operations could be designed to achieve a limited military objective, which could subsequently, as a piece of international blackmail, be negotiated or exchanged.

Fundamentally, punitive operations pose an external threat. However, if the aim is the ultimate overthrow of a nation state, there will inevitably be links with subversion and terrorism inside the opponent's country. This happened in East Malaysia and is occurring on the West Bank of the Jordan. In such circumstances, the driving force of the punitive operations may swing towards the irregular element, which will then be in a position to dictate both the pattern and the intensity of the violence used. This may happen voluntarily because of the greater constraints on governmental violence, or as a result of pressure from a revolutionary movement.

Because of the risks of escalation, which neither side will be prepared to accept, it will be incumbent on both participants, whether they be perpetrating the violence or resisting it, to restrict the level of violence used. It will be in the aggressor's interest to limit his tasks and objectives in case he may start something in international terms, for which he is not prepared and cannot sustain. On the other hand, over-reaction by the defender could force the aggressor to use greater violence than the defender could hope to contain.

Indeed, commanders on both sides will have the difficult task of achieving their military aims and rendering the other side's efforts ineffective, without using greater or more prolonged force than is necessary, and without closing the door to sensible negotiations towards an advantageous political settlement.

Each and every punitive operation must be designed to achieve a strictly limited aim and no more, and where possible should be conducted in a geographical area where escalation is not likely, such as a barren country, or in jungle or at sea. Political factors will feature very highly in military planning and success and failure will depend on the wisdom and political sensitivity of commanders as well as on their professional skill.

Peace-keeping. Any strategy of force requires a safety valve, so that those who voluntarily or involuntarily get involved in violence can have an opportunity to escape from it without undue loss of dignity and without, perhaps, abandoning some of the advantages they have gained. A nation or faction in an unfavourable military position may well wish to prevent further loss or damage. A stronger one could wish to consolidate what he had achieved, whilst reducing the economic, moral and military burden on himself. They might both, therefore, be prepared, at least temporarily, to accept the considerable moral constraint imposed by peace keeping activities under UN auspices.

These activities cover mediation and investigation of disputes by UN officials, supervision of agreements and ceasefires by UN observers and the inter-positioning of an emergency force between two hostile factions to prevent violence or further violence breaking out.

It is easy to be cynical about these operations. To launch a peace-keeping operation there has to be a degree of consent and identity of interests which is rare in international relations. By their very nature, UN operations call for a multi-national force which has been improvised at the last moment to meet specific needs, which is, therefore, unused to working together and which lacks any proper command or logistics infrastructure. Moreover, the tasks of observers and interposed forces become more difficult and dangerous in the increasingly prevalent internal and revolutionary violence. Despite these difficulties, UN operations in some form have taken place on a number of occasions in the last twenty years and have achieved significant success in preventing and calming down violence and helping to create a climate in which negotiations for a political settlement became possible.

Perhaps the most valuable contribution of all that these operations make is that they provide the machinery for encouraging nation states and ethnic communities who share the same long term goals to co-exist with dignity despite their prejudices and hostilities. This is something that the parties concerned might have neither the political courage nor the popular support to achieve, if the decision was theirs alone. In a world which is no less turbulent and competitive, but which is less inclined to destroy itself, this is a form of compulsion and restraint which cannot be ignored.

Conclusions

There will be many similarities between the international scene in the future and that of the previous decade. The seeds of conflict will not in themselves have diminished, and the influence and constraint of nuclear weapons (and others of potential mass destruction) will still make themselves felt. The world will probably remain in a more or less continuous state of low level tension. At the same time, all the various constraints on violence should increasingly impose themselves on established governments during the next ten years. The issues over which nations, particularly advanced nations, are prepared to go to war, apart from the protection of their own territorial integrity, are becoming less and less, and distinct decisive inter-state wars will have virtually ceased to be instruments of sound government policy.

Despite the limitations on the scale of violence, however, the struggle for economic power and political influence and the rivalries and prejudices stemming from race and religion will continue unabated, and force in some form will still be required whenever there is a genuine conflict of national interests. It will be required in the form of threatened violence, to safeguard territorial integrity and to achieve and preserve an acceptable balance of power, without which the constraints on inter-state violence will not be fully effective; and, if the conflict of interests is particularly deep, it may still, in the form of limited violence, be required to hurt and give more emphatic warning of worse to come. It will also be evident in the handling of revolutionary situations which are likely to prove the greatest threat to nation states in the future.

At the same time, as sustained violence cannot now be considered a sound instrument of policy, it will normally be in the interests of established governments to confine force to pre-emptive diplomacy, psychological and economic pressures or to military or economic assistance and other non-violent measures and to keep in the background, as an ambiguous but still persuasive threat, the controlled deployment of military forces.

Unfortunately, this caution and discretion will only apply at government level. To revolutionaries who feel unrepresented, or who still harbour deep social, ethnic or ideological grievances, any *status quo* will be anathema. They will see the near future as a period of intense change, and will find a number of ways of using internal violence which may not yet incur the same penalties and constraints as inter-state violence, but which will have an increasing impact on the world as a whole.

None of these changes of emphasis will make defence planning any easier or cheaper. There will be the organisational problems of reconciling the requirements of military forces which must be raised and equipped to deter and make a political point, but are unlikely ever to be used, with those which will almost certainly have to be used in the increasingly specialised role of dealing with revolutionary and particularly urban violence. And there will be the difficult strategic problem of assessing how much revolutionary violence and threats of violence around the world represent the inevitable and even desirable process of change, and how much they can be attributed to militant minorities dedicated to the disruption of the world order and the unbalancing of an acceptable balance of power.

This situation presents an intriguing prospect for all nations of the world, and it is clear that the controlled and thoughtful application of force will be no less significant than it has been in the past, nor any less of a challenge for political and military leaders.

Chapter 15

The Fifth Pillar

In March 1983 Bramall, as C.D.S., wrote to the then Secretary of State for Defence, Michael Heseltine.

Secretary of State.

UK Defence Policy beyond the NATO Area – the Fifth Pillar

1. The current Defence White Paper explained that the UK has four main defence roles and that additionally we exploit, as far as our resources permit, the flexibility of our forces to meet both specific British responsibilities and the growing importance to the West of supporting our friends and contributing to world stability beyond the NATO area. For various reasons, not least our pre-occupation with the defence budget and lack of resources, implementation has fallen far behind intention. Where action has been taken, it has been largely uncoordinated. The various constituent parts of our capability beyond the NATO area have never been placed into one coherent framework, which MoD and FCO Ministers could then direct. Moreover, the maintenance of strict priorities, with Priority 1 allocated to the UK's NATO commitment and Priority 2 to those beyond the NATO area has led, particularly at any time of financial stringency, to an unfortunate reduction in emphasis and resources to activities beyond the NATO area. The Falkland Islands reminds us of the cost of unexpected aggression and has caused us to re-appraise our approach to out of area activities.

2. The Chiefs of Staff discussed these issues on 2 March [1983] and concluded that our Defence Policy had not been implemented fully to meet the wide range of our commitments and interests beyond the NATO area where we are vulnerable to Soviet opportunism and local threats. While we appreciate that the allocation of resources must recognise clearly the primacy of the Soviet threat to NATO, and the importance of the four main defence roles, we agreed that a more flexible and co-ordinated approach is needed to the implementation of present defence policy.

3. At present, we engage in a great deal of military activity outside the NATO area. This ranges from our commitments in the Falkland Islands, Belize and Hong Kong, through loan service and seconded personnel, training

teams, assistance to sales and the provision of high calibre defence attachés, all of which are designed to maintain stability in these areas and to increase British influence. In the context of no more than a slight shift in strategic emphasis, and without downgrading our NATO capability, the Chiefs of Staff are agreed unanimously that these limited forms of involvement can represent some of the most economical and cost effective ways of meeting our commitments and protecting and advancing UK interests beyond the NATO area. But to get the maximum advantage for our foreign policy and strategic interests, and also to make best use of the limited resources, these activities need to be properly co-ordinated.

4. We have therefore given instructions for work to be undertaken by the end of May [1983] to identify more clearly all aspects of existing activities beyond the NATO area and to propose how best they can be managed and co-ordinated. In the longer term, after further study in conjunction with the FCO, we aim to establish priorities for our involvement with countries or areas outside the NATO area, against which changing demands for limited resources may be assessed.

5. I conclude that the activities and limited resources which can be brought to bear to protect our essential interests worldwide should be acknowledged as constituting an important Fifth Pillar of our defence policy, all elements of which must be considered, of course, as a whole. I would ask you to endorse this conclusion in principle because I believe it should be reflected in your forthcoming statement on Defence Estimates.

6. I have discussed all this with the Permanent Under-Secretary who is in broad agreement with this approach, and we suggest you may wish to have an early meeting with us on this subject.

25 March 1983   (Signed) ENWB CDS

Chapter 16

Military Commitments and Spending (House of Lords Speeches)

Between 1988 and 1993 Bramall spoke a number of times in the House of Lords on Defence issues. Given his recent experience as C.D.S., these were major contributions to the debates.

(a) Defence spending

His first speech came on 12 July 1988.

My Lords, each year for the past few years the Defence White Paper setting out the estimates and giving the Ministry of Defence commentary on them has been produced in ever glossier form, calling on the latest marketing techniques. There is nothing intrinsically wrong in that. It makes what could be rather turgid stuff a great deal easier to read and gives to the Armed Forces of the Crown a modern business-like and up-to-date image which they thoroughly deserve.

Our defence effort is, after all, a very marketable commodity, with Armed Forces which have seldom if ever been better, as the Falklands campaign so clearly demonstrated, and with some home built military equipment which is among the best in the world. If we can get our prices right or our customers are rich enough, it is often much coveted abroad, as we have seen recently, by those who, if and when they buy it, bring much financial benefit and employment to this country as well as, it is to be hoped, greater stability in their area.

The Government can be proud that as a result of seven years of sustained growth between 1979 and 1986, induced both by the Falklands campaign and by the Government's adherence to the NATO 3 per cent growth target (an intention, I have to say, which was first announced, as the noble Lord, Lord Mulley,[68] will know, by the last Labour Government), there is in the pipeline a formidable re-equipment programme for our forces, which for the moment at any rate is both necessary and urgent, as the Minister reminded us. It is necessary and urgent because of the technical and numerical threat which potentially still threatens us in Europe and in the Middle East, the need for continued stability in East-West relations and the very varied nature of our current commitments, from the north of Norway to the Falklands, and from Central America to Hong Kong. There is much to savour and be proud of in the White Paper, and its format and presentation bring all that to life.

Unfortunately, that is not the end of the story. What the glossiness and salesmanship cannot do, as was implied by earlier speakers, and despite the Minister's rather generous interpretation, is disguise the fact that from the point of view of real term resources and percentage of the gross domestic product we are back to the syndrome which existed in the 1970s and which was so soundly criticised by this Administration when they came to power. That was when the resources which successive governments were prepared to justify to Parliament were never quite sufficient to meet the commitments and capabilities which equally those governments thought necessary to maintain.

Today there are some additional complications. For example, whereas in the 1970s commitments were being pruned, they have now been kept at roughly the same level for the past six years and even in certain cases increased. Moreover, this Government has inevitably introduced and encouraged much higher expectations than existed in the 1970s. We are at the same time in, or edging into, a particularly expensive part of the programme such as the completion of the Tornado programme, the arrival of Trident, the rationale for which has been debated many times in this House and elsewhere, the replacement of the ageing Chieftains, the maintenance of some sort of amphibious capability to give us valuable mobility on the flanks, which we are particularly good at, and the development of the European fighter aircraft. Taken all together they will stretch the elastic to breaking point and beyond.

This Government would always want to see themselves as strong on defence. Indeed, they have done much, first, to get forces' pay on a proper basis – and here again I give credit to the noble Lord, Lord Mulley, who started the process when he was Secretary of State. Secondly, though much remains to be done, they modernised and re-equipped the forces, particularly during and in the aftermath of the Falklands campaign. Finally, they have generally made the Armed Forces, unlike the Civil Service, feel wanted and appreciated.

Despite all that, the financial squeeze in real terms is now, if anything, greater than ever. That is bound to have a harmful effect on training, activity, and professional standards, governed as they are by such things as petrol, spare parts, leading to track mileage, and ammunition – the only areas in which money can be saved in the short term. In consequence, there is an effect on morale and retention rates, which are already worsening quite significantly as the Minister recognises. That is the natural consequence of overstretch and curtailment of activity.

It is not so much the not inconsiderable sum of £19 billion plus which is allocated on paper which is the problem, though it scarcely keeps pace with inflation, if it does at all. It is much more the contrivances which the Treasury, with no longer any Government or NATO discipline of 3 per cent growth to restrain it, can use to keep down public expenditure, such as a straight cut in estimates with Star Chamber vetting. That occurred in 1979 just after the election; early in 1982, hard as the noble Lord, Lord Pym, tried to prevent it; again in 1983 just after the election, and since then quite a number of times.

Perhaps the Minister will be able to tell the House how confident he is of resisting such further inroads. If he cannot do that, it will invariably have the effect not only of squeezing the short-term cash flow – difficult as that some-times is to accommodate – but also depressing the annual out-turn figure on which all subsequent promised growth (or, more likely, negative growth) is measured. Therefore, what in the early and mid-1980s was a steadily rising graph of expenditure has now become a convex and downward curve, without in the immediate future any significant change in requirements and commit-ments which the Government will admit to.

There is also one other Treasury device which is perhaps the most dam-aging of all to the availability of the cash which Parliament thinks it has allotted for general defence needs. That is the question of funding the pay award for the Armed Forces for personnel up to the rank of brigadier or its equivalent. In a civilian business one can say to the workforce that times are hard or profits are down so that one cannot afford to pay more than so and so. With the Armed Forces it is a little different. As noble Lords will know, pay rates are judged and recommended by an independent pay review body on the basis of comparability with earnings for similar responsibilities outside. The Government are more or less committed to accepting the findings of that review body. This is clearly understood on all sides.

To recommend an award of x per cent, have it accepted by the Govern-ment, and then not pay it on the ground that there is a problem with the cash flow of the Ministry of Defence, would be a travesty of justice and virtually a breach of contract. Yet when it is awarded as mirroring the general national trend of wages and salaries, the Ministry of Defence is only compensated by the amount which reflects whatever the Treasury deems to be the going rate for public service pay, which is invariably well below the award figure.

Judging by past experience, this may mean that at least 3–4 per cent of the total award has to be carried by an already restricted budget. Put another way, around £150 million or more per annum which Parliament may be under the impression is available for general defence, particularly in the high spending equipment field, is effectively being removed from any other use than meeting the existing pay bill. So, cash absorbed by personnel costs (even when manpower has been cut to the bone, as I believe it has) goes ever upwards and money available for activity, material and equipment gets more and more squeezed, thus effectively reducing the Defence budget annually by that amount.

When I was Chief of the Defence Staff we appreciated that the Government would not wish or be able to sustain indefinitely the 3 per cent growth, however much it would be in NATO's interest to do so and would wish, in view of other priorities, to level off. Therefore, with some difficulties, we made certain adjustments which generally allowed the programme to be accommodated within a zero-growth level in real terms resources. But this further erosion which has taken place, exacerbated by the now apparent – unless the Minister reassures me – annual short-funding of pay awards has produced a new and disturbing situation. This will lead either to a defence review of capabilities and commitments which the Government, with some justification, are most reluctant to undertake, or to an even more damage salami-slicing, slipping and fudging until the moment comes when defence is so manifestly over-extended or under-funded that it loses credibility with those it has to deter, with its allies and, just as importantly, with those who stand guard on the frontiers of freedom and elsewhere and who have to sustain and implement it.

I know that some would shelter behind the facile theory that if only the Ministry of Defence conducted its weapons procurement business more efficiently, and the defence industries were not allowed to rip off the Ministry of Defence on some of its contracts, there would be more than enough money to go round. It is a good excuse, but when one bears in mind the efforts that have been made by hyperactive Secretaries of State over the past four or five years to get the best value for money, and the almost obsessional preoccupation with profit-cutting competition, this view does not stand up to close scrutiny – at least not to the major sums we are talking about; namely, shortfalls of hundreds of millions of pounds over the three-year accounting period.

Moreover, excessive competition, when combined with inherent uncertainty about future orders and defence spending in general and cautious and delayed decisions, does not always produce the most economical answer. The only sure way of getting prices down to within or below normal inflation is to have continuity, stability in programmes, early decisions, long lead times and long production lines. The best example of that is the production of nuclear submarines which are planned well ahead and where I believe prices have been reduced in real terms. It is rather like buying a colour television set today, which costs so much less than it used to.

I hope that the Secretary of State and the Minister will do all that they can to restore defence resources to at least zero growth in real terms. One of the simplest ways of achieving that would be by reaching an agreement fully to compensate the Defence Vote for any pay review body award, as I believe was done for the nurses this year and it may well be done for the police and fire services. Under the previous government, as the noble Lord, Lord Mulley, will know, it was done for the Armed Forces in his time. This will make a substantial difference.

I hope that I am pushing at an open door because with such funding I believe that with a little ingenuity the Ministry of Defence could implement the defence policy as advertised (I use the word advisedly) in the White Paper and of which I heartily approve. We shall continue to need a defence policy at least until *glasnost* proves to be on surer foundations, and while we negotiate mutual arms reductions from a position of strength. We shall need a defence policy until the Middle East becomes less volatile and dangerous with its implications for Europe. All that will take a long time to achieve.

Bramall again spoke on the Defence Estimates in the House of Lords, almost exactly a year later, on 13 July 1989.

My Lords, this is a highly interesting and also a difficult time for defence planning. It is interesting because, as has been said, much is happening which may affect the general threats and balances in the international scene. It is difficult because, although we can see things unfolding which ought to, and indeed may, require different solutions to our military problems, natural and sensible prudence and bitter experience in the past cautions us not to abandon the stability and unique advantages that we have acquired over the past forty years by membership of NATO, with its panoply of manifestly alert forward defence and burden sharing, and in the background the ultimate deterrent, as the Minister said, to man ever being stupid enough to resort again to a military option in Europe.

Moreover, although much that is happening is good, such as the undoubted easing of the East-West confrontation, not all of it can be described as comforting. Events in China have shown how quickly trends can change and there is some genuine concern as to whether Mr. Gorbachev can carry through his apparently very enlightened policies without incurring some reactions which would effectively put back the clock. In the longer term, depending I think to some extent on the success or failure of a more united Europe, it may not be possible to take for granted West Germany's key role in the NATO structure;

and we might find our country's forward defence not so far forward as we had come to expect.

Moreover, outside NATO there is a great number of more indirect and subtle threats – emanating from the carnage in Lebanon, the impasse in Palestine, rivalry in the Gulf, support for international terrorism from both North Africa and the Middle East and general instability ranging from Latin America to China – which are capable of causing our Western civilisation plenty of problems, anguish and concern in a variety of ways. The kind of situation that could arise up to and around 1997 in the South China Sea is perhaps among the most predictable of a number of yet indefinable scenarios, all of which could call for some kind of military deployment over the next two decades, whether it be prophylactic, pre-emptive or even *in extremis*, reactive.

So however high our hopes, all this calls for the continuation of balanced and all-purpose forces, capable of not only operating on the Continent and its surrounding seas, to maintain a prudent albeit perhaps changing balance of power, but also of reacting outside NATO to the unexpected emergencies affecting British and European interests with which our history has invariably been punctuated.

It may also call for a somewhat different method of funding defence. With the threat becoming more nebulous and diverse and without the discipline imposed on the Treasury by, for instance, NATO's 3 per cent real growth figure, adopted by our governments from 1978 to 1985, the funds available to defence are bound to go down in real terms, despite the fact that the increasing sophistication of equipment and higher costs of manpower have demanded at least a zero growth in real terms from a higher start point long since abandoned.

Noble Lords have only to remember – not from personal experience of course – what happened to the British Army between Waterloo and the Crimean War and again to the Armed Forces in the 1920s and 1930s, to realise that once the tap is turned off it never gets turned on again until it is too late. The only sensible way to look at defence is as an insurance policy not only against the more obvious and urgent threats but also against the less expected but still possible ones, just as we have to do in our homes and businesses. We often find the money for the premiums difficult to raise and compromises have to be made. But the premiums are invariably related to the value of the assets that we want protected and the scale of the loss that we would incur if things were to go wrong. So, I think, it should be in defence, with a finite percentage of our gross domestic product – possibly about 5 per cent to 5.5 per cent – allocated for this vital insurance. When the country's GDP rises, there would be the availability and the need for higher premiums and vice versa.

In the past, our defence expenditure has been well over 5 per cent of GDP, at one time rising to about 6 per cent – in comparison of course to the Soviet Union's figure of 11 per cent to 12 per cent. But recently we have dropped significantly below the 5 per cent figure which is likely to go down even further, as with all public expenditure. Yet with that declining figure, and however much we seek cost-effectiveness, it will be extremely difficult to maintain high quality, well trained and mobile Armed Forces capable of dealing with both sophisticated threats and unexpected emergencies, as we had to do, and indeed did do, by a very narrow margin in the Falklands.

But even with more predictable and stable funding we must consider carefully how much of our resources we need to maintain in the nuclear field. As I said two years ago, by assessing carefully what we really need those weapons to do, there is scope for reducing further the overkill situation that has existed until recently, rather than going on working from a start point of 'We are here because we're here, because we're here.'

To my mind there are still good and sound arguments for retaining some nuclear weapons for one purpose and one purpose alone – that of ensuring comprehensively that a military option would never be resorted to in Europe and that no one else would ever threaten or use first a nuclear weapon against us. For that reason, some effective and largely invulnerable submarine-launched weapon, such as Trident, remains, in the language of *Which?* magazine, 'the best buy'. So long as an adversary has a suspicion that under certain circumstances highly disastrous to you, you might just use those weapons, that would almost certainly suffice. Whether one needs any further nuclear weapons to manifest the link between any conventional resistance and the threat of a possible strategic response, so that no opponent could imagine the feasibility of a conventional military option without incurring nuclear and therefore quite unacceptable penalties, is a more difficult question.

Flexible response in nuclear terms has been described as a ladder, but one which nobody knows where you will get on or where you will get off. It certainly has never meant that you must necessarily get on at the lowest rung. For most military men, the concept of a coherent tactical nuclear battle is fairly incomprehensible (either for attacker or defender) and since such weapons even with modernisation, would inevitably fall on some German territory, their authorisation would be even more difficult than most.

Personally, therefore, I was somewhat surprised at all the fuss about the modernisation of so-called tactical or battlefield nuclear weapons. I am relieved that the subject has now been diplomatically kicked where it belongs – into the long grass of the *status quo*, merging into the mutual force reductions, where it will almost certainly resolve itself. If you must have a bridge weapon which puts the link between conventional resistance and nuclear resolution beyond all doubt – and a case can be made for it – there are other weapons which to my mind would fit the bill better and would not have the same connotation to West Germany, such as an improved air-delivered weapon for the Royal Air Force. Together with a dual capability, they would give us all the flexibility that we needed, not only in the interdiction and sub-strategic fields, but also against lesser nuclear powers whose threat one day just might need resisting.

We must assess how much we can afford to lock up in the nuclear field rather than in areas that both enhance the flexibility and mobility, and multiply the fire effectiveness of our conventional forces. My noble and gallant friend, Lord Hill-Norton,[69] has mentioned some of the areas where these resources are badly needed.

Much the most serious question facing the Armed Forces – and which the White Paper skirts around with a bare two paragraphs devoted to it (paragraphs 508 and 509) which are both misleading and totally incompatible with one another – is the manpower problem. The noble Lord, Lord Irving,[70] and the noble and gallant Lord, Lord Hill-Norton, have mentioned it. The problem arises partly from the demographic trough, which is relevant, but also from the inability of the Armed Forces to hold the manpower they have recruited and trained, with the result that they would now have to recruit more than they would otherwise have to do from a shrinking pool.

There are a number of reasons why young men are inclined to leave the service prematurely. The urgency of defence is perceived by the public to be less than it was, and the variety and interest of a military career – although still very much there in my opinion – is thought by some to be not as great as it was. It certainly requires greater effort and imagination in training, both collective and individual, to bring it about. There are now greater opportunities in civilian life for skilled and reliable manpower for which the services are renowned.

It is therefore more important than ever that the Government are seen by the Services to be a good employer who is prepared to make service to Queen and country – often under difficult, arduous and hazardous conditions, with necessarily long periods of separation, or at other times with wives not being able to work – positively rewarding in financial and family terms and in comparison with what servicemen can expect outside. It is in this area over the past three or four years that there has been a steady and significant erosion of pay and allowances.

When the Government came to power in 1979 they made great play of getting Forces' pay right, a process already started by the noble Lord, Lord Mulley. When they did do so in comparison with responsibilities outside, the manning situation was transformed, both in terms of recruiting and retention.

The Services became fully up to strength over the Falklands crisis and beyond. However, since those days, and in particular in the last three years, there has been a steady erosion of comparability in terms of the national average. The X factor, which was meant to compensate for the exigencies of the Service and to bring the serviceman comparability-plus, now means relatively nothing. Allowances have been whittled away in a number of areas. It has greatly decreased the incentive to serve and face the tempo and rigours of military life, such as living up to three months under water in a nuclear submarine, or perhaps spending twelve years on consecutive postings in Germany with frequent periods of family separation. We now hear rumours that the Treasury is proposing that the troops in Northern Ireland should be charged for their accommodation. This is quite unheard of on active service.

Perhaps the most serious weakness in the Ministry of Defence's employer's measure, and the one I still submit has the greatest influence on the premature voluntary release figures, is in the field of housing, and the disadvantage at which the servicemen and -women and families find themselves in relation to the housing market. As I suggested in a Starred Question in May, what is so badly needed now – and indeed it has been for the last ten years – is a proper house purchase scheme which would allow the servicemen and -women to save for a house towards the end of their service in a tax effective way without having to buy one prematurely when, because of service abroad, it is not possible properly to look after it, and while they are rightly being encouraged to live in Government accommodation near their place of work.

In answering my question the Minister made much play of the steps that the Government were taking to sell surplus married quarters to service people. However, after considerable research I find that at best it is only a peripheral measure and that it is not really working. Certainly, it is not working to the extent of housing the considerable number of service personnel who find themselves homeless at the end of their service and yet cannot be accommodated by local authorities. Such homelessness at the end of faithful service is hardly an incentive to stay in the service in the first place. There are many other examples where the erosion of allowances and lack of proper employer measures are encouraging good men to leave the Services. It is sad that excellent back-bench efforts in another place as yet have got precisely nowhere.

It is indeed so sad that this Government, having done so much for defence – and for whom incidentally the Services themselves have done so much – seem to have lost interest in taking on the Treasury to achieve the comparatively small amount of resources that are needed to establish their position as good employers. I hope that they will do better in future because if they do not, even with the maximum of help from the Brigade of Ghurkhas, and certainly not the minimum of 4,000, and from the Women's Royal Army Corps, they will soon be unable to man all the volunteer forces required by our current commitments, let alone any emergencies.

In the infantry alone, we are the equivalent of two battalions short on current requirements, to say nothing of the acute shortage of every kind of specialist. The battalions have a totally inadequate establishment of three companies and only 650 men. Military historians in your Lordships' House will recall that one of the main reasons that Ludendorff advised the Kaiser to sue for peace in 1918 was that the establishment of the German infantry battalion had sunk to 650 men.

Without the men, any discussion on strategy becomes academic, for the only alternative to volunteer service is some form of compulsory national service and I think that most of your Lordships will agree that that is hardly a political option.

(b) Options for Change

On 12 June 1991 Bramall spoke in the House of Lords about the Defence Review commonly known as 'Options for Change'.

My Lords, it was marvellous that my noble and gallant friend Lord Field-house[71] was able to make his maiden speech in this important debate. I wish to add my congratulations. His knowledge of these matters is formidable and his contribution to his country before the Falklands, during that campaign as Commander-in-Chief and afterwards as CNS and CDS has been outstanding. We look forward immensely to having the benefit of his wisdom and experience in the years to come.

This important debate, launched so effectively by the noble Lord, Lord Colnbrook,[72] has shown quite clearly that many in your Lordships' house are increasingly concerned at the ways in which Options for Change is developing. We have not exactly been reassured by the recent limited statement in another place on the Army.

We are not concerned because a strategic defence review was uncalled for or inappropriate. The collapse of the Warsaw Pact alone, with its impact on any imminent threat to NATO, demanded such a review. This has not been invalidated by the more recent uncertainties in the Soviet Union or surrounding the Gulf War, although these latest developments must surely influence the outcome. They occurred well after Options for Change was first conceived.

Moreover, there is, I believe, general approval for our moving from a now unnecessary and uneconomic forward defence deployment to a British-led rapid reaction force for NATO and in NATO. For reasons that do not need restating, that organisation must still remain the cornerstone of any collective security system in Europe and of a proper balance of power. All this, including stationing but one strong armoured division on the continent of Europe, seems eminently sound and sensible, particularly as our commitments in this force would give us some national capability to operate outside Europe, if there were the need, as in the Gulf.

My concern lies much more with the way the size and shape of our forces has been arrived at, which seems to indicate a clear case, as the noble lord, Lord Glenarthur,[73] aptly put it, of putting the cart before the horse. The trouble undoubtedly was that before the ink was dry on any genuine choices proffered to Ministers, the Treasury funding had been virtually removed for both the short and the longer term. It was as if all the crucial and difficult decisions on government defence policy, on strategy, on equipment policy and organisation had been taken, when, of course, they had not. So far as I can judge, in certain cases they have still not been taken. It was also as if the cheapest option and something perhaps even cheaper than that, had not been properly assessed against developments in NATO and future commitments, both inside and outside that organisation. It was as if the cheapest option had then been accepted on its merits, strategic as well as political and financial.

There is no evidence that this strategic reappraisal has happened. Nor, in the light of subsequent events and uncertainties in the world, would such what I may describe as a part-worn selection have been wise, at least without considerable modification incorporating the lessons of the Gulf. That would include the relationship between regular forces and reserves and the many other developments since Options for Change was first considered.

However, this removal of the money in advance must have greatly reduced the scope and freedom of action of Ministers and their military advisers to make sound decisions. If a yawning gap already existed between commitments and resources, and there was not even enough to meet the original cheapest option, there was not much chance of a reassessment upwards, however sensible this may have become.

If the noble Earl[74] can reassure me I should be only too delighted and relieved. It seems to be that what started out as a highly sensible and logical exercise has degenerated yet again into one of those resource-led scrambles in which, in order to balance the books in the shorter term, we first cut anything we can easily lay our hands on: training activity, ammunition, spare parts, equipment orders (running on older equipment beyond its point of obsolescence). Those are the very things which created such unreliability in what would otherwise have been good equipment in Germany. As the noble Lord, Lord Williams of Elvel,[75] pointed out, it necessitated contortions, cannibalisation and grounding of other units when we needed to send only a modest

sized force to the Gulf. Also, the overall projected numbers of the Armed
Forces were: 116,000 for the Army – 50,000 below the authorised strength at
present, the lowest figure for the British Army ever, and even 4,000 less than
was announced last July, when the world did not look as uncertain as it does
today. The number of frigates and particularly submarines is far less even than
in the heyday of what was considered to be Sir John Nott's assault on the
Navy and when the Soviet naval threat which is not dependent on the Warsaw
Pact is still *in situ*. There is the reduced number of aircraft when the Gulf War
demonstrates the crucial part which is played in combat by aircraft. Finally,
the number of Army combat units is not yet officially announced, but is said
to involve swingeing cuts of up to fifty per cent.

These figures have all been arrived at far more from what could be
squeezed into an arbitrary financial ceiling, with the Treasury well in the lead
and calling the shots, and with an apparent desire to have equal misery for all,
than from an analysis of what will be required by our ongoing commitments.
They include the only recently established dispositions and deployments
agreed by NATO; Northern Ireland, where there is acute infantry over-
stretch; and all the other uncertainties, in Eastern Europe, the Middle East
and the Far East, which bedevil the world scene. I say that as one who, in the
debate last year, warned your Lordships' House about the imminent dangers
in the Middle East.

Of course, there must be compromise. Savings emanating from the reduction of our forward forces in Germany and Berlin can and must be made.
However, if there is not some alleviation of the present level of resources
which will bring them more into line with our up-to-date commitments, and
if there is no end to the present blight on decisions on new equipment, such as
the obsolete Chieftain replacement – the noble Lord, Lord Trefgarne,[76] has
dealt with this extremely well and comprehensively – we shall end up for sure
not with smaller but better Armed Forces as promised, but with smaller forces
equally overstretched and equally underfunded. They will therefore be generally less effective than at present. As an example, I seriously question whether,
with only 116,000 in the Army, we can properly sustain operationally and
logistically the formations and units which are now apparently required by
NATO and our other commitments in the 1990s.

I hope that in the White Paper the Government will not ignore the lessons
of the past which have been pointed out in the debate. Earlier governments,
seduced by the same prospect of easing tension and the absence of any immediately definable threat, cut our operational capability so badly that when
crisis and even mortal danger loomed but a short time later, as the noble
Lord, Lord Boyd-Carpenter,[77] pointed out, we were nearly in no position to
recover or cope. It is well to remember that the quality of men and equipment

and the professionalism that goes with them that we saw in the Falklands and again in the Gulf is not something which can be manufactured overnight. It cannot be turned off for long periods and then switched on again at the drop of a hat as if nothing had happened. It needs to be nurtured. It needs a certain amount of tradition, stability and *esprit de corps*. It needs the confidence and professionalism that can only come from a credible capability and the self-respect of those who know they are appreciated.

I wish to make two further points. First, I hope the Government will not forget the great value that is provided at an extremely low cost by many units of the Territorial Army and other reserve forces. The noble Viscount has just reminded us of that fact. They can produce valuable reserves and reinforcements in an emergency, as we saw in the Gulf, when over 1,000 individual volunteers offered their services, mostly for the medical services. However, I believe a great opportunity was missed in not calling out a certain number of actual units or sub-units in the Gulf or in Germany. That would have achieved so much in terms of motivation and retention.

The reserve forces can also provide vital links and routes for the regular forces into the civilian community with mutual advantages in both directions. With some help from the regulars – extra outlets may be needed in that respect – they can make a real contribution to our defence effort. It would be a sad day if the Government failed to tap to the maximum recruitable extent this volunteer spirit for which this country is famous. Indeed, historical precedent shows that as regular forces are reduced, reserve forces are needed more and not less. We await with interest any Government announcement on this point.

While I am on the question of reserves, I sincerely hope the Government will not feel obliged to go back on their solemn undertaking to maintain a role in the British Army at a viable level for the Brigade of Gurkhas after 1997 when their essential role in Hong Kong comes to an end. I am sorry that the noble Lord, Lord Boyd-Carpenter, is not in his place at the moment. Not only does this country owe the hillmen of Nepal a quite unique debt of gratitude for all the times they have rallied to our country's side in our darkest hours and sacrificed their lives in large numbers, but they also remain some of the finest fighting men in the world. They are also a marvellous source – provided we maintain the connection – of virtually unlimited recruitment. Looking ahead to some inevitable disenchantment in our own recruiting, and in any case to a disturbingly disadvantageous demographic trend, the Gurkhas may prove invaluable to us in the years ahead. If they have to remain outside the numbers ordained for the infantry, so be it. Some of the funding for the Gurkhas is already outside the Defence Vote. I believe there are few roles worldwide they could not undertake with distinction. However, I am not sure that the story about severed heads will do the image of the Gurkhas much good with the civil servants of Whitehall. Even if that story is a little exaggerated, their reputation preceded them in the Falklands and enabled them to use minimum force when the time came. The Gurkhas constitute a formidable weapon and their reputation does no harm as it serves as a useful deterrent.

Secondly, if, after a proper assessment of commitments and of the effect that the stretching of resources will have on the Services and on redundancies – and as I have said already, I am not yet convinced that such an assessment has been properly carried out – the Government are prepared to take the responsibility for reducing our none too lavish combat units, I hope they will have the courage (such a step will take some courage as it is no good just passing the buck to the military) to stand by the Services if it makes military sense. I further hope that the Government will have the courage to produce a new organisational structure for the regular Army which is in tune with the future and which will enable that Army easily to produce full-strength units in an emergency. Such a policy can also be linked to some extent to regimental centres where families can congregate, buy houses and consistently educate their children. Such a practice is much more common in the Royal Navy and the Royal Air Force.

The regimental system with which the fighting soldier can proudly identify is important, as the Secretary of State recognised. It provides a mainspring of pride, loyalty and motivation which in peacetime makes the Army an altogether more interesting and congenial place in which to serve. That is soon to be a very important factor. In war the regimental system inspires men to even greater efforts of fortitude and endurance.

A vibrant regimental system need not depend on sticking willy-nilly to one particular title or cap-badge at one particular moment in history. If that had been the case, we would have destroyed that system many times over in the past three centuries. What are required now, perhaps more than ever, are regimental organisations which are still small enough to have a definable natural ethos of their own in terms of pedigree, regional loyalty or professional specialisation, and thus may still mean something rather special and unique to the front-line soldier from the moment he joins his depot or training centre. At the same time, regimental organisations should be large enough in terms of numbers of units within them to be able, whatever the future holds, to produce units which can provide the maximum motivation for those who serve in them and are ready for action in all respects. I believe there is scope for some positive thinking in this direction, even if the merging, let alone the disbanding, of smaller units will cause great distress, particularly among the retired. The salvation of some of the older titles in the Territorial Army may well be an excellent solution to this problem.

At the end of the day what the young want more than anything else is a proper job of work to do, a credible role and the opportunity to be part of or to command full-strength squadrons, companies, troops and platoons inside well equipped, viable units which can generate real spirit and are manifestly ready for anything. If there have to be fewer combat units – I hope the cuts will be kept to a minimum – I hope that there will be larger but more viable regiments. As a non-Guardsman, I view with absolute horror the possibility that such a famous and magnificent regiment as the Grenadier Guards might lose its second battalion when I personally believe that no infantry regiment should have fewer than two battalions. I also view with horror the possibility that the outstandingly well trained and effective Parachute Regiment should be reduced in number merely to bring it into line with other regiments. Let us try to reinforce success and not penalise it.

I hardly have to remind this House that in the past forty years the Armed Forces of the Crown have been needed in one form or another on a remarkable number of occasions. To say that they have never let the country down is an understatement; indeed, they have made an immense contribution not only to national and European security and British interests abroad but also, and increasingly, to disaster relief in many forms. Disaster relief is a topical matter. Our Armed Forces have also made a contribution to the economic life of this country and to fuller employment.

Moreover, there can be few if any national institutions which have so well preserved their reputation and integrity in the eyes of the public, many of which look to the Armed Forces as one of the real jewels in the national crown. It would be sad indeed if the only perceived reward for many thousands of men and women after all this – perhaps 10,000 to 15,000 in the Army and many others in the other Services over and above normal wastage – was to be deposited on a highly-depressed labour market with a redundancy payment which could barely meet the deposit on a house, certainly in the South-East. No patriotic citizen could wish to see that happen.

Although no one likes paying insurance premiums – that is what defence expenditure amounts to – and we bitterly resent doing so when everything seems quiet; when the winds blow and the floods come or there is a spate of burglaries or we experience the worst winter for five years, how glad we are that we did not default on our premiums. When we reflect on the effect there might have been on our country's social development and economy if our defence arrangements had gone wrong or had been unreliable over the past forty-five years, or if we had not had forty years of comparative peace in Europe, and if our military intervention in the Falklands and the Gulf had ended in disaster, we must conclude that these premiums are well worth keeping up.

(c) Commitments and resources

On 10 February 1993 Bramall spoke in the House of Lords on military commitments and resources, a theme he had taken up before, and was to again.

My Lords, this debate is extremely timely, not least because the Government's pre-emptive strike last week, although welcome, still left many key questions unanswered. It is absolutely right that commitments and resources should be discussed in tandem. The more one feels obliged to reduce one's defence expenditure in search of a 'peace dividend', even though the world has become anything but peaceful, the greater must be one's restraint on the military commitment that one maintains, let alone takes on, and the less one must be prepared to carry weight and exert influence in many areas of international affairs.

On the other hand, if it is felt that Britain's somewhat unique experience, and particularly our seat on the Security Council, makes it difficult to refuse certain obligations and involvements in the cause of international safety, then proper and adequate resources ought to be set aside to sustain the forces which will be needed. Like love and marriage, commitments and resources should go together. I mean, of course, real resources in financial terms, not just those that rob Peter to pay Paul. And if your Lordships accept my second premise, it is no good going on saying as the Secretary of State[78] said in his statement in another place – I only hope with his fingers firmly crossed – that, 'The judgements made in Options for Change remain valid.' If we want to retain our international role and seat on the Security Council, they almost certainly will not remain valid and, indeed, many of the assumptions made in that document have proved inaccurate.

Let us look at resources. There, of course, the cat is out of the bag. No one is denying that the Armed Forces, and particularly the Army, are unacceptably stretched for their everyday commitments; let alone having enough in reserve for emergencies. The Select Committee's report is critical of the Government's part in allowing that state of affairs to develop, which may have accounted for the timing of the recent statement agreeing to do something to alleviate the Army's manpower situation to the extent of two extra battalions, a 3,000 increase in the manpower ceiling and 2,000 redeployed into the Infantry from who knows where.

As far as it went I welcomed that statement, and rejoice for those who now see their proud regiments retained, even though I have to say that there will still be many deserving cases of quality throughout the Army – not least the

Brigade of Ghurkhas and the large regiments who are so infinitely better organised to face the future than single battalion regiments – who will feel correspondingly resentful and aggrieved.

But, leaving sentiment aside, that modest recognition of reality raises two important points. First, bearing in mind the glaring shortcomings of all peace-time establishments, particularly but not exclusively in the Infantry, I very much doubt if raising the ceiling by only 3,000 will be sufficient to support and maintain those extra battalions and the other two, which at the last moment were put into Options for Change without any extra manpower. I believe that we need at least double that number and if I am right all that will happen is that we will end up with extra cap badges but with the units themselves still inadequately manned for the tasks that they have to do.

My second point concerns the Right Honourable gentleman's statement that the cost of any additional manpower must be met not just from within the original Options for Change financial projection, which was severe enough; but within the much lower still financial provisions of the Autumn Statement of 1992. That means that the Government are not finding extra resources to meet increased and unplanned commitments. In fact, they are continuing to take them away even faster. They are merely shifting £80m from one part of the highly-stretched budget to another. It is all being done by mirrors.

We are entitled to know from where that money is likely to come. Will it come from the Royal Navy? That is a Service which perhaps more than any other is ideal for projecting power and bargaining clout to any crisis area, as we have seen in the South Atlantic, the Gulf and now the Adriatic, and where some degree of amphibiosity is essential to the flexibility that that Service provides. Perhaps it will come from the Royal Air Force, without which, as the Gulf War showed, our ground and naval forces cannot operate, in any conflict worthy of the name, without an unacceptable degree of risk, and whose Tornado force provides a unique, highly specialised – to pick up the point of my noble and gallant friend – and professional element in any United Nations or international task force.

I believe, as some other noble Lords I am sure would agree, that it could come from our more than adequate nuclear capacity. But sadly, if we keep anything worthwhile at all, the savings cannot be great in the shorter term. Or will the funds come from the Army, grasping at the ages old panacea of 'cutting the tail to strengthen the teeth'? There might have been something in that, if we had not been doing that for the past twenty-five years. I say that with some feeling having been involved, up until Options for Change, in every reorganisation in that period.

It is therefore my judgement that those things that we can, in financial terms, obtain from headquarters – the logistical and medical services, military music and the training machine – are all trifling compared with what we need elsewhere if we are to continue to play our part on the world scene.

That brings me to a final word on commitments. I am certainly not one to suggest that we should rush into military involvements when they are really none of our business, when our national interests are not involved, when there is no clear political objective and when military action would not work anyway. There is also much to command respect in the Foreign Secretary's[79] recent speech regarding Britain's interest in a safer world needing to be disciplined and constrained and more concentrated on the techniques of prevention.

But if, as he also said, there is a need [in] the international community for an effort comparable to that in the years after 1945 if we are to avoid a slide into disorganised chaos, then Britain should play its part and some commitments will be inescapable. If we are not careful we could be in danger of deciding our foreign policy initiative not so much on what serves best our international relations and national interest and what is achievable in military terms, but on paper plans instigated by medium grade officials heavily influenced by the Treasury over three years ago when the world scene and prospects for stability looked very different from the way they look today.

If the Cabinet cannot produce more resources or at least stop taking them away, then they must shed commitments and have the courage to do so. We must do something about Ireland. When I was the CGS, in Ireland we had 9,000 men stationed there; there are now 19,000. For whatever reason, if those commitments cannot be shed or refused – and I think that is more likely – and as a result the Armed Forces continue to be over-stretched, then it is equally their duty to obtain more real resources to correct the situation on the perfectly logical basis that the assumptions and judgements on which Options for Change was drawn up three years ago are today no longer valid.

Chapter 17

Military Strategy

(a) The military dimensions of foreign policy

In 1998 Bramall was asked to lead a discussion at All Souls' College, Oxford. The invitation came at the behest of Professor Sir Michael Howard,[80] *who was present and who had warmly commended Bramall's thesis at the I.D.C.*

I have been asked to lead this discussion on the Military Dimension of our Foreign Policy.

I will, of course, endeavour to draw on nearly eight years in or around the Chiefs of Staff Committee, from early 1978 to the end of 1985 and some earlier experience working for Lord Mountbatten when he was Chief of the Defence Staff over a quarter a century ago, and for Monty fifteen years before that, but I only hope that my personal thoughts will not be held, particularly in this tabernacle of learning and original thought, to be set on too low an intellectual plane; because you know that old story about the man who was recommended by a surgeon to have a brain transplant, which the wonders of modern science and medicine could apparently now perform, although it would be very expensive. When the would-be patient asked how much it would cost, he was told it all depended on what type of brain he wanted; for instance, he could have a legal brain for £10,000, or an academic's brain for £15,000, or an Army officer's brain for £25,000.

'That's preposterous,' the indignant patient said, 'An Army officer's brain cannot cost nearly twice as much as an academic's.'

'Oh, yes,' was the reply. 'You see, it's as good as new; it has never been used!'

So, don't expect too much.

I suppose the first thing I ought to try to establish is whether the Foreign Policy of any country, but particularly of this country, directs military strategy or whether the military and defence dimensions are the predominant factor in formulating that Foreign Policy – a classical chicken and egg situation. Well, of course there is no clear-cut answer. One would, of course, imagine that a country makes its Foreign Policy through whatever processes are traditional to it, and the military strategy is then developed from it; and you may be able to recall certain instances in modern history which could, I suppose, illustrate this – a final realisation after Munich in 1938 that the challenge of Hitler's doctrine and expansionist aims could no longer be ignored and that a stand had to be made involving a declaration of war if Poland was to be invaded, even though our military strategy to give effect to it, in terms of troops, or their peripheral and imperfect deployment was still unformed and undecided, and anyway, much lacking in resources and strength. Then the decision in the West in 1946–7, that despite being Allies in World War II, and no doubt with the implications of Yalta and Potsdam in mind, Stalinist Russia and its satellites posed a direct and worldwide threat to democratic freedom throughout the world. More recently, the Labour Government's decision in the late 1970s to withdraw military forces and bases from east of Suez, and take whatever military consequences there might be; in fact, there were very little.

But very often policy parameters change so rapidly, either because of quite unexpected hostile actions, or uncompromising opposition in Parliament to a government's declared attitude, or unexpected pleading of Allies or international bodies, or sometimes a combination of all three, that it is difficult to tell whether Foreign Policy is leading Defence, or the other way round: the Korean War, the Brunei Revolt, our presence in Belize and, of course, the Falklands War are good examples of where political parameters have changed almost overnight and a new line of defence strategy has suddenly emerged, which, for a time at any rate, has governed and forced the hand of Foreign Policy.

So I think it would be more helpful to suspend judgement on the chicken and the egg, and concentrate instead on the various constant, or at least, recurring factors on which British Defence Policy has been, and as far as I can judge, continues to be based.

First, there is always an element of 'We're here, because we're here, because we're here.' For, when you analyse it, all government machinery tends to be designed to protect Ministers from trouble and pitfalls and rough rides in Parliament, of the sort that are likely to be involved in any leap into the unknown and a rapid change of direction. The status quo and solid precedent are much safer, and the 'Yes Minister' brigade try to ensure there is not too much deviation from them. Of course, Mrs Thatcher has adopted, and certainly in some areas, a much more adventurous type of policy in Government, but even she, once a particular part of a policy has had to be defended and justified in political terms, in her case quite belligerently, finds it difficult to change direction radically, without being accused by her opponents of having got it all wrong, and having led Britain up the wrong, perhaps even the garden, path. A good example of this is [that] the so-called Independent Nuclear Deterrent, whatever its advantages and disadvantages (and I happen to think that the former – the advantages – still outweigh the latter), has rather become set in concrete, until it is eventually past the point of no return, and set in that way, as much for political as military reasons; and certainly the offshoot policy of US-based Cruise Missiles (now removed by the zero-zero INF agreement) was rushed through the Corridors of Power with very little considered military input, even though it may have achieved its political purpose.

Of course, the new Soviet attitudes to defence matters must be starting to have influence on our thinking, as must the West Germans' changing attitude to *Ostpolitik* and NATO, but old habits do die hard.

Then, secondly, there is that most compelling and understandable of all factors – the unfortunate experiences and lessons learned so painfully at the start of the two World Wars (1914 and 1939) when dithering and lack of United States commitment and, in the 1920s and 1930s, totally inadequate resources for Defence, and unilateral disarmament and appeasement actually encouraged aggression by the dictators, even, it must be remembered, from their position of military inferiority. So this experience quickly led, after World War II, to the political as well as the military view that the only way to secure peace with honour and ensure that territorial integrity and political freedom remained unimpaired was by a Collective Defence, which essentially included the United States, not present before, credible shop window conventional forces, at least to guard against surprise attack and indicate a readiness and a commitment, like a burglar alarm, lacking last time; and, manifestly linked to these, background nuclear weapons, which were able, after Hiroshima and Nagasaki, to constitute a far greater restraint and more powerful argument against aggression than had been at all possible in 1914 and 1939.

Where we did not practise what we preached (as in the far away Falklands), where there was no *in situ* deterrent at all, our territorial integrity was impaired, and we were forced to fight to get it back (which could have proved extremely difficult).

In that overall concept of graduated Deterrence in Europe, the conventional/nuclear linkage and balance came to be varied over those forty years, as thinking about the relevance of nuclear weapons in actual conflict changed, and the overall strategic balance between the USA and the Soviet Union altered.

Early on, when the United States had complete nuclear superiority (i.e. in the 1950s and '60s), the West had no qualms about planning to threaten (and if necessary to fight) both a tactical and strategic nuclear battle. And in the 1960s, and in order to save money on conventional forces, this turned into a virtual trip-wire concept in which the conventional forces would have become little more than the means of identifying the extent and direction of aggression, before triggering off early and perhaps massive nuclear release.

But that all changed when the strategic balance between the United States and the Soviet Union became one of virtual parity, and people began to realise that while a spectrum of nuclear weapons could still be of great value for imposing restraint, at every level, and therefore keeping the peace and preventing someone else using these weapons on you, their value as a war-fighting weapon was highly doubtful, if not utterly useless. So, in the 1970s a strategy of Flexible Response was adopted which extended, although not indefinitely, the ability and intention to fight conventionally, and left it uncertain when and how you moved from conventional resistance to nuclear release.

Then in the 1980s this trend was continued to include the feeling that, within the inevitable financial stringency, you should, if anything, strengthen conventional capabilities still further, to enable the Alliance to have less reliance still on nuclear weapons and to give political leaders even more flexibility in their possible response to any aggression. Nuclear weapons would still be in the background to deter and even selectively to demonstrate, with dire warnings of worse to come, but today's concept, even without any significant strengthening of conventional forces, definitely presupposes that, if ever attacked, nuclear release would be later – certainly days, more likely weeks, rather than sooner – virtually hours, as in the '50s and '60s.

So while the theology, so to speak, of nuclear deterrence has been changing, little by little all the time, the presence of background nuclear weapons, in some form and in some numbers, and even when culled by the I.N.F. agreement[81] (because the surfeit or overkill had been up to then immense) has been said [to be], and still for the time being remains, a main pillar of NATO strategy, for the simple reason that they are still thought to be fundamental to the most comprehensive and compelling deterrent to a military option ever being used in Europe.

You could agree that with the Middle East so volatile and increasingly dangerous for miscalculated Superpower confrontation; with Europe still the key area in any ongoing ideological competition and struggle; with the undoubted numerical superiority and technological potential of the Warsaw Pact, including chemical weapons (although certain proposals are in the offing), as yet undented by any balanced force reductions, and perhaps even with Mr Gorbachev still walking a bit of a tight-rope between presiding over sweeping reforms and changes of attitude, or being committed to oblivion, NATO and its supporters can hardly do less. Not, if we are to go on facing the future from a basis of continued confidence and indulge in 'meaningful' negotiations from a position of strength. And, incidentally, that it would not be safe to do anything which would risk throwing away perhaps the greatest advantage of all that we have today over 1914 and 1939 – a firm US commitment to Europe, underlined not so much by its nuclear weapons on European territory, as by its ever ready 300,000 odd soldiers, who would from Day One be in the forefront of any battle.

The next, the third, factor takes into account the undeniable historical experience that whereas Europe remains potentially because of sheer mathematics the area of greatest threat, it is events outside the NATO area, directly or indirectly affecting British interests, which are more likely to concern or embarrass our government and thus require them to deploy military forces in some capacity – prophylactic, pre-emptive or reactive; and our military history is littered with such examples, even after, or discounting, withdrawal from Empire: Korea, Brunei, Borneo, Oman, Cyprus, Lebanon, Rhodesia now Zimbabwe, Belize and of course the Falklands and, more recently, the Gulf. So while maintaining our contribution to the Atlantic Alliance, both in Central Europe where the 1st British Corps is the lynch pin of the whole framework and in the maritime areas, on and over the Norwegian Sea, where Britain provides the advance guard and screen to US Sea and Air power, the British Armed Forces, unlike, say, their German, Dutch and Norwegian counterparts, have to be ready to be deployed overseas, backed by quickly reacting forces, which can be moved and if necessary inserted by sea.

'Send a gunboat' is still a powerful instinct in any Prime Minister's repertoire, whatever his or her political persuasion, if they have aspirations for their own country's influence and for their own clout and prestige as a national and international statesman. Nor is it much good the Military turning round after a period of financial stringency and saying (and the Falklands would have been a good case in point), 'I am sorry, Prime Minister, but owing to the financial cuts and pruning down, we have had to cut this and that out of our Order of Battle of lower priority than NATO, so we are no longer in a position to react in the way you want, even though we accept it makes political and diplomatic sense.'

Because the Prime Minister would merely say, 'Bloody Hell', or words to that effect, 'We still spend x-billion pounds (over 19 billion at the last count) on Defence and when we want something out of it and require to use it, you say it can't be done. Ridiculous – get on with it!'

So Britain has to look both ways (four ways if you count nuclear and home defence) and that itself is very expensive.

This brings me on to the fourth factor which, in long periods of peace, is perhaps the most compelling of all, because it affects all the others. This, of course, is the financial factor in which it has to be recognised that by and large (and certainly this can be confirmed for the years since World War II; before that it was even worse, whether the Chancellor was Churchill or Neville Chamberlain) there is only a limited amount of money, as measured as a percentage of the GDP, which Parliament is prepared to allocate to the Defence of the Realm, and that is never quite enough to meet properly all the commitments which Parliament equally expects and insists that Britain should undertake. There are times when expenditure is marginally up, as at the time of the Korean War in the early '50s, and during and in the aftermath of the Falklands War (money being no object during the campaign itself), and when, largely because of that campaign and its legacy, the government was able to point to seven years of sustained growth between 1979 and 1986, averaging out at 3 per cent real growth per annum. And then there are times, as in the 1970s and now the late 1980s, when there is clearly a marginal decline.

Generally speaking, however, the expenditure line at constant prices is pretty level. Nor does it seem to make that much difference (or it has not done in the past) which party is in power. This is not only because there used to be, up until the end of the 1970s, a bi-partisan Defence Policy (and who knows, [there] may be again), but rather because of the various political swings and roundabouts. The Conservatives, as you know, like to be thought strong on Defence and are bullish in their approach to commitments and upholding British interests and prestige, but they are equally (at least under Mrs Thatcher) very tight monetarists with a very close hold on public expenditure. So while raising expectations and never shirking commitments, they tend to give the Treasury *carte blanche* over constricting cash flow in the short term, thus depressing start points for future calculations and generally reducing the percentage of GDP spent on Defence, as in all other public expenditure.

With Defence manpower now so expensive, even though very considerably cut, and sophisticated defence equipment to meet a potential threat so liable to be ahead of inflation, such constraints invariably have serious repercussions on the Defence programme both in the short and longer term, involving an even greater squeeze on manpower, considerable reduction in activity, which is the only area where cash can be saved in a hurry, and both of which affect standards of professionalism, and considerable slippage of in-service dates for new equipment past its effective date, while running on of old and obsolescent equipment; all leading to pressures for a Defence Review, which no Conservative likes because it looks as if they are not fulfilling their promises.

Labour, on the other hand, although they always tend to be bearish about Defence commitments, perhaps in deference to their left wing, and not averse to swingeing Defence Reviews, are also much more free and easy with public expenditure, and since Whitehall and Parliament rather take the view that what is sauce for the goose is sauce for the gander, some of it spills over on to

Defence. So, under Labour, the money supply to Defence has often, para-doxically, been more nearly matched to the, albeit lower, expectations and the reducing commitments, and was often in advance of what political statements on the subject would have led people to believe.

But this evening-out has only meant that Defence housekeeping is invari-ably a question (however much value for money is sought) of squeezing a quart-size set of commitments – including up to now a credible shop window land and air presence on the Continent, a 50-frigate Navy both for our own Lines of Communication and for the Northern Flank, and for out-of-area (outside NATO) operations, such as the Gulf, a small strategic reserve for rapid deployment, and improved Home Defence, particularly in the air, and garrisons in the Falklands, Belize, Cyprus, Borneo, still Gibraltar, and until 1997, Hong Kong, and of course, a new nuclear deterrent and even perhaps a modernised air-delivered nuclear weapon – all these into a pint pot of resources which becomes increasingly difficult, particularly as once again the pint pot is shrinking.

The trouble with the apparently obvious panacea for all this – a Defence Review which would either scrap commitments, as Denis Healey did, or a capability, as John Nott wanted to do – is that the choices which are open, which would be worthwhile in terms of savings, are so appallingly difficult to make, and if selected on military grounds are often contradicted by other political factors. Moreover, the architect of such a review, faced with such choices, can often be wrong, and be frequently proved to be so at a later date, as happened pretty quickly with John Nott.

One of the choices, although it would not save as much money as people imagine, would be the nuclear or non-nuclear one. This raises the whole question of whether Trident is really necessary, and even if it is, whether it is affordable. I have already said something about the somewhat entrenched political position on this, but, in any case, with the USA so committed to nuclear arms reductions (which, I may say, I heartily approve of because it to some extent lances the boil of real concern and alarm about the escalation of the nuclear arms race), it could be argued that Britain's Trident is even more important than ever. It provides a second European point of decision, thus complicating any aggressor's decision-making calculations, and it ties down more clearly the US commitment to Europe, whatever differences there may be in perception. It also means a real say in the use or non-use of nuclear weapons generally, and in their mutual reduction. Above all, it is that ultimate insurance that if deterrence should fail and conventional hostilities were to break out – which God forbid – and we were in that twilight period in which governments and Alliances were having to decide when and how and where to use nuclear weapons and/or bring the war to an end as quickly as possible, under not too disadvantageous circumstances, wherever else nuclear weapons were to be dropped initially, it would not be on this country because the capability for subsequent retaliation would be too great.

An expensive insurance, no doubt, but then all comprehensive insurances are, as we know in our own homes. Finally, it would not leave nuclear deterrence and the nuclear defence of Europe exclusively to the French, and who would want to do that?

Speaking of France and Europe reminds me of that rather neat if cynical definition of Heaven and Hell: 'Heaven is where the police are run by the British, the mechanics are German, the cooks are French, the lovers are Italian, and the whole thing is organised by the Swiss; Hell is where the police are run by the Germans, the mechanics are French, the cooks are British, the lovers are Swiss, and the whole thing is chaotically disorganised by the Italians.'

Be that as it may, the other choices are equally difficult. NATO requirements versus mobile forces for the rest of the world (if indeed there is a clash) ignores the facts, as I have said, that whereas NATO may face potentially the greatest threat, it is the one that is least likely to happen, and that the commonest threat of all, and the one most likely to embarrass a government and cause them to deploy forces, is the unexpected. While the choice between Central Europe and the maritime commitment involves largely unacceptable political ramifications. We are an island power and we can hardly cut our Navy below the reduced level engineered by John Nott, without wrecking the whole of NATO strategy for Forward Defence and deterrence in the Norwegian Sea and on the Northern Flank, and being unable to operate in the Gulf or elsewhere, while to pull BAOR out of the 65 miles of front allocated to them would remove a key brick from the NATO alliance and encourage others to do likewise.

So, salami-slicing, while keeping a framework of general capability, may well be the wisest and safest as well as the easiest course. At least, the capability can be quickly built upon if tension rose and the threat increased; while if you remove a complete capability you cannot rebuild it up for many, many years, and before that you may need it politically or militarily. The 1930s showed us that. But these dilemmas continually rear their heads as money becomes increasingly squeezed.

There is one final factor that you get very used to when working in Whitehall, and that is that Defence Policy is not exclusively, indeed perhaps not primarily, about defending the realm or exactly meeting military requirements and the commitments laid down in Foreign Policy. It is about sheer politics (and I am afraid this seems increasingly to apply to many other things as well). It is whether you want to be seen to be strong or whether you want to be seen to support certain strongly held beliefs in your own party, or whether you want to carry clout in international relations or reduce your spending percentage of GDP, or perhaps both at the same time. It is no good any military man not coming to terms with these realities. The best he can do is to massage military requirement and the political requirements and advantages as close together as possible; then doors, even Treasury doors, may gradually become open.

So, we return to what I said at the beginning about the relationship of Defence and Foreign Policy; and people ask me: who decides strategy in this country? Is it the Chiefs of Staff? I reply, from my own not inconsiderable experience, that they try to do so. They write papers, they assess threats and priorities where they can, and where the conflict with their own services' vested interests is not too great, they make agreed recommendations, but unless these are taken on board and given positive political approval they mean very little, and the status quo, barely modified, which is not often if there is no crisis, then goes quietly on.

What usually happens is that suddenly, as a result of something unexpected happening, the political parameters change overnight as they did in the Falklands, and then the whole machinery rushes into action on a new tack. I suppose in a democracy this is inevitable. Of course, we may stand today at a turning point or quantum leap, not so much as a result of an euphoric aftermath of the INF, or on what Mr Gorbachev may or may not achieve, but just as much due to a changed attitude in Europe, particularly in Germany, to the threat and future political groupings. We shall obviously proceed with caution on both sides of the political spectrum.

So these are the ingredients which go into the melting pot of a Defence and Foreign Policy – the military dimension if you like. It may not always seem a very rational way of going about it, but on the other hand, the achievements of that policy have not been insignificant. We probably have, for the last ten years or so, the best Armed Forces we have ever had in peacetime. We have had peace in Europe for forty years, which may not seem all that strange to some, but to my generation and my father's this represents no mean achievement. We have conducted an orderly withdrawal from Empire and we have won, or helped to win, restrict or contain innumerable small conflicts – in Korea, Malaya, Kenya, Oman, Borneo, and more recently, the Falklands, a particularly difficult operation – and we have participated in numerous peace-keeping operations in Cyprus, Sinai, Zimbabwe and Lebanon, which have brought this country considerable kudos and international prestige. It is a record of value for money. So, perhaps, we do get there in the end.

(b) A fully joined-up Strategic Defence and Security Review

This paper, written in May 2010, was intended as a 'vade mecum' of the Defence and Security thought processes needed to be followed through for the achievement of a fully joined-up Strategic Defence and Security Review. It was intended for circulation to those in both Houses of Parliament who were particularly concerned about the way that the Government went about tackling that long-awaited Review, and wished to probe and question it. It was also aimed at obtaining some sort of cross-party support for the nation's future Defence and Security policy.

National Interests

1. **National Security Strategy**. Because Foreign and Defence issues can no longer be separated from domestically-generated threats, and all events and actions abroad are interdependent with security at home, an effective and detailed Review must start with a National Security Strategy, linking all relevant parts of government and inspired by what can be agreed at the national level as the United Kingdom's true and abiding national interests. If this is to be achieved the first thing to be put in place is a new National Security Council which, having agreed on the national interests, can produce the assumptions (agreed at Cabinet level) against which a Defence and Security Review can properly take place.

2. **National Security Council**. This new committee, chaired by the Prime Minster, would become responsible for all national security policy decisions and would draw up the national security strategy. It would:

   (a) Replace any existing ministerial committee, active or moribund, (such as the Defence and Overseas Committee) on defence, security, international relations and development and civil contingencies.
   (b) Include Ministers of relevant Departments and, always in attendance, the Chief of Defence Staff and Chairman of JIC.
   (c) Be supported by its own Cabinet Office secretariat with at its head and chief of its staff, a National Security Adviser, and by a strengthened intelligence organisation.
   (d) Have the capacity to create inter-Departmental budgets.
   (e) Produce the firm assumptions on which the more detailed Review can be carried out.

3. **Considerations of factors**. However, the National Security Strategy is expressed on paper and before firm assumptions can be arrived at on which a Defence Review can be carried out, the following thought processes should be followed through.

4. **Basic commitments**. Among these must be included an acceptance of and involvement in some or all of the following basic commitments which would

include membership of international organisations and any other bi-lateral relationships, e.g.

(a) The continuation (appropriately resourced) of any current operations; and some assessment of how long these might last and at what strengths, i.e. in which way should we continue to re-focus our efforts in Afghanistan in the interests of stability and security?

(b) Home and European security, both from any external threat and from internal subversion and terrorism; and also, national resilience against disaster, natural or man-made. Some of these might require an enhanced Armed Forces involvement, particularly from the Reserves – especially in 2012!

(c) Protection of any remaining overseas Protectorates or Sovereign Base Areas and/or evacuation of UK citizens from overseas territories.

(d) Continued membership of NATO (with an updated strategy) to help European security and keep the USA interested and involved.

(e) Continued membership and furtherance of the European Union and the Commonwealth.

(f) Continued membership of the UN, with particularly a permanent seat on the Security Council and the extra obligations and responsibilities for peacekeeping, conflict prevention and resolution this imposes.

(g) Ability to trade with and/or protect vital energy supplies and freedom of the seas.

(h) Continuing commitment to curbing nuclear proliferation and eventually to achieving multilateral nuclear disarmament as soon as possible.

(j) Maximum support to any measures and initiatives likely to bring a fair and lasting peace in Palestine on the basis of a two-state solution – the key to Middle East security and stability.

5. Likely threats to international security and stability. Threats to international stability, and hence to this country's domestic security, could come from a wide variety of developments, such as climate change, globalisation, conflict between nations and ideologies, terrorism, subversion and organised criminal activities affecting national security, as well as from the proliferation of potentially hostile technologies, including cyber-attack. It might also come from small-scale aggression if the aggressor thought he could get away with it, to solve an ongoing political dispute. For the foreseeable future, however, threats to our national interests are most likely to come from those indirect forms of violence, such as subversion, international terrorism and possibly rogue attacks from the air (missile or aircraft), some of which could be difficult to predict.

6. Confronting the threats. These indirect threats would need to be confronted, deterred, contained and dealt with by the most effective means available, at a distance, as well as nearer to home. These could, in some cases should, include:

(a) Improving intelligence gathering by both security and intelligence services.

(b) Based on hard intelligence, selective pre-emption by agents, special forces or attack from the air.

(c) Helping friends with some common cause, in key areas, to help themselves, with aid, training and advice.

(d) Projection of military power in support of active diplomacy to provide deterrence to any would-be aggressor and thus prevent conflict.

(e) Humanitarian operations. These have in the past, and could in the future, include the relief of suffering in the wake of natural disasters; peace keeping between two sides which would in any dispute require mutual agreement between them, and peace enforcement when there has been abuse of an international agreement.

(f) Contributing politically, economically and, if necessarily, militarily to any international action to try to stabilise areas where terrorism is known to have roots or obtains inspiration and mainspring support.

(g) Expeditionary operations. Involvement in larger type expeditionary operations whether they be in self-defence, to recover territory illegally seized or to put right an internationally accepted wrong.

7. **Fundamental issues to be resolved**. Before going firm on, and attempting to prioritise the basic commitments, anticipated threats and possible response, there are some fundamental issues which ought to be examined and resolved:

(a) Is it accepted that the United Kingdom has a special position in the world, based on its reputation as an open, democratic society, as well as its membership of so many international organisations, and therefore has an ability to influence world events in the interests of stability? Our highly professional Armed Forces may lend added weight to this, if we are prepared to use those assets effectively.

(b) Should successive government commitments to a global foreign policy, in the interests of our influence and trade and the wider stability on which it depends, be continued, with an emphasis on strategic mobility and a global diplomatic presence?

(c) What role, if any, should national nuclear deterrence play, beyond the maximum life of TRIDENT, in the maintenance of our strategic commitments and the security of the United Kingdom and Europe? Could there be other more benign and economical ways of maintaining a psychological deterrent and uncertainty?

(d) How should affordability be measured, other than seeking to design appropriate solutions to the Review with cost-effectiveness very much in mind? Could a reasonable percentage of GDP provide a clue; or would it be left entirely to the Treasury to decide?

8. Other factors to be taken into account. There must be consideration of some other relevant factors which could influence the likelihood, extent, frequency and duration of any active operations involved in honouring commitments or containing threats. Among these are:

(a) The inherent volatility of the international scene which, in the past, has invariably produced responsibilities and political challenges utterly unpredictable in advance; thus, giving defence expenditure an element of being an insurance policy against eventualities over quite a wide range, including (although not on the scale envisaged during the Cold War era), some capability and equipment for war-fighting against a sophisticated enemy. The uncertain challenges ahead may still require some preparedness for less likely contingencies as well as optimising for the most likely ones. Particularly, equipment which may not be required for at least, say, ten years, may still require some design and development or be bought 'off the shelf' at a later date, probably from the USA and possibly cheaper, but at the expense of the nation's industrial base. Is this acceptable or is the maintenance of a comprehensive armaments industry still important?

(b) Military and Security Contributions we can reliably expect from our allies and partners which would help this country carry out any operational commitments and reduce the cost of our own involvement in them. Would it be practicable further to integrate our capabilities with those of key partners? If so, how?

(c) The part an Active Diplomacy does and should play in modern military operations, countering of threats and conflict prevention and resolution, justifying part of the FCO budget being considered in a strategic context.

(d) Economic and Political Restraints so fundamental that they need to be taken into account before any appropriate size and shape for our security forces have even been identified, let alone costed. Also, the effect of an expanding aid budget on the resources available for diplomatic and security expenditure, and the extent to which these should continue to be considered separately when development and security can only be inextricably linked.

(e) The Maritime Scene
   (i) Developments. There is likely to be more emphasis on freedom of the seas (not least piracy), power projection, strategic mobility and in any maritime warfare over (air and missile) and under the water operations and away from large scale open ocean warfare.
   (ii) Aircraft Carriers. Aviation ships are ideal for strategic mobility of aircraft and helicopters as well as providing a comparatively self-sufficient base for joint operations (amphibious or otherwise) at a distance, when because of geography, political sensitivities and indigenous threats similar facilities cannot be provided in any other way or at least not so quickly. For a variety of reasons two such ships would be ideal but two full Fleet Carriers and their essential protection can come very expensive to provide at a time when the whole defence and security programme is bound to be under intense pressure. Helicopters and VSTOL aircraft and command and control facilities could be moved and operated from smaller ships, but the more intense the operations, the more sophisticated the opposition, the more remote the conflict the more a full Fleet Carrier would be needed. As against this must be balanced the likelihood of such a conflict, certainly in the shorter term, the contribution any allies or partners even more strongly equipped in this field might make to support and enhance our own forces and the greater vulnerability of carriers compared with any land-based alternative, even with all its expensive protection.
   (iii) The Falkland Islands. A perceived continuing threat to the Falkland Islands could influence the precise balance of the Fleet, but the existence of the new airfield at Mount Pleasant, enabling it to reinforce quickly and operate high performance aircraft from it has transformed the situation, provided we can defend and hold it.

(f) The Land Battle. To prepare for any land battle certain issues could be crucial:
   (i) Full manning of establishments to curb over-stretch, invariably found in recent operations.
   (ii) Availability of a range of war-fighting equipment not only for urgent operations and training but as a basis for expansion in the event of a more sophisticated threat becoming more likely.
   (iii) Improved surveillance and intelligence gathering.
   (iv) Vehicle protection and adequate helicopter numbers for more secure mobile operations.
   (v) Greater range, lethality and precision of indirect fire weapons.
   (vi) Matching logistic and medical support for any forces deployed.

(g) <u>Air Space</u>. In any successful operation on land or at sea control of the air space could be critical. Improved ground-to-air defence weapons, the greater utility of powerful attack and anti-tank helicopters and the effectiveness of precision weapons launched from remotely controlled, pilotless aircraft may have altered the way the Air Space is used and controlled. Although any alliance will still need some counter-air capability, particularly to destroy aircraft on the ground, instances of air-to-air combat (dog-fights) will be fewer, which is likely to lead to some reduction in the number of piloted fast jets required, which in any case ought to have a dual capability. Other roles of the Air Arm – air transport for strategic mobility, logistic support and casualty evacuation, maritime aircraft to deal with any submarine threat and troop and supply-lifting helicopters may need an even higher priority.

(h) Any further developments in the <u>future character of conflict</u> and making war which may affect the application of force and the Principles of War, possible examples being:

  (i) <u>The greater complexity of war</u>, with the emphasis more on hearts and minds of people and on engaging closely with them rather than on gaining ground and destroying armies; and with much of war fought through the medium of the communication revolution. Even more, there is a need to recruit and train high level people who can learn quickly and be adaptable, becoming resilient and dedicated and are highly motivated. Training is vital and will require equipment to train in addition to that needed on operations.

  (ii) The strong advisability of trying to complete any <u>purely military</u> action in as short a period time, if it is not to attract often insurmountable follow-up problems.

  (iii) <u>Minimum force</u> may require maximum numbers.

  (iv) The importance of lengthy <u>post-war reconstruction</u> in any conflict planning, with again intense manpower implications.

  (v) <u>High Quality Personnel</u>. There is an even greater need for our Armed Forces to recruit and train high quality people who can learn quickly and be adaptable, become resilient and dedicated and are highly motivated. Training is vital and requires equipment with which to train as well as that earmarked for operations. The quality of our Armed Forces and the superb, selfless and dedicated way they carry out their complicated duties throw into sharp focus the need to maintain and continue to fund the Covenant which reflects the obligation the whole country has to their welfare.

(j) Greater Scrutiny from the media and the public, both at home and overseas, and the deepening attitude of the public and the international community towards the legality of conflict under international law. Possibly also is a greater awareness of the age old, albeit not binding, principles of a 'just war'.

(k) Any obligations to obtain as broad a consensus as possible, before any operations are embarked upon and, for any major operation, the authority or at least the approval, of the United Nations.

Decision Making

9. Assumptions. As a result of consideration of these and, perhaps, other factors by the National Security Council and the firm assumptions emanating from their resolution, the Strategic Defence and Security Review can, then and only then, go ahead.

10. Strategic Defence and Security Review. This would still be overseen by the National Security Council but should be carried out by its own Cabinet Office secretariat with strong input at official level from the FCO, the Chiefs of Staff (MOD) and Home Office, and be based on those assumptions (now agreed on by the Cabinet). The strategy itself must cover:

(a) Types of Operations which the Armed Forces and Security Forces may be required to continue or be prepared for, nationally or more likely as part of a coalition or alliance, from active diplomacy and peacekeeping, through peace enforcement up to larger expeditionary-type operations, whether these be in self-defence, to recover territory illegally seized, or to stabilise an area by force of arms. This would include an assessment of any limitations on such operations in terms of likelihood, size, frequency, concurrence and the contribution of others.

(b) In the interests of flexibility and economy the need for equipment as far as possible to have a multi-role value and for military units to have and acquire a dual capability for different types of operations.

(c) Any change in command and control which would quicken decision-making in Whitehall; speed up response time and effectiveness of the Armed Forces where they are needed, and make it more receptive to the requirements of Theatre-level plans, while maintaining clear cut chains of command and lines of responsibility.

(e) If, in the interests of economy, risks must be taken, in which area should they best fall.

11. Outcome. The outcome of the Review should be able to indicate the necessary capabilities required for the most likely operations, current and future and, in broad terms, a size, shape and equipment range for the various forces to which the individual Departments would then fill in the details, including how much of the 'Covenant' is to be maintained. The Review should be subject to updating every five years. No major war in ten years was not an unreasonable planning assumption in 1922, but wholly irresponsible ten years later, when it was still in force.

Funding

12. The outcome would then, in negotiations with the Treasury, be funded across the board, not only of the three Services, but for the whole security field.

13. Once the requirements and funding have been reconciled at the overseeing National Security Council level, either as a finite amount for each Department or as a percentage of GDP, there must be an agreement by the Treasury to which it must adhere.

14. Final Thoughts. What must be avoided at all costs is the hitherto invariable undermining by under-funding by the Treasury of whatever has been decided at the highest political level which in the past has degraded expectations, minimised political and Parliamentary intentions, stored up endless trouble for the future and rebounded disastrously not only on operational performance but, very much so, on the lives, support and welfare of the men and women of our Armed Forces and their families.

Conclusions and Summary

15. Because of the changes in the international scene there is now an urgent need to set up a new top-level National Security Council, chaired by the Prime Minister, which would become responsible for all security decisions and, based on the United Kingdom's true and abiding interests, draw up an agreed (at Cabinet level) National Security Strategy. It would achieve this by considering in depth all the various factors which have a bearing on conflict in the modern world and on the threats and responsibilities which may face us in the short and long term. As a result of this consideration it would produce firm assumptions against which the long-awaited and more detailed Defence and Security Review can properly take place.

16. The National Security Council would be supported by its own Cabinet Office secretariat, with at its head a National Security Adviser, which would also carry out the Strategic Defence and Security Review with strong input, at official level, from the FCO, the Chiefs of Staff (MOD) and the Home Office.

17. This Review would include the types of operation to be prepared for, together with any limitations in terms of likelihood, size, frequency, concurrence and the contribution of others; the need for flexibility; and any changes in command and control or in the structure of the forces which might speed up their response time and effectiveness, make them even more adaptable and reduce overheads.

18. The outcome of the Review would include the necessary capabilities required and, in broad terms, a size, shape and equipment range for the various forces, to which the individual Departments would then fill in the details. It would also make clear whether and to what extent the vulnerable 'Covenant' was to be maintained.

19. All this would then, in negotiation with the Treasury, be funded, and once this and the requirements have been reconciled, if necessary at the overseeing National Security level, there must be agreement by the Treasury, to which it must adhere, instead of, as invariably in the past, undermining by underfunding whatever had been agreed at the highest political level.

20. The Review should be subject to updating every five years.

BRAMALL F.M.
May 2010.

(c) The Operational Scenario

In a paper written in 2016 entitled 'Military Strategy or the Operational Scenario and the Conditions for Operational Success in the 21st Century', Bramall explained his thinking about modern warfare.

The surest way of safeguarding international peace in the modern world is to arrive at and to maintain a reasonable balance of power between national blocs, ideologies and religious factions with which the nations of the world should have learned to live, without conceding vital national interests. Such a balance needs to be protected by dynamic diplomacy backed by military strength, but also by International Law under the watchful eye of the United Nations and its Security Council. There should also be potentially credible deterrence in place – military, technological and financial – to discourage anyone who wants to change that balance to their advantage by state- or bloc-led military action.

This together with other constraints on prolonged war fighting has undoubtedly cut the chances of inter-state war to a far greater degree than ever existed in the past. It certainly does not mean however that some sort of military conflict has become impossible. When consolidating a particular balance some countries and factions may presume that vital interests have been lost (as seen with the collapse of the Soviet Union). Events, *coups d'état*, and 'Arab Springs' may occur in one nation from which those outside may feel it is not in their interests to stand aside. Moreover, with all the constraints on inter-state war, there will be greater incentives to indulge in proxy-wars using irregular elements within an opposing confrontational bloc to tip its balance back towards what it had been before.

Nor would a balance of power, even if broadly acceptable, impose restraint on the ever-increasing extremism as terrorism which recognises no existing national boundaries, strikes internationally and whose aims and objectives are nebulous and obscure to say the least of it; but [which] will certainly require the use of military force to bring the threat under control.

Against this background, when our military strategy and operational scenarios need to be brought up to date in order to undertake appropriate military responses to new threats, it would be necessary to take account of various considerations and ask specific questions in order to come to sound and beneficial decisions. There are seven main questions requiring answers.

First, has proper consideration been given to the 'kind of war' (as Clausewitz put it) which would be embarked upon; has it been thought through to ascertain exactly what would be entailed and where it was likely to lead?

Secondly, would firm political and military aims be in place before any action was embarked upon?

Thirdly, would the action proposed be commensurate and proportional to the situation and any counter threat?

Fourthly, can the proposed military action be considered as being in a just cause and represented as such both nationally and internationally? The term 'Just Cause' is liable to differing interpretations according to the political and ideological leanings of the interpreter. From a legal point of view one would be on very safe ground with anything which can convincingly be construed as self-defence; wars undertaken in accordance with a UN Resolution agreed by its Security Council; or indeed, one conducted by an international coalition with its own indigenous base and UN approval. The term 'Just War' could not, I submit, be applied to the export of democracy, or for that matter Communism, or any other ideology or religion by military means; nor should it cover attempts to change a nation's regime or leadership from outside for political reasons. As the great Duke of Wellington remarked 200 years ago, 'The people of that country want to do it themselves, well and good, but to do it from outside is a terrible responsibility.' Only UN-recognised ethnic cleansing would justify operations to remove the leadership on a UN or coalition basis.

Fifthly, can sufficient resources in terms of finance, manpower and equipment be provided and made available for the operation or campaign to ensure a reasonable prospect of success? In this regard, a coalition would not only broaden international support but help to guarantee the resources needed.

Sixthly, would the tactical plan envisage and be able to execute a campaign which, in the words of Frederick the Great was 'quick and lively' and thus ensure a short war? This is essential in the modern world if the military action is not to bring on its back even greater problems, as has recently become obvious.

Finally, would the campaign bring about a more benign outcome?

Many of these considerations resemble the famous six considerations for a Just War laid down by St Thomas Aquinas in the Middle Ages and still, remarkably, today represent an appropriate checklist before embarking on armed conflict. Indeed, if satisfactory answers can be given to the seven questions, and if in consequence there is a good tactical plan which takes into account the eleven established Principles of war (including a new one, 'First win the Air Battle') and also cures the aftermath, then complete success is likely to be assured. All this was evident in two completely successful operations: the reoccupation of Kuwait after the Iraq invasion and the Falklands campaign to repossess the islands after the Argentine invasion.

In Kuwait, all the appropriate conditions had been met. It was a just war with wide international support. There was a clear-cut aim which was not deviated from. The United States had taken very positive steps to make available sufficient material resources within the coalition to ensure victory over a war experienced enemy. There was an excellent tactical plan, backed by credible deception to gain surprise; and the air battle had been won first. The result was a complete achievement of the aim in a very short land battle of under a week with hardly any coalition casualties.

The Falklands Campaign also met most of the conditions for success. The war-experienced High Command knew what would be required in combat power to achieve victory and how the battle was likely to develop, and sufficient resources in materiel and manpower were available to make this possible. It was a Just Cause in terms of self-defence and had adequate UN and international backing. The aim was clear and the tactical plan was sound. The only principle of war which could not militarily be met was the newest one: 'First win the Air Battle'. This was impossible because of the proximity of Argentine air bases; while for our Task Force air parity let alone air superiority could only be won (as indeed it was) during the campaign itself, by VSTOL aircraft on our naval carriers bobbing around in the poor weather of the South Atlantic, and by ground to air missiles and our defence systems once ashore in the landing area. This posed a greater degree of risk, particularly to the naval approach and landing, than would have been normally acceptable to this type of operation. The landing area of San Carlos Bay had however been carefully chosen to reduce these risks as far as possible and once ashore the ground troops would be far less vulnerable. Having assessed the risks accurately and bearing in mind the great potential of the tactical plan and the quality and morale of our forces to be able to overcome the opposition, the Chiefs of Staff advised the War Cabinet that the risks should be accepted and the landings should go ahead. This proved to be a good decision, for after a significant number of ships were lost, our superiority was by degrees won as the ground forces pushed forward with offensive operations to repossess the islands with the greatest vigour, dash and daring. The result was the complete achievement of the aim in a very short war.

So, whenever a campaign has been embarked upon or extended as a result of careful consideration of the relevant questions and principles, success should surely come. However, when this has not been done, preferring to be unduly influenced by imagined political advantages or media contrived transitory public opinion, such interventions are likely to turn out less satisfactorily, to say the least, with the obvious examples of Southern Afghanistan, Libya and Syria.

Chapter 18

Tactics in a Modern Operational Scenario

In 2016 Bramall wrote a paper on how the modern Army should be thinking tactically at low levels.

Introduction

1. The operational scenario in which British Forces may have to deploy and carry out appropriate tactics in order successfully to achieve the stated political and strategic aim can cover a wide spectrum of threats, terrain, climates and political and ideological environments. It may also involve our forces in varied degrees of levels and intensity of conflict. These include:

(a) Containment. This is the preservation of the Status Quo within an existing and tolerable balance of power, of which the most outstanding was the 'Cold War' of the period 1947–89. In that cause the ring was held by the strategy of Flexible Response with instantly available conventional forces manifestly backed up by a credible threat of nuclear retaliation. Since the end of a land threat to Central Europe, containment in other areas could still be carried out by [one of the following]:

(i) Peace-Keeping. This would become possible when both sides confronting one another were in sufficient agreement about a disputed area to allow a neutral power's forces under UN colours to act as a buffer between them.

(ii) Confrontation. This would occur when a border or line of contention became militarily active because one or both sides want to draw attention to their political cause, and even gain some positive military advantage from it. If some positive mutual agreement could be internationally brokered, Peace Keeping, or even Peace Enforcement Forces could then be brought in to calm things down.

(b) Revolutionary operations. Originating with Mao Tse Tung in China, the major ones have become linked to the readiness, or often reluctance, of Imperial Powers to withdraw from their Empires. It is now a useful generic term to cover the whole range of operations including the use of political and economic measures inside a country to weaken and overthrow an established government. It could then involve widespread civil disobedience, or general insurgency when the insurgent factor has the support of a large part of the population, and even if the terrain is suitable, guerrilla warfare. The latter, normally conducted by small bodies of largely indigenous irregulars with considerable local knowledge, which enables them to avoid pitched battles and ambush Security Forces where and when they are most vulnerable. This has taken on a new lease of life with the so-called Arab Spring.

(c) <u>Intervention operations</u>. British Forces might be required to take part in military intervention to help with the containment of conflict, peace keeping, countering certain revolutionary operations particularly those with wider international significance, or to defend or recapture countries whose integrity Britain has a national or international responsibility for safeguarding. Any British intervention, other than for self-defence will inevitably have been asked for by the threatened country and would be likely to form part of a wider coalition or alliance effort. Preparation and the readiness to act quickly with a small balanced force is the keynote to timely and effective intervention, which in Britain's case puts emphasis on a strategic reserve and its ability to move and introduce it over long distances by air or from the sea even in the face of some opposition.

(d) <u>Limited war</u>. Any of the above operations could develop into a conflict of wider international significance, in which formed bodies of regular troops get involved on both sides. It would then take on the character of Limited War. If this came about as an extension of revolutionary operations, when an all-out effort had to be made to avoid total defeat of the government threatened, it would probably have to be fought with the added complication of having no front or rear and with guerrilla activities over a wide area. Indeed, a blend of limited and guerrilla warfare may become a likely pattern for future conflict. Limited War would certainly come about as a result of overt aggression by one country against another sovereign state, and the need, nationally or internationally, to defend the threatened country or recover it if temporarily lost.

(e) <u>General war</u>. There is always a risk that open warfare, initially limited in geographical terms by the scale of forces that both sides can or are prepared to deploy, and the types of weapons available, might escalate into something infinitely more violent and widespread. However, with nuclear deterrents in place in many areas of the world and so many other constraints on prolonged war fighting, this has radically cut down the chances of fight-to-the-finish, inter-state wars, to a far greater degree than hitherto. Today, if military aims cannot be achieved in a short period of time, political effort must be tuned on to conflict resolution, before the consequences become too serious to contemplate.

Outside influences

2. The deployment and carrying out of military force has become more complicated because of extraneous influences, some of which are more compelling than they used to be in the past. There are four main ones:

(a) Nuclear weapons. Now quite widely held, these may still exert a restraining influence against any outbreak of limited war becoming more widespread. Nuclear weapons are however essentially a political weapon designed to set up compelling doubts in those who might have their eyes on too grandiose a military objective, or who might even contemplate a first use of such a weapon. They would have no part to play in the conduct of actual operations, nor affect the tactics employed if a nuclear weapon was ever to be used once conflict had started. It would bring all operations to a grinding halt and lead to immediate negotiations to suspend all hostilities while the priorities turned to humanitarian relief.

(b) Politics. While all forms of warfare may vary, a conflict of political policies is still the background to all military action, and military action can never be divorced from them. If operations are therefore to be conducted intelligently and successfully, the political aims must always be clearly stated and understood. In addition, a British military commander, even at a low level, must understand that in today's media-dominated world most of his activities are likely to be kept under continued political scrutiny and even pressure. Although no military commander should commit his troops to a plan which is militarily unsound, and should be prepared to put forward most strongly the implications of being pressed to do so, he must take account of any political requirements and see that the political aim is not prejudiced.

(c) Public opinion. This has increasingly become a strong strategic consideration and influence. Although governments may seek to lead public opinion they are often prone to follow it, particularly if it had to some extent been contrived and given wide expression by the media. It is clear and understandable that the public now expect to be informed about the reasons for entering any conflict, and equally important that any military operation should be portrayed both nationally and internationally in the best possible light, so that there can be the greatest possible public support for the Armed Forces, who would be risking their lives. A government must be proactive in getting the public behind the National Security strategy, including any initially less popular points.

(d) Legality. With more public concern about the deployment of British Armed Forces into conflict situations, a government is likely to be far more sensitive to the strict legalities of any planned military operation than was the case in the last century, when international law often, in reality, was based on what you could get away with. Today, a country is on the safest ground if any military action is in accordance with a UN Resolution, and has widespread international support, or, of course, is clearly a matter of self-defence. The criteria for a Just War, laid down by St Thomas Aquinas in the Middle Ages (and which include a Just Cause, proportionality, last resort and the prospect of success being followed by a more benign aftermath) remain a remarkably relevant check list as to what is appropriate and what is not.

Prerequisites for success

3. Any force taking the field to fight a tactical battle, as well as being properly organised and equipped should, if possible, have a measure of superiority over the enemy. It is not always necessary to be numerically stronger, helpful though that can be; but if it is not, this must be balanced by some other form of superiority in terms of skill and technical equipment. Military operations will then need to be conducted against certain principles which have been developed from the ten historic principles of war, which cover the conduct of war in its widest sense and are particularly applicable at the strategic level. At the tactical level when condensed and where necessary supplemented, they emerge as seven prerequisites for tactical success. These are:

(a) A clear aim. In every military operation, just as in the conduct of war as a whole, it is essential to select and clearly define the aim. The ultimate aim may be heavily circumscribed by political considerations, but each phase of the military campaign and each separate operation must have a more limited aim of its own. The selection of the aim is one of the commander's most important duties. It demands clear and logical thought and above all must be practicable with the forces at a commander's disposal.

(b) High morale. Success in war is as much dependent on morale as on material qualities. Maintaining a high morale fosters the offensive spirit and the will to win, and it will often decide the outcome of a battle. A high morale is based on confidence, discipline and self-respect and it must be present throughout the chain of command from its senior commander down to the private soldier. The best way to achieve it is by success in battle.

(c) <u>Accurate information</u>. The more accurate the information about the enemy and the exact localities and progress of own troops, the more likelihood there is that a battle plan once embarked upon will fully succeed. Indeed, in counter-revolutionary and insurgency operations little of real value will be achieved unless military action is based on accurate information. Up until the end of the nineteenth century a field commander could assess what was happening and where the enemy was making himself vulnerable, by reading the battle personally from a vantage point and giving direct orders to take advantage of the new opportunities offered. Nowadays he would have to rely on radio reports up the chain of command which are likely to take too long and are prone to inaccuracies; to personal liaison officers reporting back directly to him; to air and ground reconnaissance; and on other more clandestine sources. The information gained should, if possible, then be properly processed and the right questions asked before they can be answered on hard intelligence which a commander can use with the fullest confidence. Even then, he will still need to draw on his experience of what he knows of the character of the enemy to provide possible collateral and keep his plan flexible enough to compete with any enemy action which turns out to be largely unexpected.

(d) <u>Surprise</u>. This is probably the most powerful and effective influence on the conduct of a battle of all the principles of war. It confers the initiative, threatens the enemy morale, reduces own casualties and often gives material advantages consistent with superior concentration of force. When other factors are unfavourable success may depend almost entirely on it. So, commanders at every level must constantly seek ways to mystify and surprise the enemy. Surprise can be delivered in a variety of ways but at a tactical level it is more likely to come about by the indirect rather than by the direct approach. It is compounded from secrecy, concealment, deception, originality, audacity and speed to give an enemy insufficient time to recover from it and react effectively to it.

(e) <u>Sound administration</u>. Although administration (generally described as logistics) should be the servant and not the master of the tactical plan, it is often a deciding factor in assessing the feasibility of the operation and the practicability of the aim, particularly in regard to the momentum of an operation and how long and to what depth it can be sustained. No operation can therefore be wholly successful unless care is devoted to the logistic arrangements for putting it into effect. These must be flexible enough both to allow for the unforeseen and give the tactical commander as much freedom of action as possible. Without adequate logistical support morale will soon suffer.

(f) <u>A satisfactory air situation</u>. Although an army can survive and even achieve a limited degree of success in an unfavourable air situation, particularly if the terrain is very broken and overgrown, such a situation does much to destroy an Army's mobility, its capacity to obtain timely intelligence and its ability to concentrate quickly to deliver a decisive blow. An air situation which is at least not unfavourable and would allow air superiority to be won for short periods at the decisive time and place, is undoubtedly a prerequisite for tactical success; and the longer it can be maintained the greater advantage it will offer the side that achieves it, in terms of fire power and freedom of movement. Air superiority is best achieved by attacking enemy airfields and aircraft on the ground and cutting off fuel supplies, but it can be maintained by fighter cover with air to air missiles and surface to air missiles.

(g) <u>The maintenance of balance</u>. This is another key to success, because it enables a commander to allocate the correct proportion of effort between the security of his force, offensive action, including that devoted to the enemy rear areas, and the maintenance of a reserve which can reinforce success, develop a new thrust line or counter any surprise move by the enemy, or take advantage of a new opportunity to disadvantage the enemy. To achieve balance a commander will need to think ahead to the aftermath of the immediate engagement, to intelligent anticipatory movement, planning and preparation of logistic support and to the maintenance and, where necessary, the reforming of a reserve.

Tactical functions
4. Taking account of the principles and prerequisites for tactical success, a commander will be in the best possible position to carry out the four main tactical functions of **Protection**, **Striking**, **Movement** and **Fire**. One of these, **Firing**, as well as being ever present is often the most dominant and potentially battle-winning function. When **Protecting**, defensive positions, whether temporary or permanent, should be invariably supported by defensive fire tasks which can be instantly called down by Artillery (even Naval) Forward Observation Officers, and be of variable intensity, depending on their targets. Indeed, sometimes the quickest and most economical way of writing down an enemy strength is to seize some area which the enemy will be forced to counter-attack and then to bring down on him, when he is assembling, unprotected in the open, preparing to launch such an attack, massive pre-planned defensive fire.

When **Striking**, fire power will be needed to suppress and if possible destroy, enemy resistance in fixed defences and to counter and neutralise any enemy artillery batteries capable of bringing defensive fire down on our own attacking troops. While when **Manoeuvring** in close contact with the enemy it is advisable to have 'one leg on the ground' firing, or being ready to fire, while the other 'leg' moves to envelop him and bring even greater weight of fire to bear on him to destroy him. Manoeuvre connected with any break-through or pursuit will also require strong fire support particularly from the air to eliminate and throw into confusion any resistance points which might be ahead.

Indeed, once battle has been joined its successful execution will largely depend on the proper balance and close co-ordination of fire power – direct, indirect and air support – and the manoeuvre of the combat arms. It is there-fore vital to have really good professional organisation for the planning of fire support and the closest co-ordination with the troops on the ground.

Conclusion

5. It is easy enough to list the Principles. It is much more difficult to apply them, even to decide the relative weight that should be given to each and to judge how they could be affected by extraneous influences. Each tactical situation will impose its own variations and degrees to which the appropriate principles are modified and applied. It is here that the experience, judgement and flair of the tactical commander will come into their own. He will be faced with calculating and weighing them against the chances of success, and there will be times when boldness is certainly the right answer and others when it will pay better to be cautious. In tactics, as in so many other fields of activity, everything hinges on the aim. A commander must keep a completely clear mind about this and constantly remind himself what he is trying to do. He must then, in a positive, dynamic way, which makes the best use of the time available and does not let precious hours and minutes slip away in badly organised reconnaissance, ponderous orders groups and deployment, make appropriate plans for **Protecting**, **Striking** and **Manoeuvring**, all closely co-ordinated with flexible direct and indirect fire in order to achieve his aim.

Chapter 19

The Nuclear Weapons Issue

Although Bramall had been a firm supporter of our 'independent' nuclear deterrent throughout the Cold War, by the last part of the twentieth century he felt that the threats and faces of conflict had changed so radically that the whole philosophy of the deterrent should be looked at again before any firm decision was taken on a like-for-like replacement of Trident.

(a) House of Lords speech

On 27 January 2007 Bramall spoke in the House of Lords in a debate on the Armed Forces and the nuclear deterrent. The speech had gone through a number of drafts.

My Lords, the White Paper on continuing the United Kingdom's nuclear deterrent virtually presents Parliament with a *fait accompli*, with only a few details about the number of submarines, and whether, how and when we need to refurbish the ongoing D5 missiles, to be decided. With the world as dangerous and uncertain as it is, the future so unpredictable and some volatile regimes apparently intent on doing us or our friends harm, it is so easy to say that we would be mad to forego our own ultimate weapons system and must not do so – a widely held view, to which Her Majesty's Opposition has signed up. I feel, however, that my most useful contribution, in the interests of wider analysis and debate – until now conspicuously absent – is to act as devil's advocate to that view. There are a number of other factors which the Government should consider very seriously before, as the song of *The Good Soldier Švejk*[82] read, just keeping on keeping on, almost as if the world had not changed.

First, it is difficult to see how the United Kingdom can exert any leadership and influence on the implementation of the non-proliferation treaty – if that is what we and the rest of the world want and, essentially, need – if we insist on a successor to Trident that would preserve our own nuclear-power status well into the second half of the century. On the other hand, abandonment, even before Trident finally wasted out, could be seen as a bold and striking decision intended to show that this country is resolved to return to the position of moral and ethical standards for which it was once widely recognised – and seems largely to have forgotten recently – and to exert some real leadership in the modern world, as the Right Reverend Prelate mentioned. Some major international player must take a lead in this. While making a further 20 per cent reduction in superfluous warheads may be seen as a gesture in the right direction, it hardly compares with abandoning Trident in favour of properly funding our Armed Forces with what they need to meet the commitments laid upon them, so that they can act, in that much-vaunted phrase, as a force for good.

Secondly, even our present nuclear deterrent cannot be seen as being truly independent of the United States in any substantial or useful sense. It continuously relies on the United States for the provision of components for, and the regular servicing of, the D5 missiles (although not for the warheads or the building of the launching submarines); and above all for US information on key aspects of operations, such as communications for the accurate positioning of the launching submarines and the targeting of missiles. Certainly, this country has, in theory, complete freedom of action over giving the order to fire. It is, however, unthinkable that with a terror weapon which is virtually unusable because of its catastrophic consequences on guilty and innocent alike, it would ever be launched or seriously threatened by this country, itself so intensely vulnerable to such weapons, without the backing and underwriting of the somewhat less vulnerable United States, whose nuclear arsenal is more than amply adequate in weight and destructive power to underpin any security situation to which the United States would, at least in the mind of any adversary, be credibly committed. Our defence policy does not envisage undertaking any really major warlike operations other than those in conjunction with the United States, and even the possibility that such weapons might be brought into play would certainly envisage a potentially major war situation.

Indeed, my Lords, it is not easy to assign high probability to any scenario now discernible, in terms of specific actions and places, under which it would be necessary and important to have our own nuclear capability because the United States was not somehow involved. Even if grounds of unease about Russia's internal evolution intensify, as well they might, it is hard to imagine her remaining as a military threat to the political freedom of Europe and certainly not without the United States [being] deeply concerned. While in the Middle East the United States is, for well-rooted and obvious political reasons, at least as deeply engaged as any European country, and would certainly be the guarantor of Israel if any other Middle East country seriously threatened it; while should our country become vulnerable to nuclear blackmail by some terrorist group, it must be asked in what way and at whom could our nuclear weapons be used or threatened to deter or punish?

My Lords, our present nuclear weapons system has shown itself completely ineffective as a deterrent to the threats and violence we are currently facing, or most likely to face – particularly international terrorism. Indeed, the more you analyse it, the more unusable such a weapons system appears to be, except possibly, as Winston Churchill once said, as a 'voice from the grave', when it would have failed as a deterrent and would hardly matter. To use it on those who do not possess it would be to invite the outcry and indirect retribution of the whole world, while to do so on a nuclear power by a country the size of the UK would only be to indulge in mutual suicide.

The best thing you can say about our present nuclear deterrent, itself but a minute part of the Cold War balance of terror and which, despite what the White Paper boastfully claims, would probably not have altered the course of history had we not possessed it, is that now that it is in service and as long as it lasts to 2020 or even longer, the cost is comparatively not too great and would allow us to flaunt the satisfaction of being of premier league status, without wrecking other more usable parts of the defence programme.

So, the real problem is: can we afford it? A successor to Trident, bound, as the White Paper tells us it must be, to the existing submarine-launched missile is a very different matter. It would cost at least £25 billion and probably a great deal more, with which no defence budget could cope while at the same time providing over the years the many things urgently needed in the defence field and which <u>are</u> likely to be used. Even if it were to amount to no more than 3 per cent of the existing defence budget, you can be quite certain that if that is incorporated in the future defence budget the Treasury would insist on substantial cuts being made in other parts of the programme.

Such a successor would, by necessity, be even more dependent on the United States with a significant and unsatisfactory input on a proper two-way relationship with that country, which we are seeing as so important in the future. Moreover, with potential threats so diffuse and indirect I have tried to show that it would be virtually impossible to think of any obvious targets, either in the context of threat or retribution, and even if the political will was there or there was advantage to be gained, both of which would be most unlikely.

As far as the much quoted 'seat at the top table' is concerned, I suggest that in future this is more likely to be earned by those who take a lead in reducing tension rather than those trying to maintain a threat with obsolete weapons.

My Lords, any military case for continuing our own nuclear capability would, therefore, have to be made, as the White Paper admits, on an absolutely general and long-term basis, that in an uncertain and changing world might it not be comforting in – say – twenty-five or thirty years' time to have such a powerful weapon in the armoury, just as an insurance policy against something which one hopes and has some reason to expect will never happen, and even if its purpose had become more and more obscure. Although any decision would also have to be taken against the background that to abandon it, after the current life of Trident, would have to be regarded, for practical purposes, as irreversible.

If, at the end of the day, and after the most careful thought, the British deterrent (independent or otherwise) would be seen to be more in the nature of a status symbol, like an American Express Gold or Platinum Card if you like, rather than a serious weapon of war which would add to the effectiveness of our Armed Forces and enhance the security of the nation, then £25 billion is indeed a great deal to pay for something so nebulous and doubtful; I can imagine what the Treasury's reaction would be if the argument 'you never know what lies around the corner' was used to justify a not unreasonable size, shape and balance for our regular forces which history had shown would be needed.

I hope, therefore, that the Government will continue to consider this very important decision most carefully and unemotionally, of which so far there has been little sign, before putting firm recommendations to Parliament, would look at other, perhaps non-nuclear and non-strategic options, with therefore a far greater utility factor. I believe that there are others which would truly enhance both the deterrent power and effectiveness of our conventional forces, perhaps on a European basis so as to spread the burden and thus make us less dependent on America. That, with or without a new generation of submarines, would allow us to achieve a greater flexibility than an exclusively nuclear solution can provide.

Before Parliament is asked to endorse a Trident replacement, it should not only be made aware of the realistic costs, but also how those costs are to be met and, if out of the Defence vote what compensating savings would have to be made to accommodate that replacement. Otherwise an assessment of the value and impact of such a decision would be incomplete.

(b) Discussion paper

In 1993 Bramall contributed to a debate about nuclear weapons in a paper entitled 'Getting off the Nuclear Hook'. It was initially delivered at the RUSI, and then worked up into a discussion paper, given wide circulation and later updated and amended.

Very soon the Government will have to decide whether to go ahead with a 'like for like' successor for Trident; and before that it is very right and proper, as the Government once called for, that there should be a debate on whether this country really needs and can afford to have it on military and financial grounds, or equally whether it can afford not to have it on purely political grounds.

After the American attack in 1945 on Hiroshima and Nagasaki, when atomic bombs far less powerful than the hydrogen weapons of today, revealed to the world the catastrophic consequences of ever again using them, nuclear weapons have always been of more political than military significance – something that just might be used under extreme circumstances rather than as an integral part of any planned battle plan. At the height of the Cold War, however, they were no less necessary for that. Indeed, nuclear weapons became the cornerstone of NATO's strategy, in that it was reckoned that the best way to defend Central Europe from any covetous eyes in the Soviet Union was for NATO to confront them with a sizeable but far from superior conventional force, which would initially engage any aggression but, unable to cope with the scale of the attack, could trigger the use of nuclear weapons in some shape or form. As the 'Mutually Assured Destruction' which would then have occurred would be too horrific to contemplate, it was considered highly unlikely that any aggressor would contemplate that the prize was worth the risk he would be running. As the prize, from which a potential aggressor had to be deterred, would be no less than the ideological domination of the whole of Europe, the unleashing of nuclear weapons in such extreme circumstances did carry that degree of credibility which is so essential if a deterrent is to be successful. That same credibility could also have been accorded to our own deterrent if our homeland had been threatened with direct attack.

As the Chief of Defence Staff in the 1980s I wholeheartedly supported this strategy of 'Flexible Response', and indeed believed it made a significant contribution to a stable European peace spread over a remarkably long period of time.

Now, however, the international scene has radically changed, both politically and in the scope and method of its conflicts. Even with President Putin's power manoeuvring on the very borders of Russia, there is no conventional threat to Central Europe and the threats likely to face this country more directly have also fundamentally changed, moving inexorably away from clear cut 'all-in inter-state wars' towards those which are threatened and often selectively executed by a multiplicity of ill-defined non-state terrorist movements. These could never, even if threatening blackmail with some WMD device, be countered by nuclear retaliation. Indeed, in today's intensely globalised and economically interlocked world it would be almost impossible for anyone to use such an indiscriminate weapon under any circumstances, without making any crisis infinitely worse for themselves as well as everyone else.

So with these changes in the international scene there is an urgent need, before taking a final decision on Trident's successor to take a fresh look at what other options exist for a credible deterrent; always accepting when dealing with any prospective threat that prevention, if possible, remains infinitely preferable to a sometimes messy and invariably punishing cure. Such a reappraisal needs to be considered from military, economic and political points of view.

From a military point of view the 9/11 attack on the governmental and economic heartland of the United States, and the lesser but still serious attacks on London and Paris (and now Brussels, Paris and various German cities) demonstrate only too clearly that a nuclear deterrent, however advanced and powerful, has not and indeed cannot, in the future, prevent the sort of threats and challenges we face today, and are likely to continue to confront us. Moreover, in the aftermath of those attacks there was never any question or a need to fire a nuclear weapon back in retribution because of the impossibility of selecting an appropriate nuclear target. In military terms, therefore, our so-called independent deterrent has not only completely lost its credibility, but a like-for-like successor would no longer be capable of doing the job for which it was designed. Whereas precision weapons, with a conventional warhead, supported by state of the art electronic counter-measures and greatly improved intelligence, could well regain that credibility.

Against the background of there being no military necessity, this country certainly cannot afford, in times of ongoing financial stringency, the very large (and ever rising) extra expenditure which would be required to set up and sustain an ever-ready, virtually invulnerable, replacement for Trident. This financial problem has been given added poignancy by the Treasury laying it down that such extra expenditure must come from within the limits presently set for the planned Defence Budget. This, as has recently been made clear, needs to be sustained if not increased, rather than actually being cut back by a further overloading, if the really essential needs of our armed forces and of cyber, intelligence and security are not to be dangerously underfunded. All of which gives added urgency to finding a cheaper as well as a more credible alternative for our deterrent.

This leaves the question whether holding our own nuclear deterrent still has a political value, as for instance as some sort of status symbol. In this respect, I would make three relevant points. First, for all practical and utility purposes our deterrent has never been truly independent and if we had not possessed one over the Cold War years we certainly would not be seeking to acquire one now. Secondly, even the oft-quoted status of 'having a seat at the top table' has worn very thin. Holding a nuclear weapon was never a qualification for membership of the Security Council; and today it is economic strength, wise counsel and an ever-ready ability to deploy selective military force for peacekeeping and conflict resolution which brings prestige and influence, rather than the capability to destroy indiscriminately and *en masse*.

Thirdly, if the Government is serious as it purports to be about making a positive contribution to the dialogue on the reduction and ultimate elimination of all nuclear weapons (and the continuing posturing of North Korea and earlier of Iran in this field makes this even more urgent) it would be irresponsible if the main example we set was to be a wholly negative one: retaining for ourselves, for at least another fifty years, an excessive nuclear capability which we did not really need on military grounds. It is so easy to hide behind multilateralism which has such wide international support, and others may indeed not follow any lead which we give. But you have to start somewhere and cannot for ever be waiting for others to make the first move. At least we could set an example which could well bring us considerable international kudos.

On many counts therefore there is a strong case for at least a fresh approach to the whole problem of deterrence. The trouble is that when this country, continued to maintain and develop its own nuclear deterrent, first with our air-delivered weapons from a V-bomber, through Polaris to the present Trident, it was presented to Parliament and to the country as not only a 'political weapon of last resort', but also as 'the ultimate guarantee of this country's homeland security'. Moreover, without any clear idea as to how it achieved it, these criteria became deeply embedded in the public psyche and conscience as a *sine qua non*. So, in the political world we live in, could any political party anxious not to alienate votes, be seen not to be supporting the best nuclear weapon that money can buy? Furthermore, could any government even if mindful of taking a more rational and forward looking step, defy popular opinion which could so easily be, and undoubtedly would be, whipped up, to highlight what in terms of our security we could be said to be giving away? It might become politically so much easier to go ahead with the planned successor to Trident whatever the cost and drawbacks.

In practical terms the government are on the hook as regards Trident's replacement, from which they can only be released by being provided with a breathing space. Delaying a final decision on Trident's successor and postponing any early expenditure on specialist submarines will help. But the time gained should then be used positively. To begin with we should recognise, what few would deny, that in the post-Cold War world we do not need to have a nuclear weapon-firing submarine at sea continuously for 365 days a year to demonstrate a deterrent capability. Periodically, one boat would be at sea for training purposes and at other times there could always be one at short notice to put to sea, if the threat to our homeland was considered to have increased. While at all times other nuclear powered submarines would be at sea whose exact weaponry would not be too obvious to the uninitiated.

This variable state of readiness would still maintain that important state of uncertainty; and at moments of crisis, could even emphasise our extra commitment and concern, which is all part and parcel of any deterrent. It would also lead to worthwhile savings particularly, by degrees, in the number of boats which would in turn lead to the lengthening of the lifespan of the existing Trident boats well into the next decade without any new boats being added or needed. Psychologically this would keep us longer in the nuclear club and might even sway any lingering electoral doubters.

Most importantly it would provide a necessary transitory period in which, after further urgent consideration, to perfect and adapt a more relevant, economical and useable way of keeping at bay and warding off any varied and realistic threats now facing this country. There are a number of practical and affordable options now available, to which greatly improved intelligence, both electronic and satellite, will provide the key. After all, to be forewarned is to be forearmed.

I would hope that this gradual stepping down from the no longer credible, immediate and nuclear retaliatory nature of our current deterrent could be interpreted and implemented in a way that persuaded the nation as a whole that it was a sound and progressive step designed not to prepare for past conflicts, hot or cold, which so many established aspects of the changing face of conflict show could never be repeated, but to invest in a more balanced, more relevant and effective defence programme which would better guarantee the future safety and security of our country.

(c) Valedictory speech

On 24 January 2013 Bramall made his final speech in the House of Lords, on the successor to Trident.

My Lords, as, for various reasons, this is my last speech in your Lordships' House – the last, I believe of close on 200 personal contributions over the past twenty-six years – I hope that noble Lords will be indulgent over my being given dispensation to deliver most of this speech sitting down because of my difficulty in standing without full back support for more than a few moments.

I have selected this most timely debate – moved by my noble friend, Lord Ramsbotham, whom I thank for his very kind and generous remarks – to make a final contribution for two reasons: first, because there can be no more important question facing this country than the vexed one of nuclear weapons, and in particular our country's own nuclear deterrent; and secondly, because in my maiden speech, made in March 1987 (see Chapter 5), I reminded noble Lords of the positive contribution that the possession of nuclear weapons had made to Europe in terms of its stability and an unusually long period of peace, for the simple reason that no prize that might have been gained by military means would have been worth the risk of possible nuclear retaliation.

In those days of the Cold War I therefore fully supported the generally accepted philosophy – one might almost say theology – of the deterrent, and believed that because the prize was no less than the domination of Europe, it was – just – a credible faith. On this I disagreed with my more distinguished predecessor as Chief of Defence Staff, the late Lord Carver, who I then thought was ahead of his time. I say this because, not having had any emotional antipathy to the useful possession of such weapons, it gives me, I hope, slightly greater credibility if now, a quarter century later when things have moved on, I want to deal with the practicalities of nuclear weapons and their future rather differently.

For now, with the Cold War over, the world has changed significantly, both politically and in terms of its conflicts, and is likely to continue to do so. I now feel that it is possible – indeed I would say essential – to look at the whole question from an entirely different point of view. I shall therefore ask three different but closely related questions. Perhaps I might now be allowed to continue while sitting down.

The first question, from a military point of view, is whether we still need a successor to Trident which the Government seems presently to have in mind. Will it go on being able to do the job it is supposed to do under any relevant circumstances? For all practical purposes it has not and, indeed, would not deter any of the threats and challenges – now more economic than military – likely to threaten this country in the foreseeable or even long-term future. It has not stopped any terrorist outrage in this country nor, despite America's omnipotent deterrent, did it prevent the very traumatic 9/11. It did not stop the Argentines trying to take over the Falklands, nor did any nuclear deterrent stop Saddam Hussein marching into Kuwait or firing missiles into Israel. Nor indeed, in a now intensely globalised and interlocked world, could our deterrent ever conceivably be used – not even after a serious hostile incident which it had presumably failed to deter – without making the whole situation in the world infinitely worse for ourselves as well as for everybody else.

For all practical purposes our deterrent has never been truly independent, and if this country had not had a national deterrent over the years, dominated by the formidable balance of terror between the USA and the old Soviet Union, it would certainly not be seeking to acquire one now. I see no reason why these circumstances should change, because conflict is moving inexorably in an entirely different direction. Indeed, even that often-quoted justification for such a status symbol – a seat at the top table – has worn a bit thin, with prestige and influence more likely to be achieved by economic strength, wise counsel and peace-making than by an ability to destroy en masse. Against that background, this country does not need, and really cannot afford the very large extra expenditure needed to set up and maintain an ever-ready, invulnerable successor to Trident, particularly when all the really useful and frequently needed forces and agencies, so vital for the real security of our country, are still deprived of the resources they require.

Secondly – and particularly as in the gracious [Queen's] Speech the first of only three small, rather opaque references to defence was a determination to reduce the threat of nuclear proliferation – I ask how we could possibly make any positive contribution to the current dialogue, and ultimately, one hopes, to a widespread reduction of nuclear weapons, if the only example we set is to be a wholly negative one, by going ahead with possessing for ourselves such an excessive capability for at least another forty years, and at the same time claiming, however fallaciously, that for a country like ours it is the only way that we can guarantee our security in all circumstances. I imagine that that line of argument is not lost on those who may now wish to acquire such weapons for themselves.

Other countries may not necessarily follow our example if we were to start to run down our own white elephant and be seen to be stepping further down the nuclear ladder. However, to encourage them in the completely opposite direction, to follow our particular stance, seems to me to be very irresponsible for a country such as ours, which rightly has aspirations to be a leader in international affairs.

However, my third and final question is whether, in the real political world we live in, can this Government politically afford not to be seen to have the best nuclear weapon that money can buy? Even if they were mindful to take a rational step, could they really defy any populist feeling which could so easily, and certainly would be, whipped up by those ever keen on contriving a row on key issues – and there could be no issue more key than this – that somehow the Government, however inaccurately, were giving away Britain's ultimate guarantee of homeland security, while at the same time, heaven forbid, the French may be – probably would be – holding on to theirs? It may therefore be politically easier to let a successor to Trident go ahead despite the many and considerable down sides.

Nevertheless, ever an optimist, I believe that there can be a sensible way of getting round this impasse and giving the Government the opportunity to get off the hook. For instance, they should give urgent consideration to adopting a more practical, realistic and, I hope, cheaper way of keeping at bay or warding off any likely threats to the integrity of our nation and the safety of our citizens, which at the same time would be seen to be giving a lead in the active non-proliferation dialogue. I believe that there a number of convincing and capable ways of achieving this, some of which may be expanded on by other noble Lords.

To begin with we should recognise that in today's world we do not need to have a nuclear-firing submarine ready and on station at all times to demonstrate an effective deterrent capability. Periodically, one boat would have to be at sea for training purposes and at other times a boat could be put to sea at short notice if the threat to us or to our vital interest was perceived to have increased. This variable state of readiness would still maintain some useful sense of uncertainty and could even, at times of particular tension, actually appear to enhance our commitment and resolve. Some useful economies would arise from a system of reduced readiness, which might even, by adding to the time span of the existing Trident, go some way to assuaging any lingering electoral doubters. Even more importantly, it would allow a breathing space in which to perfect – hand in hand with improved intelligence, both satellite and terrestrial – a more relevant economical and useable system, and therefore to allow work on the replacement submarines exclusively for Trident's successor to be cancelled or at least reviewed.

I would hope that this stepping down from the no-longer-credible immediate response nature of our current nuclear stance could be implemented in a way that persuaded people that it was both a sound and progressive step, designed not quixotically to re-prepare for the last war, but to present a better balanced, more relevant defence programme. Moreover, by making a further significant contribution to the general dialogue for multinational nuclear disarmament, which everyone seems to approve of, it could even enhance the value of our counsel in international affairs and as a key member of the Security Council.

In introducing this motion in the House of Lords, Lord Ramsbotham[83] *had prefaced his speech with the following comments:*

My Lords, at the start of this debate I would like to beg your indulgence if I break with tradition. Today is a sad day for the House because, during this debate, my noble and gallant friend Field Marshal Lord Bramall, with whom I had the privilege of serving in the Royal Green Jackets, having both originally joined the Rifle Brigade, although at different times, will make his final speech on its floor. Few people have contributed more, in so many ways, to the life of the nation than my noble and gallant friend as Chief of Defence Staff, Lord Lieutenant for Greater London, President of the MCC and, for the past twenty-six years, an active Member of this House. He made his maiden speech on this subject and I look forward to hearing again the views that we share, and which he has long and consistently expressed with his customary vigour and clarity.

I hope I may also share a personal memory that I suspect he may have forgotten. Almost fifty-three years ago, I first played cricket under his captaincy on our regimental ground at Winchester. Towards the end of the match I hit the biggest six of my life, and if I shut my eyes, I can still see the ball soaring over the trees at the edge of the ground. However, as I walked towards the pavilion, not out, I was taken aback not to be welcomed by my captain but rocketed for playing such an irresponsible shot when we were fighting for the draw that we had achieved. With such commitment to the cause, it is no wonder he became Chief of the Defence Staff. I am sure that the whole House will join me in thanking him for his many contributions and wishing him and Avril every good fortune in the future.

Following Bramall's speech, the next speaker was Lady Williams of Crosby,[84] *who said:*

My Lords, I do not think that I can say anything more strongly than the speech we have just heard from the noble and gallant Lord, Lord Bramall. It shows how great will be our loss in not having his company and advice on this most important of issues. We are all deeply in his debt for once again so strongly speaking truth to power, as he has done all his life, and for his illustrious and remarkable military career, starting with the Military Cross [in Normandy] and going all the way up to becoming the Commander-in-Chief of the British Land Forces and also – something which I want to mention on personal grounds – his distinguished action as Colonel of the 2nd Gurkha Rifles. I mention that because my son-in-law, who died earlier this year, was a junior officer in the 2nd Gurkha Rifles. He served in Hong Kong and in that neighbourhood, including Malaya. Over many years, he told me that nobody was more admired by the Gurkhas than the Field Marshal, the noble and gallant Lord, Lord Bramall, who did so much to help and assist them in their deep dependence on this country and their deep service to it.

Book 5

The Higher Organization
of Defence

Chronology

1946

July	White Paper on Defence Reorganization.

1957

January	Macmillan replaces Eden as Prime Minister.

1958

April	Unified command established in Aden.
July	Sandys White Paper, 'The Central Organisation of Defence', published.

1959

January	Dickson becomes first CDS.
July	Mountbatten becomes CDS.
August	CENTO established.
October	Macmillan wins general election.

1961

July	Successful intervention in Kuwait on a Joint Tri-Service basis.

1962

July	Thorneycroft becomes Minister of Defence.
November	Unified command established in Far East.
	Mountbatten puts his views to Thorneycroft on a unified MoD.

1963

July	White Paper by Ismay and Jacobs on unified MoD published.

1964

April	Unified MoD established.
October	Denis Healey becomes Minister of Defence.

1965

April	Cancellation of TSR-2.
May	Aircraft Carrier Working Party set up.

1966

January	RAF win Carrier debate.

1967

July	Withdrawal from East of Suez by mid-1970s announced.

1970

February	Single Service Ministers abolished.

1977

January	Humphreys dies in post as CDS, temporarily replaced by Ashmore.

1981

January	John Knott becomes Secretary of State for Defence.
May	Dismissal of Minister for the Navy, Keith Speed.
June	John Knott's 'The Way Forward' published.

1983

January	Heseltine becomes Secretary of State for Defence.

1984

April	Heseltine proposals for Ministry of Defence reform.
July	Chiefs' meeting with Prime Minister on the reforms.

1985

January	Reorganization of Ministry of Defence.

1986

January	Heseltine resigns over Westland affair, succeeded by Younger.

Introduction

As an introductory comment to this chapter it is worth recalling a story told by that great figure, Field Marshal Sir William Robertson, the only man in the British army ever to hold every rank between private and field marshal, and C.I.G.S. 1916–18. He tells us in his autobiography of a conversation with a senior General:

> Never forget, Robertson, that we have two Armies – the War Office Army and the Aldershot Army. The first is always up to strength and is organised, reorganised and disorganised almost daily. The second is never up to strength, knows nothing whatever about the first and remains unaffected by any of these organising activities. It just cleans its rifle and falls in on parade.[85]

Bramall became involved in the higher organization of Defence at an early point in his career. In 1947 he served in a policy branch of the War Office when Montgomery was C.I.G.S. and advocating more centralized powers across the three Armed Forces: no doubt with thoughts of himself as the supremo! Then in 1963 Bramall was posted as a Lieutenant Colonel to the personal staff of the C.D.S., Admiral of the Fleet Earl Mountbatten of Burma, with special responsibility, reporting directly to him, for setting up a unified Ministry of Defence which centralized military policy and financial control, created a central Defence Staff and co-located the management staff of the three separate services in one building.

Mountbatten, with his enthusiastic energy, original thought and vision and ability to get things done, was a most charismatic figure. Moreover, the immense prestige he had acquired as a result of his wartime and Viceregal service in India, together with his close contacts at the highest level, gave him great political clout. This was good for Defence as a whole. Bramall was to learn a great deal from him about the best way to ensure the new MoD conducted its business positively and efficiently, and particularly how the Chiefs of Staff Committee and system should best work, as it had so brilliantly in the Second World War. This was to prove invaluable when Bramall himself occupied some of the top posts in the MoD and ultimately took over the C.D.S. post which Mountbatten had himself held twenty years before. As

C.D.S. Bramall was therefore an ideal person to work with the Secretary of State, Michael Heseltine, who was determined, partly for political reasons, to carry out another fairly substantial reorganization of the MoD and take the Mountbatten reforms one stage further, as Mountbatten himself might have wanted, thus enhancing still further the political, financial and even military controls at the centre. This was achieved reasonably successfully and certainly helped with more effective budgetary control, but by removing the Service Vice Chiefs it weakened the influence of the Single Service Chiefs of Staff. This makes Bramall's analysis of the current state of the Chiefs of Staff system, and its input into future policy, particularly relevant and topical.

Before the original Mountbatten Review was started there had already been a successful attempt to integrate overseas commands with a Joint Head-quarters and a single Tri-Service Commander-in-Chief. Such a command was first established in Cyprus in 1960, then in Aden in 1961 and Singapore in 1962. These Tri-Service commands necessitated a small operational exec-utive in the MoD at Storeys Gate to communicate with them and to give operational direction. This was to prove its worth in 1961, when Britain rapidly deployed an amphibious Brigade to defend Kuwait and, in practice, deter aggression.

The Mountbatten Reorganization was to go further, as Bramall describes in Chapter 10 of his book, *The Chiefs*. Bramall also put forward his own views on further improving the higher organization of Defence, emphasizing the urgent need for a National Security Council.

Chapter 20

Designing a Unified Ministry of Defence

(a) The Mountbatten era

In The Chiefs *Bramall wrote about the Mountbatten era, when he had served as Mountbatten's personal representative on the main steering committee restructuring the new unified Ministry of Defence. This is a condensed version of Chapter 10.*

By the summer of 1962 Watkinson had been replaced by Thorneycroft[86] and pressure was building for another step towards unification of the Service Ministries. Not only had the Kuwait intervention shown the success of the tri-Service command structure, but it had also shown up the inherent inefficiencies in mounting quick reaction operations through the Admiralty, War Office and Air Ministry. Irritating inadequacies were also emerging in the weapons procurement field where each separate ministry had a different perception of conflict. Thorneycroft's triumvirate of advisers in the MoD – Mountbatten, Zuckerman[87] and Sir Robert Scott,[88] who had replaced Playfair – all felt it was time to move ahead on this front, and they were supported by Macmillan, who extended Mountbatten's tenure as CDS to five years specifically to allow him to drive this through.

Two problems immediately presented themselves to Mountbatten: how sweeping should his reforms be, and how should they be launched? Paradoxically, Mountbatten was both the generator of the unification proposals but also the biggest hindrance, as the three Chiefs regarded him with great suspicion, and particularly viewed any proposal from him with opposition. They viewed three basic principles as sacrosanct: corporate responsibility; independent single-Service management; and a firm linkage between power to advise and responsibility for implementation. If Mountbatten was to dent those three, let alone breach them, he needed firm Cabinet backing, and Macmillan therefore asked him to prepare a paper, through Thorneycroft, setting out his personal views on the future organisation. It took him three months to write it, and he was only helped by his personal staff as well as Scott and Zuckerman.

He started with a rehearsal of all the weaknesses of the current system: how the formulation of broad defence policy was frustrated by narrow single-

Service interests; how this exacerbated the already difficult budgetary situation; and how it divided the loyalties of Service Ministers, the Chiefs and their staffs. He then went to his main conclusion and the key to the rest of his paper: nothing short of the abolition of the Service Ministries and the creation of a single Ministry of Defence which would eradicate the deep-seated weakness of the defence organisation as it stood. He discarded the notion of a single unified defence force, as in Canada, although he believed it should be the ultimate solution. He went on to give a broad outline of his new-style unified ministry. There would be one Secretary of State, assisted by Ministers of State, with functional, rather than single-Service responsibility. The Naval, General and Air Staffs would be integrated into one Defence Staff, responsible to the CDS, who would be advised by the three single-Service Chiefs of Staff on sea, land and air matters, as the heads of their sections of the overall Defence Staff. The CDS would have clear paramountcy over them, not just as their chairman, but in his own right, and the Service Chiefs would lose their status as professional heads of their Services, which would be taken over by three Commanders-in-Chief or Inspectors General of the Navy, Army and Air Force, who would act as the principal Personnel Officers of their Service, responsible for their general wellbeing, taken to mean their management, training, morale and operational efficiency.

Mountbatten undoubtedly proposed much of this in order to rid the Chiefs of their parochial single-Service thinking and to encourage them to think nationally across the board. However, it was a near fatal error as he was attempting to overturn the three principles which the single-Service Chiefs deemed non-negotiable, and he was undermining the very foundations of the Chiefs of Staff system.

Thorneycroft treated the paper with interest, but no more, while Macmillan welcomed it. However, the Chiefs were outraged, viewing it with anger, alarm and varying degrees of personal animosity towards Mountbatten. In their hysterical reaction, they received support from a number of past Chiefs, notably Harding, Slessor and Portal. They put forward a counter-proposal which accepted the principle of unified commands overseas, and agreed to the strengthening of the Central Staffs shown to be necessary by the Kuwait crisis, and by technological problems over nuclear delivery systems. However, they were adamantly opposed to any downgrading of their corporate responsibilities as military advisers to the Government, or as professional heads of their Services.

Macmillan played a master stroke in setting up an independent inquiry on the Cabinet's behalf into this conflict of views, and asked Lord Ismay and Sir Ian Jacob[89] to carry it out. It was an authoritative and impressive team, and was thoroughly approved of by Mountbatten, who realised that this would take the heat off his paper, and saw that the inquiry would report direct to the Cabinet, making it constitutionally difficult to muster support against their conclusions. Amazingly, Ismay and Jacob wrote their report in six weeks. It was highly critical of the existing system and put forward three possible solutions for the Cabinet to consider.

The first option did little more than tinker with the existing structure and they did not recommend it because it did not go far enough in tackling fundamental weaknesses, but it stressed the importance of strengthening the CDS's position. The second option was the collocation of the three Service Ministries with the Defence Ministry in one building. A Secretary of Defence would be in overall charge, with the Service Ministries reduced in status to that of departments of the new super Ministry of Defence, each under a junior minister. The Board of Admiralty, Army Board and Air Council would be downgraded and subordinated to a new Defence Council, and there would be some strengthening of the Central Staffs, but the Chiefs would retain their corporate responsibilities and remain the professional heads of their Services. The third option was a fully integrated and functional Ministry of Defence, with all officers of two-star rank and above merged into an Armed Forces Staff and wearing a common uniform. Service identity would be retained up to one-star rank.

Ismay and Jacob believed that the third option would be premature and recommended the second to the Cabinet, not only on its intrinsic merits, but also as a stepping stone towards the third option. It was accepted by the Cabinet with alacrity as an elegant and eminently sensible solution, breaching none of the Chiefs' sacrosanct principles, but bringing the Services much closer together. They ordered it to be implemented with full collocation by spring 1964. Mountbatten set about implementing it with characteristic energy, aiming to win as much power for the CDS and degree of functionalization for the new Ministry as he could wring from the broad principles laid down by the Cabinet. The Chiefs, relieved that they had retained their own positions and decentralised Service management, were equally determined that Mountbatten was not to be allowed to use the thin end of several wedges to achieve his covert aims. Mountbatten's Byzantine tactics to get his own way infuriated the Chiefs, which he ignored, believing he was right and they were wrong!

On one important issue Mountbatten was defeated. Most of the new Ministry was organised on a joint, not an integrated basis. That meant that sections of the Naval, Army and Air Staffs with similar responsibilities remained separate within their own Departments, but were brought together in joint committees. Most of the co-ordinating work was done by the civil servants of the PUS's Defence Secretariat. Four new integrated staffs were

created: the Defence Operations Executive, the Defence Operational Requirements Staff, the Defence Signals Staff and the Defence Intelligence Staff.
Mountbatten hoped that they would be the start of further integration.

The new Ministry of Defence opened on All Fools' Day 1964 in what
became known as the MoD Main Building. The building was sliced like a
layered cake. The vertical slices were by Service: Air Staff at the Parliament
end, Army and Central Staff in the middle, and Navy at the Charing Cross
end. The horizontal layers were by function: The sixth floor was the principal
floor, housing Ministers, Chiefs, senior Civil Servants, the Chief Scientist
and their personal staffs; the seventh floor was for personnel and logistics; the
fifth for operational staff, including the new Joint Operational Centre; the
fourth for Intelligence; and so on. Mountbatten chaired the first Chiefs of
Staff Committee meeting in the new purpose-built conference room on the
fifth floor on 7 April 1964.

If asked the question 'Had the drama and acrimony been worthwhile?',
the answer must be 'Yes'. It was the logical next step in the development of
the Chiefs of Staff system. Collocation alone turned into an enormous asset,
with questions being answered by the simple expedient of walking from one
office to another, instead of by telephone or reams of paper. The allocation
of financial resources was much more accurate and positive. The position of
CDS was strengthened, without weakening the managerial powers of the
Service Chiefs, and decision making at all levels was improved by the inter-
departmental co-ordination of the PUS's unified Defence Secretariat. The
reforms went as far as the perceived wisdom of Whitehall and the Defence
establishment would allow, and were to survive virtually intact for the next
twenty years, evolving all the time as each new generation of Chiefs brought
their own experience to bear on the crises of the day. It was, said the historian
Michael Howard, 'An administrative revolution unparalleled since the days of
Cardwell.'[90]

[It was to prove vital, eighteen years later, in guaranteeing the closest possible cooperation in mounting the extended Falklands operation.]

(b) Looking back from the 1990s: one step too far?

In The Chiefs *Bramall wrote about the period between the Falklands War in 1982
and the fall of the Berlin Wall in 1989 (the chapter, 'Heseltine Makes His Mark'),
for the earlier part of which he had been CDS. He also wrote an Epilogue, of which
this is a condensed version, looking forward to what might happen.*

One requirement stands out above all others in the working of the Defence
decision-making system, and that is the need for balance: balance between
the politically desirable and the militarily practicable, or vice versa; balance

between the needs of the three Services, operating together although in the three very different environments; and balance between central policy-makers, who, as the old adage puts it, tend to know less and less about more and more, and the experts on naval, land and air warfare, who have the opposite skills, knowing more and more about less and less, but who are vital in deciding what is practicable in war and peace.

The quest for balance has taken place over three consecutive periods in the evolution of the Chiefs: 1904–23, 1923–64 and 1964 onwards. The ground rules for politico-military balance were evolved by the Committee of Imperial Defence and had been firmly established by 1923 when the Chiefs of Staff Committee was formed. It was the formation of the RAF as the third Service that impelled that establishment, and began the quest for inter-Service balance. Finally, it was Mountbatten's drive for unification of defence decision-making in the early 1960s that triggered the current search for balance between central policy makers and the managers of the Service Departments.

The critical factor common to all three periods has been the span of responsibility that ministers and their professional advisers have been deemed able to handle. Paradoxically, despite the increasing complexity of warfare, which should have enforced decentralisation, advances in communications and electronic command and control systems, have been even more rapid. They have made centralisation ever more practicable and, indeed, more necessary for operational efficiency and economic management.

In the first period, which really began in the nineteenth century, the problem was how to achieve naval and military efficiency without surrendering political control. The Admiralty Board and the Army Council systems were already in place to provide separate collective professional advice to ministers on sea and land warfare, and for the internal management of the Navy and the Army, but there was no governmental machinery for developing national strategy on which the allocation of resources between the two Services could be based. There was some hankering for the appointment of a Minister of Defence, but the task was considered too big for one man.

Rather than a General Staff, as chosen by Germany, which smacked too much of a dictatorship, the more politically acceptable Committee of Imperial Defence, chaired by the Prime Minister, was established in 1904, and had to serve as a substitute for a British General Staff. Although the CID was replaced by various forms of War Cabinet during the First World War, and its secretariat became the Cabinet Secretariat under the ubiquitous Maurice Hankey, the principles needed for balance in politico-military relations had been firmly established by 1923.

The two most important of those principles were, firstly, that only the Prime Minister in Cabinet had the mandate to take the major decisions of

Defence Policy. A deputy, or later a Minister of Defence, could be tasked to carry some of the burden in peace, but the ultimate responsibility for the security of the realm rested with the Prime Minister. Second, that the tasks of the Chiefs were to tender collective and individual military advice to the Government, and, as the professional heads of the Navy and Army and later RAF, to maintain their battle-winning efficiency and high morale. These principles hold good today.

The Navy and Army fought hard during the second period to overturn the 1917 decision to form the RAF as an independent Service, but they could never counter the Trenchard philosophy of the indivisibility and independence of air power. With sea and land warfare straddled by the air, the replacement of the defunct CID by the Chiefs of Staff Committee was the logical outcome of the Salisbury Commission's deliberations. Opinion in Whitehall and Westminster in the 1920s still saw the appointment of a Minister of Defence as politically undesirable, as it was too wide a remit for one man to handle, and would anyway give him too much power. The possibility of appointing a Chief of Defence Staff was not even considered.

The Chiefs of Staff system proved itself under Churchill and Alanbrooke during World War II, and it was copied, almost *in toto*, by the Americans, with one important exception. With Churchill combining the roles of Prime Minister and Minister of Defence there was no lack of political direction but doubts were expressed occasionally about the British habit of rotating the chairmanship of the committee, instead of appointing the equivalent of a CDS, as the Americans did with Admiral Leahy. [Alan]Brooke and his colleagues rejected such an appointment on the sound principle that it is always unwise to divorce military planning from responsibility for execution, or policy from management. The principle holds good today, and its breach would spell disaster in war.

The post-war explosion in weapon technology and the acceleration in the rate of military change with its related defence costs inflation, enforced the appointment of Ministers of Defence and Chiefs of Defence Staff, with stronger supporting staffs, and prepared the ground for the third period, starting with the Mountbatten reforms of 1964. Economic decline and the consequential shrinkage in resources available for Defence added to the pressures for greater centralisation of policy to neutralise the intense rivalry which grew up between the Chiefs as they fought on behalf of their own Services for the lion's share of the smaller Defence cake.

In creating the unified Ministry of Defence in 1964 Mountbatten was stopped well short of the total functionalisation of the ministry and the unification of the Services. The power of the CDS flowed from his chairmanship of the CoS committee. The only staff that he was allowed was his personal briefing staff: the newly created Defence Staff was responsible to the Chiefs of Staff Committee *per se*. Power still rested with the Chiefs, who, as the managers as well as the policy makers of their Services, could wield the veto in the CoS Committee, whose views the CDS was constitutionally responsible for representing, rather than tendering advice to the Government in his own right.

The system worked unscathed for almost two decades, but in that time two new centres of power gradually developed within the MoD to cater for the explosion in weapons technology and the consequential financial stresses: the Chief Scientific Adviser's staff and the Permanent Under-Secretary's empire, consisting of the Defence Secretariat, which provided the co-ordinating nervous system for the Ministry, and his financial staffs. Both had centralising instincts and motivations. By the beginning of the 1980s the ground was ready again for another step forward towards greater centralisation in the short term and perhaps unification of the Services in the more distant future.

The successive Lewin and Heseltine reforms have strengthened the Centre at the expense of the Service Departments. Advising the Secretary of State and thus the Government, there is now a triumvirate at the highest level: the Chief of Defence Staff, the Permanent Under-Secretary and the Chief Scientific Adviser, although he is in fact subordinate to the PUS. The Chiefs in their collective capacity have been reduced to a subordinate advisory level, and in their individual capacities they are now on a lower management tier. If that centralising trend continues, they could become Commanders-in-Chief out-side Whitehall, like Wolseley in the 1880s, or even Chief Personnel Officers of their own Service within the MoD, as has been mooted in some quarters. Divorced from their formulation of Defence policy, and denied their Vice-Chiefs, they could even have difficulty in finding out what is being planned and prepared in the Centre, let alone making an early and significant con-tribution to the process.

In the actual conduct of the Gulf War – admittedly mainly a United States responsibility – the Service Chiefs were kept more on the fringes of opera-tional policy and planning than would have been the case in the past. The CDS alone advised the Government, and although he debriefed the Chiefs after meetings of the War Cabinet, he did not draw on their wider experience or expertise before the event, relying more on the briefing of his own central staff. The Chiefs were confined to planning and organising the deployment of British forces, and to making the complex movement and logistic arrange-ments involved. This was in marked contrast to the all-British Falklands Campaign of eight years earlier, when the Prime Minister, at times, drew on the experience and ideas of all the Chiefs, and when the CDS always consulted them before War Cabinet meetings.

The key questions now therefore are: has centralisation been taken too far? Is policy becoming too divorced from management? And are the Chiefs' days numbered? What are the Chiefs' strengths and weaknesses?

Since their inception the chiefs have been, individually, the chief executive of their own Service, and, collectively, the professional advisers to the Government. Like all human beings they are fallible, though much less so as a collective body than individually. They can never forget that they epitomise the hopes and fears of their own Service; but they have shown themselves capable both of evolution and of operating effectively within the political and financial constraints properly laid down on them by the Cabinet and Parliament; and they have worked in reasonably constructive harmony with their civilian and scientific colleagues. They can claim considerable achievements since 1945, and despite some anti-nuclear sentiment within the electorate, the stock of the Armed Forces has rarely stood higher.

The principal criticism levelled at them is that when resources are tight, as they usually are, the Chiefs tend to eye each embryonic change of strategy, organisational initiative or breakthrough in weapon technology from the point of view of its impact on their own Service's programmes, rather than in the wider context of national security.

The Chiefs' collective and individual responsibilities do therefore sometimes clash, and this can lead to divided loyalties, but there is a reverse side to this coin. If the Chiefs were not to make their parochial points, particularly in a climate when there are seldom enough resources in any Service to match existing commitments, let alone the unexpected, and risks have to be taken, critical considerations could go by default. Those who talk glibly about a 'best' defence solution to which the Chiefs should be ready loyally and enthusiastically to subscribe, are not necessarily referring to what is best in military terms. They are probably describing the politically most attractive course; or one that conforms to the view of Treasury officials, who, as has so often been said in the past, are better at assessing the cost of things than their relative value to the nation; and who cannot escape the blame for Britain's military plight in 1939. The political and financial factors are certainly important, and ultimately may have to be overriding, but the military voice must be clearly heard and understood in the corridors of Whitehall, albeit not necessarily in the country at large, where presenting the case for Defence must be the prerogative of Ministers.

Even if there were no inter-Service arguments, there would be others on less easily accessible and manageable lines of antipathy within a functional organisation, such as personnel versus equipment or equipment versus barracks and pay and so forth. The apparent weakness caused by rivalry within the Chiefs of Staff system can, therefore, be far from unproductive, provided there is the central machinery with the knowledge and determination to cut Gordian knots. This is where the CDS, his Vice-Chief and the Defence Staff play their crucial role, interacting with the PUS's largely civilian-manned Office of Management and Budget. The Chiefs still have their right of access to the Prime Minister, who can overrule or support them if the centre, in some exceptional case, has not been able to resolve the issue within the Ministry.

A study of the Chiefs also shows that they have never been particularly innovative. All their background and training, and the professional briefing they receive from their staffs, tend to make them err on the side of caution both in peace and war. While Churchill often railed against their caution, the Chiefs did curb his more impracticable ideas. It was this balancing of his restlessly innovative mind by the more cautious professionalism of the Chiefs, who had to weigh the risks and bear the responsibilities for executive action, that ensured the coherent and dynamic direction of the Second World War, which contrasted so sharply with the conduct of the First, when the Chiefs of Staff system did not exist.

Certainly, if the chiefs are to give of their best, particularly in active operations, there must be a linkage of mutual respect between their expertise as professional advisers and the drive of a decisive Prime Minister capable of delivering Parliament and the country, without whose support the Armed Forces of the Crown cannot operate effectively. This was the secret in the Second World War, and it was repeated with great advantage in the Falklands Campaign.

Under purely peacetime conditions the Chiefs may seem themselves too much as the guardians of what they believe is worth preserving within their own Service to espouse very willingly some novel proposal from which one other Service or another might suffer. They are highly suspicious of politically or financially inspired initiatives and they dislike reformers like Sandys, Nott or Heseltine with political ambitions, whose tenure of office can often be much shorter lived than the damage that they can inflict. The prime example of the Canadian experiment in unification stands as a warning of what can sometimes happen. The instigator left public life shortly after, never to reappear, but the Canadian forces were stuck with his unsound system for many years.

So perhaps it is not surprising that Ministers treat the Chiefs with a certain wariness, often believing that if they take them into their confidence too early, they use the time to take up entrenched positions, rally arguments and gather outside support. Ministers feel more secure with a small caucus of civil servants beholden only to them. Michael Heseltine's decision not to take the CDS into his confidence until the eleventh hour before revealing his plans for the 1985 reorganisation may well be a case in point. He, no doubt, thought that if he revealed his plans earlier the CDS would be in duty bound to inform the other Chiefs and this would make it more difficult for him to achieve what he wanted. On that occasion, he may have done the Chiefs less than justice since they showed themselves to be constructive in discussions with him, and they made no attempt to gather outside support against him.

But old habits die hard. There have been plenty of clashes with Ministers in the past and wariness persists. The latest study, Options For Change, has again been carried out largely by the centre and away from the Chiefs' machinery, but in his case, there seems to have been no clear ministerial view of the way ahead or of what the government wanted to do.

At the root of the matter lies the fundamental difference between sea, land and air warfare, and in the types of men and women and the equipment they need, which must never be overlooked. Although there has been a growing together in weapon technology, logistic support, and general inter-Service co-operation, the three Services still fight under very different operational conditions, which require diverse techniques handed down from one generation to another. It takes a lifetime's experience to master war in one environment. It is only possible in the last half of an officer's career to achieve a broad understanding of the problems of fighting in the other two environments. Brilliant though a tri-Service commander may prove himself to be, he still needs expert advice on the other Services' capabilities in the same way that a brigade commander would be lost without his gunner and sapper advisers. The same applies to the CDS, who will usually have proved himself already as a tri-Service commander, but is still dependent on the advice of First Sea Lord, CGS and CAS.

So it is in their collective capacity that the Chiefs have the greatest part to play in the development of national security policy and in crisis management. It is they who bring to bear the whole weight of experience accumulated over the centuries in their own Services to ensure a full debate on the complex issues, which are the day-to-day fare of any Ministry of Defence. Four minds (or five, now that the VCDS is a full member of the Chiefs) are invariably better than one in an assessment of military options and their attendant risks.

The final argument in favour of curtailing the swing away from the Chiefs of Staff system is that if an effective military voice is to be heard in national affairs, the CDS needs to be seen to be able to call upon the full support of his professional colleagues, each at the head of his Service and with its full weight behind him. The CDS is not there to ride roughshod over them, but rather to provide the central dynamic; clarifying issues, identifying genuinely alternative points of view, giving his own objective thoughts on issues, and stage-managing and presenting the whole spectrum of military advice for political decision. He has to do this with foresight and in a way that ministers understand; and whenever possible, in a way that harmonises with political objectives. But he may on occasion have to take an opposing line, and then, like any other national leader, he needs a power base if he is not to be ignored. The Chiefs of Staff Committee, as the collective military heads of the Armed Forces, undoubtedly provides the CDS with that base. Without it, the CDS is little more than the head of a purely bureaucratic structure subject to political manipulation. Nor would he have the ability to demonstrate that his advice could only be discarded at national military peril and, hence, political risk.

For over a quarter of a century, the chiefs have provided, under the direction of the CDS, the ideal forum for thinking through strategy and other Defence policy issues, and for measuring possible solutions, plans and recommendations against practical reality and manageability; and for establishing a proper dialogue with ministers. Such a forum will be as important as ever in arguing through new strategic policies in response to the dramatic changes in Eastern Europe and events in the Middle East. It is the Chiefs' duty, directly and indirectly, to advise the Government on the shape and size of our Armed Forces, which must be capable of quick expansion in an emergency, be highly mobile and-hard hitting, and above all confident, contented, fully manned and armed with up to date weapons, tactics and techniques. This is no easy task to fulfil in a climate of constant financial stringency.

Moreover, the human factor must never be overlooked. Each Service is a living organism with all the collective strengths and weaknesses of the men and women who wear its uniform, and who, like any team, will only give of their best if properly led by a captain in whom they have trust and confidence. There have been times when, if it had not been for the leadership of the Chiefs as professional heads of their Services, those organisms would have wilted and died through lack of confidence. They would not have withstood the constant salami-slicing of expenditure; the counter-productive contracts moratoria; the savage reductions in training activity with depressing reductions on sea miles steamed, track miles travelled and flying hours flown; the never ending administrative cheese-paring and reduction in operational reserves; and the frequent failures to maintain pay comparability. It is the Chiefs who have maintained morale and made successes like the Falklands and the Gulf possible, but it has often been a close-run thing. Without the leadership that the Chiefs have provided, the fighting experience and the professional skills of the services, accumulated over the centuries, would have been dissipated, and backing for British foreign policy lost.

Defence is an on-going and ever changing business, requiring high morale that comes from good leadership. The Chiefs must not be allowed to wither on the vine through over-pruning of their powers and responsibilities in favour of a bland central staff organisation, and isolating them from the mainstream of Defence policy. For in spite of the political character of military operations at the end of the twentieth century, depth of realism and professional expertise is still vital when conflict looms. Bureaucrats, working in the interests of expediency, must not be allowed to take over from the doers. The dire consequences could be a rerun of the 1920s and 1930s.

Much will depend on the selection of successive CDSs. While the CDS must rightly have the ultimate responsibility for advising the Government on military policy, it will be to the advantage of his own authority and to the quality of the advice he brings that he brings the other Chiefs into his deliberations. He will naturally try for a consensus on policy, which is easy enough when adequate resources are available, but far less so under the more normal conditions of inadequate funding. When consensus lies beyond his grasp, he should concentrate on identifying the different points of view and the respective risks for ministerial decision, annotating them with his own hopefully more objective assessments. This is the way the Chiefs have worked in their more successful moments.

There should be little difficulty in developing future defence policy, provided CDSs, even if chosen from a wider field, are men who can keep their colleagues 'in on the act' while they themselves take the initiative in strategic thinking and give objective advice to ministers. Under such leadership, a proper balance between policy and management should be maintained, and the Defence voice should remain strong in the corridors of power, whatever the future may hold.

Defence policy is not just about defence of the realm. It is also about the projection and protection of British interests world-wide; about the support of British foreign policy in this unstable world; and about what Britain wishes to be seen by others to be able to do in the development of a new world order. The Chiefs of Staff Committee provides the forum for debate on strategic issues and the dynamic to implement measures needed to ensure that Britain's armed forces are such that they are sought by allies and feared by opponents, not so much for their size, but for the impact that their fighting qualities can make upon the balance of power.

Chapter 21

The Importance of the National Security Council

On 12 November 2010 Bramall spoke in the House of Lords on the higher organization of Defence.

My Lords, one of the most important parts of the strategic defence and security review was the establishment of the National Security Council, chaired at the highest level by the Prime Minister with his own designated staff, whose task it would be to develop and, one hoped, to oversee an updated national strategy. It was to cover, among other matters, vital interests, likely and even possible threats – international and domestic – and a range of state powers that we had to be prepared to take in the short and longer term. It would also lay down what the country might require its Armed Forces and the other complementary agencies to be able to do.

I greatly welcome this innovation, because it should have produced the planning assumptions in terms of priorities, scale, warning time, concurrency of possible involvements, reliable allied co-operation and broad financial restraints without which no detailed review could be coherent or relevant. It also had to be the only way of trying to balance the strictly military requirement to defend the realm and its established interests, together with any other aspirations in the international arena, against the resources that Parliament would be prepared to allot and above all to sustain.

The trouble was that such a fundamental and intricate exercise needed not only considerable thought, realistic insight, vision and some grasp of history by wise clear-headed people but also, inevitably, a reasonable amount of time to think things through properly. Yet, in parallel, there was an even more urgent exercise designed, irrespective of any strategic guidance and with a black hole of overspend to be eradicated, to secure an arbitrary cut of 10 per cent, or whatever, by certain dates from all vote holders, which often produced completely conflicting answers.

It would have been surprising if this exercise, rushed through in barely four months, came up with a blueprint that was truly in the up-to-date national interest. The fact that in the light of all the factors and pressures – political, strategic, economic and industrial – the review has come up with, at least for the moment, perhaps as good an optimum solution as could be expected owes much, I believe, to the direct interest and involvement of the Right Honourable gentleman, the Prime Minister,[91] the urgent and compelling requirements of Afghanistan, if we are to successfully complete our vital work within five years, and a general realisation of how invariably this country has needed really effective professional Armed Forces.

As far as I can judge, the NSC, although not properly constituted and not fully effective – I hope that it will become both those things – and however rushed, has come up with some helpful strategic guidance and assumptions. The operation in Afghanistan is to have the highest priority and is even in equipment terms to be enhanced. The cost of actual operations is to continue – I hope that everyone will note this, because the Prime Minister said so – to be met out of the Treasury reserve.

The review naturally highlighted good intelligence as being all important and often by far the best way of heading off the most urgent threat to us at the moment of international terrorism. It itemised the range of state powers that this country has, under various circumstances, to be prepared for. That ranges from active dynamic diplomacy through power projection for conflict prevention, humanitarian operations and peacekeeping, to limited and highly selective – and perhaps pre-emptive on hard intelligence – military action, and even, almost always with allies, larger scale intervention in order properly to protect our established interests.

Secondly, in giving broad guidance on size, shape and equipment type required, the review made a distinction between what is manifestly needed now and in the foreseeable future and that which, because of the volatility and uncertainty of the international scene, is required more in the form of a firm and experienced base for expansion and equipment development in the longer term, after a degree of notice and warning time but possibly against more sophisticated opposition. Of course, because you can often get these things wrong, as we have in the past – you can back the wrong horse – there has to be an element of flexibility. The point has been made that the review must be redone every five years if not even more regularly.

On the review itself, I personally can find nothing to be concerned about. The decision on the exact successor to our present Trident nuclear deterrent, which after all could be extended to serve effectively for at least another fifteen years, has been put off to 2015. This interim period will at least give us much needed flexibility diplomatically in negotiations on non-proliferation and multilateral disarmament. It also gives us an opportunity to examine whether there are not other, cheaper, more usable and therefore more appropriate and relevant ways of, with allies, deterring and, I hope, stopping likely threats to us in the future.

Yet some misgivings undoubtedly remain. There are misgivings about the carrier muddle and the shortage of destroyers and frigates, misgivings about the heavy reductions in the size of the Army and the future of the reserves and misgivings about where the covenant exactly stands at the moment. There is also sadness and sorrow about the early retirement of the highly versatile Harrier. However, as these things have been dealt with by other noble Lords at some length, because of time I will not deal with them any further.

The Nimrod saga was clearly a disgrace and should, among other things, be studied carefully when the whole structure of the Ministry of Defence, which has been for some time strong on second-guessing and bureaucratic procrastination and very weak on dynamic and effective action, is examined by my noble friend, Lord Levene.[92] For the moment – this is what is on the table – the SDSR [Strategic Defence and Security Review] has left us with, and in many places enhanced, a viable Armed Forces presence capable of playing, at short notice, an appropriate role in the protection of our country's interests overseas and nearer to home. Also, in conjunction with allies, but if necessary on our own, it can be well led, as our service men and women have [done] and continue to do. They will still, most importantly, be able to display that remarkable degree of motivation and dedication that sets them apart as professional forces in this troubled world. That does not happen by accident; it happens only because of the way that they have been trained, led and organised over a number of years.

I hope that the review will be looked on in a positive way and implemented with a will. Many of us who have had a great deal of experience in this field can give it a measure of encouragement and support. There is, however, one important caveat, which I want to stress. The National Security Council took a conscious decision and announced publicly that Defence and Security should be cut less than the activities of other departments and, presumably, less than the Treasury had at first demanded and that the NATO figure of 2 per cent of gross domestic product should be held to. Some might say that this is little enough in all conscience. These changes, both reductions and enhancements, must have been costed and have contributed to the 7.5 per cent in the defence budget which is what the National Security Council agreed at the highest level. The Treasury must now be held to that and must not, as has invariably happened in the past – usually before the ink was dry – start to undermine the whole review by further restricting the cash flow by various means. Every review over the years – some of them have been very good – has been immediately affected in this way, which has had an appalling effect. It has downgraded the expectations announced to the public, minimised political and parliamentary intentions, served up endless trouble for the future, which is partly why we have this yawning black hole, and rebounded dangerously, not only on operational performance but very much on the lives, support and welfare of the men and women of our Armed Forces and their families – on the covenant, in fact – to whom this country owes so much.

I hope that Ministers will take heed of these words, which are based on long experience, because with the Treasury short of its full pound of flesh, it is all the more likely that the money will not be there to pay for the changes in the defence review. The Government say that they are cutting this and bringing that down and getting rid of *Ark Royal* and that we will be left with this, that and the other, but we will find, if we are not careful, that the money will not be there to pay for even that. That would be absolutely disastrous. This has to be fought at the very highest level in the Cabinet, and by the Chiefs of Staff in the Ministry of Defence. Ultimately, we have to not just hold the line as it is at the moment, but in the future, do very much better with the financial resources, or the whole pack of cards will collapse and we will be in for real trouble.

Book 6

Leadership

Introduction

Bramall is particularly well qualified to talk and write about military leadership. Not only was he required to exercise it at every level of military field command from Platoon Commander to Commander-in-Chief, but his heritage as a Rifleman centred around an original and unstereotypical approach to military problems, not least the leadership of soldiers. This dates back to his original regiment being formed in the eighteenth century from settlers to fight the French and their Indian allies in the forests of North America, to the stimulating ideas of Sir John Moore, under whom the Rifles served in the Light Brigade, and later to Wellington, under whom they served both in the Light Division and skirmishing in front of and on the flanks of the main battle line in the Peninsular War.

Bramall used the bicentenary of the Battle of Waterloo and the legacy of Wellington, without whose leadership the battle would not have been won, to speak on British generals and generalship in the twentieth century; some of these generals Bramall knew and served under. Earlier he had written a very specific booklet on Junior Leadership for the benefit of officers joining a battalion for the first time. His papers with a leadership theme also include the eulogy he gave at the Memorial Service for a brilliant frontline leader and double VC winner, the New Zealander Charles Upham; one of the speeches Bramall gave at the Sovereign's Passing Out Parade at the R.M.A. Sandhurst; and his address at the Medal Parade of 2 Rifles on their return from Afghanistan in 2010.

Chapter 22

Generals and Generalship

In a public lecture entitled 'Generals and Generalship', given in September 2014, Bramall gave his views on the generals of the British Army in the twentieth century and their performance. He started with the qualities a general needs and went on to look at key generals of both World Wars, and their immediate pre-history.

With our minds and emotions focused this year on the centenary of the start of the Great War, which destroyed so many lives, and next year on the bicentenary of that decisive Alliance victory at Waterloo which certainly could not have been won without the personal presence and leadership of the great Duke of Wellington, it was thought you might be interested to hear from a long-time professional soldier some personal observations and assessments of British Generals and Generalship since Wellington, and on how [these men], some of whom I met and served under, performed in subsequent conflicts in and up to the end of the twentieth century,.

The first thing to be realistic about is that although the British Army has long been admired and respected throughout the world, it has been more for the steadfastness of its infantry in defence – 'the thin red line', you might say – the reliability of its NCOs and warrant officers, within a unique regimental system, and perhaps its junior leadership as developed at the Royal Military College and then Royal Military Academy, Sandhurst, rather than for the quality and tactical sense of its generals, some of whom, frankly, have been fairly indifferent. Our military history has been punctuated with such names as Braddock, Cornwallis, Chelmsford, Hamilton, Townsend and Percival, whose qualities of generalship, or lack of them, have contributed to serious military defeats. There have of course been marked exceptions.

Before Wellington the only commanders of note were Cromwell, who was a part-time soldier,[93] and the great Duke of Marlborough with his talent for allied command, grasp of logistics and calm control of the battlefield. In one campaign each the short-lived Wolfe, and the brilliant, much admired if ill-fated Sir John Moore, demonstrated great talent. The rest of the nineteenth century was inhibited by a lack of any reform after Wellington, while the prolongation of the system of purchasing commissions until the Cardwell reforms in the 1870s, and having supreme command mostly in the hands of the Royal Family, all meant that the best brains did not necessarily rise to the top at the right time. Also, the lack of sophisticated opposition, did not, until right at the end, throw up any really significant military figures.

Wellington, of course, possessed in full measure all the basic qualities required of any good and successful general; and it might be helpful first to analyse these, so that one can more easily see how subsequent generals measured up to them.

There are, I think, six essential qualities. The first, undoubtedly, is robustness in mind, body and spirit. The commander must be strong enough physically not only to be able to compete with prolonged campaigning in often arduous and unhealthy environments, but also to withstand the various shocks of war, which go hand in hand with conflict, even with the best laid plans, not excluding political pressures, and above all responsibility for men's lives. Youth may be a bonus to contribute to all-round good health – both Napoleon and Wellington were in their early to middle forties – but many good generals have been a lot older, and youth has to be balanced against important experience.

Next I would put courage, again, both physical, enough to ensure coolheadedness and clarity of orders and direction, whatever the imminent dangers; and moral, the willingness to take urgent, if unpopular decisions. Wellington was, of course, an outstanding example of all this. He was always at the right place, at the right time in a battle to demonstrate calm and confident leadership, whatever personal danger to himself (having many of his staff at Waterloo killed or wounded right beside him) and he is on record, when asked what was the greatest quality of a general, as saying, 'Knowing when to retreat and having the courage to do so'.

Next I would stress professionalism, by which I mean a sound knowledge of the whole mechanics of war, giving him a sense of what is practical operationally and what is not, and an ability to control, co-ordinate and most importantly keep supplied a large force of all arms, of whose special strengths and weaknesses he would be well aware. Wellington was a consummate professional, who had learned his trade in the unsuccessful British operations in Flanders and later in the exacting and demanding conditions in central India. He then consistently displayed and developed that professionalism in the six-year campaign in the Peninsular War against some of France's finest generals, or rather *maréchals*. But a general needs more than just professionalism, and a feel for how long everything takes, if he is to rise above being just 'a good plain cook' (as Montgomery unforgivably said in public of General Anderson, commanding the British 1st Army in Tunisia) and reap the proper rewards. He needs an acute tactical sense, a certain flair which would give him a 'nose' for what the enemy might have in mind; can spot opportunities which, if acted on quickly and with vigour, can be used to his great advantage, as Wellington showed at Salamanca ('*Marmont est perdu*')[94] and also at Oporto against Soult; and it also gives him a feel for the ground. Wellington demonstrated this so well at Waterloo in choosing the ground on which he was to do battle, and realising the great advantage of the sunken road and the reverse slope to help his army cope with the powerful French artillery bombardment and their massed cavalry charges. (My own experience many years later was that the Germans were equally good at using reverse slopes and the British, then, notably bad, but I digress!)

Then it is difficult to think of a good general who did not possess a keen intellect, which would enable him to be crystal clear about his priorities and his sustainable aims, and which should also have given him a good understanding of human nature so as to get the best out of his subordinates and allies, [something] at which Wellington was particularly good.

Finally, and above all, he will require the quality of leadership, the character to know what he wants and the determination to get it, and the ability to dominate and to inspire those under him, because there must be no doubt as to who is the boss, whose orders, once he has made up his mind, must be obeyed and not treated as a basis for discussion.

There can be quite a variation as to how individual commanders exercise that leadership. Some can almost rely on example and charm alone. Others, at the other extreme, perhaps rely on force of character and even fear. Some will want to inject an element of personal, almost theatrical showmanship to gain the attention and confidence of those under him. Wellington, of course, was no showman and could be particularly reticent, but he exercised his leadership by making all those under him feel that as long as he ('Old Nosey' as they called him) was there, they would have all that was needed in terms of supplies and tactical direction to ensure they could overcome whatever the opposition threw at them. This is crucial because, whatever method is used, exuding confidence is the essence. Soldiers do not win battles just because they are fighting for a good, or better, cause; they win, generally, because they are stronger in men and material; although sometimes it can be because they have been given the confidence to feel stronger by their leader, sufficient to carry them forward to victory.

With these pointers, perhaps I could now run the rule over British twentieth century generals to see how they measure up and what they achieved. I will look first at two essentially Victorian characters, Field Marshals Lord Roberts of Kandahar and Earl Kitchener of Khartoum, who qualify as twentieth century generals because they both took over in the Second South African War, when other generals had been found wanting. Both, of course, won their combat spurs against unsophisticated native opposition: Roberts with his great march from Kabul to Kandahar in 1879, and Kitchener at Omdurman near Khartoum in 1898, when his well-disciplined infantry was able, with some help from Beatty's gunboats on the Nile and the Maxim heavy machine gun, to kill literally thousands of Dervishes and hold their line with the loss of only twenty-seven killed. Both had the essential qualities of a good general: Roberts was exceptionally brave, winning the Victoria Cross (as did his son), warm and considerate, with an exceptional ability to win the respect and love of those under him – 'Bobs Bahadur' his adoring Ghurkhas called him. Although neither he, nor the colder, more austere and autocratic Kitchener, initially acting as his chief of staff, showed outstanding tactical sense in South Africa, Roberts did have the clarity of mind, having assembled sufficient force, to make a sound strategic plan to outflank the Boers in the Transvaal and stick to it. This ended the main war, and Kitchener showed energy and outstanding, if ruthless, organisational ability to bring the war to an end and ultimately defeat the Boers' guerrilla [action].

When the Great War broke out a decade later and Kitchener had come home, having been Commander-in-Chief in India, where he had argued with and got the better of the Viceroy, and [been] appointed Secretary of State for War in the political crisis of 1914, he showed a much clearer understanding than anyone else of how the war would develop and what would be needed in terms of manpower and munitions, and he created those Armies in a remarkably short space of time. Indeed, he may have prevented the Germans from capturing Paris when he ordered the Commander-in-Chief of the BEF (Sir John French) to conform to the French retreat to the Marne instead of pulling the BEF out to refit after Mons and Le Cateau, as the latter wanted. Both Kitchener and Roberts must be considered fine soldiers and significant military figures. Roberts, who became the last Commander-in-Chief of the Army before the post of CIGS was introduced, died in his eighties within the sound of the guns while visiting the BEF at St Omer in 1915, while Kitchener was killed at sea on his way to Russia in 1916.

[This] brings me to the First World War, and militarily it must be appropriate initially to consider the clutch of senior generals emerging, as a group, because they showed many common strengths and weaknesses. First, they were all products of the late Victorian and Edwardian age in which honour and the defence of the Empire, without counting the cost too much, was all that mattered, and indeed was sufficient reward for those who followed this heroic path. Yet soon they all came to be judged by the very different standards of a very different age in which it was no longer enough to win, which a number actually did, but [where] the cost, consequences and impact on the individual became all important and resulted, over the years, because of the appalling loss of life which most of their battles involved, in a tarnishing of their reputations (the 'Lions Led by Donkeys' and *Oh! What a Lovely War* syndrome). In addition, all had held more junior commands in the South African War with its wide-open spaces, and many, being cavalrymen, had become obsessed with mobility and the need to let the cavalry 'crack about' in the enemy's rear areas, which these open spaces had made possible. They failed to realise, or only slowly came to the realisation, how much the imped-ing qualities of barbed wire, massed machine guns and heavy artillery were to demand a completely new technique for the trench warfare that developed. So it wouldn't be until the last few months of the war that thanks to a positive learning curve and a change in ground conditions their efforts were able to bring sufficient success and indeed victory.

Of course, some of these generals were better than others because their learning curve was quicker, their planning more scrupulous and professional and their tactical instinct better developed. Amongst those I would single out the infantryman, Plumer, who despite looking like Low's Colonel Blimp, and indeed having some responsibility for the Passchendaele fiasco (the mistake was not in the strategy or in his handling of it, but the decision – not his – not to call it off when prolonged and torrential weather turned the battleground into a death trap) was in fact a very sound professional.[95] Then there was the cavalryman Byng, whose leadership made a great impact on the Canadians. They called themselves 'Byng's Boys', and he commanded the Canadian Corps with success at Vimy Ridge in 1917, and later became Governor-General of Canada. Even Rawlinson, who as commander of the Fourth Army presided, rather reluctantly as regards methods, over the Battle of the Somme and its 60,000 casualties on the first day, came into his own in the much more open warfare of the late summer and autumn of 1918. I think I should also mention Rawlinson's best friend and fellow Rifleman, although in the Rifle Brigade not the KRRC, the maverick Henry Wilson, who, although in no sense a commander, must be considered a significant military figure because it was his energy, determination and foresight, as a senior staff officer, which was largely responsible for the British Government finally deciding to send a BEF to France when the Germans invaded Belgium, and [for the fact]that it arrived professionally and administered by a good staff. Much later he was to mark himself as the only military man Lloyd George would deal with, con-firming his reputation as something of an intriguer, both militarily and polit-ically. A staunch Ulsterman, he was assassinated by the IRA in 1922 having earlier finished his career as CIGS.

But standing out above all the other generals on the Western Front must be Douglas Haig, who having commanded 1 Corps competently in the retreat to the Marne and then in the vital First Battle of Ypres, which probably saved the Empire, was to command the First Army, and then relieve the dashing and, in

South Africa successful, cavalry leader, Sir John French, later the 1st Earl of Ypres, who had proved himself to be above his ceiling as Commander-in-Chief of the BEF. Haig finished commanding five Armies and about 2 million men, over a sustained period of four years, leading through his perseverance, some foresight and a positive learning curve, to victory over a still formidable foe.

Douglas Haig was a professional soldier through and through; almost certainly the most qualified in the whole British Army at the time and recognised as such throughout. Even at the end of the war and after four years of hostilities, no military man seriously doubted that he was the best, perhaps the only, man who could lead the BEF on the Western Front. Most also believed that there was no one more deserving of victory when it came. A view, I must say, to which the Field Marshal, with his great self-confidence, would, I am sure, have subscribed! Indeed, though not a very charismatic, indeed a very reticent, leader there was no doubt about his complete authority, and indeed it should be recognised that even after all that his troops had been through, particularly in 1916 and 1917, he still retained their full support and loyalty. He certainly had the necessary robustness of body, mind and spirit to withstand the burden of four years of intense and costly warfare and the inevitable political and Allied stresses and strains – and one can only imagine how heavy that burden must have been. He also had courage, both physical, which he displayed personally on a number of occasions, particularly in November 1914 when, mounted, he rode forward to rally any stragglers, and again in the summer of 1918, when he did much the same thing, while giving his 'backs to the wall' order to ensure that the German breakthrough got no further; and moral, sticking to his view, which was correct, against much political opposition, that the war could only be won on the Western Front by the side which stood up best to the hard pounding and lasted longest. Although essentially an orthodox soldier, he consistently developed a more flexible tactical sense so that by 1918 the British and Dominion divisions had been raised to the cutting edge of the Allied armies on the Western Front, for example by the reorganisation of infantry tactics and more intimate support the infantry could expect from artillery and tanks, the greater use of radio in motorised units with aircraft, in the ground attack role, operating ahead of them [and] disrupting enemy troop movements. It was almost a forerunner of the German Blitzkrieg in World War II, and Haig was behind all that.

Although history may never let Haig and his subordinate commanders escape criticism for some of the technical and tactical errors which led to the horrendous casualties of 1915–16 and some of 1917 (suffered also, I may say, by the enemy), when you add to his performance in 1918 the size and tenure of his command over four bitter years, he must rank in the very top flight of British generals. And, of course, he had the intelligence and status and strength of character when the shooting stopped, to make an inroad into the social structure of this country through the setting up in 1921 in England, Wales, Scotland and Northern Ireland the organisation of the British Legion, to care for the needs of returning soldiers who had served him and their country so well.

There was one other World War I general who needs a specific mention and this was the cavalryman, Sir Edmund Allenby, later Field Marshal the Viscount Allenby of Megiddo. As he did not get on well with Haig, he was more easily selected to leave the Western Front to command our Army in Egypt, which had, prior to 1917, performed indifferently against the Turks under his predecessor. Allenby had many of the qualities necessary for higher command: certainly robustness. Nicknamed 'The Bull' for his uncertain temper, and with the ability to be decisive, given time to make up his mind, there was no doubt about who was the boss! But with this he had the character and personality to exercise confident leadership, which greatly impressed and inspired the Australians and New Zealanders under his command, who were not always easily led. Freed from the restraints of ground and trench warfare, where he had not particularly distinguished himself, he was able to display professional skills and tactical insights to great advantage, winning, with the help of carefully concealed deception plans and sound logistic planning and backup, two notable victories at Gaza and later Megiddo; these he brilliantly exploited first, with some help from Lawrence of Arabia's Arab Revolt, to capture Jerusalem and then later Damascus and Aleppo, 400 miles to the north, which put Turkey out of the war. At the end of the war he had the status and intelligence to make an effective High Commissioner of Egypt and the Sudan. All round, he must be considered one of the very best British generals of the twentieth century.

Now let us turn to the generals at, or coming to, the top twenty years later, with World War II about to break out. It is appropriate to consider that there were some extraneous factors which would have a bearing on where and how these generals operated. First of all, there would have been the experience in one form or another of the enormous casualty lists seemingly synonymous with the battles of the Great War, and this would have left a deep impression on them, to see if this could be avoided in future conflict. Secondly, because the Army was virtually forgotten about in the 1920s and on into the 1930s, it was starved of manpower (the Geddes Axe) and equipment, with a hesitant, desultory mechanisation programme,[96] so there became a tendency to look upon the joining of the British or Indian Army as something of an oppor-tunity to indulge in sport, particularly the equestrian variety, foreign travel, adventure and delightful and stimulating regimental ritual, rather than taking up a serious long-term profession which needed to be studied in depth. This led to a somewhat amateurish approach creeping in at every level, in marked contrast to Prussian militarism, which had remained in place even after the German defeat in 1918.

This had not been prevalent before the Great War thanks to the Staff College, which continued to do its best, and there were of course exceptions amongst those rising very slowly up the promotion ladder; but these tended to stick out a bit like a sore thumb, and were not always popular with their contemporaries. 'Too keen' was a criticism sometimes levelled at contemporaries, and some regiments frowned on any officers wanting to go to the Staff College.

Another factor which influenced the deployment of generals at the start of the war was the appointment as Secretary of State for War in 1938 of an ambitious, publicity-seeking politician named Leslie Hore-Belisha, who had made his name as Minister of Transport ('Belisha Beacons' at pedestrian crossings). He quickly got the impression, probably correctly, that the Army had a good deal of dead wood at the top, and in order to make a dramatic political gesture decided to fire the existing CIGS, Sir Cyril Deverall, a Yorkshire infantryman who had been a successful divisional commander in the First World War. (His sacking was conveyed to him by a letter he found sitting on his desk.) Hore-Belisha set out to dig down the promotion list to select a fairly junior new broom as replacement. Unfortunately, instead of selecting one of the true rising stars, like the infantrymen Wavell or Dill or the Gunner Alan Brooke, who had been put in charge of the experimental, rickety Mobile Division, he picked someone whom he knew, because he had been his own Military Secretary. This was the Guardsman, Gort ('Fat Boy' Gort VC, so named for his extreme fitness and slim physique), a very brave fighting soldier who although unlike another earlier Guardsman whom a bright military contemporary later described as 'as out of place as CIGS in the War Office as a nun in a night club',[97] was somewhat out of his depth and was soon transferred more logically to swap with Ironside as C-in-C (Designate) of the BEF.[98] 'Tiny' Ironside (he was well over 6 feet), [who had] seen much active service, including in North Russia at the end of the Great War, and was said to be the role model for Bulldog Drummond,[99] was himself much more of a commander than a staff officer, and was to prove no match for Churchill when the latter became Prime Minister, so he too was relieved, first by being made C-in-C Home Forces and promoted Field Marshal, and later retired to become Baron Ironside in the House of Lords. Although one of his Corps Commanders rather snidely remarked that Gort seemed more concerned as C-in-C with what the men had in their water-bottles than with strategy, he should not be written down as a commander of the BEF because, mindful of

Wellington's remark about 'knowing when to retreat and having the courage to do so', he was the one who quickly decided that his only hope in June 1940 was to try to evacuate his outnumbered and grossly under-equipped BEF from Dunkirk before they were completely overwhelmed. He was later (May 1942) sent, most appropriately, to be Governor of the George Cross Island of Malta[100] in the vital struggle to maintain itself as a thorn in the side of Rommel and his supplies.

So then, after a certain amount of 'Box and Cox', our senior generals were, at the start of the war, deployed as follows. As CIGS, the top man, there was John Dill, a recent corps commander in the BEF and a thoroughly good professional soldier, who seemed eminently qualified for the job. Unfortunately, his robustness and stamina were not sufficient to prevent him from being driven to a virtual nervous breakdown by the buffeting he received from Churchill, with his many unreasonable demands and his criticisms of the generals in the field. But later, Dill was to play a vital role as Britain's representative with the US Chiefs of Staff, and when he died in 1945, as a mark of their respect he was buried in Arlington Cemetery.[101]

In his place, late in 1941, came that formidable Gunner and master of strategy, Alan Brooke. Long destined for high office, he had been a corps commander in the BEF in 1939–40, and C-in-C Home Forces at the time of imminent invasion, and he certainly had the robustness to stand up to Churchill. Indeed, he had already had the courage to tell him, with some asperity, when ordered to lead British troops back to France after Dunkirk so as to make the French feel we were supporting them, that it would be impossible to resurrect a corpse! With his intellect and clear, incisive mind he could communicate directly with Churchill on equal terms and keep the Prime Minister's inspirational, war-winning leadership within practical bounds. When discussing the appointment of Dill's successor with the VCGIS, Archie Nye, Churchill said, 'When I thump the table and push my face towards him what does he do? Thumps the table harder and glares back at me! I know these Brookes – stiff-necked Ulstermen and there's no one worse to deal with than that.'[102] Undoubtedly, because of his grasp and influence on strategy, with the Americans as well as ourselves, no military figure did more to help win the war. But he never had, of course, the opportunity, after Dunkirk, to command troops in the field, since an American was bound to be selected for the supreme command of the invasion of Europe. He could not therefore be rated as a commander in the field on a par with Wellington, but he was a very significant military figure nonetheless.

But of the effective field commanders after Dunkirk the one that most quickly comes to mind is the C-in-C Middle East (the main, indeed only, and far-reaching[103] active command at the time), the highly intelligent and cultured Wykehamist, Archie Wavell, to whom, incidentally, we are all indebted for his wonderful anthology of verse *Other Men's Flowers*,[104] all of which he could at one time recite by heart, [and] who was, with the cards he had to play, a skilful military practitioner with an original approach, a great sense of history and a keen tactical sense, who could seize opportunities when they existed, as he showed with his comprehensive defeat of the Italian army in Cyrenaica in 1940, which he exploited out of what was originally planned as a strong frontier raid. He was physically tough and robust, but the trouble was that his leadership was somewhat tinged with pessimism, or perhaps excessive realism. And his demise had to come, not because of a later defeat in the Western Desert, for which he was not entirely to blame, but because of his long silences and monosyllabic responses when called upon to report, and a complete inability to communicate with Churchill, who liked a battle of words in debate as much as he almost enjoyed every other sort of battle. 'Nothing is so invigorating', he used to say, 'as being shot at without results.' So again, he had to go, first to be C-in-C India, and from there to command in South-East Asia,[105] where he was too late to influence the military disasters which were occurring in Burma, Malaya and Singapore, and afterwards to be a statesman-like Viceroy of India. However, in different circumstances he might have proved to be, and been recognised as, one of this country's very best generals.

Wavell was relieved by the C-in-C India, Claude Auchinleck, a sound professional soldier who himself had the robustness and stamina, as he showed later by holding Rommel at the first battle of Alamein. But he was a poor picker of subordinates, and was too easily influenced by clever advisers without proper professionalism.[106] And, to a great extent the to-and-fro battles in the Western Desert in 1941 and the summer of 1942 were influenced by a certain lack of professionalism throughout the chain of command. There was uncertainty and disagreement about the best way of handling armour in the prevailing conditions, co-operation between arms was poor, and the giving and receiving of orders over the radio was in its infancy. As a result, formation headquarters were not capable of delivering even the best-laid plans without getting them confused and delayed. To confound it all, there developed a chaotic command organisation to lead Operation CRUSADER, the counter-offensive to Rommel's earlier threat, and still rather premature, due to Churchill's pressure. To lead it Auchinleck had picked General Alan Cunningham, who had done well in East Africa against the Italians. But when his operational plans began running into trouble and his rear areas became threatened by a daring, if injudicious, Rommel thrust, he began to lose his nerve and his health, and Auchinleck rightly decided to remove him because the battle was there to be won. But instead of taking command of the Desert Army himself, he introduced a newly-arrived member of his staff, his DCGS,

Lieutenant-General Neil Ritchie, who had no experience of field command, let alone in the desert. Ritchie was a good man, a protégé of Wavell and later a steady corps commander in North-West Europe, but he was junior in rank and age to some of the other desert generals who were now subordinate to him. These included the very rapidly promoted, but desert-experienced 'Strafer' Gott, the Indian cavalryman Messervy, and the cavalrymen Norrie and Lumsden, all admirable men, albeit with some professional weaknesses, who naturally resented and mistrusted Ritchie; they complicated his orders and questioned them, making them the basis for discussion. To make matters worse, Ritchie never felt himself a free agent, with Auchinleck indulging in back-seat driving and constantly giving him advice. The result was uncertainty and misunderstanding, and although the Germans were pushed back and Tobruk relieved, which said much for the fighting spirit of our troops, particularly when taking account of their generally inferior equipment, the technically victorious battle left a feeling of lack of confidence and uncertainty. This no doubt contributed to the later major defeats at Gazala and El Adem, where instead of defeating Rommel, who had got himself into a very vulnerable position on the wrong side of a minefield, he was allowed to push on through the now too dispersed and ill-coordinated British and South African forces and capture Tobruk, throwing the Desert Army into headlong retreat right back to the Egyptian frontier and beyond. Here, Auchinleck, now in sole command, held him at a small railway station called El Alamein, under a hundred miles from Alexandria. But after this serious defeat he, too, had to go because the army had lost all confidence in its leadership and in its ability to defeat the charismatic Rommel.

And this is where Montgomery came on the scene. Churchill, against Brooke's advice, had wanted the desert-experienced and most popular of the remaining desert generals, 'Strafer' Gott to take over, he whom Mike Carver once described as 'all that was best in the profession of arms'. But Gott was desperately tired after nearly three years of continuous fighting, and it is doubtful if he could have revived the confidence of the Desert Army, which had been so shattered; then, of course, he was shot down in an aircraft returning to Cairo for leave before taking command.

Montgomery, on the other hand, who had been strongly backed by Brooke, had all the qualities for army command at such a crucial time. He was a consummate professional, who had studied his profession in the greatest detail and he knew, as few other British generals did, how to manage a large battle and to co-ordinate all the elements of the Army to the best advantage. He had proved himself commanding 3 Division, under Brooke's command, during the retreat to Dunkirk. He also realised that, at this moment, getting over to the dispirited Desert Army optimistic confidence would have to be the key to his leadership and to achieve this he was prepared to use a large element of personal contact and showmanship, at which he was very good, to give them that confidence. He left nobody in any doubt as to who was the boss whose orders had to be obeyed without any argument or, as he described it 'belly-aching'. Rommel could be defeated and indeed would be defeated by him, by Montgomery.

Having had the drive and authority to put in place the forces needed, he exemplified to them that confidence by, before the main battle of Alamein itself, decisively defeating Rommel's last attempt to reach the Delta by successfully holding the key and vital ground at Alam Halfa and inflicting very severe casualties on him. It is often said that Montgomery's tactical sense bordered on the cautious, but this is not entirely borne out by his record. It is true that what he did prefer was the set piece battle, when everything was in place as he wanted it, with a proper balance of advantage in men and fire power. But he went on to win two more important battles on the border of Tunisia, the defensive battle of Medenine and an imaginative break into the Mareth Line. Successfully he had, alongside the Americans, invaded Sicily, and then started with his Eighth Army the long slog up the east coast of Italy as far as the Sangro River, seizing the all-important Foggia airfields. But I have no doubt that his finest hour came with the invasion of Normandy, for which he had been appointed the Land Commander-in-Chief. What Monty did was to inherit a plan that would not have worked, convert it into one on a wider front that would, and produce exactly the right amount of confident and competent leadership when so many others had doubts, and to inspire those taking part. And, of course, I was one of those who listened to one of Monty's 'pep talks', which always filled us with enormous confidence that he knew exactly what he was doing and that all would be well. Quite different from what I heard from a corps commander, who rather delightfully and modestly ended his speech with the words 'Well, gentlemen, I know whatever the balls-up I may make of it, you will see me through!'[107] That was not quite what we wanted to hear! Above all, Monty produced a sound and indeed brilliant master plan: to hold down and write down most of, and indeed the best of, the German divisions at the key east end of the bridgehead in front of his British and Canadian troops, so as to make it easier for the Americans to break out to the west, and thus provide scope for an encircling movement to cut off the Germans' determined forward defences west of the Seine or closer in. And that is exactly what happened. As a result, the Allies lined up along and indeed across the Seine within three months of D-Day, exactly as Monty had predicted, and with two whole German armies virtually written off in a catastrophic defeat in the Falaise pocket. It was a masterly performance and was to lead at once to a blitzkrieg-like, albeit latterly hazardous, exploitation through northern France and Belgium to Antwerp, and the attempt to cross the Rhine, which became 'a bridge too far'. No one could say that this was not something of a risky gamble, and it was then followed by a hard winter break-through of the Siegfried Line, followed by an immaculate set-piece crossing of the Rhine itself, which was right up Monty's street. This led to the final clearance of north-west Germany. In all of this, Monty in his own Army Group sector, and, at one crisis period, the Battle of the Bulge, in part of the American sector as well, kept tight operational control, albeit often influenced and motivated by his determination for his Army Group to be in the pole position for the final advance to the Elbe or to Berlin.

Although Monty had a keen and crystal-clear intellect, he was, unlike Wellington, extremely bad over his relations with his allies. His patronising attitude to his Supreme Commander, General Eisenhower, and sometimes other US generals, was intolerable, and he often tactlessly insisted to Supreme Headquarters, and others, that all his battles had gone exactly according to the original plan, when as so often in war, particularly when there is such determined resistance, this does not happen.

He always had the robustness and clarity of vision, however, after any tem-porary setback to make the necessary adjustments in thrust lines and tactical innovation, to see his overall aim was never lost sight of, and the enemy were kept pinned down and written down by our vastly superior fire-power, and with our casualties kept as low as possible. This was essential because the British were very short of infantry reinforcements. Considering the quality and fanaticism of the opposition it was still a formidable achievement, with Allied forces gaining in professionalism and experience as the days and weeks went on. To this Montgomery himself contributed by bringing in personally selected commanders at army, corps and even divisional level, prepared to operate strictly under his tight direction: Dempsey (Second Army), a resusci-tated Ritchie (XII Corps), Leese (Eighth Army in Italy, after XXX Corps in North Africa), Crocker (I Corps), Horrocks (XXX Corps) and Roberts (7 Armoured Division), the victor of Alam Halfa, who seized Antwerp in 1944 by a bold *coup de main*. These changes improved the detailed planning and execution of those tactics which were to be found successful: accepting more limited objectives to save excessive casualties, frequently changing the thrust lines to draw in more enemy reserves, and using our overwhelming fire power and air power, not only to break in but to destroy the inevitable counter-attacks, until the enemy cracked. There are similarities to the bite and hold tactics towards the end of World War I here.

Montgomery was undoubtedly a master of the battlefield and made a major contribution to winning the war, and so must rank up with Wellington as a field commander. Indeed, like him, he can be said to have won a major

Alliance victory, in Normandy, which was to change the face of Europe. There is a nice little anecdote about Montgomery, in quite a different, non-combat setting, to illustrate his skill at making speedy adjustments if he ran into trouble. At the end of World War II he had been asked by the Second Master at Winchester College, who had been one of his liaison officers,[108] to inspect the CCF there.

Going down the line of boys, Monty asked the first one, 'Who was the greatest general in the Second World War?' only to receive the not entirely expected reply 'Alexander, Sir'.

Monty's immediate response of 'Quite right, quite right! He always did everything I told him!' shows him up well, as a tactician, if not as a person!

Which anecdote brings me to Harold Alexander, later Field Marshal Earl Alexander of Tunis and Governor General of Canada, widely known simply as 'Alex'. From a young age, this brave, debonair and immaculate Guardsman had been groomed for high command, commanding a Guards battalion and a brigade on the Western Front in his mid-twenties, and seeing service not only on the Western Front, but also in North Russia. As commander of the 1st Division he commanded the rear-guard for the evacuation at Dunkirk. Then for a short time he was sent out to try to stabilise the situation at the start of the British and Indian retreat in Burma, but was shortly withdrawn to be made Commander-in-Chief in the Middle East, when Monty took over the Eighth Army. He therefore became Monty's boss, although knowing Monty (the two had been divisional commanders together under Brooke in II Corps, 1939–40), he gave him full rein to fight the battle of Alamein in his own way. After the Eighth Army had advanced into Tunisia and joined up with the Americans and the British First Army, who had landed in Algeria and Morocco, he took command of 18th Army Group for the final breakthrough and the removal of all Axis forces in Tunisia, with the capture of well over 200,000 German and Italian prisoners. This too was a formidable achievement, as Hitler had insisted on continuing to reinforce the experienced Afrika Korps until nearly the very end.

After this Alexander became Eisenhower's land Commander-in-Chief, taking a loosely (some would say rather too loosely) co-ordinating role over Montgomery's and Patton's armies in the invasion and occupation of Sicily, and he then did the same for the hard slog up Italy, inspiring the troops in the hard-fought Salerno bridgehead, but doing little to galvanise the sluggish and initially unopposed landings at Anzio. In fact, no great credit can be attached to him for his attempted breakthrough of the Gustav Line around Monte Cassino when more effort should have been made and devoted to the out-flanking position through the mountains. After the capture of Rome by the Americans, under his overall command, Alexander's forces, which had already drawn off many German divisions away from the Normandy landings, were progressively reduced to allow for a second invasion in Southern France, and yet he still had to battle northwards and into the Gothic Line through the mountains and in terrible weather conditions so as to keep the Germans pinned down. By early 1945, however, he did manage to break through and achieved a significant victory in the Po valley so that the German forces in Northern Italy were the first to surrender in May 1945, again a considerable achievement, considering his comparatively limited resources.

Alexander may not have been as clear-headed a tactician as Montgomery. It was said that he needed a good Chief of Staff[109] to help him formulate and carry through a battle. But his relaxed leadership and charm won much devotion from subordinates, and the Americans trusted him completely. Indeed, Eisenhower would have preferred him to Montgomery to command the invasion land forces in Normandy. And there would never have been a question of an American general refusing to serve under him, as was threatened later with Monty after the Battle of the Bulge. His modesty was in marked contrast to Monty's egotism, and there is a good story to illustrate this, when after the war there was a reunion of the top brass.

Prime Minister Harold Macmillan said to Alexander, 'Alex, wouldn't it be wonderful if we could have our lives all over again?'

To which Alexander replied, 'Oh no, Harold, that wouldn't be at all a good idea. We might not do nearly so well next time!'

He undoubtedly was a great captain of whom this country should be very proud, which leaves me only one other who might aspire to that description. This is Bill Slim, commander of Fourteenth Army in Burma, and, much later, CIGS and finally Governor General in Australia. 'Uncle Bill', as he was always affectionately known by his troops, was very much a soldiers' general, who exercised his leadership through, with his straight from the shoulder approach, their feeling that he was very much one of them, who would always be with them however tough the going got. A Ghurkha, he had won his spurs commanding a brigade in East Africa against the Italians. But as a more senior officer he presided over and kept some control over the long retreat of BurCorps through Burma to the Indian border. With his Fourteenth Army, he held the Japanese in desperate defensive battles at Kohima and Imphal, and then when the time was right and when more resources became available, he clearly defeated the Japanese, now greatly overextended, using a variety of innovative tactics: Chindit operations behind the enemy lines, wide outflanking movements across the Irrawaddy river, often having his troops supplied from the air in country devoid of proper communications, and amphibious operations, progressively to clear the whole of Burma and recapture Rangoon. It was a first-class practical piece of generalship, carefully controlled, which took account of all the relevant factors and achieved complete success. The new Army Group Commander for the recapture of Malaya, Oliver Leese (one of Monty's boys), tried to relieve Slim on the grounds that he felt he was worn out after continuous fighting, and he had, it is believed, some support for this from Mountbatten, the Supreme Commander South East Asia, although Mountbatten afterwards hotly denied this. There was such an outcry that the Army Group Commander went instead, and Slim took his place for the forthcoming invasion of Malaya.[110] Slim was a highly intelligent man with a good literary bent, and after leaving the army, and for a time running the railways, was brought back by Prime Minister Attlee to be CIGS, at which he proved to be a truly outstanding incumbent, far superior to Montgomery who, having no political antennae, believed he could behave in Whitehall just as he had on the battlefield, laying down the law and expecting the whole Whitehall machine to comply!

Since the complete and ultimate success of World War II the British Regular Army has achieved and maintained, I believe, a very high degree of professionalism, and the General Officers and Joint Commanders for the most part, have been found fully up to the operational responsibilities imposed on them, but I must end with the twentieth century generals as promised.

There were significant military figures who could not be judged on field command alone, but who made a major contribution both to the reputation and progress of the British Army, and amongst these I would include Roberts and Kitchener at the beginning of the century, Wilson in the Great War, and of course, Brooke, the master of Allied strategy in World War II. Then there were any number of subordinate army and corps commanders who were essential executors of their overall commander-in-chief's design for battle planning and carrying through their plans to conform to the pattern and aims he had laid down. These were good, professional commanders (those who did not come up to scratch had been removed) and who, as the wars progressed, introduced much closer co-operation between all arms and far more effective planning and implementation of operations generally.

Finally, we have the comparatively few who may be worthy of the mantle of Wellington. All possessed the basic qualities required of a good general, although not all to the same degree. All made mistakes; most generals do, but all of them achieved significant success against formidable opponents, which others might have failed to achieve, and all contributed to their county's success on the field of battle in the two World Wars. They are, in no particular order, Haig, Allenby, Montgomery, Alexander and Slim. Certainly, all can be said to have been masters of the battlefield. I believe no others qualify to the same extent, but there may be others on the fringes whom I have not had time to mention, and I am happy to deal with them in questions.

Chapter 23

Field Marshal Earl Haig KT

In a lecture to the Haig Fellowship in 2009 Bramall delivered a broad survey of Sir Douglas Haig, entitled 'A Field Marshal on a Field Marshal'. It was his first public attempt to sum up the qualities of the controversial First World War Commander-in-Chief.

I feel greatly honoured to have been invited to be the Douglas Haig Fellow for 2009 and to address you at this annual lunch; but the theme I have been given, 'A Field Marshal on a Field Marshal', fills me with great humility because only in our common rank can there be any similarity in our experience, achievements and impact on our country's history.

In the early part of our careers, up to perhaps even Brigadier (or Brigadier-General in his case), we may have had some similar spells of sustained active service, and experience of warfare of one sort or another, but the Field Marshal always seemed to be playing more significant roles, which were marking him down, with the most senior commanders in the British Army, for rapid advancement, achieving major-general at the very young age of 43; I had to wait another five years! And after that, my command of a division in the Cold War, the British Forces in Hong Kong, Home Commander-in-Chief and, finally, eight years on the Chiefs of Staff Committee, three of them as head of the Army when it was not much more than 200,000 and with but one proper, and then very short, conflict, the Falklands, doesn't begin to compare with the command of a Corps during the retreat from Mons to the Marne and at the First Battle of Ypres, followed progressively by the command of, first, an Army and then five Armies and almost 2 million men, over a sustained period of over four years, all leading through his foresight, steadfastness and perseverance to complete victory against a very formidable foe.

Afterwards, of course, the Field Marshal, rightly elevated to an Earldom, was for the rest of his life to make an enormous impact on the social structure of this country through the organisation he set up in England, Wales and Scotland[111] to care for the needs of the returning soldiers who had served him and their country so well to the very end. So my humility has plenty of substance and my assessment of him is made as a student of military history rather than in any sense as an equal.

The trouble has always been, for the Field Marshal himself and for all those who have so respected him, that in every sense he was a product of the late Victorian and Edwardian age, in which honour and defending the Empire, without counting the cost too much, was all that really mattered. Indeed, it was in itself sufficient reward for those who followed this heroic path. Yet, he and his contemporaries soon came to be judged by some very different standards of a very different age, in which it was no longer enough just to win. The costs, consequences and the impact on the individual became all important. So it is right that, from time to time, the record has to be re-balanced in its proper perspective, something he never bothered to do in the less than a decade he lived after the Great War. He kept a dignified silence. Anyhow, this is what I will now endeavour to do, covering ground many of you will know well.

Douglas Haig was, of course, a professional soldier through and through, probably the most professionally qualified in the whole Army; and indeed, recognised as such throughout the Army. He had studied his profession intensely and had carried out important tasks both in command and on the staff on the various rungs of the military structure. Indeed, to the end of his career no military man seriously doubted that he was the best and indeed perhaps the only man to lead the BEF on the Western Front, or one who more deserved the victory when it came. A view to which the Field Marshal, with his great self-confidence, would, I am sure, have entirely subscribed! Although a very private person, difficult to get close to, he was so very self-assured and self-reliant that he didn't really need encouragement and assurance to bolster his morale or to advise him on things on which he had already made up his mind. He was completely confident in his professional ability and qualifications and, I have not the slightest doubt, believed that Destiny had had a part in bringing him to the role he was about to assume, just as Winston Churchill felt in 1940. All this, of course, actually strengthened his hand as a commander and his ability to ride through 'the slings and arrows of outrageous fortune', which are inevitable in so protracted and bloody a conflict.

Douglas Haig, who had done well in the smaller but more flexible and wide-ranging conflict in South Africa, first came to prominence and under the national microscope as a top battlefield commander when, at the outbreak of the war in August 1914, and as a Lieutenant-General, he took I British Corps to France as part of the BEF, under his old South African War cavalry boss, Sir John French. After the retreat from Mons to the Marne, and the bounce back to the Aisne and further north still, his Corps held the Germans at the First Battle of Ypres. This battle had started as Haig thought all battles should start (indeed, he tended to judge his subordinate commanders almost exclusively on, to use his own phrase, whether they showed 'a sincere desire to engage the enemy') with an attempted offensive to drive the Germans before them. But it soon became clear that the enemy were in far greater strength than expected and indeed were on the point of launching, with fresh divisions, a major offensive themselves, designed to separate the British from the French and drive them back to the sea.

The attack when it came was massive and prolonged for one whole month (mid-October to mid-November 1914). The enemy's artillery support was overwhelming, yet somehow, thanks to the great heroism of I British Corps units, some of them fighting almost to the last man, the line held, which probably saved the Empire. Haig had handled all this, as he did his Corps' part in the retreat from Mons, with cool-headedness, determination and firm control; and he himself was often under shellfire, e.g. once occupying and often visiting the chateau on the Menin Road where two of his divisional commanders were mortally wounded. Indeed, at the critical point in the battle when it looked as if the Germans had indeed broken through, at Geluvelt, a key village on the Menin Road, which was miraculously recaptured by a brilliant charge by the Worcestershire Regiment, he mounted his charger and rode down that road towards the enemy to encourage and inspire those still fighting so hard and to rally the inevitable stragglers. This was a device he was to repeat over three years later after the German offensive at Saint Quentin which so nearly captured Amiens, when he issued his memorable Order of the Day, with the immortal phrases 'With our backs to the wall and believing in the justice of our cause each one of us must fight on to the end.' He had come through his baptism of fire in that new type of warfare which earned him the gratitude of his C-in-C and promotion to full General. After this promotion, first to command of an Army, and then, in December 1915, to be British and Dominion Commander-in-Chief, he followed the only path he thought right, which was to defeat the enemy.

This was his one and only aim. Throughout 1916 and 1917 he based his strategy to achieve that aim on three golden rules: (a) the war could only be won on the Western Front, (b) it could only be won by attrition, by the side that lasted the longest, and (c) the best way to achieve this was by continually attacking the enemy, to wear him down and, if possible, to do this with such speed and to such depth that the cavalry could be released into the enemy's rear areas, thus forcing him to commit even more of his precious reserves. He was also very ready to come to the assistance of his French allies whenever he could, so that they, too, could play their full part (often a major part) in the attrition battle.

On the first two he was proved right, although on the third there were doubts (since increasingly expressed) as to whether prolonged and continuous attacks with deep objectives were the best way of achieving attrition, rather than short sharp attacks followed by consolidation and destruction, by fire, of the inevitable enemy counter-attacks.[112] But certainly, at the Battle of the Somme, ever on the conscience of the British people, in which the British suffered horrendous casualties, the Germans suffered even more heavily. If Haig had a marked tactical weakness, it was his conviction that battle should, and indeed could, still be finally won by the shock action and deep penetration of horsed cavalry – the cavalry charge, if you like. This was no doubt encouraged by the wide-open spaces of South Africa (his most recent war experience) when cavalry did have that free reign, e.g. capturing Kimberly. Later, of course, military thinkers, who were able to substitute tanks and motorised infantry for horsed cavalry, followed a similar concept very successfully. Anyhow, all those battles, largely offensive against the Germans holding more dominating ground, continued, to varying degrees, because lessons were being learned all the time, to show the strength and weaknesses of the C-in-C's strategy, and all those battles contributed (at a price) to the attrition and eventual downfall of the enemy.

But, in the time I have, I want to concentrate mostly on the events of 1918 which, a year earlier than had been intended, but which he himself had predicted, brought the war to an end, and in which Haig's reputation and right to be considered as one of the country's greatest commanders should have been well and truly enhanced; and for which he has never really had the full credit he deserves.

As the Commander-in-Chief dressed on the morning of 21 March 1918, immaculately, as always, in boots and breeches, he received the news that the major German offensive on his front, which he had anticipated, had begun, with a massive onslaught 43 miles wide, the weight of which fell on General Sir Hubert Gough's Fifth Army, on ground recently taken over from the French. Its aim was clearly to split the Allied front and cut off the BEF from the Channel ports. In complete contrast, only six days before, he had received far more welcome, and for him, momentous news that his wife had borne him a son. He was 57 and had almost lost hope of there being an heir to the title of Laird of Bemersyde. His biographer, Duff Cooper, recounts how Haig, usually a taciturn and undemonstrative man, had embraced the Medical Corps colonel who had been in attendance and to his astonishment kissed him, like a Frenchman, on both cheeks! And not long ago we happily marked Dawick Haig's ninetieth birthday. But I digress slightly.

Yet it was desperation as much as anything else that had turned the German Chief of the General Staff of the Field Army, Field Marshal Hindenburg, and his Chief of Staff (or Quarter Master General) Ludendorff, away from the shrewd, largely defensive strategy on the Western Front. The vast cost in men and crucial resources which was to result from the March 1918 offensive was really forced on them by the Kaiser's approval of unrestricted submarine warfare, and the subsequent sinking of neutral shipping, together with the madcap scheme, which came to the ears of the Americans, to create a diversion in conjunction with Mexico in the event of that provoking the United States into declaring war, as of course happened. The Germans felt that they had to do something before the Americans could arrive in sufficient strength to tip the manpower balance; and if they couldn't win they had, to their mind, lost, not being interested in a negotiated peace for which they might have been in a strong position.

Haig's generalship in readiness for the offensive could hardly be faulted. He positioned his reserves in the north, where the front was 25 miles from the sea at its nearest point and, anticipating the main German attack in the south, ordered Gough's Fifth Army to give ground but to keep his front intact, while striving to maintain contact with the British Third Army on his left and the French Sixth Army on his right.

Gough, whom I once met when he was very old but as sprightly as ever, was, of course, to be made Lloyd George's scapegoat for the British casualties sustained and the ground lost, but his withdrawal was in exact accord with the instructions Haig had given him. He handled his divisions like a flexible chain. When it broke, as it often did, in places pretty chaotically, he cobbled it together, often using dismounted cavalry or improvised groups of lines of communication troops, to grant Haig time to bring the French to his aid over the ground they had held until recently.

On 23 March Ludendorff, the *de facto* commander of the German forces in the West, delivered a new attack with fresh divisions in the north of the BEF front at Arras, but this brought him little more than crippling casualties. In his sop to public opinion, Lloyd George had insisted that Gough be replaced by General Sir Henry Rawlinson and the Fourth Army staff, but by then the worst was over in the south. The BEF, still remarkably effective after four years of war, had fought six gruelling defensive battles between 21 March and 5 April, retreating almost to the gates of Amiens.

Ludendorff then swung further north still against Ypres and Hazebrouck, where the BEF fought eight more costly battles. The total bill for March and April was 40,000 dead, 180,000 wounded and 93,000 missing, from every part of Britain, Ireland and the [Empire]. They had had to bear a very heavy burden, but the endurance of the survivors had thwarted the breakthrough on which Ludendorff had so depended.

Foresight, resolve and persistence were being rewarded. Ludendorff conceded the BEF was too much for him, turned on the French, and Haig began preparations for his ultimately decisive offensive in August, in concert with

Foch, who was now co-ordinating the whole Allied effort on the Western Front.

This began on 8 August 1918, the day which Ludendorff described as 'the black day of the German Army'. In this so-called hundred-day offensive, which ultimately brought the Great War to an end, the BEF, including many fine divisions from the Dominions, won the Field Marshal and his Fourth Army commander, Rawlinson, the greatest succession of victories in the history of the British Army. During those hundred days, they engaged ninety-one German divisions, some more than once, and by the Armistice in November had taken 188,700 prisoners, captured 2,840 artillery pieces and defeated the formidable Imperial German Army. No mean achievement. This performance cannot, of course, be seen in isolation. The Germans had themselves prepared the ground for their own defeat, in that Ludendorff, having exhausted the German Army's resources with not nearly enough to show for it, now left himself vulnerable to counter-attacks over country much more conducive to manoeuvre and exploitation. On the Allied side, the Americans, Belgians, Portuguese and, of course, the French Army, nursed back to discipline and full effectiveness by the humanity and leadership of Pétain, all made key contributions.

There was also the part played by the confidence, optimism and determination of Foch, who had been named, at Haig's insistence, at the crisis meeting at Doullens in March, as General-in-Chief of the Allied Armies in France. It was he who, with Haig, shaped the winning strategy of attacks at different points along the whole front, from the Argonne Forest in the south to Ypres in the north, to be followed by the *coup de grace* on September 29, when the BEF's Fourth Army, supported by the American First Army, stormed the Hindenburg Line. In the following week, the German High Command could only advise the Kaiser to seek an armistice.

And here it is important to dismiss the myth of the German Army being 'stabbed in the back' by the failure of its manufacturing base and supply organisation. In March and April 1918 irreparable damage had been inflicted on it by first the blunting and then the halting of Ludendorff's offensive in Picardy and Flanders which had denied it an opportunity to divide the BEF from the French; but much of the German Army was still fighting in that autumn with all the tactical skill and tenacity that characterised the German soldier in both World Wars. But in November 1918 there was no doubt that the enemy was being defeated in the field. As Haig put it, they were capable neither of accepting nor refusing battle.

Although Haig himself was by nature very much an orthodox soldier, not prone to risky flights of imagination, his victory had, in fact, been the product of a steep learning curve from December 1916 after the Somme, which had raised his British and Dominion divisions to the tactical and technical cutting edge of the Allied Armies on the Western Front. It could be seen in the re-organisation of infantry platoons and in small unit tactics, using new infantry weapons; in the greater use of wireless, motor machine gun units, armoured cars, and of aircraft in the ground attack role, disrupting enemy troop concentrations and movements ahead of any advance, the forerunner of Blitzkrieg. In particular, tanks were used tactically in co-operation with the infantry as well as in mass for the initial shock action, while 'silent registration' by the artillery, obviating the need for compromising preliminary bombardments, and new fire control techniques, now allowed creeping barrages of great weight and accuracy to lead the infantry and now tanks on to the very edge of their objectives. Even the maligned staff officers made a vital contribution.[113] Sustaining an army of nearly 2 million men in the field was a colossal commitment, not least in the final weeks of the war when Haig's divisions were almost constantly on the move.

Even if Haig and his army commanders may never escape entirely criticism for the mistakes, technical and tactical, and the horrendous casualties of 1916 and 1917, mirrored, I may say, by [those of] the Germans, they do deserve full credit for the successes they achieved in 1918. Haig himself, having displayed the character and fortitude needed to bear the burden of Commander-in-Chief over the three and a half hard fought years, had been proved right in his unswerving conviction that the war could be won only on the Western Front and by the side which sustained the pressure and lasted the longest.

And just ponder for a moment what a burden it was – the strategic and tactical problems, the ghastly casualties, battle after battle, because deep down, as revealed after the war, he was not by any means an insensitive man; dealing with Allies of whom he had to take full account; and then the 'frocks', or politicians, who naturally saw everything rather differently, ever breathing down his neck, and some seeking to remove him. It was all there, combined with perplexing and contradictory intelligence; intricate negotiations and difficult personal relations, all weaving a web of heavy and persistent anxiety. And the Field Marshal bore it all with detached and majestic equanimity, never complaining, never departing from his convictions, never courting popularity or losing heart, just continuing to apply himself with all his vigour to the task he had set himself. And never, and this was remarkable over such a prolonged and dangerous period, losing the support of his soldiers, which had never wavered. In all this he displayed personal character, fortitude and determination of the very highest order.

Essentially, the Allied victory was won by the prolonged and persistent courage and endurance of the soldiers from Britain, France, Belgium, Australia, Canada, New Zealand, Newfoundland (then still independent of

Canada), India, Portugal, South Africa and the United States. The greatest disservice that we can do to their memories nearly a century on, is to allow their final victory to be submerged by endless recrimination; to forget that in 1918 they, Haig and his Army, actually achieved what they had been fighting for; and fail to acknowledge the part that not only their endurance and courage but also the foresight, steadfastness and increasingly professional skill of Haig and his senior commanders had played in that victory, in itself quite enough, I would say, particularly when you take into account the size of the command and the length of the tenure to put the Field Marshal in the very top flight of British military commanders over the last 300 years; and certainly none would deny that his character both as a soldier and as a loyal subject of his King and Country still remains today a strong example to us all.

Chapter 24

Field Marshal Viscount Montgomery KG

Bramall gave a public lecture on Field Marshal Montgomery in 1992 on the fiftieth anniversary of the Battle of El Alamein.

I was lucky enough to meet Field Marshal Montgomery of Alamein on two or three occasions. The first time was during the campaign in North-West Europe in 1944–45; and before I was ushered into the Field Marshal's presence I was told by a Staff Officer that the Field Marshal will ask if you have met him before. He does not mind you saying 'yes' or 'no', but he does not like you saying 'I cannot remember'!

Cannot remember! How could anyone ever forget that small, alert, supremely self-confident and ever positive and professional commander, who made such an outstanding contribution to our victory in World War II?

His military achievements were indeed remarkable, starting with his highly professional command (rather a rarity in 1939) of 3 Division in the retreat to Dunkirk and his invigoration of this country's defences in South-East England under threat of invasion. Before that, after service in World War I in which he nearly died on the battlefield of Ypres and won a DSO, he had a conventional, albeit sometimes controversial career. He was looked on as somewhat unorthodox, but clearly a man to watch. He certainly didn't hide his light under a bushel.

But of course, he particularly came to the fore in 1942 (when he was in his early fifties) after all that inconclusive fighting in the Western Desert in 1940–41 between Britain and her Empire on the one hand and the German and Italian Axis on the other, which by mid-1942 had brought the latter, led by Field Marshal Rommel, deep into Egypt, less than 100 miles from Alexandria and the Nile Delta. It was he, then Lieutenant General Bernard Montgomery, who was sent out by Churchill, after the latter's first choice, 'Strafer' Gott, had been killed, to take over the somewhat dispirited and certainly confused Eighth Army and gave that formation the smack of firm professional leadership, by someone who really did know how to manage and control a major battle. This he was to do, proving himself every inch a match for the highly professional Germans.

General Montgomery, 'Monty' as he became so widely known, tore up any plans to evacuate, if necessary, the Delta, which would have given Hitler free access to the Middle East with disastrous consequences, announcing, in a remarkable speech, that if the Army could not stay there (at El Alamein) alive, they would stay there dead. He then proceeded to hold Rommel in a classic, tightly controlled defensive battle on the ridge at Alam Halfa, which Monty had appreciated with his clarity of mind that Rommel had to take if he was to continue his advance eastwards. He therefore deployed his own armour in good hull-down positions and in depth to protect it; an ideal use of armour. This saved Egypt, and he then went on, between 23 October and 4 November 1942 comprehensively to defeat Rommel in one of the decisive battles of World War II, known simply as Alamein. This was the turning point of the war as far as Britain was concerned. Before it, as Winston Churchill said, we had never had a victory (well, hardly any) and after it virtually never had a defeat. Not the beginning of the end, but the end of the beginning.

Mind you, Monty ought to have won at Alamein. He insisted, despite urgings from Prime Minister Churchill, on waiting to start the battle until new equipment and fresh formations had arrived and the old hands, sometimes to their chagrin, had been put through intense periods of retraining; and in men, tanks, guns and aircraft he outnumbered Rommel, who was in any case away sick for the first two days of the battle – his stand-in dying of a heart attack on the first day. The Germans and Italians were also experiencing serious logistic problems with their lines of communications across the Mediterranean seriously harassed by the Royal Navy and Royal Air Force, and as a result were short of ammunition and petrol.

But whereas other desert generals might well have frittered away some of these advantages, as they did in the earlier Battles of Gazala and El Adem, and so produced a less conclusive result, Monty, with his singleness of purpose, his strict adherence to the principles of war (not least the Maintenance of the Aim); his fighting of divisions as divisions with maximum fire support; and his ability to impose his will on his subordinates and tolerate no bellyaching, made no mistake about the victory.

With the help of a good deception plan, Monty attacked at the very heart of the German defences, and brushing aside perhaps understandable complaints from his armoured commanders, forced the armour through the infantry's half-made gaps in the extensive minefields to occupy key ground. This forced the Germans to counter-attack and thus wear down their own armour; while the infantry continued crumbling operations on the flanks. In all this Monty was helped by Hitler ordering Rommel to continue the battle long after it was wise to do so.

By 4 November, twelve days after it started, the dog fight was over, the Italian Corps had been destroyed or captured, the Afrika Corps broken with its commander, Von Thoma, a prisoner of war, and the Army had broken through to the open desert. The victory was complete.

Casualties, not surprisingly in such an intense and lengthy battle, were not light. The British lost 13,000 and half their tank force of 1,000 tanks, but these, unlike the men, could be and were quickly replaced. But against this you have to put the 55,000 Germans and Italians killed, wounded or captured, and also compare it with the 56,000 casualties of the first day of the Battle of the Somme and 35,000 over a similar period during the Third Battle of Ypres, with virtually nothing to show for those appalling losses.

Alamein precipitated Rommel's long retreat through Libya to Tunisia with Monty again defeating the Afrika Corps at Mareth by a skilful outflanking manoeuvre combined with a frontal assault, and led to the Eighth Army (made up of its splendid Australian, New Zealand, South African, Indian and Ghurkha, as well as British troops) linking up with the Anglo-American landings from Algiers to bring about the total surrender of 250,000 Germans and Italians in North Africa. Monty then went on, after superficially improving and strengthening the staff-made plan, to lead his victorious Eighth Army in the successful Anglo-American invasion of Sicily, a campaign marked by the tiresome rivalry, which the Army Group Commander, Alexander, failed to grip, between Monty and Patton, and which the Germans eventually abandoned when the Italians pulled out of the war, and then across the Straits of Messina, taking them up the east side of Italy against ever increasing resistance as far as the river Sangro and the German Gustav Line, seizing the all-important airfields at Foggia.

Then, at the end of 1943, Monty, by then a charismatic public figure with his distinctive black beret with two badges on it, was selected for what was probably his finest hour, the master-minding and land command of the whole of the 'Second Front', both British and American, the invasion of Normandy, which, if it had failed, could have put back the end of the war almost indefinitely. In this great enterprise it was his personal contribution, his self-confidence and his professional leadership which were to prove major factors in ensuring victory in Normandy in less than three months, exactly as he had predicted. For what Monty did was to take the planners' plan that would not have worked, convert it with the Supreme Commander Eisenhower's full support, into one on a broader front (five assault divisions instead of three, and three airborne divisions instead of three brigades), with a quicker build-up which would work, and at the same time, invigorate and give firm directions to a staff which was confused and uncertain. Then, by endless morale-boosting visits to military and civilian audiences alike, culminating in an epic briefing at St Paul's School in London, in front of His Majesty the King and the Prime Minister, he convinced everyone – commanders, all of us taking part, and the country at large – that the Second Front was a feasible operation and was going to be successful. Many who served under him in those days will remember being exhorted to break ranks and gather round the Commander-in-Chief, a small alert figure in his black beret. The Prime Minister had had some doubts about Normandy, so had the Chiefs of Staff; Alan Brooke, the CIGS, was particularly pessimistic, as well as the Supreme Commander Eisenhower, but Monty's self-confidence never faltered – we were going to win – and he inspired us all through what could have been, and indeed for a time was, a close-run thing. And he emphasised that confidence by putting his own headquarters ashore early on D+2, in close proximity to the front line, under direct shell fire and in front of many of his subordinate commanders. It was leadership of the highest quality.

The Battle of Normandy did not, in terms of timing, go exactly according to plan, as many of us realised only too well at the time. The Germans, with their large preponderance of fanatical Waffen SS divisions put up a very fierce and determined resistance. But the Commander-in-Chief's overall design for the battle, of keeping up pressure and drawing the bulk of the German armour and divisions onto the eastern, i.e. British and Canadian, flank and using that as a hinge on which the whole Allied line pivoted, thus allowing the Americans to break out against weaker opposition and envelop the Germans from the west, and even, as it turned out and with the full encouragement of the C-in-C, from the south, which they did quite brilliantly, was carried through as planned. Moreover, after the Falaise pocket was virtually closed by the Poles from the north and the Americans from the south, with vast German losses in men and materials, the Allied Forces were able to line up along the Seine well within the three months of the landings in Normandy, exactly as he had predicted. It was indeed a most impressive victory, both in its design and, considering how short Monty was of infantry, in its execution.

The only sad thing, as far as his military reputation was concerned, revealed both one of his weaknesses which did not always endear him to his allies and to those he had to answer to, and paradoxically one of his strengths, which sometimes gets forgotten. [The] weakness was that he would never accept criticism or admit that everything was not working out exactly as intended, particularly when failing to take Caen early on, as he had planned. Although you have to remember that he had to maintain the morale and the confidence of the troops under some very tough conditions. And you could also say that one of his strengths was that despite setbacks and the best laid of plans not surviving in their original form the vagaries of battle (as they never do), he was still able to make the necessary adjustments, remain balanced, and exploit the situation in a different way in order to keep control and maintain his overall aim – the mark of a good commander.

After the successful outcome to the Normandy campaign, and having somewhat reluctantly but at the insistence of the Americans, handed over command of the Allied Land Forces to General Eisenhower, whom, as Supreme Commander he felt was too remote, excellently though he handled the political side of things, and too inexperienced in field command to control the land battle decisively, the Field Marshal, as he had now become, led his British and Canadian 21st Army Group with considerable dash through Belgium and southern Holland, capturing Antwerp, Eindhoven and Nijmegen, before in the cold damp early spring of 1945, invading Germany itself, crossing the Rhine and ultimately advancing over the North German plain to the Elbe and the Baltic, taking the surrender of all the German forces in the north at Lüneberg Heath in the first week of May 1945.

Earlier, around Christmas and New Year in 1944–45, when the Germans made their unexpected last fling attack through the Ardennes, threatening to cut the Allies in two and even capture Brussels and Antwerp – the Battle of the Bulge – Monty took command of all Allied troops, British and American, north of and directly in line with the German penetration. In doing so, with great clarity of thought and using his liaison officers to find out exactly what was happening, whereas the American chain of command was bewildered and out of touch, he tidied up and gave stability to the defence in depth, preventing any needless panic in the rear area (although much damage had been done to Allied aircraft in low level air raids) and any hope of the Germans achieving their objectives. Unfortunately, in doing this he gave the Americans the impression that he was being brought in to sort out their amateurish muddle and mess (over which there was an element of truth) and was putting their military affairs into the hands of a master tactician. This did not endear him to our Allies, and it took some time for Eisenhower to agree to Monty assuming control in the north, as it was really the heroism of the American GIs, particularly at St Vith and Bastogne (after all, they lost 60,000 to the British 10,000), the absurdly over-ambitious objective set by Hitler, and the might of the Allied airpower, once air conditions improved, which together 'did' for the Germans and sent them back to their start line with 100,000 casualties, many of them frozen to death. For a time, the American Corps commanders appreciated the clear orders Monty gave them.

In fact, in the whole of the last six months of the war, the Field Marshal only had one set-back, and that was at Arnhem, which under the circumstances prevailing at that time was definitely a gamble, and almost bound to be 'a bridge too far'. It was perhaps uncharacteristic of Monty that he did not appreciate the difficulties of ground and stiffening resistance, and was not prepared to settle for something slightly less ambitious, perhaps concentrating on clearing the banks of the Scheldt and opening up earlier the much-needed port of Antwerp. Yet had it been politically and logistically possible to concentrate both his 21st Army Group and the greater part of Bradley's 12th US Army Group in a concerted attack north of the Ardennes towards the Ruhr, as Monty himself had so strongly advocated, it might have been much more successful, and even ended the war earlier.

As it was, Eisenhower did order Monty to go for the Ruhr rather than the Scheldt estuary and gave him the Airborne Army, in fact an Airborne Corps of three Airborne divisions and some, but not enough, extra logistics to help him. Having advocated a northern thrust so strongly, it was too late for Monty to pull back and accept a secondary role, even though the airborne planners' sensitivities were taking him further from the Americans and down a narrow canal and river-crossed axis with both his flanks exposed, and with resistance manifestly stiffening with Student's Parachute Army and the two SS Panzer Divisions fortuitously resting and re-equipping at Arnhem.

I think Monty realised that this audacious plan of dropping a carpet of three Airborne divisions[114] over which 30 Corps of one armoured division and two infantry divisions,[115] would drive to relieve the furthest Airborne Division, Britain's 1st at Arnhem, wasn't going to be 100 per cent successful, perhaps not even 90 per cent as he later claimed; and again rather uncharacteristically he took little part in the command of Market Garden, as the Arnhem operation was called, leaving it to 2nd Army Commander, Miles Dempsey, and the 30 Corps Commander, Brian Horrocks.

But as it was, at the end of the day, what the British Second Army achieved, in trying unsuccessfully to relieve the bridge at Arnhem, gave the Germans a very nasty fright, stopped any counter-attack against Antwerp and provided a firm left flank and a useful launching pad for subsequent operations against the Siegfried Line and the crossing of the Rhine. So the sacrifice at Arnhem did make a marked contribution to the military successes in the early spring of 1945 and to final victory in Europe in May. It was probably worth the gamble, and Monty certainly did not want, at that stage of the war, for either he or the British to be seen to be playing second fiddle to the Americans

None of this – three years of more or less constant fighting – could have been achieved against such a formidable foe, who often fought so fanatically and recovered so quickly, and on such brutal battlefields as Alamein, Mareth, Italy, Normandy, south Holland, the Reichswald Forest and the Rhine crossing, without the resolution, persistence and courage of the soldiers of so many diverse races and nationalities who fought under him. But equally, the Allied team could not have done without the Field Marshal's consummate professionalism, first as an Army Commander, then as a Commander-in-Chief, and his general mastership of the battlefield, which always included a clear design for battle, a definite aim of which he never lost sight, and an ability to be able to think about, plan for and regroup for the next battle, while he was fighting the current one. Although preferring not to strike until everything, in the way of equipment and logistics, was in place so as to reduce the risk to his soldiers to the minimum, he was quick to exploit enemy weaknesses and he showed he could be daring when circumstances justified it, as at Mareth and in his advance into the Low Countries.

Of course, his style of command was refreshingly different. First, he commanded, in every sense of the word. No question of using orders as a basis of discussion, as had happened in more amateurish circles:

> 'Well, look, old boy, I want you to do so and so.'
> 'Well, as a matter of fact, Harry, that isn't the way we normally do it. We'd prefer to do it this way.'
> 'Well, that's OK, provided you do so and so.'

That sort of dialogue had lost us the Knightsbridge battle early in 1942. In Monty's case he made it clear exactly what subordinates were to do, and there was to be no bellyaching about it.

Secondly, he didn't trust either the chain of command or the communications which linked it, to tell him in good time and accurately what was happening. Instead he sent out his own young liaison officers to all parts of the battlefield to report exactly what was happening on the ground, and how individual commanders were coping with the situation. When they returned they were intensely cross-questioned, and this meant that Monty was always ahead of the game and often at least one jump ahead of his junior commanders, the handling of the Ardennes being a good example of this.

After the war, Monty became the obvious choice to take over as C.I.G.S. from Lord Alanbrooke, but Whitehall was not really his scene, with him still imagining he could give orders as he had on the field of battle and failing to realise how much more complicated it was than that in the political atmosphere of Whitehall. He rowed with the other Chiefs, attended as few of their meetings as possible, and spent much of his time travelling and meeting world leaders like Mao Tse Tung and the Pope, sometimes to the alarm of the Foreign Office. But when he went on to organise European, and later NATO defence with the title of Deputy Supreme Allied Commander, Europe, he in fact did invaluable work laying the whole foundation for Western defence and the confrontation with the Warsaw Pact, including nuclear deterrent strategy to prevent war actually breaking out.

As a person, Monty was not at all easy. He could be petty and small-minded in his personal relations and he liked adulation. Because of his consummate self-confidence, he was invariably an awkward subordinate who often held his contemporaries and superiors (with the marked exceptions of Winston Churchill and the C.I.G.S. Alan Brooke) in scarcely concealed contempt. But he evoked enormous admiration, respect and trust amongst those he led. They knew that he would plan their battles properly, would not be wasteful of their lives and would keep them in the picture about what was going on. He also inspired great affection among his personal staff to whom he showed considerable concern and kindness and even, as he grew older, a puckish sense of humour.

Altogether, he was exactly what the rather amateurish British Army, which for two decades in the 1920s and 1930s had been starved of money and equipment, needed to take on the well prepared and intensely professional and fanatical German war machine; and he will, I believe, be rated as the greatest professional soldier since the great Duke of Wellington.

Chapter 25

Leadership the Green Jacket Way

This booklet on regimental leadership was written by Bramall when he was the Commanding Officer of the 2nd Battalion the Royal Green Jackets in Penang in April 1966. It has been reissued to new officers to the regiment, and its successors, The Rifles, ever since. It could comfortably be adapted to teach leadership in almost every sphere of modern life.

FOREWORD

When a young officer first joins a Battalion, he is often, I believe, confused about how he is expected to handle his platoon. He has presumably basic leadership qualities (otherwise he would not be there), and he has certainly been taught something about command at Sandhurst or Mons; but he does not yet understand the basic philosophy of the regiment he is joining nor will he know of the particular whims and idiosyncrasies of the Battalion to which he is posted.

He may be nervous at being thought too zealous by his brother officers and diffident about throwing his weight around with a comparatively experienced platoon and an even more experienced platoon sergeant. He will almost certainly be uncertain of the type of discipline and degree of strictness required in his platoon, and he will be acutely aware that his platoon will be watching carefully the actions he takes and the decisions he makes in the first few weeks.

Altogether the new officer will be naturally and understandably unsure of himself and may well be hoping for some positive guidance which will help him to act in the approved way and allow him to take the right decisions. He may get this from his Company Commander or Adjutant or even CO, but a suitable opportunity does not always present itself and before it does, he may find himself 'putting his foot in it' and getting a number of 'rockets', all of which will increase his confusion and uncertainty. It is so easy for people to assume that he will soon pick it up as he goes along, as so many have had to do before him, but this is not really a very helpful attitude.

It is therefore for the benefit of these young officers who may be seeking guidance that I have prepared this short booklet. The ideas advanced are not revolutionary but represent what I have always believed to be the genuine Green Jacket philosophy and approach to matters of leadership, discipline, man management and training. Ever since their formation, the Regiments which now make up the Royal Green Jackets have been ahead of their times. It is not surprising, therefore, that their way of doing things remains completely up to date and in tune with modern conditions and requirements. I hope that this booklet will help the young officer face the challenges of his new command with greater confidence and understanding.

Dwin Bramall
Borneo, April 1966

THE AIM – HIGH MORALE

When you take command of a platoon or later of a company or even a battalion, you should always have one constant aim: that is to ensure that the men for whom you are responsible have, what is generally described as, a 'High Morale'.

If you achieve this you will be doing your job; for if there is high morale, it means that not only are all ranks individually and collectively contented, but that they have also acquired that spirit of service and self-discipline which is so necessary if they are to carry out their duty properly and stand up to discomfort and danger. A body of men with high morale is both happy and efficient and in every way capable of carrying out the demanding military commitments of the 1960s. Nothing less will suffice and no officer should rest or be content until he is quite satisfied that he has achieved this aim. The challenge is exciting, but will demand hard work and dedication and a thoroughly professional approach to the job. On the other hand, the fruits of success will be infinitely rewarding.

There is nothing particularly complicated about high morale. Its main ingredients are:

    I. Confidence
    II. Discipline
    III. Self-respect

I. CONFIDENCE

The confidence required is bred from an appreciation by all ranks of the all-round efficiency of the unit or sub unit and of its leaders. It can only be brought about by a properly planned and supervised training programme which is demanding, progressive and interesting and ultimately, by success in active operations. It also requires the leader to exercise his leadership in a positive and dynamic way.

Training.

The first thing you must do as a leader is to see that the training of your men is right, so that they will become and remain proficient in their military skills.

These will include amongst other things, shooting and weapon training, fitness and agility (including marching and swimming), first aid and health training, map reading and navigation, signals, tactical training, and certain special skills applicable to a particular theatre of operations such as the jungle or the desert. Soldiers must not only be taught their trade but must also have complete confidence in their own and their comrades' skill. This will not happen by accident, but will be achieved if the training is carefully and imaginatively conceived, clearly explained, is interesting and progressive, and leads up to a real challenge which offers, when met, a proper sense of achievement. Officers who believe their soldiers will be grateful for soft and easy training do not understand human nature and will never succeed in producing high morale. The expert trainer of troops is the one who, despite the protestations of the Jeremiahs, can select an objective which, although it appears unobtainable, is in fact just within the capabilities of his soldiers. Then having won through, his men will feel that they have done the impossible and their sense of achievement and morale will be correspondingly great. The difficulty in peace time is thinking up tasks which can produce sufficient challenge without any undue risk to life and limb; and one normally has to fall back on tests of endurance in adverse weather conditions. Crossing of water obstacles and scaling cliffs are also good training provided that an expert and necessary kit are available and elementary precautions are taken. There are also certain 'tricks of the trade' with live firing guns which can make field firing appear dangerous to the participants when, in fact, there is no risk whatsoever. All these and other ways of encouraging self-reliance help to make training realistic and build up confidence. In an active service theatre of operations, operations and training often overlap and there is no difficulty in producing the necessary 'needle' and risk and therefore the maximum sense of achievement.

A good trainer, like a good organiser, must think every training session or exercise right through to the end. In this way every development is anticipated, the timings are realistic and go according to plan and every training aid and piece of equipment required is readily available. The training will then be fully appreciated by the soldiers who will have confidence in its value and realism. A good trainer will also take the trouble to brief his troops beforehand on what is expected of them, and to discuss the exercise at a postmortem at the end, in order to bring out the lessons and ensure that the soldiers fully identify themselves with the training and appreciate the progress being made.

Training syllabuses will usually be laid down by the CO or the 2 i/c and training programmes will normally be the province of the Company Commander, but as a Platoon Commander you will often find spare time on your hands when you will have a chance of showing initiative and of originating useful and interesting training. Some of the types of training for which you are responsible are discussed below.

Shooting. In a Green Jacket battalion shooting naturally has a very high priority and this will always remain so. The advantage of competition shooting is that it enables a Regiment to maintain a well distributed shooting elite who are enthusiastic about their shooting and ready to pass on their skill and enthusiasm to young soldiers. This helps to raise the standard of every type of shooting.

When preparing for active service however, it is not enough to classify once a year, shoot the non-central matches and send a well-trained team to Bisley and Command Rifle Meetings. Shooting must, under these circumstances, have a practical application to the sort of conditions which are likely to be met. After all, all tactics are valueless if when we meet the enemy at close quarters we fail to kill him, and the trained soldier should be given a regular diet of handling his weapons from cramped battle positions, at realistic combat ranges, and at night. In addition, and with the help of the shooting gallery type of range, steps should be taken to make shooting interesting and enjoyable for everyone.

Weapon Training. Weapon training, particularly the advanced handling of weapons (e.g. safety stages, firing from cover, reloading etc.) represents one of the basic infantry skills which must be continually practised. Weapon training, however, must never be allowed to degenerate into something which merely fills in the gaps in the programme. It must always be progressive and taught as part of a syllabus or series of tests, and lessons must be fully prepared by the instructor. As an officer, you will usually supervise but you must be prepared to take a lesson yourself.

Fitness and Toughening Training. A fit soldier can meet most of the demands made on him, including competing with the elements. If he is unfit, he will probably collapse under conditions of extreme heat or cold as well as being a liability in battle. You must therefore aim, from the start, at a state of affairs in which every man under you, whatever his rank, feels that he has a personal obligation to keep himself fit; and as a result, will take exercise on the playing field and in the gymnasium, swimming pool or squash court of his own accord. Exercise which strengthens the upper limbs (to help in carrying heavy weights, roping down from helicopters and crossing obstacles) and builds up stamina should be particularly encouraged, and unarmed combat and swimming are also important. As the tone of physical fitness comes from the top, all officers and senior NCOs must set an example. A good opportunity to do this occurs if an officer will play games with his men. Sports and games not only increase fitness but also build up high morale in other ways, and soldiers have a right to expect plenty of time to play games in the Army, and a high standard of organisation. By fully identifying yourself with these games as a player, referee or failing that as a consistent watcher you will help to foster enthusiasm and a good team spirit.

First Aid and Health and Hygene Training, Map Reading and Signal Training. These are all subjects which to some extent should be mastered by all ranks, not only by NCOs and specialists. They build up confidence.

Current Affairs. Giving him some knowledge of the world around him is a useful method of building up a soldier's self-respect and maturity. Moreover, the modern professional soldier needs to have a proper understanding of the people and problems of the areas of the world in which he may have to fight. But care must be taken to see that these subjects are not put over in an amateurish and slipshod way. Too often in the past Current Affairs periods left to Platoon Commanders have produced varied and erratic results, with barrack room lawyers taking control. Either the subject must be meticulously prepared or outside lecturers, who are experts on these subjects, must be brought in to give the instruction.

Drill. This is another subject which must be approached with caution and a real understanding. Close order drill is no longer a major factor in building up battle discipline, as indeed it was when it was first introduced. It is however very necessary in order to maintain a smart public appearance (as is expected of the British Army by the British Nation) and in preparation for some special parade at which the Battalion wants to show itself off to its audience. In this context, Riflemen have always demonstrated their ability to drill hard for a special performance when required. Drill is a contributory factor in building up pride and self-respect, particularly among junior NCOs. Drill should therefore not be ignored but must form part of a definite programme working up to a definite objective. At times when there are more pressing operational matters only sufficient drill should be done to keep up an acceptable standard of bearing and turnout and to ensure that the techniques of close order drill is not lost completely, and can be easily recaptured when the need arises. Morning muster parades and a simple guard mounting drill are normally sufficient to achieve this.

When drill is done, just in the same way as weapon training, it must never be allowed to become a stop gap in the programme, or something which the NCOs can take without preparation, or a period which the Platoon Commander feels he need not attend. That sort of drill makes no contribution whatsoever to the professional efficiency of the soldier or to his morale.

Tactics. Finally, there is the question of tactical training which is the officer's main responsibility. The successful teaching of tactics depends on the enthusiasm and an ability to get realism into exercises. A good tactical trainer should possess or acquire the imagination to think up tactical situations which could well occur and confront his troops at some future date, and should then reproduce these as realistically as possible in the training he has planned. Time spent in stage managing background incidents, e.g. producing character sketches of 'wanted terrorists', or dressing up characters who will contribute to the realism of a situation, will not be wasted because the heightened atmosphere will make the soldier give that much more in his training, will highlight the lesson and will enhance the sense of achievement. Instruction on tactics will vary from theatre to theatre and you must try to cover all the situations that your sub-unit is likely to face, but the following general principles may be helpful:

a. Patrolling in section or half platoon strength should be given a very high priority.

b. Tactical exercises with troops (if the aim is to teach rather than to test) should, where possible, be preceded by TEWTs [Tactical Exercises Without Troops] or model exercises over the same or simulated pieces of ground or, if this is impossible, by officers' and NCOs' discussions. This will ensure that officers and NCOs develop their full potential and fully understand what they are doing, and that the soldiers in consequence get the maximum value out of the training exercise.

c. All advance and attack training should be based on the principle of Fire and Manoeuvre or skirmishing, i.e. manoeuvring into a position from where our own weapons can be brought to bear on the enemy with maximum effectiveness.

d. All defence training should include the digging of fire trenches and, where possible, the provision of overhead cover. This is a science often neglected on training but reverted to quickly enough when the shells and mortar bombs are landing in earnest.

e. As large a proportion as possible (up to 25 per cent) of tactical training should be conducted at night. Rather like jungle training, nothing will build up confidence (and morale) quicker than coming to terms with this rather unnatural but effective way of operating against the enemy.

Success in active operations

However well an officer trains his soldiers there will be no substitute for success in the face of the enemy in building up a truly high morale. Although naturally if the training is well done the better will be the chance of achieving this success. Because the results of an engagement on active service have such a significant effect on soldiers' morale, it is important that when troops are first committed to battle they are given tasks which are fully consistent with their training and experience, and, where possible, are allowed to progress steadily from strength to strength and from small successes to larger ones. In this way, and in each operation, the soldiers and their leaders will have the sense of achievement derived from an earlier encounter to inspire them in their task and give them confidence. This will not always be possible, and the urgency of the threat may justify risks being taken, but it is the ideal. Many a commander in the past has carefully engineered a comparatively easily won and minor victory early in his command, in order to produce the necessary sense of achievement and pride which can act as a springboard for the greater and more important challenges ahead. This is sound practice and commanders at every level should be looking for ways for their men to 'win their spurs' without undue cost. Once they have a sense of achievement in battle, there should be no problem about morale and they should be ready for all challenges ahead.

Leadership

Leadership must always be executed in a positive, personal and dynamic way. A leader must not only have a policy and be capable of leading but he must be seen to be doing so. It is no excuse for you as a young officer to plead that you have not made much contact with your men, because they do not really wish to see you all that much, or because you are shy or bad at addressing men in public. If you take this line you will never get your personality across and never be recognised as living up to your responsibilities. It is up to you to cure yourself of your shyness and rid yourself of your inhibitions.

A leader requires certain basic qualities – courage, robustness, judgement, to name three, but it is likely that every officer possesses these to some degree otherwise he would not be where he is. But these qualities must be fully recognised by the men, if the necessary confidence is to be there; and in the early days of command a certain amount of showmanship may be required to get these points across. Until you are fully accepted you may have to work harder, expose yourself (not your men) to more risks, take more trouble and show more versatility and endurance than are strictly necessary for the carrying out of your command function. This is in order for you to imprint your personality on your men. The important thing is that when you order your men to do anything tough or risky, they must not have a moment's doubt that you are capable of doing such a task yourself and have probably done so many times before. If they are doubtful you must show them.

If you are already well known for some achievement in another field, such as athletics, mountain climbing, skiing, shooting, boxing, to name but a few, this will be all to the good, as the prestige that results from these will help you get fully accepted.

In leading men and in war generally, one needs a certain amount of luck, although luck normally comes to those that deserve it and particularly to those who have thought carefully and anticipated most eventualities. Certainly, an officer need not have misgivings about recognising his luck, because to have the reputation among soldiers of being a lucky commander is one of the highest compliments possible. Once success has come in a unit, whether it be operational success or of another type, it never hurts for a commander to remind men of their past achievements together, and of the benefits obtained under his leadership. Men will only have faith in a leader who himself is confident and has faith in himself.

To sum up, leadership is exercised first and foremost by example, secondly by successful results, thirdly and most importantly by the spoken word in briefing men about the future and reminding them of past achievements and lastly, and to a lesser extent, by the written word. As a leader, you must cultivate all these methods if you are to put across your personality, exercise your leadership and win the men's confidence to the fullest extent.

II. DISCIPLINE

Once the training is developing on the right lines, you should turn your attention with a critical eye to the discipline of your men, and here you may well run into a maze of uncertainty and conflicting standards.

What constitutes discipline? What are the standards worth keeping and what should be discarded in the interests of progress? Certainly, the methods of instilling discipline have changed, as indeed they must; otherwise we would still be in the era of the lash and the gun wheel. But the need for discipline is as great as it ever was, and must never be neglected or lost sight of when commanding men. Soldiers will never go happily into a battle unless they know themselves to be a disciplined body of men, in which every member of the team is to be trusted. In fact, without discipline they rapidly become a collection of frightened and unhappy individuals. In barracks discipline is necessary if soldiers are to project a good public image and be respected by the local inhabitants.

Discipline on active service means having the capacity to carry out an essential, irksome or arduous task without supervision; keeping going and staying awake when fatigue is overpowering; obeying unpleasant but necessary orders; and above all continuing to fight when the instinct of self-preservation is advocating something totally different. Discipline in barracks implies an absence of crime and displaying a good soldier-like appearance to the outside world. A smart bearing, good manners and good saluting are an outward and visible sign that all is well, and if the discipline is right, these things should follow without too much of a conscious effort being made. The problem is how to instil the necessary discipline in the most economical way and in a way that does not insult the intelligence of the normal soldier of today.

In the Green Jackets we rightly put the emphasis on self-discipline rather than the imposed variety favoured by some others. We seek, by good leadership, example, explaining what we are doing and generally treating those under us with humanity and common sense, to evoke a loyal response and produce the sense of responsibility needed. This is a policy to be proud of and it has proved to be extremely effective. The end product is more deep seated because it is based on the individual's own will power, and it usually creates a fine atmosphere of trust and mutual respect which manifests itself in a sensible adult approach to problems and marked absence of crime. At the same time the leader must be careful not to deny the weaker and more rebellious characters the stiffening discipline without which they cannot come up to scratch; and he must remember that the battlefield requires men who are mentally as well as physically tough, and that this cannot be achieved by excessive leniency. The build-up and the maintenance of discipline therefore, like so many other things in life, demands a middle but consistent course to be found and followed. This course should be one that encourages self-discipline, whilst at the same time giving the individual man plenty of opportunities to prove he is worthy of this trust. It should also make provision for 'turning the screw' (by increasing punishments) if results are not being obtained, collectively or individually, or if a certain aspect of discipline is particularly important, needs stressing or is being neglected. Examples of this are a lapse in the alertness of sentries on active service, a prevalence for accidental discharges, or a fall in standards of turnout in a place like Berlin. Officers and NCOs can then be ordered to tighten up on the particular point. The important thing is to keep the aim always in mind and not get obsessed by the means to an end. Drill, and ultra-high standards of turnout, are not an end in themselves. A man with a shaven head will not necessarily be a more disciplined man than one with a normal haircut, nor a man with 'dagged' boots better than one with clean boots; although a generally dirty man and untidy man will almost certainly have poor self-discipline and require checking. What is required is a reasonable standard of turnout with special pre-announced spurts if special results are required, or if there is an indication that discipline is suffering. This also applies to drill, where there should be a reasonable constant emphasis with a special drive on occasions.

Discipline, however, is far more easily 'caught' than 'taught'. Men will react to some degree to the threat of punishment, particularly pay stoppages, to a much greater extent than having it explained to them why certain orders and routines are necessary both in the field and in barracks; but most of all to seeing that those who administer discipline and give them orders are disciplined men themselves, with all that implies in terms of punctuality, turnout and obeying themselves the orders they enforce. The rest will then follow provided they are given the opportunity to display their discipline and are taken to task whenever they fall down on what they are supposed to do. What must be avoided at all costs is the bullying, blustering type of junior leader who covers up his incompetence and lack of leadership by shouting and swearing. That is not discipline under any circumstances.

Although the ways of enforcing discipline may be varied from station to station, and in the light of the end product, there must be consistency for a particular period, and the men must know exactly where they stand. It is up to the officers at every level to make it clear from time to time the standards which they expect in the various fields of military conduct and routine such as the instant obedience to orders, alertness of sentries, cleanliness and serviceability of weapons, personal and room hygiene, and behaviour, bearing and turnout in public. For infringement of these and other things which may be applicable at the time, it is wise for any commander to announce penalties which will be well known to all ranks and will help clarify the issues on which no compromise is possible. If you are uncertain of the strictness to be imposed you should get guidance from the commander above you.

To sum up, as a leader you should explain what is necessary and announce your standards, set an example, give your men the opportunity to do what is required of them without bullying, and then 'hammer' them with a fair but stern punishment if they do not make the grade. The chance is that next time they will. To put it another way, you should decide where to draw the line and make it clear to everyone where that line is and what will happen to them if they cross it. There can be no uncertainty or misunderstanding.

III. SELF RESPECT

The final ingredient of high morale is what can best be described as self-respect – the individual soldier's conviction that he is a respected member of a respected and honourable profession with a worthwhile job to do. This self-respect or healthy personal esteem will of course be greatly helped by the other two ingredients which have been discussed – by the confidence each man feels and by his intelligent discipline which each man acknowledges and is proud to possess. It can also be acquired and improved by other ways, and every officer, whatever his rank, has some responsibility for seeing that the following conditions are met.

Information. First and foremost, positive steps must be taken to see that all ranks are kept informed about the Battalion's policy, and the reasons for it, and about what is expected of them. This has already been mentioned in connection with the building up of confidence, the exercise of leadership and the instilling of discipline. But it is also a significant factor in building up of self-respect. It invokes appreciation and co-operation on the man's part out of all proportion to the effort involved. This may well be done by the Commanding Officer or a company commander at frequent informal talks and question periods, but it is the duty of every officer, within the bounds of security, to pass on to his men what he knows, and to keep them 'in the picture' about what the future may bring.

Living conditions. Secondly, there is the question of high living standards in barracks. Men will not respect their occupation or themselves unless their life and their training is varied, interesting and tough; but this toughness should not extend to conditions in barracks. Here they should be provided with a high standard of feeding, sleeping accommodation and amenities and recreation facilities generally. The young officer should take, and be seen to take, an interest in these and should be prepared to tangle with authority in fighting for the best possible conditions for his men. There is also the question of really well run messes for warrant officers, sergeants and corporals, with ever rising standards of taste and dignity. These help in building up the self-respect of the NCO and also help him maintain that slight but significant psychological separation from other ranks, without which the implementation of even the most humane and intelligent discipline becomes difficult.

Public relations. Next there is the need for good lively public relations. Everyone likes to know that their activities are appreciated, and soldiers are no exception. Both morale and recruiting benefit if articles and photographs of a unit's activities can be got into the national and local press. In the past, officers have shown a hostile and suspicious attitude to journalists, but by doing so have defeated their own ends. It is a laudable aim of any young officer to show off his command in the best possible light and, again within the bounds of security, get them the type of publicity which will enhance their pride and influence others to follow the same calling. Within a unit there is also scope for some private publicity in the form of a newsletter or news sheet. This enhances the family spirit and keeps men and their families informed in a light unpompous way of what is going on in the rest of the unit.

Families. All the above conditions apply equally to married men and their families – an ever-increasing company in the modern army. Married men should not, under any circumstances, get preferential treatment in their share of military duties, but no effort should be spared in seeing that they and their families live happy, comfortable and civilised lives. The families need to be kept in the picture about a unit's affairs just as much as the men (particularly as married men are notoriously bad at passing on information to their wives). The living conditions of families are also every bit as much the responsibility of a unit as those of the single men, and there must be in every unit a good welfare organisation to give really speedy practical help, if it is required, both with quartering and other human problems. The young officer can act as a link with this organisation, as can the wives of senior ranks, who can bring sympathy, understanding and a helping hand to families with welfare problems. All this contributes towards the married man's peace of mind without which he cannot have confidence in himself as a soldier.

Punishment and the redress of grievances. Then there is the question of dignity of punishments and of redress of grievances. Leniency for proven prevalent and significant military offences will incur no respect from well trained and disciplined men, but punishments should be constructive and not debase the human spirit. Hit his pocket, restrict his privileges, and toughen him up on useful training – yes; but degrade him – no. It must not be forgotten that a man is innocent until proven guilty at his summary trial and should be treated with this in mind. It should be appreciated also that however fair the administration of justice may be in a unit, there are bound to be the odd injustices and misunderstandings which if allowed to persist may cause quite unnecessary discontent. If the only method of drawing attention to them is by asking for an interview through 'the usual channels' – i.e. the same machinery used to punish him – a man may feel that he is not in a position to get a square deal. Besides, the matter may be confidential and he may be diffident about raising it through the usual channels (although he should always be encouraged to do so). As a result, a small irritant which could be disposed of early on, may easily become a smouldering ulcer without anyone knowing much about it. It is therefore the duty of every officer, from the Commanding Officer downwards, to be approachable so that a man can feel that he can have a private talk without a formal application for an interview. It is very unlikely that this concession will be abused and quite unnecessary, if the officer handles the interview intelligently, for the wires to get crossed or disloyalty to be condoned. The officer should naturally not commit himself too much until he has investigated the problem with all concerned, but he should convince the man of his readiness to hear him and help him if he can. In this way, the officer helps activate a very useful safety valve as well as, in the case of a Commanding Officer, keeping in close touch with many aspects of Battalion life. The principle of direct access to officers has been accepted by the Green Jackets for many years and has always worked most effectively.

Addressing Soldiers. Finally, there is the small but significant question of the way that officers and senior NCOs address the ordinary soldiers. The surname alone is of course the conventional way, but these days this might be thought to have a rather patronising and peremptory ring to it. After all, a man expects to be given the prefix 'Mr' in civilian life, whatever his position. The use of a Christian name on the other hand as well as being novel, would be interpreted as being familiar rather than friendly. This form of address could certainly not be reciprocated without familiarity and ill-discipline creeping in and, unless it was used consistently and impartially, it would also lead to charges of favouritism. The use of the rank followed by the surname (e.g. Rifleman Jones), however, provides the ideal answer. The term 'Rifleman' is a proud and honourable one, and by so addressing a soldier you give him a certain status, prestige and dignity which is often quickly reflected in his behaviour. Although this form of address seems strange at first to someone who is unused to it, it quickly catches on (after all, NCOs have always been addressed in this way). Soon the soldiers start addressing each other in this manner and then you get the very healthy use of rank titles downwards and sideways as well as upwards, with a very beneficial effect on the general self-respect of all ranks.

CONCLUSION

This then is the Green Jacket way – pride in fighting qualities and professional skill, intelligent and humane discipline, sympathy and understanding between all ranks and concern for the individual for his welfare and for that of his dependents. The young officer who applies the ideas in this booklet should have no difficulty in having a platoon which has a high morale and a healthy self-esteem that they are the best platoon, of the best Battalion, of the best Regiment in the British Army. A Battalion committed to these principles could well be reported on in the words Lieutenant General Sir John Moore used when inspecting the 52nd (now the 1st Battalion the Royal Green Jackets) in Sicily in 1807:

> I have the pleasure to observe that this Regiment possesses an excellent spirit and that both officers and men take a pride in doing their duty. Their movement in the field is perfect. It is evident that not only the officers, but that each individual soldier knows perfectly what he has to do. The discipline is carried on without severity. The officers are attached to the men, the men to the officers.[116]

This must represent what all officers are seeking to achieve, for it is impossible to think of a higher compliment being paid to a Regiment. Results like this should be a reward in themselves for all the hard work and dedication needed to achieve them, but for officers who are looking for further incentive or sense of purpose perhaps this final quotation (from the *Seamanship Manual* of 1865) may have a message despite the rather dated and rather pedantic language:

> Remember, then, that your life's vocation, deliberately chosen, is war – war, as I have said as the means for peace, but still war, and in singleness of purpose, for England's fame, prepare for the time when the welfare and honour of the service may come to be in your keeping, that by your skill and valour when that time arrives, and fortune comes your way, you may revive the spirit and perpetuate the glory of the days that tingle in our hearts and fill our memories.

It must be the aim of every officer holding the Queen's Commission that they and their men are, in all senses and in every way, ready for that moment when it arrives.

Chapter 26

Eulogy and Parade Addresses

(a) Eulogy to Charles Upham VC & bar, 1995

On 5 May 1995 Bramall gave the eulogy at the memorial service at St Martin-in-the-Fields, London for Charles Upham VC & bar, the only combat soldier ever to be so decorated.

I only met Charles Upham once, and although that for me was a very significant and memorable experience in itself, I do feel very unqualified, as well as most unworthy, to talk about his qualities as a soldier (a truly remarkable wartime one) and as a man, and I am sure that others among you will share my misgivings.

I have, however, been asked to say something about the impact of his deeds and warrior reputation on the traditions and inspiration of the profession of arms, in which I have spent over forty years, and this I am proud to attempt, perhaps most particularly as we are starting the 50th anniversary commemoration events, when to the older generation memories of World War II inevitably come flooding back, and when everyone, of all ages, will be remembering with thankfulness and pride the efforts and sacrifices of those, under the Crown, who made victory possible.

What, of course, all of us here this afternoon know, without a shadow of doubt, is that Charles Upham had all the qualities and indomitable spirit of the true warrior – the will to face danger, take risks and overcome obstacles; the will to decide under pressure and the will to win; and above all in the execution of his perceived duty as a New Zealand officer, at war against the most evil regime, something in which he believed passionately, and in support of his comrades for whom he felt a total responsibility, the will, if need be, to lay down his life.

As a result, although by nature a very shy, modest, at times almost gentle person, he became on the battlefield, with his men's lives at stake and duty to be done to the utmost, a warrior of heroic proportions – always remaining to fight with his men without any heed whatsoever to wounds or any debilitating illness, however severe these might be, and, apparently, utterly indifferent to danger and his own personal safety.

As a result, he was able, in a way that would have eluded so many lesser men, to seize fleeting tactical opportunities and, by remarkable personal feats of bravery, to achieve significant local success for his unit in the face of very considerable odds. These encounters, against a brave, determined and resourceful enemy may not have changed the course of any campaign, but in the New Zealand Expeditionary Force, itself remarkable for its gallantry and battlefield effectiveness, they became a byword which inspired all ranks to even greater efforts.

Not surprisingly therefore that a New Zealand General[117] told the late King, George VI, that in his opinion Captain Upham had earned the VC not just twice (a feat achieved only twice before, by two medical officers) but several times over.

This is really the point, because however much Charles Upham would have been horrified with any undue fuss being made over him, or any over-the-top glorification of his prowess on the battlefield, always preferring to be treated, in his own immortal words as a true West Coaster Kiwi, 'like any other bastard', his memory will always be held in awe and admiration by those who admire courage, patriotism and unselfishness, and who look upon the bearing of arms in the service of your country as an honourable estate.

We all need heroes to look up to, to point the way and set us an example to try, however inadequately, to follow. Nations need them to foster national pride and *esprit de corps*, although more and more of these, perhaps thankfully, will in future be emanating from the sports field rather than the battlefield; and armies, navies and air forces certainly need them to incorporate into their traditions of service and sacrifice and to provide inspiration for future generations; for without them, and the events surrounding them, something will always be lacking in the creation of the highest morale and loyalty to the group or unit which is so essential to success in battle.

As the famous old song, *The British Grenadiers*, goes:

Some talk of Alexander, and some of Hercules,
Of Hector and Lysander, and such great names as these.

This reference to, and seeking after, heroes has continued throughout history. Look how Nelson has inspired and motivated the Royal Navy for nearly two centuries, and how the names of Ball, Bader, Gibson and Cheshire will never be forgotten by future members of the Royal Air Force. While the Army's history from Hougoumont to the Falklands, and from Rorke's Drift to Sidi Rezegh, Kidney Ridge and Arnhem is littered with events and heroic deeds occurring within them which have made the Regiments and Corps what they are, and this inspires recruits from the moment they join not only to do their level best but to put duty and service to their units and their comrades before the purely selfish ones of self-preservation. The strength of any unit depends so much on what has gone before, good and bad, and the more good and gallant there is to record with honesty, the stronger that unit will be in the service of its country, and often of mankind – not only on the battlefield but in peacetime and when peacekeeping as well.

So, whether he likes it or not, Charles Upham VC and bar has now entered the military Valhalla, and, long after the actual engagements in which he took part with such professional skill and ferocious dedication have been absorbed into the mists and the myths of history, his name will be remembered by the military profession with awe and the greatest respect.

As one who could not possibly have emulated him, but, knowing something of the pressures and environment of the battlefield, admires him more than I can possibly say, I, on behalf of the British Armed Forces, salute him.

(b) Address to cadets at RMA Sandhurst, 1985

On 9 August 1985 Bramall, as C.D.S., represented the Queen at the Sovereign's Parade at RMA Sandhurst, and spoke to the cadets. He performed this task three times, which is probably some sort of record![118]

This is the second time that I have had the immense privilege of taking the Salute at this Parade as the representative of the Sovereign; but of course, there have been many other occasions over the years when, with my wife, I have watched it as a spectator, and it never ceases to impress me; and this time has certainly been no exception, as I am sure everyone watching would agree. As usual you have carried it out immaculately and with great pride, and I congratulate all of you most warmly on your drill, and your bearing; particularly of course those passing out, including those from overseas whom we are so very pleased to welcome amongst us and for whom I hope the friendships forged here will last for many years to come to the mutual benefit of our countries; also the student Officers and Officer Cadets of the WRAC who, though they have appeared on this parade before, have marched past today for the first time, and so very well if I may say so.

I assure you that the understandable pride of all of you passing out, at reaching this milestone in your lives, is shared by all of us watching you today. By your instructors who have shown you what you yourselves can do; by your parents and friends and no doubt admirers, for whom your commissioning in the Service of your Queen and your country must mean so much; and most certainly by me who, as I approach the end of nearly forty-five years in the Armed Forces of the Crown, can take such comfort that their future is in the promising hands of the likes of all of you, with your lives and careers ahead of you.

What can I possibly say to you on an exciting day like this with the weather threatening which might just be of some help as you start the adventure of a military career?

The answer is probably precious little; and the one thing I can say without fear of contradiction, is something of which many of you hardly need to be reminded, and that is that you are going out into the most professional and generally most respected and admired Army in the whole wide world. An Army which for the last forty years, in the form of the highly regarded British Army of the Rhine, has been making such a well-trained and increasingly well-equipped contribution to the defence of Europe and the prevention of war; and an Army which at the same time, all over the world, and in the protection of our nation's interests and our friends' interests, has done everything that could be expected of it, and more, from Central America to Korea, from the Arctic Circle to the Falkland Islands, from our own Northern Ireland to Central and Southern Africa, and from the Middle East to South East Asia, in a variety of conflicts, crises and emergencies, all involving considerable risk and danger, but equally requiring restraint, moderation and compassion as well.

In the Falklands, when the honour of our own country came so suddenly to be in the keeping of our Armed Forces, all ranks of all three Services, working in great unity and whatever their Arm or Corps or Regiment, fully lived up to the confidence that the whole country had placed in them, and showed that they did indeed have what we have all been trained to have, the true and indomitable spirit of the warrior – the will to take risks, the will to overcome obstacles, and the will to face danger – the will to decide and the will to win. So, you need have no qualms about the purpose, value and quality of the profession you have selected. If in future you are asked what you do, you will be able to hold your up head in any company.

But perhaps I should also remind you that these things – the professional quality of the British Army, its high reputation within our country and the incomparable strength of the Regimental system – don't happen by accident or continue just of their own accord, but only because each successive generation builds on the foundations of the ones before, and, I like to think, actually improves on them.

This then is now your heritage, the ball is so to speak in your court; and it is up to you to see that what has been so good in the past, and is today is perhaps even better, will in the future, thanks to all of you, become even better still. And if the prospect of all this daunts you, well, all I can say is that you will be given a great deal of help. You will have the advice and support of high grade warrant officers and non-commissioned officers such as you have known here. You will have the strength and practice and experience of your Regiments and Corps behind you; and your training will be amongst the best in the world, and you will be obeyed by those under your command who, given half the chance, will give you their undivided trust and loyalty. But you will have to go on earning that trust remembering, as I am sure you have been told repeatedly, that leadership is not just a matter of transmitting orders from behind a comforting barrier of rank, but ultimately one of sharing and caring; sharing the same risks and hardships and the same sporting and adventurous activities as your soldiers and getting them to do, not just what you tell them to do, but especially what you are showing them how to do and frequently doing yourself. And then really caring – understanding that the people for whom you are responsible matter, and matter a very great deal. For they will have emotions like you, develop hopes and aspirations for themselves and their families, similar to yours; have a desire for appreciation and thanks, just as I am sure you all possess; and an inquisitiveness to know what the hell is happening, just as you do. All this will, I hope, be familiar to you, but it is worth restating because those below you will certainly deserve, within the bounds of that all so necessary military discipline, to be treated in the sort of fair, sensible but above all stimulating way you would expect to be treated yourself, if you were in their shoes.

It is basing our leadership on this mutual respect between ranks which so often gives our Army a head start over so many civilian occupations and organisations, which fail to realise this simple truth, and indeed over other Armies as was shown so markedly in the Falklands.

My final word to you would be, don't forget to grasp the opportunities the Army will sensibly give you, has perhaps already given you, to live life to the full, to cultivate outside interests and pursuits, both adventurously active and intellectually reflective, and to go on learning more about the world around you and the real people who live in it. For these are the things which develop character and judgement, which enable you to acquire a sense of proportion, perspective and humour, and to see the broader picture as well, not only those matters of your immediate concern, and which will, incidentally, make you to others (of both sexes) that much more interesting a person.

So, remember, your heritage is priceless, don't neglect it; rather build on it and try to make it better. Live life to the full, and never discard your sense of humour nor forget that people matter. Then you should find your future taking care of itself.

Have a good holiday and enjoy yourselves and very good luck wherever your service to the Crown and your soldiering takes you.

(c) Address to 2 Rifles Medal Parade, 2010

Bramall visited and addressed the men of 2 Rifles, and their families, at a medal parade in Ballykinler on their return from Afghanistan in 2010.

Riflemen of the Second Battalion, The Rifles, My Lord Lieutenant, Ladies and Gentlemen,

It is such a privilege for me to take the salute at this Medal Parade, forty-five years after I took command of a Rifle Battalion, also on operations, which was one of your forebears; and particularly, of course, to be able to welcome you home after a most arduous, intense and dangerous tour in the harshest possible terrain and environment, and with hardly any respite in the whole six months.

Like fellow Riflemen before you, the determination and resolve all of you – individual Riflemen, fire teams, sections right up to Battalion level – have been fully tested, in your case under constant fire when facing insidious and corrosive threats of IEDs and when taking the fight to the enemy. It's clear to me you have not been found wanting. I salute you and can tell you that your fortunes have not only been followed with pride by the rest of your admiring Regiment but also by the public at large, as must have been obvious when you marched through Croydon and Liverpool.

You were at the very heart, the focal point, of NATO's strategy in Helmand Province, Sangin, which you held throughout, defying all the efforts of the Taliban, who threw everything at you, to dislodge you; and as a result you brought greater protection, stability and economic improvement to the Afghan people in the area, so vital to the future security of not only the whole region but to the wider world. Indeed, in furthering that aim I believe your bravery, tenacity and, indeed, sense of humour will not have been lost on the Afghan people. Hardly ever can a campaign medal have been more deserved than the one that has just been given to you.

With your recent tours in Iraq and, before that, Kosovo, ten years with active service in every year, you are one of the most battle-hardened and experienced battalions in the whole British Army. So I congratulate you most warmly. You have proved yourselves, and if anyone is unwise enough to try to provoke you now that you are back, into anything which might undermine the admiration that the whole country feels for you, just tell him to get some service in.

But we are all too painfully aware that your gallant efforts have not been made without substantial personal sacrifice. You have lost, killed in action, thirteen brave and much respected comrades in arms, all good men and friends. We greatly mourn them and we will never forget them. I am humbled to see almost every bereaved family represented here today, and I want to reassure them that as a Regiment we are not only very proud of them and the supreme sacrifice they made, as soldiers and warriors must be prepared to do, but also of you as you had to come to terms with your very great loss.

You have also had a large number of others wounded, some very seriously. The courage of the wounded at the time and subsequently has been quite outstanding, as was that of those who got them to safety and evacuated them. I had a chance to see for myself some of that grit and determination shown by the wounded when I visited some of them at Selly Oak – a clear illustration of the indomitable spirit of your battalion. To all of them, as well as to all the bereaved, led by our Colonel Commandant who himself with his wife have had a Rifleman son seriously wounded, the Rifles Family extends our sympathy and our understanding in these difficult days, and our continuing support.

This gives me an opportunity to say a special word to all the families of the Second Battalion, The Rifles. Although as an old soldier I am understandably particularly proud of the performance of the Battalion on active service, I am no less proud of the families left behind in Ballykinler. The strain and tension of waiting for news of your loved ones, and sometimes having your fears realised, can have been no less great than that which is inevitably experienced at the front in the face of the enemy; the way you have had to come to terms with all that, kept up your spirit and morale and continued to give your men encouragement and support has been magnificent and most impressive, and I thank you all from the bottom of my heart and wish you wherever possible, joyous reunions, which in themselves, of course, may require a sympathetic understanding on both sides. Soldiers who have been in close contact with a fearsome foe sometimes find it a bit difficult to readjust immediately to a more benign and loving environment, and wives and families, too, will certainly want to have it appreciated that they, too, have been through a very tough time. But given affectionate understanding there should be a good chance of that past rather traumatic separation actually deepening relationships. After all, as the old saying goes, absence makes the heart grow fonder.

So, well done everybody in The Rifles – those at the front who in an exemplary manner have done their duty and proved themselves as professional soldiers in the service of their Regiment and their Country, and those keeping the home fires burning, amongst which I include the Rear Ops team who have coped brilliantly with the many and varied challenges involved in the support of the families, wounded and the bereaved. You can be very proud of our new modern Regiment, The Rifles, to whose history you have added an important chapter, and the Regiment can be very proud of you.

Appendix

Holders of Office, 1945–2017

Prime Minister

Winston Churchill	May–July 1945
Clement Attlee	July 1945–October 1951
Winston Churchill	October 1951–April 1955
Anthony Eden	April 1955–January 1957
Harold Macmillan	January 1957–October 1963
Alec Douglas Home	October 1963–October 1964
Harold Wilson	October 1964–June 1970
Ted Heath	June 1970–March 1974
Harold Wilson	March 1974–April 1976
James Callaghan	April 1976–May 1979
Margaret Thatcher	May 1979–November 1990
John Major	November 1990–May 1997
Tony Blair	May 1997–June 2007
Gordon Brown	June 2007–May 2010
David Cameron	May 2010–July 2016
Theresa May	July 2016 –

Foreign Secretary

Anthony Eden	May–July 1945
Ernie Bevin	July 1945–March 1951
Herbert Morrison	March–October 1951
Anthony Eden	October 1951–April 1955
Harold Macmillan	April–December 1955
Selwyn Lloyd	December 1955–July 1960
Earl of Home	July 1960–October 1963
Rab Butler	October 1963–October 1964
Patrick Gordon Walker	October 1964–October 1965
Michael Stewart	October 1965–August 1966
George Brown	August 1966–March 1968
Michael Stewart	March 1968–June 1970
Sir Alec Douglas Home	June 1970–March 1974

James Callaghan	March 1974–April 1976
Anthony Crosland	April 1976–February 1977
David Owen	February 1977–May 1979
Lord Carrington	May 1979–April 1982
Francis Pym	April 1982–June 1983
Sir Geoffrey Howe	June 1983–July 1989
John Major	July–October 1989
Douglas Hurd	October 1989–July 1995
Malcolm Rifkind	July 1995–May 1997
Robin Cook	May 1997–June 2001
Jack Straw	June 2001–May 2006
Margaret Beckett	May 2006–June 2007
David Milliband	June 2007–May 2010
William Hague	May 2010–July 2014
Phillip Hammond	July 2014–July 2016
Boris Johnson	July 2016–?

Minister of Defence

Clement Attlee	1945	Francis Pym	1979
A.V. Alexander	1946	John Nott	1981
Emanuel Shinwell	1950	Michael Heseltine	1983
Winston Churchill	1951	George Younger	1986
Earl Alexander of Tunis	1952	Tom King	1989
Harold Macmillan	1954	Malcolm Rifkind	1992
Selwyn Lloyd	1955	Michael Portillo	1995
Sir Walter Monkton	1955	George Robertson	1997
Anthony Head	1956	Geoff Hoon	1999
Duncan Sandys	1957	John Reid	2005
Harold Watkinson	1959	Des Brown	2006
Peter Thorneycroft	1962	John Hutton	2008
Denis Healey	1964	Rob Ainsworth	2009
Lord Carrington	1970	Liam Fox	2010
Sir Ian Gilmore	Jan. 1974	Phillip Hammond	2011
Roy Mason	Mar. 1974	Michael Fallon	2014
Fred Mulley	1976		

Chief of Defence Staff

Sir William Dickson	1957	Sir Peter Hill-Norton	1971
Earl Mountbatten	1959	Sir Michael Carver	1973
Sir Richard Hull	1965	Sir Andrew Humphrey	1976
Sir Charles Elworthy	1967	Sir Edward Ashmore	Feb. 1977

Sir Neal Cameron	Aug. 1977	Sir Charles Guthrie	1997
Sir Terence Lewin	1979	Sir Michael Boyce	2001
Sir Edwin Bramall	1982	Sir Michael Walker	2003
Sir John Fieldhouse	1985	Sir Jock Stirrup	2006
Sir David Craig	1988	Sir David Richards	2010
Sir Richard Vincent	1991	Sir Nick Houghton	2013
Sir Peter Harding	1992	Sir Stuart Peach	2016
Sir Peter Inge	1994		

First Sea Lord

Viscount Cunningham	1943	Sir Henry Leach	1979
Sir John Cunningham	1946	Sir John Fieldhouse	1982
Lord Fraser	1948	Sir William Staveley	1985
Sir Rhoderick McGrigor	1951	Sir Julian Oswald	1989
Earl Mountbatten	1955	Sir Benjamin Bathurst	1993
Sir Charles Lambe	1959	Sir Jock Slater	1995
Sir Caspar John	1960	Sir Michael Boyce	1998
Sir David Luce	1963	Sir Nigel Essenhigh	2001
Sir Varyl Begg	1966	Sir Alan West	2003
Sir Michael Le Fanu	1968	Sir Jonathon Band	2006
Sir Peter Hill-Norton	1970	Sir Mark Stanhope	2009
Sir Michael Pollock	1971	Sir George Zambellas	2013
Sir Edward Ashmore	1974	Sir Phillip Jones	2016
Sir Terence Lewin	1977		

Chief of the (Imperial, until 1964) General Staff

Viscount Alanbrooke	1941	Sir John Stanier	1982
Viscount Montgomery	1946	Sir Nigel Bagnall	1985
Sir William Slim	1948	Sir John Chapple	1988
Sir John Harding	1952	Sir Peter Inge	1992
Sir Gerald Templar	1955	Sir Charles Guthrie	1994
Sir Francis Festing	1958	Sir Roger Wheeler	1997
Sir Richard Hull	1961	Sir Michael Walker	2000
Sir James Cassels	1965	Sir Mike Jackson	2003
Sir George Baker	1968	Sir Richard Dannatt	2006
Sir Michael Carver	1971	Sir David Richards	2009
Sir Peter Hunt	1973	Sir Peter Wall	2010
Sir Roland Gibbs	1976	Sir Nick Carter	2014
Sir Edwin Bramall	1979		

Chief of the Air Staff

Viscount Portal	1941	Sir Keith Williamson	1982
Lord Tedder	1946	Sir David Craig	1985
Sir John Slessor	1950	Sir Peter Harding	1988
Sir William Dickson	1953	Sir Michael Graydon	1992
Sir Dermot Boyle	1955	Sir Richard Johns	1997
Sir Thomas Pike	1960	Sir Peter Squires	2000
Sir Charles Elworthy	1963	Sir Jock Stirrup	2003
Sir John Grandy	1967	Sir Glenn Torpy	2009
Sir Denis Spotswood	1971	Sir Stephen Dalton	2013
Air Andrew Humphrey	1974	Sir Andrew Pulford	2013
Sir Neal Cameron	1976	Sir Stephen Hillier	2016
Sir Michael Beetham	1977		

Permanent Under Secretary, MoD

Sir Henry Smith	1947–8	Sir Clive Whitmore	1982–8
Sir Harold Parker	1948–56	Sir Michael Quinlan	1988–92
Sir Richard Powell	1956–9	Sir Richard France	1992–5
Sir Edward Playfair	1959–61	Sir Richard Mottram	1995–8
Sir Robert Scott	1961–3	Sir Kevin Tebbit	1998–2005
Sir Henry Harman	1963–6	Sir Bill Jeffrey	2005–10
Sir James Dunnett	1966–74	Dame Ursula Brennan	2010–12
Sir Michael Cary	1974–6	Jon Thompson	2012–16
Sir Frank Cooper	1976–82	Stephen Lovegrove	2016–?

Vice Chief of the Defence Staff

Air Chief Marshal Sir Alfred Earle	1964
Lt. General Sir George Cole	1966
Vice Admiral Sir Ian Hogg	1967
Air Marshal Sir John Barraclough	1970
Lt. General Sir John Gibbon	1972
Air Marshal Sir Peter Le Cheminant	1974
Vice Admiral Sir Henry Leach	1976
Vice Admiral Sir Anthony Morton	1977
General Sir Edwin Bramall	1978
General Sir Patrick Howard-Dobson	1979
Air Chief Marshal Sir David Evans	1981
Admiral Sir Peter Herbert	1983
Air Chief Marshal Sir Peter Harding	January 1985
Air Chief Marshal Sir Patrick Hine	August 1985
General Sir Richard Vincent	1987

Admiral Sir Benjamin Bathurst	1991
Admiral Sir Jock Slater	1993
Air Chief Marshal Sir John Willis	1995
Admiral Sir Peter Abbott	1997
Air Chief Marshal Sir Anthony Bagnall	2001
General Sir Timothy Granville-Chapman	2005
General Sir Nick Houghton	2009
Air Chief Marshal Sir Stuart Peach	2013
General Sir Gordon Messenger	2016

Notes

1. Churchill to Eden, 11 July 1944, quoted in Martin Gilbert, *Winston S. Churchill; The Road to Victory*, p. 847.
2. Richard Morgan, Headmaster of Cheltenham 1978–90 and Warden of Radley 1991–2000.
3. Or, even better, in the opening scenes of Steven Spielberg's *Saving Private Ryan*.
4. In fact, the 101st Heavy Tank Battalion, which consisted of five Tiger tanks, commanded by the famous Michael Wittman.
5. This particular argument was still being had when Bramall became G.O.C. 1st Armoured Division in BAOR in 1972. See M. Tillotson, *Dwin Bramall*, Chapter 10.
6. The US Airborne Divisions were even more widely dispersed than 6th Airborne. The 82nd and 101st Airborne were so scattered that men of each division often fought intermingled in whatever groupings could be formed.
7. The Heritage Lottery Fund eventually contributed £12.6 million.
8. Among these were Lord Wolfson, who pledged £1 million, and Stephen Rubin, a similar donation.
9. Colonel Roger Plowden was the Chief of Staff 1st Armoured Division.
10. Tom Jackson was a fellow Green Jacket, and the chief administrative officer of 1st Armoured Division.
11. Sonnet 16, *Cromwell, Our Chief of Men*.
12. The Annals of the King's Royal Rifle Corps, Volume VII, 1943–1965, edited by Major General G.H. Mills (Celer et Audax Club, 1979).
13. Winston Churchill, Secret Session speech, House of Commons, 25 June 1941, Martin Gilbert, ed., *The Churchill War Papers, Volume III, The Ever-Widening War, 1941*, William Heinemann, 2000, p. 858.
14. HRH Prince Charles.
15. Alan Campbell, Baron Campbell of Alloway, (1917–2013) was a prisoner of war in Colditz 1940–5. A barrister and QC, he became a judge in 1976 and was created a peer in 1981. From 2012 he was the oldest sitting member of the House of Lords.
16. Vincent Bramley, *Excursion To Hell*, Bloomsbury, 1991.
17. Lieutenant Colonel (later Lieutenant General Sir) Hew Pike KCB, DSO, MBE.
18. Sir Nicholas Lyell (1938–2010), MP 1979–2001, Attorney-General 10 April 1992 to 2 May 1997.
19. The chief legal officer in Scotland. In 1994 it was Lord Rogers of Earlsferry.
20. Lord Mackay of Clashfern.
21. Lord (Douglas) Hurd (born 1930), Conservative MP 1974–97, Foreign Secretary, Home Secretary and Northern Ireland Secretary in Thatcher and Major governments.
22. Marshal of the RAF Sir David Craig, CDS 9 December 1988 to 1 April 1991.
23. Lord Waddington.
24. General Colin Powell. Professional soldier for thirty-five years, ending as National Security Adviser to President Reagan 1987–9, and then Chairman of the Joint Chiefs of Staff

1989–93. Rarely advocated military action as the first solution to an international crisis, preferring diplomacy and containment. However, when force had to be used he believed in using overwhelming force. He was Secretary of State 2001–5 under President Bush Jr.

25. Marshal of the RAF Lord Tedder (1890–1967). Enlisted in the Army 1914, joined the RFC and then, in 1918, the newly formed RAF. Made his name commanding the Mediterranean Air Forces in 1943–4, and then became Deputy to Eisenhower at SHAEF 1944–5. CAS 1946–50. Chairman of the British Joint Services Mission, Washington, 1950–1. Usually disagreed with Montgomery.

26. Major General (later General Sir) Rupert Smith commanded 1st Armoured Division in the Gulf War.

27. Founded in 1870 by Colonel Sir Charles MacGregor, originally in Simla, moved to Delhi in 1953 and into purpose-built present home in 1996. Initially, it had 215 members; now it has 13,300. It is the principal national security and defence think tank in India.

28. General Norman Schwarzkopf (1934–2012). Commanded US Central Command, 1988–91, including eventually commanding all Allied forces in Saudi Arabia (750,000). Designed and led Operation Desert Storm, liberating Kuwait.

29. Rossbach (4 November) and Leuthen (5 December).

30. At Gaugamela Alexander lost somewhere between 100 and 500 casualties, inflicting a decisive defeat on the Persians, who lost a minimum of 40,000. At Omdurman Kitchener lost 47 dead to 12,000 Sudanese.

31. General Sir Peter de la Billière, Commander-in-Chief of all British forces in the Gulf, 1990–1. Effectively, second in command to Norman Schwarzkopf.

32. Air Chief Marshal Sir Peter Harding, CAS 1988–92.

33. USS *Missouri*, launched in January 1944, colloquially known as 'The Mighty Mo', was the last battleship commissioned by the US Navy. She was the site of the Japanese surrender in 1945 and fired her weapons in anger in six decades. Decommissioned 1992, she is now a tourist attraction at Pearl Harbor.

34. Lord (David) Owen (born 1938), MP 1966–92, Labour Foreign Secretary 1977–9. Founder member of the Social Democrats in 1981. Chairman of the EU Conference for the former Yugoslavia 1992–3.

35. Lord Callaghan (1912–2005) had been Labour Prime Minister 1976–9. The only man to have held all four of the senior offices of state: Home Secretary, Foreign Secretary, Chancellor of the Exchequer and Prime Minister. Many have held three.

36. Bramall's four commanding officers 1944–5 were W. Heathcoat-Amory (died 1982), R.B. Littledale (killed in action 1944), R.H.W.S. Hastings (died 1990) and C.d'A.P. Consett. By a process of elimination, it must have been the latter's funeral.

37. Lord (Francis) Pym (1922–2008). War Service in North Africa and Italy in 9th Lancers. Conservative MP 1961–87, Foreign Secretary, Defence Secretary, Northern Ireland Secretary and Leader of the Commons in Thatcher Governments.

38. Ivor Richard, Lord Richard of Ammanford, born 1932, Labour MP for Barons Court 1964–74, British ambassador to the UN 1974–9, European Commissioner for Employment and Social Affairs 1981–5, Leader of the Opposition in the House of Lords 1992–7, Leader of the House of Lords 1997–8.

39. Mark Schreiber, Baron Marlesford, born 1931, farmer and journalist, worked in Conservative central Office. Created a life peer in 1991.

40. Lady (Shirley) Williams (born 1930), Labour MP 1964–79, Education Secretary in Callaghan government. Founder member of Social Democrat Party, 1981, MP 1981–3. Life Peer 1993.

41. Anthony Eden.
42. The most highly decorated soldier in Israel's history. Born 1942, Chief of General Staff 1991–5, Minister for Internal Affairs 1995, Minster for Foreign Affairs 1995–6, Leader of the Labour Party 1996–2011, Prime Minister 1999–2001, Minister of Defence 2007–13.
43. Field Marshal Lord (Gerald) Templer (1898–1979), GOC 56 and 1 Division in Italy, 1943–4, DMI, 1946–8, VCIGS 1948–50, High Commissioner Malaya 1952–4, CIGS 1955–8.
44. Lord (Andrew) Phillips of Sudbury was a solicitor, specialising in charity work. A Liberal Democrat peer since 1998, Chancellor of the University of Essex 2003–13.
45. Julian, 3rd Baron Grenfell (born 1935) educated Eton, commissioned into the KRRC, worked for the World Bank 1965–95. Entered House of Lords 1976 and left in 1999, along with most hereditary peers, but created a life peer in 2000.
46. Field Marshal Lord (Richard) Vincent (born 1931), commissioned 1951 in Royal Artillery. Master General of the Ordnance 1983–7, VCDS 1987–91, CDS 1991–2, Chairman of the NATO Military Committee 1993–6.
47. Hugh Thomas (1931–2017), historian and writer. Created life peer 1981, initially as a Conservative, then Liberal Democrat, then a crossbencher.
48. Jack Straw was Foreign Secretary 2001–6.
49. Admiral Sir Michael Boyce, CDS 2001–3.
50. Winston Churchill, *My Early Life*, (1930) p. 246.
51. The leaders of the UN weapons inspectors in Iraq looking to see if Saddam Hussein had weapons of mass destruction.
52. Lord (Geoffrey) Howe (1926–2005), Conservative MP 1964–6, 1970–92, Chancellor of the Exchequer, Foreign Secretary, Leader of the Commons and Deputy PM in Thatcher governments. Ennobled 1992.
53. Decisive battle in 1954 in which the Viet Minh, commanded by Giap, defeated the French and forced them to renounce their Far Eastern empire.
54. See *The Chiefs*, ch. 8.
55. See *The Chiefs*, ch. 12.
56. Field Marshal Lord (Charles) Guthrie (born 1938), commissioned 1959, Welsh Guards. Two tours with 22 SAS, commanded battalion 1977–9, GOC 2 Infantry Division 1985–7, ACGS 1987–9, GOC 1 BR Corps 1989–91, C-in-C BAOR 1991–4, CGS 1994–7, CDS 1997–2001. Ennobled 2001.
57. General Tommy Franks (born 1945), enlisted in US Army 1965, GOC 2 Infantry Division 1995–7, C-in-C 3 US Army 1997–2000, C-in-C US Central Command 2000. Led the invasion of Afghanistan 2001, overthrowing the Taliban government, also 2003 invasion of Iraq. Retired 2003. Declined to accept the position of Chief of Staff.
58. Field Marshal Lord (Peter) Inge (born 1935), commissioned 1956 into Green Howards, GOC 2 Infantry Division 1984–6, GOC 1 BR Corps, 1987–9, C.G.S. 1992–4, C.D.S. 1994-97. Life peer 1997.
59. Geoff Hoon (born 1953), Labour MP 1992–2010. Defence Secretary, Leader of the Commons, Europe Minister, Chief Whip, Transport Secretary in Blair and Brown governments.
60. Lord Saville (born 1936), barrister, appointed judge 1985, Lord Justice of Appeal 1994. The Saville Inquiry was set up by PM Tony Blair in 1998.
61. The decision to use 1 Para as the arrest force was taken by the Commander Land Forces, Northern Ireland, Major General Sir Robert Ford. He held the post between 1971 and 1973.

62. The Rules of Engagement card, carried by every soldier in Northern Ireland. Described by Bramall later in this speech as 'Not Holy Writ, but more like the Highway Code'.
63. Commanded by Major Ted Loden MC, later murdered in Kenya in 2013.
64. Lieutenant Colonel David Walford OBE.
65. Brigadier Pat McLellan, commander of 8 Infantry Brigade.
66. David Cameron.
67. General (later Field Marshal) Sir James Cassel.
68. Fred Mulley (1918–95) was a Labour MP 1950–83 and Secretary of State for Defence 1976–9. He famously fell asleep during the Queen's Jubilee Review of the RAF in 1977. Created a life peer in 1984.
69. Admiral of the Fleet Lord Peter Hill-Norton (1915–2004). War Service as Gunnery Officer on cruisers and battleships and in the Admiralty. C.N.S. and First Sea Lord, 1970–1 and C.D.S. 1971–4, following the unexpected illness and retirement of Sir Michael Le Fanu. Chairman of the NATO Military Committee 1974–9.
70. Sydney Irving (1918–89). Labour MP for Dartford 1955–70 and 1974–9. Created Baron Irving of Dartford 1979. Not to be confused with Derry Irvine, Lord Irvine of Lairg.
71. Admiral of the Fleet, Lord (John) Fieldhouse (1928–92). Joined RN 1944, submariner, commanding Britain's first nuclear powered submarine *Dreadnought* 1964–6, Flag Officer Submarines 1976–8, Controller of the Navy 1979–81, C-in-C Fleet 1981–2 (including commanding the Falklands Task Force), First Sea Lord and CNS 1982–5, CDS 1985–8.
72. Humphrey Atkins, Lord Colnbrook (1922–96). Served in Royal Navy 1940–8, Conservative MP 1955–87, Chief Whip 1973–9, Northern Ireland Secretary 1979–81, Lord Privy Seal 1981–2. Resigned, with Lord Carrington, over the Falklands in 1982.
73. Lord (Simon) Glenarthur (born 1944), commissioned 4th Hussars 1963. Served as Minister of State in DHSS, Home Office, Scottish Office and Foreign Office in the Thatcher and Major governments.
74. Frederick Curzon, 7th Earl Howe, Minister of State in Ministry of Defence in Major and Cameron governments.
75. Lord (Charles) Williams of Elvel (born 1933), National Service, 1955–7 in KRRC, first class cricketer for Oxford University and Essex. Businessman, 1977–9 chairman of the Price Commission, created life peer 1985.
76. Lord (David) Trefgarne, Conservative whip in the House of Lords 1977–9, Under Secretary of State for Trade 1981, Foreign Office 1981–2, Health and Social Security 1982–3, MoD 1983–5, Minister of State MoD 1985–9, Trade and Industry 1989–90.
77. Lord (John) Boyd-Carpenter (1908–98). War Service with the Scots Guards. Conservative MP 1945–72. Ministerial office under Churchill, Eden, Macmillan and Douglas-Home. Life peer in 1972. Great supporter of the Gurkhas.
78. The Defence Secretary in 1993 was Malcolm Rifkind.
79. The Foreign Secretary in 1993 was Douglas Hurd.
80. Professor Sir Michael Howard OM, CH, OBE, MC (born 1922). War Service in Italy with the Coldstream Guards. Founder and head of the War Studies department at King's College, London 1962–8, Chichele Professor of the History of War 1977–80, Regius Professor of Modern History, Oxford University 1980–9, Robert A. Lovett Professor of Military and Naval History at Yale University, 1989–97.
81. Intermediate Range Nuclear Forces Treaty, signed in 1988 by Reagan and Gorbachev, eliminating all nuclear and conventional missiles with ranges of 500–1,000km and 1,000–5,500km, excluding sea-launched missiles. By May 1991 2,692 missiles had been destroyed.

82. *The Good Soldier Švejk*, written by Jaroslav Hašek (1883–1923), published in three of an intended six volumes 1921–3. It is the most translated of all Czech novels (58 languages in 2013).

83. General Lord (David) Ramsbotham (born 1934), National Service in the Royal Artillery then read History at Christ's College, Cambridge. In 1958 appointed as a Lieutenant in the Rifle Brigade. M.A. to the C.G.S., Lord Carver, 1970–3. Commanded both a battalion and a brigade in Northern Ireland, before becoming Director of Army PR during the Falklands War. Commanded 3rd Armoured Division in Germany, and then was Commander UK Field Army 1987–90, and finally Adjutant General 1990–3. Upon leaving the Army he was Chief Inspector of Prisons 1995–2001. He was created a life peer in 2005 and is the only living founder member of The Grannies Cricket Club.

84. Lady (Shirley) Williams, born 1930. Labour MP for Hitchin 1964–79. Secretary of State for Education 1976–9. Founder member of the SDP 1981, MP for Crosby 1982–3. Life peerage 1993, Leader of the Liberal Democrats in the House of Lords 2001–4.

85. William Robertson, *From Private to Field Marshal*, Constable & Co, 1921, p.159.

86. Harold Watkinson (1910–95) was Minister of Defence 1959–62 and was sacked by Harold Macmillan in 'The Night of the Long Knives'. Peter Thorneycroft (1909–94) was Minister of Defence 1962–64.

87. Sir Solly, later Lord, Zuckerman (1904–93) first came to public notice as a scientific adviser to the Allies on bombing strategy in World War II, with his Transportation Plan. He was Chief Scientific Adviser to the Ministry of Defence 1960–6, and to the Government 1964–71, and an ardent proponent of a centralized Ministry of Defence under a strong Chief of Defence Staff.

88. Sir Robert Scott (1905–82) replaced Sir William Playfair as Permanent Secretary at the Ministry of Defence. Any centralization of power in the MoD would undoubtedly strengthen his position.

89. Lord Ismay, formerly Sir Hastings 'Pug' Ismay (1887–1965), had been Chief Staff Officer to Churchill as Minister of Defence 1940–5. He provided the oil to ease the frictions that existed between Service Chiefs and political leaders, and was trusted by both sides. First Secretary General of NATO 1952–7. Sir Ian Jacob (1899–1993) was a career soldier, who served as Military Assistant Secretary to the War Cabinet throughout the war. In charge of the BBC World Service, and then Director General of the BBC 1952–60.

90. Michael Howard, *The Central Organisation of Defence*, p.19.

91. David Cameron.

92. Lord (Peter) Levene (born 1941), personal adviser to Michael Heseltine in MoD, served as Chief of Defence Procurement and later as adviser to John Major as PM. Life peer 1997. Member of the Joint Committee on National Security and chairs the Defence Reform Group.

93. Part-time, maybe, but Cromwell was a great trainer of his troops in the New Model Army, and in many ways a professional soldier. He was definitely 'the boss' in his army.

94. 'Marmont is lost'. Said of the French marshal by Wellington to his Spanish liaison officer at a crucial moment in the battle.

95. Plumer and his Chief of Staff, Harrington, believed his Second Army was successful because his staff worked with the motto 'Trust, Training and Thoroughness'.

96. The 'Geddes Axe' refers to the drive for cuts in public spending recommended in the 1920s by the committee chaired by Sir Eric Geddes. Despite the mechanization programme being 'desultory', the British Army was the only army to go to war in 1939 almost entirely motorised.

97. J.F.C. Fuller on Lord Cavan.
98. In fact, Gort became C-in-C of the BEF, not designate, and Ironside assumed he was the designate C-in-C BEF, when he was Inspector General of Overseas Forces, the post held by Sir John French before he became C-in-C BEF in 1914. The change came on 3 September 1939, the day Britain went to war. Ironside was generally seen as even less suitable to be CIGS than Gort.
99. Usually thought to be the role model for Richard Hannay in John Buchan's novels.
100. Malta had received its GC shortly before he became Governor.
101. The only Englishman to be so honoured, and the only equestrian statue in that vast cemetery.
102. Quoted in David Fraser, *Alanbrooke*, citing an unpublished memoir by General Sir Archie Nye.
103. Wavell was controlling campaigns not only in the Western Desert, but also in East Africa, Syria and Iraq against the Italians and Vichy French.
104. Published in 1944 and never out of print since.
105. Not to be confused with the later SEAC set up under Mountbatten; Wavell's command was ABDACOM, standing for American, British, Dutch and Australian Command.
106. Such as 'Chink' Dorman-Smith.
107. This was Richard O'Connor, GOC VIII Corps in Normandy and NW Europe.
108. Tom Howarth, later High Master of St Paul's and Senior Tutor at Magdalene College, Cambridge.
109. He certainly had an outstanding one in Harding.
110. It is said that Leese sent Slim a telegram saying, 'You're not sacked; I am'.
111. The British Legion.
112. What came to be called 'bite and hold' tactics.
113. Also, the gradual development of an official doctrine on how to fight both offensive and defensive battles at both divisional and battalion level had been disseminated from GHQ.
114. 82nd (US), 101st (US) and 1st (British) Airborne Divisions.
115. Guards Armoured, 50th (Northumbrian) and 43rd (Wessex) Divisions.
116. Quoted in J.W. Fortescue, *History of the British Army*, vol. VI, p. 410. Fortescue finishes his tribute to Moore thus: 'No man, not Cromwell, not Marlborough, nor Wellington, has set so strong a mark for good upon the British Army as John Moore.'
117. Major General Howard Kippenberger.
118. Bramall acted as the Sovereign's Representative at RMAS on 8 August 1980 as C.G.S., 9 August 1985 as C.D.S., and on 9 August 1997.

Editor's Acknowledgements

Editing the Field Marshal's papers has been not only a privilege but, more importantly, a means to repay some of what I owe to a most generous friend and mentor. Apart from typing up all the contents in electronic form, I have given certain of the House of Lords' speeches brief introductions and the occasional footnote to place them in context. I have provided rather more extensive footnoting for his Normandy campaign recollections and the chapter on *Generals and Generalship*. The only piece of joint writing is the Prologue, which was drafted by the Field Marshal before being expanded on by me.

I am grateful to four books for guidance. Two provided me with an understanding of much of the background to modern campaigns: *High Command, British Military Leadership in the Iraq and Afghanistan Wars* by Christopher Elliott (Hurst and Co., 2015) and *British Generals in Blair's Wars*, edited by Jonathan Bailey, Richard Iron and Hew Strachan (Ashgate, 2015). The former, in particular, explained much that had been obscure before, and made it easier to understand the thrust of many of the speeches which appear in this volume. I am also indebted to Michael Tillotson's biography of the Field Marshal, *Dwin Bramall* (Sutton Publishing, 2005, later reissued as *The Fifth Pillar*) and the Field Marshal's own volume, *The Chiefs* (with Bill Jackson, Brassey's, 1992).

Due acknowledgement is made to the Imperial War Museum (whose trustees Lord Bramall chaired for ten years) for use of photographs 4–8, 19, 20 and 23; to General Sir Peter de la Billière for photograph 15; to Jan-Dirk van Merveldt and The Rifles for photograph 29; to the Press Association for photograph 22; to Alamy.com for photographs 16 and 31; and to Sir Max Hastings for permission to use maps from his books *Overlord* and *The Battle for the Falklands*.

I owe thanks to Henry Wilson at Pen & Sword and to George Chamier for all their help in getting the volume to the start line; to Sir Anthony Seldon, the distinguished former Master of Wellington College and now Vice Chancellor of Buckingham University, who was a firm backer of this volume and was kind enough to contribute the foreword; to Professor John Adamson and Dr Lloyd Clark, both of Buckingham University and, respectively, Peterhouse College, Cambridge, and RMA Sandhurst, for timely help and advice. Paula Lees,who acts as part-time secretary for the Field Marshal, deserves great thanks for all her efforts and generous spirit. The same applies to my wife and children, who lived with this project for well over a year without any complaints.

If there are mistakes in the transliteration of the Bramall Papers, they are undoubtedly mine; conversely, any credit must go not to the editor, but to the Field Marshal. These are, after all, his Papers. That they display such a remarkable understanding and a grasp of modern defence policy should not surprise anybody. After all, he served more time on the Chiefs of Staff Committee than any of his predecessors or successors.

Robin Brodhurst
Stanford Dingley
June 2017

Index